How Fantasy Becomes Reality: Seeing Through Media Influence

How Fantasy Becomes Reality: Seeing Through Media Influence

KAREN E. DILL

OXFORD
UNIVERSITY PRESS

2009

OXFORD

UNIVERSITY PRESS

Oxford University Press, Inc., publishes works that further
Oxford University's objective of excellence
in research, scholarship, and education.

Oxford   New York
Auckland   Cape Town   Dar es Salaam   Hong Kong   Karachi
Kuala Lumpur   Madrid   Melbourne   Mexico City   Nairobi
New Delhi   Shanghai   Taipei   Toronto

With offices in
Argentina   Austria   Brazil   Chile   Czech Republic   France   Greece
Guatemala   Hungary   Italy   Japan   Poland   Portugal   Singapore
South Korea   Switzerland   Thailand   Turkey   Ukraine   Vietnam

Published by Oxford University Press, Inc.
198 Madison Avenue, New York, New York 10016

www.oup.com

Library of Congress Cataloging-in-Publication Data
Dill, Karen E.
    How fantasy becomes reality : seeing through media influence / Karen E. Dill.
       p.   cm.
    Includes bibliographical references and index.
    ISBN 978-0-19-537208-3
    1. Mass media—Social aspects.   2. Mass media—Psychological aspects.   3. Social
psychology.   I. Title.
HM1206.D55 2009
302.23—dc22
                                                                          2008052692

27.95

1   3   5   7   9   8   6   4   2

Printed in the United States of America
on acid-free paper

To Jay, Jason, and Regan, the brightest stars in my universe.

Acknowledgments

This book would not exist without Lori Handelman, my editor at Oxford University Press. Every academic wants to write a book—someday, as I did. I had no plans to write one *now*. But Lori asked me and before I knew it, this project came to life. She encouraged me and shared in my joy at every turn. I remember well that exciting morning, waking up in a hotel in South Korea to an e-mail from Lori telling me my book proposal had been enthusiastically accepted. Lori, your grace and energy are inextricably bound to this book. Warm thanks to you, my editor and friend. Thanks also to the many others at Oxford who made this project successful.

A special thank you goes to Brad Bushman. Brad was one of my original three peer reviewers on the book proposal and also was peer reviewer for the complete book. His enthusiasm for the project, and his promise to use my book for his media effects course at the University of Michigan helped me craft a book that I hoped would be at home both in the classroom and with a broader general audience. Brad, I have always loved your research. I feel so fortunate to have had the benefit of your expertise on my first book and I will never forget the help and encouragement you gave me.

I couldn't have written this book without the support of my colleagues in media psychology; you have to be the best colleagues in the whole wide world. I can't possibly name them all here, but I want to at least mention a few.

To Craig Anderson, my mentor and friend these past twenty years. You showed me what it means to be a social psychologist. For modeling excellence, for giving me great opportunities, and for all your contributions as a scholar to the media psychology literature, many thanks.

To Russ Geen, a mentor and friend to me since graduate school. Your influence on me has been truly important. You are with me whenever I teach the history of psychology. Your intellect, wisdom, and kindness are some of the many things that make me so fond of you.

To Dorothy Singer, for seeing something in me that I did not yet see. Your support is invaluable to me, as is your kind friendship. To Jeanne (Funk) Brockmyer, the best roommate in all Budapest! In graduate school when I was citing your work, I never dreamed I'd both collaborate with you and call you a good friend. Warm thanks, Jeanne, for everything.

Thanks to Dave Walsh, one of the peer reviewers on the book proposal. You are one of the rare ones who combine excellent science with excellent communication—just what I meant when I discussed great scientific communication in the final chapter of the book. And to an anonymous peer reviewer whose insightful comments and suggestions encouraged me to take this book to another level. You are an inspiration!

To my closest research collaborators: Melinda and Stephen Burgess, Carlo Fabricatore and Ximena Lopez, and again to Jeanne (Funk) Brockmyer. You all bring happiness and inspiration to my life both as friends and as colleagues.

To my friends in Chile, especially Ana Maria Delgado Morales and the staff at ENLANCES. The people of Chile and your country both are so lovely. I hope to make many more visits and continue my connections with Chile and the ministry of education.

To Francesc Pedro at the Organization for Economic Cooperation and Development in Paris. Thanks for all your work and for involving me in your expert meetings both in South Korea and in Chile. Can't wait for the next meeting!

To my professors and other teachers who made a difference in my life. Thanks to the aforementioned Craig Anderson and Russ Geen, and also to B. Ann Bettencourt, Alan Strathman, Tom DiLorenzo, Mary Heppner, Nelson Cowan, Chuck Borduin, Doug Krull, Michael Robbins, Bill Benoit, and Mike Stadler. Thanks to Bill Bondeson and Ted Tarkow, Jo Pollack, Jim Christ, Ray Adams, Sue Merkel, and Aileen Smith.

Great thanks to the many students who have inspired me over the years and made my job as a professor the happy experience it is. Special thanks to those students who have collaborated closely with me on research: Kathryn Phillips Thill, Brian P. Brown, Michael Collins, Jessica Rowe, Matthew M. Smith, and Jacob Blackstock. Also to those who were grad students with me, especially Kathryn Anderson, Deb Hume, Jim Lindsay, Bruce Bartholow, Darrin Erickson, Nancy Dorr, and Michelle Sherman. Kathryn, you were my first female role model in social psychology and I have always looked up to you. I miss you. Nancy, you and Mary Heppner helped me learn how to be a teacher and I am grateful for that.

Warm thanks to my colleagues and friends at Lenoir-Rhyne University and in North Carolina, especially Kathy Ivey, Dale and Jean Bailey, Gail Summer, Gary Broyhill, Jennifer Heller, Brandon Lee (thanks for inspiration on political comedy, Brandon and Jen), Lisa Miller, Jane Everson, and Liza Shaw. Warm thanks to Beth Wright and all my colleagues on the third floor, and to David Ludwig, Bob Spuller, Lowell Ashman, and Larry Yoder.

There are so many more who are too numerous to name, but thank you all for your support and friendship.

With love to my whole big, huge, enormous family, most of whom reside in St. Louis, Missouri. Special thanks to my parents—Leo, Joan, and Bob—to my grandparents, and to Christine and Bob Jr., but also to all my aunts, uncles, cousins, and my good friends Mariko Tada and Dianne Prewitt.

Major love and thanks to my favorite people in the world: my husband Jay, and my children, Jason and Regan. Jay, no one can make me laugh like you do. You are the smartest, funniest, quirkiest husband ever and I love you! To Jason, who was seven when I started writing this book: you are my bright, outgoing little star. You have a special place in my heart. To Regan, who was three when I started writing: you are fun and quirky in the best way like your dad. You are a sweetheart and you fill my heart with happiness. Big, big, hugs to all of you!

Finally, sincere thanks to all my readers. To quote Jason Mraz's song "Wordplay," thank you for taking "a dive into the deep end of my head."

Karen Dill, December 2008, North Carolina

Contents

*How Fantasy Becomes Reality: Seeing Through
Media Influence*

Section One

MEDIA PSYCHOLOGY

One

FANTASY AND REALITY: A PRIMER ON

MEDIA AND SOCIAL CONSTRUCTION

Right now, at this moment in history, Americans are having a love affair with mass media. While this romance is sometimes sublime, as with many affairs of the heart, many of us are still seeing the object of our affections through rose-colored glasses, unable to acknowledge the flaws that may end up hurting us. On the other hand, the reason we fell in love with the mass media in the first place is understandable. It's like one of those relationships where the chemistry is good, so we ignore those niggling problems that are always in the background. We know we should do something about it, but we just keep muddling through, hoping for the best. But if this is going to be the kind of relationship that adds to who we are, rather than one that does more harm than good, the relationship is going to need work.

This book is essentially about media influence—its power and our propensity either to deny that power or at least to fail in understanding fully how to deal with it. Both of these common stances—denial and impotence—raise many issues that merit further exploration. Throughout this book, I view the role of media in our culture through a wide-angle lens, telling the story of what social scientists have learned about the psychology of the mass media. Exactly how and why do the media change us and mold us? And mold us they do. A broad premise of the book is that mass media are a persistent and pervasive influence in our lives and that their influence is meaningful. Though far from the only factors that influence our behavior, the effects of media are not trivial. Early in the book, I explore several reasons for a persistent dichotomy: if media are indeed so influential, why are many of us are under the impression of being almost entirely unaffected by media exposure? And before we're through, I'll give concrete suggestions about how we can become much more savvy about how we use media and how it uses us. There are many positive uses and effects of media, and I explore these as well.

Have You Noticed the Revolution?

Is there such an animal as a subtle revolution? Over the last fifty years, and most especially in the last decade, there has been a revolution in the way we Americans spend our free time. How many hours per week do you think the average American child spends staring into an electronic screen? Take a guess. Currently the statistic stands at about forty-five hours per week of what is now termed "screen time." All told, American children spend more time watching TV and movies, playing video games, surfing the net and the like than they spend in school each year. When you factor in going to school, sleeping, and basic maintenance tasks like grooming and chores, it's easy to see that American kids are basically devoting their lives to consuming media. When they have a choice about how to spend their time, they almost always choose media.

Wake Up and Smell the Water

What about statistics that include adults? According to data from the last U.S. Census (www.census.gov), the average U.S. citizen spends 3,700 hours per year using mass media. If you are like the average person, you spend about two-thirds of your waking hours using media in one form or another. Americans spend more money annually on entertainment media than they do on health care and clothing. What's your impression? Do you think we realize just how much time and energy we devote to media? As media critic Marshall McCluhan famously asked, "Does a fish know it's wet?" In other words, we probably fail to notice just how much we are immersed in media for the very reason that they are so pervasive.

Since we live in a culture where clearly the great majority of our free time is spent staring into electronic screens, don't you think it's about time all of us were taught to think intelligently and critically about our media diets? Like the saying goes, knowledge is power. In a country where we are free to choose, we should marry that freedom with some wisdom to help guide us in making those choices. We've turned a major corner with media use in America—in terms of both the percentage of our lives media use occupies and the diverse forms of media now available to us—and it's time we followed those major changes with some major changes in how we understand the psychology of how we are affected by media. These are just some of the many issues to ponder as we explore what it means to be a social creature in a media-saturated world. Before we continue these explorations, let's look at a road map for the rest of our journey together.

The Magical Mystery Tour Is Waiting to Take You Away

When I read a book, I see it as taking a trip with the author. Reading an author's thoughts means looking out at the world through that person's eyes for a short time while still using your own head to filter the author's perspective. Because you are climbing on board with me, let me tell you more about your traveling companion.

First, I'm a social psychologist. Social psychologists mostly study how people influence each other. My special area of interest is media psychology, which involves understanding how social influence is carried out through the mass media (TV, the Internet, video games, music, etc.) rather than in face-to-face interactions between people. Much of my research has centered on understanding how violence and stereotypes in the media affect people. For example, when we see a stereotype in the media (an African American woman playing a maid on TV or a woman who says "no" when she means "yes" in a movie), often the effect is for the stereotypical idea to be reinforced and acted upon. This is a great example of how social psychology and media psychology come together. The social aspect involves learning a stereotype by watching others. The social interaction was mediated; and since a medium is something in the middle, a mediated interaction involves something coming *between* the people in question. In other words, two real people didn't interact, but rather someone watched a television show or movie and learned through a representation about what other people are like.

On the positive side, a landmark television show like *All in the Family* can change viewers' thoughts, feelings, and even behaviors toward people from other races. Did you know that by simply being exposed to a show in which people of different races form friendships, viewers develop more positive feelings about members of the other race and can more easily see themselves interacting with members of the other race in their own lives? The viewer, by engaging in the simple act of watching a television show, has learned a valuable life lesson: that African American and White people really can break down racial barriers and become friends. *All in the Family* was therefore not "just a TV show" but was in fact a real force for social change. Some people missed the joke, but many did not. Who knew that Archie Bunker, that stereotype of stereotype holders, could be such a powerful influence for positive change on untold numbers of viewers? But indeed he was.

Since this book is a social psychological analysis of the mass media, I will use many examples like this, including both research findings and real-world illustrations, to show the power the mass media exerts in our individual lives and in our culture, affecting us in both positive and negative ways. For example, movies like *The Shawshank Redemption, The Color Purple,* or *Talk to Me* make us feel the power of oppression, injustice, and discrimination. Just as strong is the feeling of inferiority we get from the illusions often conjured in the media of people who have something we want desperately, whether that be social status, beauty, or popularity. And as sad as it may be to realize that the people who make commercials, for example, really would sell us out (defined as jeopardizing or damaging our well-being and our pocketbooks), we must face the fact that even though it is sad and pathetic, it's still true. The good news is that we do have power and that power starts with acknowledging plain truths such as these. I hope that what you gain from reading this book is a savvy, progressive perspective on the role of media in modern life.

Media Criticism Makes for Strong Opinions

Every college professor hopes that her dissertation will (a) be published and (b) be well received. When my dissertation was published in the top journal in social psychology, I was thrilled. Having exhausted myself to produce the best research I could manage, I hoped my colleagues would notice. Well, they did. Some days it seems that everybody noticed. My dissertation became the most-cited paper in the field on the effects of violent video games on aggression. When it was published, the American Psychological Association put out a press release. My phone rang nonstop for two weeks. I did interviews with CNN, *Time* magazine, and *USA Today.* The Japanese broadcasting company (NHK) sent a crew to North Carolina to film a documentary on my dissertation, and a company in California also shot documentary footage for a video on research methodology, now packaged with one of the most popular introductory psychology textbooks in America. To this day, I still get calls for interviews that begin with, "I was just reading your dissertation..." (to which I mentally reply, "Oh, I'm sorry!" because I realize that dissertations are generally regarded as pretty dry stuff and that I am among the few living people who actually *like* reading research reports.)

Some years and two U.S. congressional testimonies (not to mention two children) later, I have a perspective on the field of media psychology that comes with international exposure to people from all walks of life. I have spoken about my research and about media psychology in South Korea and South America, in front of television cameras and senators, in high school classrooms and churches, on sidewalks and in bathroom stalls as well as in my own college classrooms. Because of the intense interest in these issues and because of their potential to polarize, I have been vilified and deified by various stakeholders and in the end have been left with the unmistakable feeling that there is something fundamental about mass media that we're not quite getting yet as a society. I hope this book will sharpen the dialogue about the role of mass media in our lives and our understanding of how that relationship works.

> The most effective kind of propaganda is that which is not recognized as propaganda.
> —Jean Kilbourne, *Can't Buy My Love*

Now let's focus more deeply on the paradox that we live in a culture where we are powerfully influenced by messages from the mass media but where many of us misread that influence because we think we are invulnerable to it. I believe that when we deny our own vulnerability to media we are actually increasing the degree to which we can be manipulated. If you do not know you are vulnerable—indeed, if you think you are invulnerable—you will not think and act in ways that protect you. Two basic errors in judgment that we make are (1) believing that fantasy stories in no way shape our realities and (2) believing that media's reason for being is to entertain rather than to persuade us.

Jean Kilbourne has written best-selling books and videos and lectured widely about the many ways advertising influences us. In her award-winning film, *Killing Us Softly 3*,[1] she says that wherever she goes, people always tell her that they are not affected by advertising—that they don't listen to or remember ads at all. "This usually comes from a person wearing a Gap t-shirt," she quips in the film. I certainly identify with both her experience and her incredulity at the extent to which people seem unaware of their own very obvious manipulation. How is it, do you think, that advertisers make such enormous profits if indeed none of us is influenced by advertisements? Where is this silent majority of malleable individuals?

My own experience is very much like Jean Kilbourne's. Everywhere I go, people tell me that exposure to media violence does not cause increases in aggressive thoughts, behaviors, or feelings. And this is not just my experience. Research also shows that, by and large, people believe that entertainment media have no effect on them. Teen video game enthusiasts look at me with thinly veiled disgust and say, "It's only a game." (Subtext: Chill out, lady. You are so uncool.) I testified before the U.S. House of Representatives subcommittee on Commerce, Trade and Consumer Protection in 2007,[2] speaking about the effects of sexist and racist stereotypes in the media. A rap singer who was there giving testimony threw his hands up in the air and said, "It's only a song." Recently, a friend told me that he mentioned my name to a student and the student responded that he was so angry with me for doing media violence research that he wanted to make a version of the violent video game *Grand Theft Auto* where I shoot everyone. (At this point, I'm just glad he didn't want to make me the victim.) To me, the passion behind people's rejection of the premise that media affect them is very telling.

Affected by Media? Not Me!

Recent research out of the University of Maryland[3] reported that college students, in general, are apt to think of media as "just harmless entertainment." Young people were asked whether "it matters" if there are violent scenes or sexist stereotypes in video games. Most did not believe that this violent or sexist content could possibly change people's behavior or attitudes. Even more interesting, those who played violent video games *the most* were also *the most likely* to see media violence exposure as consequence-free. The more we do something that is regarded as controversial or potentially harmful, the more we need to justify doing it. It's also true that the less we really think something is harmful, the more we can feel free to do it. Opinion polls have documented that many Americans believe media exposure is harmless. For example, one poll showed that 57 percent of American adults and children believe that playing violent video games is "safe" for children.[4] (Hmmmm, do you smell a psychological explanation coming? I do!)

These studies are consistent with a large body of research documenting what scholars call the "third person effect." The third person effect is the phenomenon that people believe others are affected by exposure to media, but that they personally are not affected. If you probe more specifically, you will learn that many people believe the only ones subject to media effects are basically young children.

What do scholars think? I'll completely ruin any suspense by saying that most mainstream scholars believe the exact opposite of what the general public tends to believe about the effects of media on people. "Okay, well, how exactly do media affect people?" you might be wondering. Let's take a look at an intriguing study reported by Glasser in *Television and the Social Construction of Reality.*[5] It occurred to Glasser that while people watch a lot of TV shows about cops and lawyers, the average person (perhaps mercifully) does not actually have much direct experience dealing with either the police or the judicial system, especially when it comes to relatively serious criminal activity. So he asked everyday people some specific questions about how the criminal justice system in America works. He found that people believe things work the way they see them on TV, which turns out to be consistently different from the way they work in real life in a number of documentable ways. For example, on TV the detective often knows "who dunnit" right away and spends his time trying to "get his man." As a matter of fact, in the seriously less glamorous world of actual police work, cases have a bothersome tendency not to resolve themselves neatly, to involve "victimless" crimes and tedious duties such as arresting disorderly drunks and filing paperwork. On TV, being a detective is way cooler. For famous TV detective Lt. Columbo, all he has to do is have a two-minute conversation with someone and he immediately knows he has found his perpetrator. The same is true for the USA Network's obsessive-compulsive detective, Adrian Monk. Monk will inevitably discover a quirky clue about the way the murderer ate his sandwiches or tied his shoes and he'll throw out his catch phrase, "He's the guy." And Monk is never wrong. Columbo is never wrong. And what do we believe, fantasy or reality? Fantasy. Every time. If someone asked us where we get our facts about police work, would we ever say, "I learned it by watching TV?" You know we wouldn't. We wouldn't know that we learned it from watching TV, and we would think the very notion was absurd.

Craig Haney and John Manzolati also recognized the pervasive role of television in informing us about crime. In their article "Television Criminology: Network Illusions of Criminal Justice Realities,"[6] they relate how crime depictions on TV are often very different from real-life crime. For example, the crime we usually see on TV is street crime, including violent crime like murder. Very little crime on TV is white-collar or corporate crime. The truth, however, is that these (possibly less dramatic) crimes are vastly underrepresented on TV and street crime and murder are vastly overrepresented. And it follows that Americans are very concerned about street crime as opposed to white-collar crime. This is because TV is constructing a reality where street crime is rampant but white-collar crime is almost nonexistent. Similarly, TV criminals are often motivated by a pathological level of greed, or they commit the crime because they are insane. In real life, anger and frustration brought about by realistic circumstances—such as stealing caused by chronic unemployment—are far more likely than the "made for TV motives" we've grown accustomed to seeing. We see it on TV, so we think it is real. And still we don't understand or admit that we learned about crime by watching TV, when that is precisely what we have done. This is how it is in our relationship with mass media.

Fantasy and Reality

When I discuss the effects of exposure to mass media with various audiences, one of the comments I hear most often is that anyone old enough to "know the difference between fantasy and reality" is not affected by media content. In other words, fictional stories do not influence us because we "know they are not real." This fantasy/reality argument represents a major misunderstanding of the psychology of the media. In fact, it is so pervasive that it merits a thorough discussion.

First, let's look more closely at the words "fantasy" and "reality." When an adult says she knows the difference between fantasy and reality, how is she defining each word? I think by fantasy she means fiction. According to dictionary.com, the word "fiction" has a variety of meanings. Fiction can mean a creation or an invention of the imagination. Fiction can mean a lie. Stories are classified as either truth or fiction, literature as nonfiction or fiction. When someone says media do not affect him because he knows the difference between fantasy and reality, I think he means by "reality" that people and situations on TV are contrived or invented. We know, for example, that the TV show *Friends* was a fictional story about the relationships and exploits of a group of twenty-somethings. In what ways is the story based in fiction rather than fact? Well, the adult audience is aware that the people in the stories are actors who are paid to play parts. A young woman whose name is Rachel in the story is played by an actress named Jennifer Aniston, for example. The "apartments" that the characters live in are actually sets. The friends' dialogue is the creation of professional writers.

So the stories on *Friends* were products of the imagination of the writers and producers of the series. When we watch a fictional TV show, we're essentially imagining "what if" these were real people and these situations and events really took place. We are entertained by a story that we imagine in our mind's eye as really happening. I don't think people would be much entertained by fiction if they thought of it purely as a lie that could never happen. I think the truth is quite the opposite: to the extent that we believe these characters and their circumstances and relationships are plausible and valuable, we take an interest in them. To the extent that we buy into the fantasy, we are drawn into the show.

So where does the reality come in and what is a more meaningful definition of "reality" in this context? The reality of a fictional story is not whether it is a fantasy or a creation; it is whether it is believable and attractive. One definition of fiction (again from dictionary.com) is something artificial or counterfeit—specifically, a likeness made to pass for the real thing. So fiction can actually mean a story created to pass for the real thing. Paradoxically then, the best kinds of fantasies are the ones that strike us as in some way real or genuine. I think one of the joys of experiencing really good fantasy and fiction is the very fact that they allow us to imagine "what if"—to feel as though a very interesting or gratifying story could be true.

Research has documented the persuasive power of fictional narratives. Studies have shown that if you build false information into a fictional narrative, people actually come to believe the false information. For example, in one study,[7] German college students read a fictional story called "The Kidnapping" into which either true or false information had been inserted. A control or comparison group read a comparable story without the assertions inserted. One true assertion was that exercise strengthens one's heart and lungs. The false assertion was this statement's opposite—that exercise weakens one's heart and lungs. Results showed that the college students were persuaded by the factual information in the story regardless of whether the information was true or false. So, if you read in a fictional story that exercise weakens your heart and lungs, you are persuaded that this is true. These researchers also studied a phenomenon called the sleeper effect—that persuasion through fictional narratives increases over time as the source of the information becomes remote. While at first the students' confidence in their newly formed attitudes was relatively low, two weeks later their confidence had returned to baseline levels. What this research shows is that we can be persuaded to believe false information that is inserted into a fictional story. Also, over time, we forget where we learned this information and our confidence in its truth increases. As another example, reading romance novels has been shown to increase negative attitudes about using condoms. So, misleading information can be stated as a fact or woven into the story line. Also, to the degree that one forms an emotional connection with a character, the persuasive power becomes stronger. So, if a reader is attached to a character in a novel who dislikes using condoms, that can change the reader's own attitudes and behaviors.

The theory explaining why people are persuaded by information in fictional stories is called transportation. People reading a book, watching a movie or TV show, or playing a video game become transported, swept up, or lost in the story, even feeling like they themselves are part of the story. This is one of the appealing properties of media: being transported is a state of flow in which the person loses track of time because of deep engagement. When a fictional story transports us, we are persuaded rather uncritically because transportation decreases counterarguing (questioning assertions) and increases connections with the characters and the sense that the story has a reality to it.[8] Engaging with a story means we have suspended our disbelief, and this facilitates our persuasion to points of view embedded in the story. In fact, some theorists believe that we accept beliefs not only uncritically but involuntarily.[9]

This discussion of fantasy and reality reminds me of a funny story line from the movie *Galaxy Quest*. *Galaxy Quest* is a good-natured spoof of popular science fiction and its fans. Basically, *Galaxy Quest* asks what if *Star Trek* were real? In the film, the actors who play science fiction characters become embroiled in a real-life encounter with aliens and spaceships. When the situation becomes life threatening, the "commander" enlists the help of some extremely devoted fans he's met at a sci-fi convention. Earlier in the story the fans had indicated that they knew the spaceship and its crew's adventures weren't really real. However, when the commander needs their help, he tells them the news that those things that were supposed to be fantasy really are real. The fans reply with great excitement that they knew it all along! I think fans of *Star Trek* and similar shows and films found this scene amusing because they've personally experienced what it's like not only to wish that the fictional universe really existed but actually found it so compelling that somewhere deep in their psyches it really is real to them. We want Spock to be real. We want beaming from one place to another to be real. And there is another gray area in the fantasy/reality distinction. In the 1960s, the communicators and computer disks used as props in the show did not have real-life counterparts, but later in history these things really did come to fruition in the form of real mini-disks and cell phones.

Speaking of *Star Trek*, Nichelle Nichols, the actress who played the role of Lt. Uhuru on the original series, often speaks of another kind of reality her appearance on the show created. In the fictional universe of *Star Trek*, people believed in the notions of interracial harmony and equality. The ship's officers who were from a variety of racial backgrounds exemplified these values. Nichols the actress has told of a conversation she had with the late Dr. Martin Luther King Jr. in which she told him she was thinking of quitting the show. Dr. King reportedly responded that she could not because her being in a respected position in this fictional story was affirming and uplifting for African Americans in America. Whether they watched the show or not, it was part of our culture and having an African American officer on *Star Trek* was a real victory for civil rights.

How Fantasy Becomes Reality

What Martin Luther King Jr. understood about the positive influence of an African American actress on real American race relations is a great example of how fantasy becomes reality. When writers produce a fictional story that asks, "What if an African American woman were an officer on a futuristic space ship? What if people in the future really acted as if they were color-blind?" this excites the imaginations of those who watch the show and even those who know of its existence. Seeing a story about racial equality demonstrates that it *could* happen, and maybe too that it *should* happen in real life. So you see, on one level we know that *Star Trek* isn't real, but on another level it is very real. Real people have been changed by watching *Star Trek*, or even by hearing about it. Dr. King understood that.

And what about *Friends*? As one of the most popular television shows in recent history, *Friends* has not only influenced fashion and hairstyles, but it has even influenced the way we speak. Researchers at the University of Toronto[10] argue that *Friends* both reflects changes in American language usage and has *caused* changes in that usage. For example, *Friends* is credited with influencing the American usage of the word "so" in the sense of totally and completely as in "you are *so* dead." This is a great example of a fairly subtle, but direct, media effect. Everyday people watching *Friends* were exposed to a novel way to use the word "so" and started to imitate it. [Wow, we are *so* influenced by media!] Part of the power of social influence behind that change was undoubtedly that the people on *Friends* are seen as hip and therefore imitating their speech, manner-isms, dress, and so forth would presumably make the imitator seem more hip to her actual . . . well, *friends*.

This social influence extends, of course, to other attitudes and behaviors. For example, the actresses in *Friends* were examples of Hollywood's thin beauty ideal for women. An educational video I sometimes play in my college classroom refers to a billboard that featured the female stars of *Friends* with the caption "Cute anorexic chicks." You may know that many studies document how exposure to very thin women in the media has a host of negative effects on both female and male viewers including increasing eating disorders, body dissatisfaction, mate dissatisfaction, feel-ings of guilt and shame, and desire for oneself or one's mate to undergo plastic surgery. This is another example of watching stylish people in the media and wanting to imitate them. Do you think the latest actresses are just as thin as the stars of *Friends*, or do you imagine it is getting worse? How would you compare Evangeline Lilly from *Lost*, Keira Knightly from the *Pirates of the Caribbean movies*, or Katherine Heigl from *Grey's Anatomy* to the female stars of *Friends*? How about to the top actresses of decades past?

> People living their lives for you on TV
> They say they're better than you and you agree.
> —Jewel, *Who Will Save Your Soul*

The idea that viewing a steady diet of underfed actresses and models can make us feel fat and unattractive is an example both of the pervasiveness of certain media messages and of the power of those messages to affect us. There are myriad other ways media exposure affects us. How about our view of the standard of living and habits of people we see on TV? Did you ever notice that people's houses and apartments on TV and in the movies never look much like the places real people live? If you've never noticed, take a close look at the digs of your favorite characters next time you are watching TV. Apartments have more in the way of architectural and design elements than real dwellings almost ever have. Think about your first apartment and how it looked before you moved in—probably it featured box-like rooms with standard ceiling heights, plain windows, white walls, and beige carpet. Even the humblest characters on TV and movies have interesting, chic apartments. My husband and I were watching the detective show *Monk* recently and noticed that the apartment of a supposedly shifty character featured a very spacious living room with wood floors and an artfully designed color scheme and his kitchen boasted a beautiful vintage oven. This apartment was supposed to be in San Francisco, no less, where such an apartment would be beyond most people's means. As for Rachel from *Friends*, ask a real Manhattan resident what the apartment of a waitress looks like, or how many roommates she would need to be able to make rent in Manhattan.

What does all this mean from a social psychological perspective? When we watch TV, we don't think we are actively learning anything, but in fact we are. One thing, for example, we learn from watching *Friends* is that you can be a waitress and live in a nice apartment in Manhattan. As for lifestyle, notice that on TV people regularly hang out in interesting places during the day having long, funny conversations with their friends. For the *Friends*, these conversations often took place at their favorite coffeehouse, the Central Perk. On *Frasier*, it was Café Nervosa. In the end, what this amounts to is the projected image that other people's lives are more interesting and rich than our own. We naturally compare ourselves to others; this is a basic premise of social psychology known simply as social comparison theory. When watching these stylized, idealized lives play out before us, we wonder why we can't get as many dates with glamorous, educated women as *Frasier* does, why our conversations are not as witty, our jobs as interesting, our standard of living as high. In short, watching idealized lives makes real lives seem substandard and can result in a personal sense of dissatisfaction or ennui. This dissatisfaction is a blow to our personal well-being, but a boon to advertisers who want to sell us more products than we can afford by marketing the promise that their products will make us happy and fulfilled.

Unintended Consequences

Now we come to an important and recurring theme in media psychology. Namely, that very real media effects can absolutely be unintended consequences of media producers' desire to get our attention for their advertisers. Producers want us to enjoy watching *Frasier*, so they give him a splendidly decorated apartment, witty repartee, and gorgeous dates. Many times, I don't imagine the producers do this with the goal of making us feel inferior (although the advertisers do have that as an explicit goal); those feelings are an unintended consequence of the natural process of social comparison meeting the plastic world of Hollywood where appearance is everything and where depth and substance don't translate as well.

Media Psychology Meets Evolutionary Psychology Or Darwin Didn't Anticipate Hollywood

According to evolutionary psychology, we are motivated most deeply, albeit unconsciously, to procreate. Therefore, we are naturally attracted to anything that will help us do that. For example, men are attracted to youthful women because younger women are more likely to be able to conceive and give birth to healthy offspring. Women are attracted to men with the resources to sustain children more than they are attracted to youth. This is, in part, because older men are perfectly capable of impregnating women, and more experienced men may actually be better at protecting and providing for offspring. Furthermore, women are attracted to socially dominant men for the same reasons. Psychologists have actually analyzed what men and women say in personal ads[11] and found that women emphasize their good looks while men emphasize their material resources and social status. From an evolutionary perspective, this makes total sense.

Now, enter Hollywood, and Darwin gets thrown on his ear. If you think about it, we human beings were designed under the premise that we'd be interacting with other real live humans (Insert booming voice from above saying, "Well, duh!"). For example, we were designed to function in a system where we choose mates from the group of people around us. And, true enough, before modern media we were pretty much only exposed to other real-live people in our communities. Now many of us spend more time with media images than we do with real people (so sad!). The—again, I think largely unintended—result is that we've unconsciously changed our standards to encompass media ideals.

What are the consequences of exposing oneself to a steady diet of images of people created artificially and for other purposes altogether? What are the consequences of this to an entire society? If you want to know, then read on, we will discuss more of those consequences— what psychologists call "media effects." In fact, we've already talked about a number of them. Let's take a closer look at one consequence relevant to our last example of mate selection. Scientists from Arizona State University[12] showed undergrads photos and profiles of young people of the same sex, supposedly for the purposes of evaluating the formats used by a dating service. Actually, the researchers were interested in seeing how the viewers' perceptions of their own "market value" as a mate changed in comparison to the competition. What they discovered was that women felt their market value decreased after seeing photos of physically attractive women. Not so for men. Young men felt their market value took a punch after reading about socially dominant young men (for example, a leader who was the editor of the university newspaper). In a nutshell, people see themselves as less desirable mates if the competition is steeper. The authors point out that in the past, nature provided the competition whereas now the media provide us with "massed exposure to desirable others.[13]" In fact, we may see in the course of one hour of screen time competition at a level our ancestors weren't likely to see even in the course of one lifetime. If we operated purely on logic, when a woman saw Angelina Jolie or a man saw Bill Gates on TV, they would mentally stamp these individuals as crazy-unfair competition and make no adjustments whatsoever to their image of themselves as desirable mates. But that's simply not the kind of animal we are. We were created under a system where it made sense to compare ourselves to the competition that we *saw*. No adjustments have been made to that system to accommodate modern media exposure and the corporate desire to get our attention by any means possible in order to make large profits. In sum, we simply weren't designed to navigate this media-saturated environment in which we find ourselves.

Let's think about this more deeply for a second. Let's assume Darwin and contemporary sociobiologists are right and our primary goal in life is to produce healthy offspring. We aren't so much consciously aware of this, but it is the deepest unconscious motive of our lives. Part of the drive to produce healthy offspring includes assessing the competition and positioning ourselves favorably within it. So, if other eligible mates are physically fit, we are motivated to keep ourselves fit as well. Our competition comes from within our own gene pool and shares our environment, so comparing our physical desirability to that of other suitable mates from within this group seems fair. Within this system, keeping ourselves fit is adaptive because it tends to increase our likelihood of winning a suitable mate. Now imagine moving from this set of rules where our desirability as a mate was compared to that of our neighbors to one in which we compare ourselves to the top actors and actresses, models, and business tycoons. How can we compete with the best in the world? What does this do to our sense of self-worth and desirability? The situation sounds pretty grim for us. But let's move a little deeper into the picture. If we assume that it is adaptive to make ourselves as desirable as we can as mates and that this is not really a choice but a biological imperative—and then suddenly we feel woefully inadequate, that makes us vulnerable. We are now vulnerable to sales pitches that promise to make us more slim and attractive or to make us more successful and socially dominant. You see where I am going with this. Mass media provide us with images of extreme people—extremely beautiful or extremely successful people. That gets our attention, which means we are watching the commercials, which means we are more likely to buy the advertised products. Now we are feeling vulnerable and inadequate. What do the media do next? Why, they provide us with a host of products and services that promise to make us beautiful and successful. To complicate matters, they also sell us images of delicious looking foods that will make us feel fat and unattractive, and this just adds to the vicious cycle. So the mass media play on our deepest needs, creating needs and selling products to meet those needs, but this is a vicious cycle and most of us end up simply caught up in the cycle—unhappy with our progress but unable to escape. Do we react, as a society, by condemning this unhealthy struggle? Do we ask for reform in the media, or at least demand that our schools educate our children about the vicious cycle? A few do, but for the most part we pretty much do the opposite. Since we, by and large, do not accept the idea that the media manipulate us, we do not find fault with this painful cycle of creating need and providing empty promises of fixing those problems that media created for us. In the next section, let's explore why that might be.

Just Say NO to Pinocchio

Let's review the facts. Fact 1: We spend most of our waking hours watching media. Fact 2: Research shows clearly that media are powerful and affect us in many ways. Fact 3: Many of us passionately disbelieve Fact 2. Where does this leave us? Well, it leaves many of us with a condition I like to call *Media Manipulation Denial Syndrome*. *Media Manipulation Denial Syndrome* happens when a puppet bounds across the puppet stage bragging that nobody pulls his strings.

When people passionately deny that media affect them, another interesting state of affairs takes place, namely, that these same people start to defend media executives. I call this condition being a *Media Apologist*. Now "apologist," I know, is a funny kind of word because it sounds like it means exactly the opposite of what it does mean. If you remember (and this might come under the category of what Michael Feldman, host of NPR's *What Do You Know?* calls "Things you should have learned in school, had you been paying attention"), a Christian apology is a defense of the Christian perspective. Likewise, a "media apologist" defends media producers' rights to basically do whatever they want to do to make money. So, we are being manipulated out of sheer greed for profits by big business, we don't realize we are being used and abused in order for them to make these profits, and not only do we not realize it, but we defend their right to use and abuse us. Ironically, in part this springs from a desire to feel that we are not being manipulated. The further irony, though, is when we let ourselves be manipulated, do not realize it is happening, and then go so far to defend big business's right to manipulate us, we become the perfect pawns of the profiteers. We let them stick it to us, and we jump to their defense when anyone questions it. This is a sad state of affairs. I think those of us who can see through this smokescreen ought to do something about it. We ought to educate others about the power of the media and the absurdity of becoming a media apologist.

This reminds me of something that happened when I was giving expert testimony before a congressional committee about the power of sexist rap lyrics. During the conversation, we heard truly dark and vulgar hardcore rap lyrics such as "if your daughter is 14, I'm gonna rape her." One congressman defended the media corporations' rights to produce any musical content they saw fit. He said simply, "If you don't like the song, turn it off." I replied in my testimony that "you can turn off the song, but you can't turn off your culture." I will talk more about both media apologists and media producers later on, but first I want to address the reasons I think we have become pawns caught in the vicious cycle of vulnerability to the greed of big business, even to the point of becoming media apologists.

The Psychology of Why

What are the social psychological reasons for being influenced in a myriad of ways by the mass media, but yet simultaneously not understanding or even actively rejecting the notion that media influence us at all? Below I explore a number of social psychological explanations for being caught in the cycle of media manipulation. These explanations are, for the most part, not mutually exclusive, but they often do coexist and interact with each other. I also want to stress that there are undoubtedly more reasons for this phenomenon than the ones I list below. In fact, I sincerely hope this book will start a conversation about why the current state of affairs exists and what we can do to move on to a new era in our relationship with media.

Cognitive Dissonance

In the 1950s, social psychologists Festinger and Carlsmith[14] brought naïve college students into their lab and asked them to do boring, repetitive tasks. Then some of those students were offered a trifling $1 to lie to other students by telling them the experiment they were about to do was enjoyable. Others were offered a better reason for lying, namely $20. Funny thing, the students who told these lies for no good reason ended up reporting that they actually liked these boring tasks, at least more than students who were given a good reason for lying. Why would students suddenly think boring tasks were not so very boring after all? Because of "cognitive dissonance" — the idea that mental inconsistencies cause discomfort that we are motivated to change, often through rationalization. The idea that we would lie to our peers and that we had no good reason for doing so makes us feel uncomfortable and maybe even immoral or stupid. We make ourselves feel better by rationalizing; in this case, we soften the extent of the lie—"oh, the tasks weren't really that bad," we tell ourselves.

If Sigmund Freud (or more properly, his daughter Anna, but that's another story) had been alive to read social psychologists' work on cognitive dissonance, he probably would have explained that this is a psychological defense mechanism. Our egos can be quite fragile and we human beings are motivated to defend ourselves from, well, from ourselves. We don't want to think we are bad people, so often we rationalize. There are many ways to do this. We can tell ourselves we didn't have a choice. We can trivialize our behavior, for example, by saying that, in perspective, the behavior wasn't that bad. We can remind ourselves that we are generally good people and/or that other people are much worse than we are. We can deny responsibility for our actions (in this case, we could say that the experimenter made me do it).

Freedom of Choice Does Not Mean Freedom from Consequences

As cognitive dissonance researchers from the University of Paris[15] point out, responsibility is the consequence of making a choice. These dissonance researchers had Parisian university students write arguments in favor of a new application process for French universities. The students were given either a choice or no choice about writing these arguments. Parisian students are generally Universalists who oppose an application procedure for universities and this attitude is tied to their general moral beliefs in justice and equality; therefore, the arguments they wrote were against their beliefs. Results showed that those not given a choice about writing these immoral arguments reduced their dissonance about having done so by denying personal responsibility (again, the experimenter made me do it). Furthermore, the authors noted that this denial of personal responsibility was a stronger rationalization than trivializing their behavior ("it's no big deal"). For all the students, once they rationalized sufficiently, they no longer felt bad (guilty, ashamed . . .) about their behavior.

So how does dissonance reduction apply to our media habits and our views about those habits? If we spend most of our free time using media and if media exposure exerts powerful consequences on us, changing our attitudes, feelings, and behaviors, and if some of those changes are negative (such as negative body image, increased eating disorders, and increased aggression), then knowledge of these phenomena undoubtedly produces dissonance. If we are to protect our egos, it is quite likely that we will resort to rationalization. One rationalization for concerns about our media diet is to deny that media exposure affects us. Ah, but what consequences this brings! If we can't face the truth of our own manipulation, then we open ourselves to becoming pawns of big business, vulnerable to their many attempts to manipulate us. Paradoxically, the stronger our unconscious fear that we might be the victims of harmful manipulation, the more powerful becomes our drive to reduce dissonance and therefore defend media. Thus some media apologists are probably those who experience the most cognitive dissonance and therefore among those with the most powerful needs to rationalize their behavior.

(Others are probably those who are truly ignorant that they are manipulated and thus have no dissonance to reduce.) When some media apologists passionately defend big business, what they're really doing psychologically is defending their own egos by rationalizing behavior that they themselves are not comfortable with.

An alternative to rationalization, of course, is to change our attitudes or behaviors. Instead of defending the right of big business to manipulate us and denying that media affect us, we could face the truth and take steps to do something positive about it. But that would require real strength—strength of character, strength of intellect, and the strength to make real social change. I think many of us are strong enough and savvy enough to do this. I bet, in fact, that if you are reading this book and following my arguments, you are just the person I want to talk to about this. Maybe you, like me, have come to the realization that we are raising our children in a media-saturated environment that makes them vulnerable to manipulation and that it is time we all got smart about it. It's time for us to become more powerful and less vulnerable to manipulation. Rationalization will, after all, get us only so far. It's at best a short-term fix that will keep the symptoms at bay, but it won't cure the underlying problem. Like staying in a bad relationship, we can ignore it for only so long before it blows up in our face.

In the end, whatever your viewpoint on media effects, we must come to understand that when addressing our media diets, freedom of choice does not translate into freedom from consequences. All things considered, negative choices most likely lead to negative consequences, whether we want to believe it or not. A subtly different point is that regarding the choices we make concerning media consumption, freedom of choice also does not mean true liberation. Simply put, poor choices do not free us; they ensnare us with their consequences. As great parents have been explaining forever, "just because you *can* doesn't mean you *should*." For example, research shows that small children who watch more television enter schools with lower vocabularies than their peers who watch less television. Choosing poor media habits did not liberate these children. Just the opposite: it put them at risk for failure.

Truth and Consequences

Another reason people don't clearly see how media affect them involves another kind of perception of choice. We have the feeling that we freely choose what media to expose ourselves to. We decide when to turn the TV, game, or movie on and off, for example. *We* decide. No one forces us to buy a particular video game or to go to a certain movie. We also believe that when we choose freely, those choices cannot affect us.

How true is it that we choose our media diet freely? When U.S. adults were surveyed about their TV viewing habits, the majority said they watch more TV than they want to watch.[16] Wait a minute—they watch more TV than they *want* to watch? How is that possible? Who's forcing them to watch? Well, I don't think anyone is forcing them, in the traditional sense of the word. No one is strapping them into their Lazy Boys and forcibly directing their eyes toward *America's Funniest Home Videos*. But mass media's job is to suck us in—to get our attention at a deep, emotional level. At this level, our viewing is not actually a 100 percent rational choice. To use an extreme example, this argument strikes me as being like the alcoholic who says he chooses to drink and that he can stop drinking at any time. How likely is the average American to stop "choosing" to plug into media so much that it takes up almost all his spare time? How likely is he even to significantly reduce the amount of time he spends with media? Kubey and Csikszentmihayli noticed a phenomenon that happens daily in living rooms across America. The television is on and people are talking. During the conversation, something happens on the TV, and all eyes go to the screen in a reaction called the orienting response (like when we turn our head toward a sudden noise). This is because TV is produced to get our attention. The methods for doing this will be discussed later. For now, let me just say that the mass media artfully, skillfully, and adeptly use knowledge of human psychology to get our attention, and yes, even when we don't necessarily "want" to give it. In their article, "Television Addiction Is No Mere Metaphor," Kubey and Csikszentmihayli[17] put it well—and with a nod toward evolutionary psychology—when they said, "Perhaps the most ironic aspect of the struggle for survival is how easily organisms can be harmed by that which they desire. The trout is caught by the fisherman's lure, the mouse by cheese. . . . Realizing when a diversion has gotten out of control is one of the great challenges of life."

And what of the notion that anything that is freely chosen cannot harm us? To push the alcohol comparison further, it would be like the alcoholic deciding that drinking will not damage his liver or shorten his life span—that he somehow had control over the effects of the substance on his body and mind. This would be a dangerous fantasy, but one that is quite compelling. It's so tempting to believe a lie that covers up our messy problems, like sweeping dirt under a rug. It's probably why we believed cigarette executives for so many years when they told us that cigarette smoking does not lead to lung cancer. It's easier to believe it than to face the truth. In fact, some of the top media violence researchers[18] have suggested that the link between media violence exposure and aggression is comparable to that of smoking and lung cancer. Again, put this in the context that a large percentage of Americans do not believe there is any connection between media violence exposure and aggression, recognizing that this belief is in direct contradiction to our best scientific evidence, and it is also what media executives and advertisers want us to believe.

There is another reason for this belief that our freely chosen habits do not harm us. This reason relates to our political perspective, placed in the context of recent world history.[19] When we think of manipulation, we are likely to think of strong-arm techniques: fascist dictators and terrorists manipulate and they do it with an iron fist. Think George Orwell's *Big Brother*. Think of the motto of the Borg on TV's *Star Trek: The Next Generation*: "Resistance is Futile." Think Hitler, Stalin, Saddam Hussein, Osama Bin Laden, or the general view Americans had of Russia in the mid-twentieth century. The idea is that we'll know when people want to manipulate us because they'll publicly declare their intention or brag about how we're powerless against their strength.

This is actually similar to how villains operate in the movies, on television, and in video games (and in "professional" wrestling, for that matter). In the *Die Hard* movies, we know when someone wants to control the nice people by the way he hijacks their building, terrorizes them, shoots some of them, and brags about his domination over them and his evil scheme for great personal profit. And, in true American cowboy form, we fight back with one rugged, wise-cracking individual who can overpower an entire militant organization with a wry smile and a little "Yippee-ki-yay Motherfucker."

This vision of conquering the brutal, heartless thieves and avenging the innocent victims is a compelling fantasy. I understand, believe me. *I* want to be Bruce Willis. *I* want to run unflinching in bare feet over broken glass while firing my weapon *and* my witty retorts. *I* want to see clearly who is good and who is evil and always have the power to take down the bad guys—and look cool while doing it. I think we all do. What I'm saying is that when people want to take our money and manipulate us, they generally don't show up in our building with a German brute squad and a pithy, high-tech-savvy sidekick. The truth is much more boring: they generally manipulate us through our hands-down favorite pastime: the media. They make TV commercials and print ads designed to make us feel bad about ourselves and give us the illusion that if we buy their stuff, we will be happy. And rather than responding by opening fire at them, we're more likely to defend their right to manipulate us for all we're worth.

FIGURE 1.1A AND 1.1B. Americans have an Orwellian view of manipulation—that if I want to control you, I'll strong-arm you like the iconic villains in the *Die Hard* films. This leaves us vulnerable to the more subtle forms of mass media manipulation that are more likely to take our money and change our minds.

Mass Media, Automaticity, and Mirror Neurons

In 1890, the great American psychologist William James wrote about the principle of "ideomotor action"—the idea that just thinking about a behavior makes you more likely to do it. Research shows that we unconsciously imitate the behaviors of those around us. A baby imitates her mother's smile. If your date rubs her nose, you will probably unconsciously rub your nose too. But if someone were to ask you about it, you'd probably say that you didn't notice you were doing it. The reason is that the behavior is outside of conscious control—we do it automatically and we're not aware of it. Scholars think we're hard-wired to imitate because it helps us learn adaptive behaviors and survive. Socially, it is also the glue that can bind us to other people, in part because people like others who act the way they do. Social imitation, then, is often unconscious and it is often adaptive.

Exciting new research has identified what may well be the physical structures in the brain responsible for our ability to imitate and our inclination to do so. Called "mirror neurons," these complexes of feeling, thinking, and doing help us imitate actions. Simply put, when we see another person doing something, it is reflected directly in our mirror neurons. In fact, seeing someone else perform a behavior provokes a response in our brain very similar to the one that occurs when we ourselves do the behavior. Watching you sew on a button creates an image in my mind very similar to what occurs when I sew on a button myself. Scientists think there are several reasons for this. Mirror neurons help us empathize. In fact, the word "empathy" originally meant the ability to directly imitate a behavior. Today we use it to refer to the ability to feel what someone else feels. When my brain mirrors what you do, I understand your perspective.

Mirror neurons then are neural structures that help us empathize and imitate. Interestingly, this imitation is outside of conscious control. We don't know we are doing it. According to psychologists John Bargh and Tanya Chartrand,[20,21] people are not comfortable with this notion because we like to believe we are autonomous. We will strongly deny being manipulated unconsciously. You can see how this applies to the media. For example, when we watch someone hit another person on TV, our mirror neurons respond as if we had done it ourselves. In fact, the response is so powerful that there is evidence the muscles we would use to strike out actually are affected. Unconsciously we are now more inclined to do that behavior, and at the same time, we are not aware of this stimulus toward aggression. Here again is an explanation of why people deny media effects—they sometimes threaten our sense of autonomy on the one hand, and on the other hand, sometimes we are genuinely unaware of what's going on inside our brains as we watch other people's behavior via the media.

Recall also the research, cited above, that shows how people are persuaded by factual content that is embedded in fictional stories. We become transported into the world of the story, we become emotionally attached to the characters—sometimes identifying with them—and we do not critically process the messages that are embedded in the story. Exposure to an attitude or idea of a fictional character can change our minds about using condoms or the health benefits of exercising or any other attitude or idea. I want to point out that persuasion through fiction is powerful by its very nature. We are processing emotionally and uncritically, suspending our disbelief, and we may, as theorists note, be persuaded involuntarily. Over time, we forget where we learned the persuasive information, but hold on to the beliefs, whether true or false.[22,23]

We Really Don't Know Why We Do What We Do

This argument wouldn't be complete without telling you about one of my favorite psychology studies of all times.[24] It is an all-time favorite of mine because—like the research on unconscious imitation—it tells us something fascinating about the human mind that I think many people simply won't or can't believe about themselves. In this now-classic research, psychologists put people in a room and gave them a problem to solve. Two strings were attached to the ceiling and the task at hand was to tie the strings together. But you couldn't reach one string if you were standing and holding the other. What to do? A variety of objects were in the room, including a pair of pliers. The solution was to tie the pliers to one string and to swing them, then to go grab the other string and grab the swinging pliers, thus enabling you to tie the strings together. Half the people in this study were given a hint: a man stood in the room with them swinging a metal nut on a string like a pendulum (which was supposed to suggest that they use the pliers as a weight on a pendulum). The other half did not get the hint. Results indicated that those who got the hint of the swinging pendulum were much more likely to solve the problem. Keep in mind that no one was told directly that the man swinging the pendulum was supposed to be a hint.

Okay, so far so good. Next, the researchers asked the participants how they solved the problem. Here's where it gets fascinating. Turns out that pretty much no one said that the hint helped him or her solve the problem, even though we know from the evidence that it did help. Were these people liars or cheats? No. They just didn't realize that they were given a hint and they didn't realize that the hint had materially helped them solve the problem. Why not? Psychologists think it is because often, simply put, people do not know why they do what they do. And what do we do when we don't understand the causes of our own behavior? Well, it turns out that we make up reasons that sound good to us.

Let's take another example. In another study[25] subjects were given different pairs of pantyhose and asked which pair they thought were the best. Subjects made their choices then were asked to explain why they liked their favorite more than the others. They gave lots of reasons: their favorites were softer, stronger, silkier, and so on. The catch is that the pairs of pantyhose were all the same: same brand, size, fabric. It turns out that most people preferred the rightmost pair of pantyhose even though it was identical in every way to the other pairs of pantyhose. This is because of a general preference people show for the rightmost item in a group of items. But did anyone say, "I like these pantyhose because they were the furthest to the right on the table"? No. They didn't realize that was the reason for their preference and when asked for reasons that they did what they did, they simply made up what sounded like rational reasons. Too bad these supposedly rational reasons were totally bogus.

These studies illustrate how we can be completely unaware of the factors that influence us. They also illustrate how we can be convinced of our motives even when our explanations are patently false. We don't always know why we do what we do, but we are perfectly happy to make up reasons that sound good and to believe them as if they were the gospel truth.

Another important factor in understanding the things that influence us can be illustrated by the public conversation that followed the death of Princess Diana. Many refused to believe that Diana's death resulted from a simple car crash. Some suggested that her death was the result of a conspiracy. Why did people think this way? Social psychology provides us with one reason: people tend to believe that a cause and an effect should be similar in magnitude. So, a major event like Princess Diana's death cannot logically be caused by something minor like a simple, everyday car accident. Likewise, racial prejudice or an eating disorder can't be caused by something as innocuous as television shows or magazine pictures. Trivial things don't result in meaningful consequences. I wish it were true. But since it isn't, we have to understand this and teach our schoolchildren to understand it as well.

Also, to the extent that we can mentally reverse an outcome, we feel more strongly about it. Any time we can say "if only" about a something bad that happened, we are more distressed. "If only" he hadn't played so many violent video games, maybe he wouldn't have hurt that other child. "If only" he had concentrated on learning to play music or baseball, things might have been different. Compound the trivial cause with the "if only" negative event, and we have an especially maddening situation. "If only" he hadn't played so many violent video games...Playing games...what a trivial cause for an important negative outcome like harming someone else. I can understand why we don't want to believe it. I can also understand why those who want to sell us something can have such an easy time convincing us that bad habits don't result in bad consequences.

I took an entire course in graduate school called *Human Inference and Social Judgment*[26] that was all about the psychology of how people make decisions and how we understand our own motives and decisions. In the class, we read about countless research studies on these topics. What I learned vividly from all this research is that people often make irrational decisions but are just as passionate about these wrongheaded decisions as they would be about wise decisions. Turns out, according to our current understanding, the best decision making involves both the head and the heart. However, we are still vulnerable to making poor decisions, and these vulnerabilities are very predictable. The renowned social psychologist Phillip Zimbardo once wisely said[27] that there are more people who profit from understanding human psychology than there are using psychology to better the human condition. My hope is that reading this book will help you deal effectively with those who are using what we know about psychology against you for their profit and your loss.

Two

CHALLENGES AND OPPORTUNITIES OF GROWING UP IN A MEDIA-SATURATED WORLD

Not long ago at a conference, a presenter told a story about his teenaged daughter who had been calling him franticly all morning. The daughter had planned on going to a concert that night, but while she was dressing that morning, she had dropped her cell phone in the toilet. When her attempts to dry the cell phone with her hair dryer had failed, she freaked out. Her problem, according to her dad, was that she could not fathom how she could go out without a cell phone. Her bemused father finally talked her down by suggesting she borrow her sister's cell phone, but remained intrigued by the idea that for his daughter, leaving home without a cell phone simply did not compute.

There is no job as hard as parenthood. (Can I get an AMEN?) Today as technologies evolve at breakneck speeds, both parents and children struggle with the issues and at the same time revel in the fun and excitement that these new technologies bring. Even before I got pregnant with Jason, our first, I consulted a Web site called Babycenter.com looking for advice about being a new mommy. Babycenter.com and its partner site Parentcenter.com host articles by experts, blogs from parents, and links to online shopping. Parents can log on and read an article by a nutritionist about getting a toddler to eat his veggies, then commiserate with other parents about failing to get a toddler to eat his veggies, and finally order a Splat Mat (for when little Jason throws his yummy green beans) all from the same site.

Recently I got an e-mail from Parentcenter.com[1] entitled "7 ways to be a better parent." Number four on the list was "watch less TV" (directed at both parents and kids). The fact that I can get such helpful information from a Web site, while at the same time overuse of media is a key parenting issue, strikes me as illustrative of the mixed bag that is parenting in this age of new media. It also highlights the many ways that our current level of media exposure brings with it both challenges and opportunities.

Psychological Research on Media and Children

Yale psychologists Dorothy and Jerome Singer have addressed the issue of managing children's media use and why it is important to do so. In their 2006 book *Play = Learning: How Play Motivates and Enhances Children's Cognitive and Social–Emotional Growth*,[2] Dorothy Singer and her colleagues say that we have lost sight of the importance of play in children's healthy development. Active play with peers increases social skills, creativity, attention spans, and academic skills while staving off obesity. When children play with other children, they learn to deal with their emotions, delay gratification, and get along with other people. In schools, play has sometimes been written off as wasted time. At home, play has been largely supplanted by media use, which does not offer the same kind of opportunity for development as play does. As Marshall McCluhan, considered by some to be the father of the electronic age, noticed, "The television generation is a grim bunch. It is much more serious than children of any other period—when they were frivolous, more whimsical."[3] Both Dorothy and Jerome Singer[4] have argued that while there is a role for positive use of media in children's lives, there is no substitute for plenty of unplugged, old-fashioned playtime. I couldn't agree more.

National Television Violence Studies (NTVS)

Another source of scholarship that is pertinent to raising children is the National Television Violence Studies.[5] In the early 1990s, with concern about media's influence on children widespread, Senator Paul Simon challenged the television industry to commission a comprehensive set of studies to be conducted by top social scientists, independent of industry influence. The result was a three-volume set of books exploring factors ranging from television ratings to an in-depth analysis of the impact of violence as related to the ways in which the violence was portrayed. A number of clear conclusions emerged from this research. First, the group of top scientists responsible for this research concluded that television violence poses a serious issue of harm to children. Of particular importance in their analysis was the idea that television presents violence in ways that encourage children to behave aggressively and to increase their aggressive thoughts and attitudes and their fears. In other words, it's not just violent content that matters; what is of concern is the fact that violence on television is specifically portrayed in ways that are harmful to children. For example, the studies concluded that violence on TV is often glamorized, sanitized, and presented as humorous. "Good" characters are quite often the perpetrators of violence and even when perpetrated by "bad" characters, most violence on television goes unpunished. According to the NTVS, most children's programming contains violence and about two-thirds of the time, the violence is presented in a humorous context.

Researchers at the University of California-Santa Barbara—some of the senior research scientists on the NTVS—concluded that there is a "high-risk factor" type of media violence—one that is most likely to cause child viewers to learn aggressive attitudes and behaviors. "A high-risk portrayal includes all of the following elements: *(1)* a perpetrator who is attractive; *(2)* violence that seems justified; *(3)* violence that goes unpunished; *(4)* minimal consequences to the victim; and *(5)* violence that seems realistic to the viewer."[6] Realistic, justified aggression by an attractive perpetrator— all these elements encourage imitation. Realistic cues from the victim, such as suffering, act as cues to decrease attack. Minimizing reasons to stop aggression will tend to support and encourage aggression.

Media Exposure and Fear Reactions

Have you ever been disturbed by images you saw in a movie or on television? I have. There is a scene from the movie *The Fisher King* that has stayed with me to this day in which a character played by Robin Williams watches his beloved wife suddenly and brutally murdered before his eyes. And there is a scene involving the raping of children in *The Prince of Tides* that has stayed with me as well. Joanne Cantor has studied fear, anxiety, and other mental disturbances induced by mass media. Cantor and her colleagues have found that it is common for people to experience sleeping and eating disturbances and mental preoccupation with disturbing material, and even to avoid the situations dramatized in the offending media. In one study, over a third of her respondents who reported being frightened by media said the effects of that fear lasted more than a year. And a fourth said that they still felt the emotional ramifications of the fear-inducing media, even though it had been viewed an average of six years earlier.[7]

A random national survey[8] revealed that 62 percent of parents said their child had been scared that something they saw in the media might actually happen to them. In an experiment, children who saw frightening scenes involving house fires or drowning said they worried that something like they saw might happen to them. The children were also less willing to take part in situations related to the fear-inducing scenes they saw in the media. For example, children who had seen a media depiction of a deadly house fire were less likely to want to build a fire in a fireplace. Children who had seen a media depiction of drowning were less willing to go canoeing than children who did not.[9] Of course, these fear reactions make sense. It is adaptive to avoid situations that might harm you. What's interesting from a media psychology perspective is that the children digested the fictional information as realistic and important to apply in their real lives.

Cantor also notes that children at different developmental stages are frightened by different aspects of media stories. Three- to eight-year-old children are more likely than older children to be frightened by things that look strange or by sudden movement. As older children come to understand more social nuances, they tend to focus more on threats of injury and destruction. Adolescents are sensitive to social fears and can start to understand more global, political, and economic threats. So while smaller children might be frightened by ghosts and ghouls, older children would be frightened by potential harm and teens by broader social fears. Cantor[10] gives a great example of this. Since a sizable proportion of parents she surveyed mentioned that their children feared the Incredible Hulk, she investigated further how these fears differed by age. She discovered that the younger children were frightened by scenes in which David Banner transformed into the Hulk because they found it physically strange and grotesque. The older children, however, were not as frightened by the transformation because they understood that in the context of the story Banner had good intentions and when he transformed he fought evil. The effectiveness of coping strategies also differs by age. Younger children cope better with fear-inducing media by being distracted, by covering their eyes, or by hugging a toy or blanket. Older children do better with cognitive strategies like telling themselves the situation is not real or that it probably will never happen to them personally.

Cantor offers advice for parents based on research. Her tips include limiting TV viewing, especially before bedtime; not allowing children to have TVs in their bedrooms; watching what your children watch in order to familiarize yourself with the content; and also being aware of what you watch and how much of it your children see incidentally. For anyone who wants to know more about mass media and fear reactions, I recommend Cantor's book *Mommy, I'm Scared: How TV and Movies Frighten Children and What We Can Do to Protect Them.*

Media Exposure and Attentional Problems

The brains of very young children grow and develop rapidly in a relatively short period of time and are influenced profoundly by their daily experiences. We know that children are exposed on a grand scale to mass media and we also know that TV is produced to be fast paced and attractive. Putting these facts together then, media are shaping children's cognitive development and one important way may be that the fast-paced nature of TV takes a toll on their attention spans. Wanting to tackle this issue, a group of pediatricians studied the effects of early childhood television viewing on later attentional problems.[11,12] The researchers tracked children across time and found that hours of television viewing at ages one and three were associated with attentional problems at age seven. In other words, toddlers who watched too much TV had trouble paying attention and concentrating in elementary school. Kids' media diets had an influence on their brain development. This carefully conducted research took into account other relevant factors such as the number of children in the family, the amount of support and stimulation the child received from the family and even the mother's psychological profile. The pediatricians reckoned that for every hour per day a preschool child watches TV, his risk of later attentional problems increases by 10 percent.

What about research on kids and the Internet? Recently, the academic journal *Developmental Psychology* published a special issue devoted entirely to the ramifications of Internet use by children and adolescents.[13] The report explored research on both the pros and cons of youth Internet use. The studies indicated that between 75 percent and 90 percent of U.S. teens use the Internet for e-mail, instant messaging, chatting, and exploring Web sites. In terms of the positive impact of youth Internet use, low-income children who used the Internet at home improved their school achievement, perhaps due to increased time spent reading. The journal also reported that youth also use the Internet as a source of critical information. For example, low-income youth in Ghana searched the net for sensitive information about sexually transmitted diseases— information that would likely have been more embarrassing or difficult for them to access elsewhere.

An interesting study conducted by scientists at Cornell University examined teen use of Internet message boards related to self-injurious behavior[14] (often called "cutting" in the vernacular). On the positive side, these online interactions provided social support to a vulnerable population. When you think about it, in the past it would have been difficult or impossible to find a group of friends knowledgeable and empathetic on such a sensitive topic. The Internet also provides some privacy for people to interact yet keep their distance. On the negative side, such online communities may actually normalize cutting behavior and end up encouraging it as well. This reminds me that once during a discussion about research on eating disorders, some of my students told me that when they were researching the topic online, they found a number of pro-anorexia or "pro-an" Web sites. On these sites were pictures of anorexic models and people sharing so-called tips about unhealthy dieting practices and extolling the supposed virtues of anorexia. I couldn't believe what they were telling me. When they showed me the Web sites I was stunned. Anorexic swimsuit models that looked more like concentration camp victims than bathing beauties showed off their emaciated bodies.

Both these examples show that the Internet is a social forum with unique characteristics. Certain sites can sometimes comfort people, providing a kind of informal group counseling, but they can also sometimes support extreme and unhealthy behaviors. Social psychologists have long studied a concept called deindividuation—the idea that people engage in more extreme behavior when they don't think they will take so much of the blame for that behavior. Deindividuation takes place in these types of electronic forums as well—whether it be blogs, Web sites, or other electronic social settings. A person hiding behind the relative anonymity of a screen name might be harsher (i.e., by making mean or insulting comments in a blog) and also more extreme (i.e., advocating unpopular positions) than they are face-to-face. In live social encounters there are consequences for such behavior that are less likely to be in place in electronic social forums.

Social Learning and Mass Media

As social animals, we grow up comparing ourselves to others to get feedback about a host of social variables. Am I as smart or as talented as the other kids my age? What is considered cool? What do the people around me think I should do, think, and be? We probably do not question it as we grow up, but we're not as independent as we think we are. Quite the contrary, really.

We are absolutely social creatures, designed to judge our successes and failures and to make our choices all in the context of other people. Social psychologists call these processes social comparison. Just like whether I am a good runner depends on how fast my peers can run, I judge other social variables based on how I think my peers will react and on how my peers actually treat me.

You might be thinking that people are a bunch of conformists. What about the rebels? Well, even anticonformists are heavily influenced by society. If you think about it an anticonformist is someone who goes against the grain, who defies the status quo. Well, to defy something you must know about it, care about it, and keep track of it. If, for example, it is the fashion to wear sports apparel—football jerseys, rugby shirts, tennis shoes—and a rebel decides to wear leather and chains to be different, then he is doing just that: actively deciding to watch what others are doing and do something essentially just to be different, to stand out, to give the impression to others that he refuses to conform. In a twisted way, then, even anticonformity is a sort of conforming social behavior. True enough, there are some people who are less affected by social influence than others. The great humanist psychologist Abraham Maslow wrote about a few individuals he called "self-actualized"—those high-achieving, highly evolved people who seemed to walk their own paths without sweating what other people thought about it.

But the rest of us vastly outnumber those who are genuinely immune to such influence—the true independents. And as developing children, we are even less likely to show this kind of social immunity. If viewed through the lens of biology, this makes an extraordinary amount of sense. We are social creatures. We live together, we mate and reproduce and help each other survive and thrive. As the esteemed social psychologist Elliot Aronson[15] put it, we are "social animals." Although the notion of conformity is decidedly un-cool—perhaps especially for Americans—following social rules and "sticking with the group" is often efficient and adaptive.

There are implications both for our society and for our kids that life—even social life—has largely gone digital. Much of our kids' socialization is influenced by or supported by various forms of media. This explains why it is crucial to understand how kids learn social lessons from the media (e.g., watching celebrities), how they are affected by socializing through the media (e.g., social networking sites and text messaging), and also to scrutinize what the most common media messages are.

Sex and violence in the mass media are the topics that have generated the most interest, controversy, and research. It is understandable that we would be drawn to tackling some of the most blatant and potentially harmful effects of media first. But I think we have largely missed, as a culture, some of the more subtle issues, including issues of social learning from the media. For example, many people reject the notion that watching TV can change our feelings toward a person, group, or idea. But just like real social interactions, these mediated pseudo-interactions teach kids social lessons. Before undertaking a more in-depth analysis of these social issues, I want to put this in the context of the current statistics of American children's media use.

Life on Earth—Today It Means Staring at Screens

Earlier, I referred to some current media use statistics. These kinds of statistics vary from study to study for a variety of reasons including the nature of the specific questions asked in a given study and the people who were questioned or observed, so I'll offer some more statistics for your consideration. According to Potter's 2008 report,[16] the average American watches TV about four and a half hours per day and spends over two hours a day with the computer (not counting computer time at work). And research indicates these numbers are rising steadily. College students have a unique set of media habits. American college students spend about three and a half hours a day on the computer doing activities like e-mailing and instant messaging; they spend another seven and a half hours a day with other forms of media including TV, books, and music.

Kids and Media in America[17] is a detailed profile of American kids' media use. Authors Roberts and Foehr found that American children use media an average of 6.5 hours per day, not counting media use for school or media multitasking (e.g., looking at a Web site while simultaneously watching TV), with older children consuming media on average about seven to eight hours per day. American kids most often watch TV alone or with peers, rarely with parental supervision. Only 5 percent of American children use media for an hour or less on any given day. About half of American children aged eight to eighteen say they live in *constant TV homes*—homes where the TV is on constantly whether anyone is watching it. Two-thirds of these children also say that the television is usually on during mealtimes.

TV viewing is the most common media activity of most American children, on average taking three to four and a half hours of a child's day. One would think that these statistics mean that children enjoy watching TV immensely. But there's a fascinating paradox about TV watching. When you ask children about their enjoyment of TV, you get some interesting responses. Most say that TV is not all that stimulating and, in fact, they often watch TV simply to kill time. Furthermore, research shows[18] that heavy TV viewers say they enjoy watching TV *less* than light TV viewers. Research also shows that most kids say they watch more TV than they *want* to watch. I think these statistics show that media is attention-grabbing and that it sucks us in, even more than we really want to be sucked in. That's because the primary motive for producing media is to attract an audience for advertisers, so media producers make media that they believe will be most likely to grab their audience's attention.

I wonder if maybe we hear so many statistics that we get a little numb and are not able to fully appreciate what they mean. So, let's put this in context. The brilliant and unpronounceably named psychologist Csikszentmihayli[19] has written about how we human beings spend our days, including work and free time, and how we feel about these different activities. Roughly speaking, daily life is divided into three equal eight-hour periods dedicated to sleeping, working, and leisure time. Considering that we have eight hours a day to do more or less whatever we choose, let's put those media use statistics in that context. Out of eight hours of leisure time, the average American spends about four and a half hours watching television and another two on the computer. New research out of Ball State University[20] in Muncie, Indiana, confirms that media use is, by *far*, the most common waking activity. In fact, these researchers found that average Americans spend about nine hours per day using media. According to the Ball State study, 30 percent of a person's waking day involved media use as a sole activity and another 39 percent included media use combined with another activity. Taken together then, about 70 percent of our waking time is spent using media in one form or the other. As Csikszentmihayli notes, one also has to consider that there are a number of maintenance activities in one's day including personal grooming and activities such as driving to work and grocery shopping. Given that people sleep, eat, work, and perform maintenance activities, if you combine that information with the media use statistics reported here, I would argue that almost *all* of the time we have a choice about how to spend our time, we choose to plug into media.

Let me repeat that: almost every time we have a choice about what to do with our lives, we choose to stare into a screen. Be it the television, computer, cell phone, or Blackberry, *our lives are spent staring into electronic screens.* Now, I don't know where you are right now, but I am imagining you sitting somewhere calmly reading this information and I don't know if I am communicating to you how un-calm I feel about it sometimes. I wonder if we are too complacently plugged into *The Matrix*, without sufficient knowledge of its power over us.

In the 1960s, Marshall McCluhan understood this and wrote a masterpiece that is eerily relevant today, despite the changes in technology. If you've never read *The Medium Is the Message*, you should. Even if you expect the intellectual depth of the work, its artistry may surprise you. McCluhan's words were directed mostly toward television and the general increase in communication speed, but they apply to our modern technology explosion as well: "All media work us over completely. They are so pervasive in their personal, political, economic, aesthetic, psychological, ethical, moral, and social consequences, that they leave no part of us untouched, unaffected, unaltered. The medium is the message. Any understanding of social and cultural change is impossible without a knowledge of the way media work as environments."[21]

We watch reality shows that purport to track people living their daily lives. It occurs to me sometimes that watching people live their daily lives in America today would largely mean filming them as they stare at the TV or computer. We really need to think about this. It's ironic, in fact, that we're strangely drawn to watching other people supposedly living their real lives, while we spend all our time . . . well, watching.

I know that some might read my reaction to American's super-duper-heavy media use statistics as the sick ramblings of a humorless, finger-wagging granny. (Read the following in your best finger-wagging granny voice:) "You kiddies with your iPods and your MySpace! and your *Grand Theft Auto*! You're turning into a bunch of slack-jawed zombies!" Well, I'm not trying to be anyone's granny, but I do confess I want to make people think. (I'm a professor. Isn't that in my job description?) It seems to me that if most of us are plugged into electronic media virtually every time we can be that there are ramifications we should consider, not the least of which is whether we wouldn't like to be spending more of our lives doing something else. I offer up the following list of questions as conversation starters about mass media's role in our lives and the lives of our children.

1. If virtually every time we can choose what to do with our free time we choose mass media, what else aren't we experiencing enough?
2. If children spend virtually all their free time plugged into media, shouldn't we teach them to be more savvy media users?
3. If we tend to be media apologists—those who reject the notion that media affect us in potentially detrimental ways—then aren't we more vulnerable to manipulation by the big businesses that produce

mass media messages? Aren't we their dream customers, not only open to their manipulation, but naïve enough to defend their right to manipulate us and even attack those who criticize them?

4. In what ways is the brain of a child raised on a heavy diet of today's common mass media different from those of children who are not?

5. If you could design the ideal media diet for your (real or hypothetical) child or for yourself, what would it look like? What free time activities do you think would make for the happiest, healthiest, most interesting and fulfilling lifestyle? (And, of course you can actually do this.)

    a. How many hours a day would you devote to TV watching? What kinds of things would you choose to watch?

    b. What would you do with personal time that is media free?

    c. What media activities would you want to keep in your daily life and why?

6. Will there ever again be a human society whose free time is not dominated by the use of mass media? Would we ever choose to have such a society? Why or why not?

Media Literacy 101

Given that most of us are growing up spending a great deal of time with mass media, given the media's power to influence us, and the common misunderstandings about media power, some education is clearly in order. I suggest that media literacy be made part of our school curricula. But perhaps I am getting ahead of myself. Maybe you have never heard the term "media literacy" and therefore a definition is in order. Being media literate means understanding the messages being transmitted by mass media and how those messages affect our culture and its members. One of the basic tenets of media literacy is that literate members of a society are more powerful and more liberated.

I also like the perspective of Dorothy and Jerome Singer, that being media literate can also be thought of as being a *critical viewer*. Let's extend that notion to include the newer forms of media (audio and video podcasts, social networking, etc.) and call it being *critical users* of media. This new model means moving away from passively accepting all media messages as harmless entertainment and moving toward an active model in which we assume that media influence us. What we're currently doing as a society of relatively passive users would be like taking a politician's rhetoric at face value, trusting that he or she has our best interests in mind instead of critically analyzing the politician's behaviors, motivations, and persuasive efforts. To extend the analogy, an informed voter understands the persuasive elements of a political campaign and then chooses to vote for the candidate or not, but she is making an educated choice, not a naïve one. In our current media-saturated culture, we need to move from a society of naïve users to one of more sophisticated consumers.

In his book *Media Literacy*, James Potter talks about an issue that's especially relevant to children and adolescents, namely, the way exposure to lots of mass media messages shapes the way we think about ourselves. He discusses how advertisers expressly try to program how we think about ourselves, specifically wanting consumers to feel uneasy and self-conscious. Why would media executives want their viewers to feel bad about themselves? The answer is because if you feel lacking, you are more motivated to buy some product or service to try to fix yourself. Children and teens are especially vulnerable to such manipulation. Part of the psychology of teenagers, for example, is that they think everyone is looking at them and judging them. Of course, social approval is extremely important to teens, making them a population particularly vulnerable to this type of manipulation.

There are other developmental issues, both maturational and physical, that suggest teens process media messages in unique ways—ways that definitely affect their evolving self-concepts and their thinking and decision making. David Walsh's book *Why Do They Act That Way?*[22] elaborates on these issues. As a brief example, did you know that while adults tend to do their advanced information processing with the frontal cortex, the brain's advanced information processing center, teens tend to process information in the amygdala, an area of the brain dedicated to emotional processing? The amygdala is specifically associated with the emotion of anger. This may explain why starting an innocent conversation with a teen sometimes results in tears or screaming. If it helps, keep in mind that when a teen screams, "I hate you," it's really just her amygdala talking. As far as I understand, like the old saying goes, she probably *will* grow out of it.

Now one maturational goal of teen-hood is to move toward being able to successfully separate from one's parents—to become independent. This probably explains why teens prefer to be viewed as young adults and also why they don't want to be seen in public with their parents (in the role of children). Within this context of development, let's now overlay the issue of the digital divide. Kids are now known as digital natives, meaning they grew up with technology and are likely more comfortable with it. I'd take this further by saying that for a teenager, part of his identity is his media diet—his musical and communication preferences and exploits, for example. On the other hand, parents who've learned new technology are called digital migrants. In recent years, as everyday technology has evolved particularly rapidly, the digital divide has broadened substantially. We could now call it a digital canyon. (How about digital crevasse? Try it, it's fun to say—digital crevasse.) On the one side are teens, their thumbs flying as they text a friend, while Mom feels good that she knows how to google something, and the neighbor feels left out because he doesn't know all these terms he hears bandied about on TV—like blog and avatar. I actually can't tell you how many colleagues have privately confessed to me that they have no clue how to use an iPod. (My dear colleagues, I am more than happy to give you a free and confidential iPod tutorial. Hint: stop trying to ram your 8-track tape into the thing!) In the end, younger people identify with digital technology while older people often feel dumb and ignorant (which are, of course, two different things) around technology. I imagine there are also differences in technology use by career and education level as well as other factors. But for parents and kids, one result of the digital canyon separating them is that parents may not feel able to monitor some of their kids' media use. Heck, they may not even know that some of it exists. This situation wasn't the case for other generations of parents and kids.

A Classic Media Literacy Lesson: Don't Believe Everything You Read

Critical users of mass media have the skills to gain control over the meanings of the media messages they encounter. There's an old saying that you shouldn't believe everything you read. The same is true for "reading" the messages a movie, commercial, or video game is sending you. It begins simply by knowing that messages are designed to persuade and by asking yourself if you agree or disagree with the message you are reading and if you want to be persuaded on the particular matter at hand. An incredible amount of power and strength comes from acquiring some basic knowledge about how media work.

Yale psychologists Victoria Brescoll and Marianne LaFrance[23] studied how newspapers report science and how readers learn about science from newspapers. They found that newspapers with a more conservative political stance were more likely to report that gender differences are biological, whereas more liberal papers were more likely to report that gender differences are learned. So, the attitudes of the papers and their reporters changed their conclusions about scientific research. This finding is fascinating. Then these scientists took it to another level. They looked at how these different styles of reporting about gender affected the views of the readers. They made up fictional stories about gender differences in identifying plants. In some of the stories they said women were naturally better at identifying plants, in other stories they said the women were socialized to do the task better. Their results showed that the readers believed whatever explanation they were given. These studies tell us that science is filtered through the sieve of the reporter's biases. They also tell us that readers, at least in some cases, really do believe what they read.

We can apply the findings of this research to a relevant set of findings about media violence. In their *American Psychologist* article "Media Violence and the American Public," social psychologists and media experts Brad Bushman and Craig Anderson[24] explain that the American public doesn't know what to believe about media violence. Americans are confused, in part, because journalists often write media violence stories using the premise that every story has two equal sides. In other words, the best scientific knowledge is weighed as equal to anyone who disagrees—even if the person disagreeing makes his money from the media.

Believe me, I've been the scientist who was interviewed for stories like this enough times to know how it goes. And I've watched my colleagues go through the same thing. The scientist explains some high-quality, painstakingly conducted research and makes what she thinks are reasonable conclusions from the work. Then someone else—a media producer, a caller on a radio show—chimes in and says he doesn't believe that research. Speaking for myself, at this point I marvel to myself at the extreme amount of time, energy, expertise, and other effort that went into the research I just summarized and I mentally compare that to the work it took to blurt out "I don't believe it!" And then maybe it's worse when that kind of response comes not out of genuine ignorance but out of motivated self-interest. When someone wants to sell you something, the lure of profits can and does make him justify saying just about anything.

Bushman and Anderson also documented a bias in journalistic coverage of media violence research. While the scientific data linking media violence and aggression has grown stronger over time, journalists have changed their stance on the issue over the years, most recently trending toward reporting that there is a weak link between media violence exposure and aggression. Clearly, there is ample opportunity for confusion. Some of this, the authors note, may be caused by the fact that the newspapers reporting these stories may also be owned by large conglomerates that sell violent video games and the like. As Bushman and Anderson note, we scientists could do a better job at translating the research to the public. It's also true that consumers who are more media literate will be better equipped to see through some of these issues. To that end, I turn now to a more detailed discussion of increasing one's sophistication as a media consumer.

Increasing Your Sophistication as a Critical User of Mass Media

Let's consider some specific examples of levels of persuasive information present in media messages. This analysis applies equally to a film, a political flyer you receive in your mailbox, or to the advertisement that appears on your screen as you cruise Facebook. Let's begin with noted communications scholar James Potter's notion that media literacy is multidimensional.[25] A media message is multidimensional in that there are several layers of meaning constructed in any single message. An analogy might be helpful here. Take a face-to-face conversation: two friends are talking about a third friend who they think has a drinking problem. One says to the other, "I'm worried about Carrie. She's going to go to that party tonight and drink, and who knows who she is going to end up going home with." Let's look at the different levels of this communication. Potter identifies four dimensions of mass media communication—the cognitive, emotional, aesthetic and moral dimensions—and these apply to our conversation as well. On the cognitive level, we have the information that is being shared: an expression of concern for a friend and some reasons for that concern. On the emotional level, we can interpret a variety of feelings felt by the communicator including worry and anxiety. The aesthetic dimension includes judgments about the communicator's artistry, from her strength as an orator to judging whether what she says is genuine, or whether she is trying to make it appear genuine. Finally, the moral domain relates to values: what judgment is the speaker making about the kind of behavior that is proper for her friend?

Now, moving back to media criticism, one can judge a media message on those four dimensions as well. Why don't we use as an example something most of us have seen many times: an e-mail advertising a "male enhancement" drug. On the cognitive dimension, a critical user can analyze the factual information in the e-mail on many criteria, including the following: What does the drug promise to do? Is it likely that the drug delivers on these promises? What about the assumption that one would need what the drug offers? Moving to the emotional dimension, as a reader you can analyze how the producers of the e-mail wanted you to feel. Did they hope you would feel anxious about your own—ahem!—personal characteristics and therefore that you would send them money? Did they hope you would—ahem!—get excited about this product changing your life? On the aesthetic level, were there pictures (Yikes!), text in ALL CAPS, or other aesthetic features designed to motivate your interest? Did you get the feeling the producers were laughing at consumers while they wrote this ad—or at least thinking about playing to their vulnerabilities? Did the aesthetics make you feel dirty or embarrassed for reading the ad? Finally, on a moral level, what do you think the producers intended for readers to take from the ad? Should one feel that it is "every man for himself" and that to compete with other men in terms of sexual prowess, a man needs this drug? As Potter[26] notes, when we can perceive the values that underlie media messages, "the more sophisticated and reasoned our judgments about those values. It takes a highly media-literate person to perceive moral themes well."

Of course, not all media manipulation is as insidious as the ubiquitous male-enhancement e-mail. Let's take an example of an iconic moment in American media and examine it using Potter's principles of media literacy. In the late 1970s, the miniseries *Roots* aired. Based on the novel *Roots: The Saga of an American Family* by Alex Haley, *Roots* was a story based on Haley's ancestors and their experience as African American slaves. *Roots* received several Emmy awards and is the third most watched TV event in American history, gaining the interest of Americans of all racial backgrounds and drawing their attention to issues of prejudice and discrimination. In a famous scene from the miniseries, a slave named Kunta Kinte (played by LeVar Burton) is whipped brutally for refusing to take the slave name Toby. In that moment in screen history, we can see several messages being sent. There is information (cognitive dimension) that slaves were severely beaten for disobedience, mixed with the emotions engendered by watching this scene, the moral message that such inhumane treatment is reprehensible, and the more general message that when the status quo is morally flawed, one must take action. All of this is delivered in an aesthetic context: the depiction of the skin on Kunta's back as it is lashed relentlessly by the whip, his cries of pain, and the tears in his eyes as he undergoes the experience. Again, a very powerful set of messages has been produced and communicated to the viewer, who interprets all this. In today's media-rich environment, viewers of the program could also share views through blogs or social networking pages that might discuss some of these elements.

These are some lessons in the critical use of media. Active, critical media users think more deeply about media messages; they don't just absorb them without questioning. Critical users understand the notion that media is produced with an agenda in mind. Often the agenda is simply to capture the audience's attention so that the audience will be there to view the advertising that is associated with that particular TV show, Web site, video podcast, and so on.

I can't tell you how many times, as a media researcher, people have told me that the purpose of media is simply to entertain. As we move toward becoming critical consumers of media, we must reject this notion as the hopelessly naïve premise that it is. The primary reason people produce media is to make money. From what I've seen, those producers work fiercely to defend their bottom lines. Now that does not mean that there is no meaningful content in media. As discussed above, there are plenty of positive and entertaining messages in the media. In addition to analyzing media messages for their potential impact, another one of the marks of a media literate person is the ability to make active choices about what media to consume. If you think you watch too much TV for your own good or your own comfort, then you can make it a point to watch less, and/or to be more thoughtful about what you do watch. According to the research, you will most likely be happier and healthier for grabbing hold of the wheel yourself and taking charge.

Without adequate skills in media literacy, your natural inclination will be to digest media messages as you would a real-life experience. If a movie plays sad music to evoke a sad feeling, the naïve viewer's reaction is to simply feel sad and not to be analytic about it or to be aware that the producers are creating a scene in order to evoke an emotion. Now let's look more deeply at another social psychological issue—a broad analysis of how the media messages common to everyday experience contribute to the formation of culture.

The Social Construction of Culture

One of the basic tenets of media literacy is that what we experience via the media plays a large part in creating our culture. To better understand this view, we must begin with a definition of culture. Our culture is our shared reality, created and maintained through common experience and through communication. Culture includes socially constructed meanings including shared beliefs, values, and rules. A swastika, for example, is a symbol that is understood throughout the world to represent the Nazi movement. The same is true for fantasy objects that were created by the media. If I walked into any elementary school classroom, college dormitory, church, or shopping mall in America with a light saber and showed it to the people who were there, would they understand what it was? I am willing to bet that almost every person I encountered would recognize a light saber as an object from our culture, even though it is a fantasy object created by the media. Taking this concept to another level, there are also Star Wars light saber toys for sale, so an American boy may have grown up playing Luke Skywalker versus Darth Vader with his brother using light saber toys. Though Luke and Darth and their light sabers are all fantasies constructed by mass media, they are also all cultural icons—recognizable pieces of our shared culture.

On Power and Liberation

Often those who sell media or those who defend media makers' right to include objectionable content say that they want to encourage freedom. Freedom, in this case, refers to the freedom of expression of the media producers. Media makers also tend to support this view of freedom by labeling any media criticism an attempt at censorship. Is discouraging objectionable content or limiting broadcast hours for this content really censorship or is this a term that serves those who profit from media sales?

This is an excellent time to talk about "framing." When those who make their money from media call media criticism "censorship," they are "framing" their argument, or hoping audiences will view it in the way they've defined it. Framing uses powerful, often emotional language to manipulate the impression the message makes. In this case, media representatives understand that the concept of censorship goes against the American grain. We're a culture built on freedom and the term censorship implies a type of authoritarian denial of liberties that we find repulsive. Using the words "censorship" and "freedom" then, are ways of framing the issue to their advantage. Actually, social psychologists who study persuasion tactics know that this type of framing specifically manipulates those members of society who are *less* knowledgeable. Let's explore why.

John Cacioppo and Richard Petty (no, not *that* Richard Petty) are social psychologists well known for their joint research on the psychology of persuasion. According to Cacioppo and Petty, audiences usually take either the "central" or the "peripheral route" to persuasion. In the central route, one considers the content of the message, or the message's arguments. In the peripheral route, one considers more shallow or tangential information. Consider, for instance, that you want to buy some hand sanitizer to send to school in your child's backpack. If you are persuaded to buy *The Germinator* brand hand sanitizer (*The Germinator* terminates germs—patent pending) because you saw a commercial showing a warm, attractive mother giving her child *The Germinator*, then peripheral cues have influenced you. If, however, you read a *Consumer Reports* article that summarized factual information about hand sanitizers (such as the type of germs they kill and the speed at which they work), then central, or meaningful cues, motivated your purchase.

If we go back to the argument about media criticism being censorship then, we can see that those moved by that argument are more likely to be those reacting to the peripheral cue that censorship is a dirty word. A censor removes material that he finds objectionable; therefore, he restricts other people's freedoms and makes ethical choices for them. Media criticism is not censorship, or imposed restrictions. Rather, it involves understanding, questioning, and suggesting possible consequences of media consumption. Those who wish to profit by manipulating consumers use emotional, hot-button words like "censorship" to accomplish their goals. Another tactic they employ is to claim that media research is faulty or that media research does not show that media affect us. Both assertions are unfounded. Ironically, as discussed in Chapter 1, it is *because* people do not want to feel manipulated (censored, restricted, affected by media) that they end up defending those who actually *are* manipulating them—manipulating them for their money. What a perfect situation this is for those who profit from media revenues! Those who are most vulnerable to their manipulations are those who end up being some of their greatest defenders. The only way out of this trap is through increasing our own knowledge and understanding of how media work and how media messages affect us—in other words, when we become more media literate we put both the power and the freedom from manipulation back in our own hands.

"Censorship" is not the only hot-button term used to frame media debates. Another typical attempt at manipulation is to call media critics "alarmists" or to say that we are *trying to scare people*. If a doctor informs you that eating an unhealthy diet may put you at higher risk for health problems, is she trying to scare you? No, at least not in any gratuitous sense of the word. When experts give information, it doesn't make them alarmists. Here's a media literacy fact: among children starting school, the more television a child watches, the lower his vocabulary. Do I, as a psychologist, tell you that to scare or alarm you? No. I'm an educator and I tell you that to educate and empower you. Psychologists want people to be healthy. We are fortunate in this country to have freedom of choice, but freedom of choice should not be confused with lack of consequences for those choices. Uninformed choices can lead to debilitating consequences. Free choice doesn't always lead to liberation.

More on Fantasy and Reality, or Storytelling Revisited

In Chapter 1, I spoke about the myth that if people understand media stories to be fantasy—in other words, fiction—they are not affected by the content of those stories. Because of how common this misconception this is, I will spend some more time further elaborating on the role of this "fantasy/reality media myth" and how it relates to storytelling. So get comfortable, and settle in with me to what we might consider an alternative version of TV's *Myth Busters*.

The first step to debunking the fantasy/reality media myth is to think about what the essence of modern media is and what it has replaced, or at least augmented, from our past. The most popular forms of modern media (television, movies, video games) are essentially high-tech forms of story-telling. Noted media scholar George Gerbner spoke often about media taking on the role of storytelling. David Walsh's work emphasizes these points as well. People have always told stories; storytelling is a fundamental element of a social system. A movie, like a book or a play, tells a story about people's life experiences. To understand the social power and influence of mass media, we need to go back and ask ourselves some basic questions about storytelling. Why do we tell each other stories? Who are the story-tellers? What are the storyteller's goals? Who are the listeners? How are listeners affected by stories?

Let's examine some classic story forms from the past and relate them to modern storytelling through the mass media. For example, one form of storytelling kept alive through generations is the parable, such as the para-bles of the Bible. One such story is the parable of the Good Samaritan. This familiar story is one of an injured man in need being refused help by a number of seemingly upright men and being shown kindness from someone who wasn't expected to help. Parables have morals. In this case, one moral of this story is that people who are supposed to be upright do not always act accordingly. Why does Jesus tell this story, and why do others who come after him repeat it? The purpose of the parable is to teach important lessons. Why not just deliver the moral and not tell the story? Because stories have the power to engage the listener and to help the listener more deeply understand. When listening to a story, we identify with the characters and their predicaments. We imagine what we would do in their situations. Stories are metaphors and people understand metaphors at a deep level.

Now consider another type of story, common throughout human history—the fable. Aesop's fables are a collection of stories designed to teach lessons through metaphor. For example, consider the fable of the *Fox and the Grapes*. A thirsty fox spies some delicious grapes hanging from a tree and tries to eat the grapes, but cannot reach them. Walking away, the fox says that the grapes were probably sour anyway. The moral of the story? It is easy to despise what you cannot have. Again, why tell this story? When we hear the tale of the *Fox and the Grapes*, we empathize with the fox. We know how it feels to be thirsty. We know how frustrating it is to try and get something you need, only to be denied. We understand what it feels like to want something so badly that you can taste it and then to come away empty-handed. Listening to the story, we put ourselves in the fox's shoes (or in his paws, I suppose), including the feeling of "sour grapes"—of wanting to reject something simply because you know you can't have it. Facing that loss is too painful, so we try to convince ourselves we no longer want the object of our desire. Once again, it is not enough to simply relate the moral; there is something about telling the story itself that makes the moral that much more rich and meaningful. Simply put, storytelling is a way to share someone else's experience vicariously. We feel what the story characters feel. We live that situation through them. Most of all, for our purposes, the experience has meaning for us and we are changed by sharing it with the characters.

Social Learning through Media Imagery and Storytelling

Other than some children's programming such as *Sesame Street* or *The Magic Schoolbus*, we usually do not think of media as educational. But media are great teachers. What specific kinds of lessons do we learn as we soak in media's typical messages? Let's say we watch a television comedy that showcases a group of friends and their wacky exploits. This is just entertainment, isn't it? What could we be learning while watching this show? There are many social lessons to learn and we are, in fact, astute observers of this information. For example, are members of the group sleeping together? Do they sleep with multiple members of the group? How does their friendship circle react to this? Do they respond with humor? How do they perceive casual sex? What are the consequences? Are there unwanted pregnancies or sexually transmitted diseases? And how do the characters look? Are they attractive, thin, muscular, well dressed? How do they spend their time? What do they think is funny? Whom do they ridicule? What do they value? A new study found that watching TV with sexual content is a risk factor in teen pregnancy. One problem is that the shows do not show realistic consequences of sexual activity.[27]

You see, in many ways, we learn how we should act from watching social interactions on television. We learn what behaviors are reinforced. Psychologists call this vicarious reinforcement. If I see a television character being rewarded for sleeping around, I learn from a distance that young, attractive people value this behavior. I also learn vicariously that there are few negative consequences to promiscuity. Research shows that kids who receive these kinds of media messages actually change their own interpersonal behavior based on what they witnessed in the media. So people learn values—both what is socially acceptable and what is rewarded—through the media. They also learn expectations of others and consequences of behaviors.

Are media stories fantasy? Well, yes, in that the specific stories and characters are fictional. Does that mean these stories and images are not real? Not at all. The stories are very real to the viewers in that they represent what the viewer imagines to be the way real people do act or should act and the way real people are rewarded or punished for behaviors. We know that a television actress is playing a role, but we also understand that the story she is acting out has meaning. Why is this? Again, before mass media were so pervasive in our lives, we relied on real, face-to-face social interactions to learn social information. We watched what other people in our village or town did, how they looked, what they valued, and how others reacted to them and their behaviors and we learned from what we saw. This is the basic idea behind the concept of social learning—we look to others for examples of appropriate social behavior. One global reason we do this is because it helps our society run more smoothly. When all the group members understand the group values and roles, the group can live and work together more efficiently.

Also, from an evolutionary perspective, learning appropriate social behaviors is adaptive. For example, let's say that sexual promiscuity tends to cause negative outcomes such as sexually transmitted diseases, unwanted pregnancies, and jealousy. To avoid these problems, a society might choose to punish sexual promiscuity for the good of the group at large. Therefore, members of the group must be taught to value and support monogamy or more sexually conservative behaviors. In the past, this social learning took place within a small group of people. With modern media, we've expanded our role models, so to speak, to include anyone we can see through the media. And media do not portray role models with the goal of presenting behaviors that are most adaptive for the social group. Rather, they choose behaviors designed to get our attention (more on this later). The end result is (sometimes unintended) learning to value more extreme behaviors because we are exposed to them more often, and they therefore become more normal to us.

There are many more lessons—both subtle and not-so-subtle that we can learn from watching social interactions in the media. We've already discussed the transmission of values through the media. How about the effects of representations of group members, such as women and minorities, through the media? Again, when the media represent images of women, for example, they do so to get the attention of viewers, but they can also present a stereotypical and damaging view of women at the same time. Later in the book, I will discuss the research on the effects of this artificial construction of gender in the media.

Pararelationships or "Do I Know You?"

When we spend more time staring at screens and less time with actual people, one result is the strange feeling of having pseudo-relationships with mass media figures. Communications scholars call these "pararelationships." We might also call them mediated social interactions (with the medium—the television, for example—being the go-between). For example, we may feel like we know Bill Clinton after reading his biography. We might daydream about Jon Stewart of the *Daily Show* laughing at our jokes, or secretly fantasize that our attraction to Johnny Depp or Gwyneth Paltrow might someday be returned. Psychologically speaking, this feeling of having relationships with media figures actually makes some sense. As biological organisms, we weren't designed for this paradoxical social situation where we feel that somehow we get to know people personally from afar. When you've watched an actor laugh, cry, and share secrets through the media, it makes sense that you feel you know that person. After all, your brain wasn't made to tell the difference between watching Gwyneth cry on the screen and watching her cry while sitting beside you. Still, one question we can ask is what are the consequences of replacing some of our real relationships with mediated pseudo-social interactions? Among other consequences, we spend less time interacting with the real people in our lives and more time watching others live their lives—or pretend to—from afar. We are also exposed to different information, values, beliefs, priorities, and people than we would otherwise encounter and this exposure can have consequences.

The Social Psychology of Social Networking Sites

Appearing on the scene in the last five years, social networking sites (SNSs) such as MySpace and Facebook are now part of the landscape of how young people interact with each other. If you don't know what a social network site is (you're probably an old fart—just kidding!) it is essentially Web space where individuals can post a personal profile and communicate in a variety of ways with other users. On Facebook, for example, you can write on your friend's "wall" which means you can post a note on an electronic blackboard that that person's other contacts will also see. You can tell all your friends what you are doing right now, updating this as often as you like. You can post information about what music or movies you like or what political candidate you are backing. Similar sites for younger kids are also emerging such as WebKinz, where kids buy a stuffed animal and then access a matching character online. While MySpace has 100 million users, Disney's Club Penguin, which media psychologist David Walsh calls "MySpace for the grade school set" now has four million subscribers.[28]

In December of 2007, a branch of the *Pew Charitable Trusts* called *The Pew Internet and American Life Project* published a research report about teens (ages 12–17) and social networking.[29] According to the report, 93 percent of American teens use the Internet, with 55 percent actively using social networking sites. Twenty-eight percent of teens also have blogs (short for Web log, a blog is a kind of online diary). More teen girls than teen boys have joined the blogosphere (kind of like cyberspace, the blogosphere is the world of blogging) and teen girls are also more likely to use social networks than are teen boys. What are the teen boys doing? Uploading videos on video sharing Web sites like YouTube—teen boys are more likely than teen girls to do so. Parents, by the way, think their kids spend about half as much time online as they actually do.

The Pew researchers asked the teens how they socialize with their friends on a daily basis. Teens reported their preferences in this order: landline phone, cell phone, in person, text messaging, instant messaging, sending messages on social networking sites, and, last *and* least—e-mailing. For "multi-channel teens"—those who have cell phones and use other high-tech forms of communication—they preferred cell phones and text messaging, but still ranked e-mailing last. In fact, when this report was released, word hit the press that "e-mail is for old people." (Dang it, young people! That hurts!)

What's interesting to me as a social psychologist is why teens prefer cell phoning and texting to e-mail: because they want to reach their friends right away, wherever they are. It's also interesting that multi-channel teens preferred talking to friends on their cell phone two to one over spending time with friends in person. In fact, talking to friends in person was low on their list of priorities, only ranking higher than e-mailing.

Services such as social networking sites and photo and video sharing sites have the advantage of letting people carry on a conversation about something with all their friends, albeit not in person. For example, if you post a video on YouTube of your college roommate singing in your dorm room while wearing a towel, then all your friends can make comments that the others will see. According to the Pew survey, almost 90 percent of teens said that when they post photos, people make online comments. With cell phones, you can send out a photo or a video to all your friends simultaneously as well, and you know they're likely to all get it right away, and they can reply to just you or to a whole group of friends. Kids enjoy that kind of immediacy and access to a group of friends simultaneously that these new technologies provide.

I have a profile on Facebook. At first I resisted joining in on the social networking craze. Frankly, as a college professor, I had the vague apprehension that if I logged on to a social networking site, I would be inundated with compromising photos of my students (illicit drinking photos; images of female students in revealing clothing). I just didn't think I wanted those mental images as I walked into the classroom. I'm not the only teacher who feels this way. Recently, an eighth grade teacher wrote an article about social networking in which she began by saying that the first time she perused MySpace, she saw profiles of her students who claimed to use hardcore drugs, claimed to be very much older than they actually were, and so on. She realized after working with these sites and talking to her students that kids do the things they've always done, they just do them in new ways now. For example, kids brag about illicit things that they haven't actually done (of course, some have done them). Kids try to claim their individuality by liking the band that's cool to like (so, they're individuals because they're like everyone else—an age-old teen characteristic). In other words, same stuff, different day.

When I first logged on to MySpace, I cruised around and I did see a lot of trashy pictures and references (though I didn't see any from my students, thankfully. Students, your reputations are still intact—at least with me!). I checked on some of the public social groups that were advertised and quickly found a public group dedicated to young people who claimed to want to have impersonal "hook ups." When you clicked on the group name, a cartoon played accompanied by an adolescent song that said something to the effect of "I don't want to talk to you. I just want to . . . " blah, blah, blah. The thought of my kids getting the social message that this is what the cool kids do was a little unnerving.

On the other hand, I've had good experiences on SNSs too. As someone who does research on video games and interactive media, I get to cruise Facebook and play *Guitar Hero* as "part of my job." (And yes, my friends mock me for this.) The first twenty-four hours I was on Facebook, I was completely addicted. I started marking countries that I had visited on a virtual map of the world. I wrote online reviews of some of my favorite movies. I became an official "fan" of the "Flight of the Conchords"—the award winning comedy team from New Zealand. At that point, I had to swear it off for a while and get back to . . . you know, work. So, to my fellow old people, there is, in fact, a lot to like about SNSs.

It's an axiom that the teen years are times when we all do stupid things. There are many ways that as social interactions go digital, those stupid things are more accessible to a wider range of people for a much longer period of time. Simply put, some of these newer technologies make it easier for kids to make mistakes that will end up publicly embarrassing them or otherwise doing them harm. A friend of mine who teaches high school English recently told me that a female student was the talk of the school because she took nude pictures of herself with her cell phone and sent them to her boyfriend's cell phone. You guessed it: the boyfriend promptly put the pictures on his computer and e-mailed them to . . . basically everyone (have *you* seen them yet?).

Another social psychological aspect of online social networks is that face-to-face social interactions have characteristics that differ in a number of ways from cyber socializing. As mentioned previously, several authors have noted that people can be very mean-spirited online—meaner than that same person would be to your face. Why do you think that is? Well, for one thing, you don't have the immediate facial expressions, body language, tone of voice, and other cues that would be typically done to let someone know when they have gone too far. Also, on a blog or in a chatroom, anonymity can embolden people to say things they wouldn't say if they had to take personal responsibility for them, or if they had to carry on a long-term relationship with that person. A hastily typed comment that makes it to a literally worldwide Web site can take on a gravitas that might be tempting for the perpetrator, and particularly crushing to the receiver.

OMG: My First Meeting on Skype

There are other ways social interactions differ in RL (cybergeek code for real life) as compared to in cyberspace. For example, there are new access points to adult content in cyberspace. As a case in point, I'll tell you about my first meeting on Skype. Skype is an Internet service that allows you to chat (write messages), talk as you would on the telephone, and even send and receive a live video feed from anywhere to anywhere and for free. My friend and colleague Dr. Carlo Fabricatore is the CEO of a video game development company in Rome, Italy. When we began a research collaboration, Carlo suggested we have virtual meetings on Skype. It was a great idea and a great example of how the Internet and new technologies can make so much possible. Carlo was in Italy and I was in the United States, but we could have research meetings almost as if we worked in the same city.

I'd never used Skype before, so I got online, downloaded the required free software, and set up an account. At the appointed time, we both logged on and began talking. There was a lot going on. We were designing some research studies. Also, Carlo, being a very talented person, was speaking about these issues in English—his third language after Italian and Spanish. Furthermore, he is a computer scientist and I am a psychologist, so we bring different perspectives to the table. I was thinking about all of this and was totally unprepared for what happened next. I began getting suggestive chat messages from strange men from different countries. Next, I heard calls ring in with men greeting me. I closed windows and hung up on calls. Carlo, not knowing any of this was going on, continued to talk about research. As if this weren't distracting enough, I was completely unprepared for what happened next: strange men from around the world started to send me pornographic videos. Now you may be wondering what I mean by porno-graphic videos. Just to make this clear, they were naked videos where the camera was trained right on their penises. So, I'm trying to talk about research with my colleague, and chat windows are opening up with mes-sages like, "Hey, pretty lady, you want to talk dirty?" Meanwhile, I am hearing phone calls engage and men saying, "Hello, hello!" and then videos of penises are popping up on my screen. All the while I am frantically closing windows.

Eventually, I had to explain this to Carlo and we had a good laugh about it. He helped me look through my settings and try to find the problem. I thought I had made it so only my contacts could see my information (a brief profile and photo). It turned out that I had done this, but I had neglected to change one setting. Seems that from a list of choices I had selected "Skype me," which apparently is a euphemism for "send me naked videos." Carlo was very good-natured about it and teased me about solving my "popularity problem." I changed the setting and we were able to continue our Skype meetings uninterrupted. Who would have ever thought that anyone would have to deal with the issue of trying to have a meeting while pornographic images and messages popped up all over your computer screen? Again, this new form of technology provided us with great opportunities, but also new challenges.

So I end this chapter as I began it, with the notion that there are ample reasons for both excitement (no pun intended) and concern when it comes to navigating in our ever-changing, media-rich world. For those of us who are parents, this is going to mean taking the time to familiarize ourselves with the technology our kids are using. I know people feel inadequate sometimes when it comes to learning new technologies, but take heart: if our kids can use it easily, believe it or not, we can too. As with all things when it comes to new technologies, knowledge is power, and making an effort to be active and involved is always better than choosing to be left behind.

Section Two

ISSUES AND CONTROVERSIES IN
THE SOCIAL PSYCHOLOGY OF
MASS MEDIA

Three

MEDIA VIOLENCE: SCHOLARSHIP
VERSUS SALESMANSHIP

The *Grand Theft Auto* games such as *Grand Theft Auto III, Grand Theft Auto: San Andreas* and *Grand Theft Auto: Vice City* are perhaps the most widely known video games, making their mark in pop culture due to record-setting sales, critical acclaim in the gaming community, and controversial content. On April 29, 2008, Rockstar games released the much-anticipated sequel *Grand Theft Auto IV* to unparalleled critical acclaim as well as to controversy over violent and sexual content, now de rigeur for a title in the series. That week I got an e-mail from Nicole, a former student of mine. She asked me if I knew that they'd named a car after me in *GTA IV*, telling me to go to YouTube and search for "Karin Dilettante."

I got on YouTube and watched the video—a humorous promotion for a hybrid car described as a "seriously bad, morally good, fully customizable luxury V.I.P. style hybrid sedan: the Karin Dilettante."[1] At first I couldn't quite believe it. I asked some of my friends and colleagues who are video game violence experts if they thought this *Grand Theft Auto* car was really named in "honor" of me. They said they thought it was. Come to think of it, naming a car in a violent video game a variation of Karen Dill is a pretty unlikely phenomenon, unless you take into account that a media violence critic is named Karen Dill. Considering I have publicly critiqued the *Grand Theft Auto* games in various media outlets, in scholarly journals, and in front of Congress—okay, yeah, I see.

FIGURE 3.1. A screen shot of my "namesake" the Karin Dilettante—a car in the videogame *Grand Theft Auto IV* by Rockstar Games, distributed by Take Two Interactive.

Now, if you're not familiar with the term, a "dilettante" is basically an amateur who pretends to be a professional. In other words, a dilettante is someone who thinks she knows what she's talking about, but really doesn't. The word comes from a root meaning to be delighted, and applies especially to a superficial admirer of the arts.

So apparently the guys at Rockstar games were teasing me about critiquing their art with my pseudo-knowledge or faux expertise, if you will. I actually think it's a pretty subtle and sly lampoon—in my opinion, quite clever. I don't mind being teased—in fact, I enjoyed it immensely. You might say I was quite *delighted* (or is that *Dill*-lighted?) by the satire.

Media Industry Spin: Scholars as Dilettantes

But of course, this does beg the question: are media violence experts like myself really dilettantes? Media violence is a controversial topic to be sure, with outspoken, passionate advocates sitting on both sides of the table. In a recent poll of parents of teenagers, about 6,000[2] adults were asked whether media violence exposure (specifically violent video games) affects children's behavior. Fifty-eight percent answered "yes," 31 percent answered "no," and 11 percent didn't know. How would you interpret these results? First, one might note that the majority of the people surveyed believe media violence exposure affects children negatively. But a roughly 60/30/10 breakdown is far from a unanimous interpretation of the evidence. Broadly speaking, there are people who believe media violence exposure harms children and another sizable group believes the opposite. These data were collected on a parenting Web site, so they were probably biased toward more concerned parents. People who clicked on the poll were probably interested in the topic. Why do these people believe what they do? Who is right, if there is a right answer? Is this even the right question?

One very important aspect of a poll like that is it asks people to make a judgment about how other people are affected by mass media. Because of the third person effect, we know that people are more apt to think that others are affected than to think they themselves are. Since most polls ask about people in general, theoretically the numbers would be much stronger than if polls asked people if they personally felt influenced.

An interesting place to gather some relevant information is the Web site whattheyplay.com—billed as the "parents' guide to videogames." Whattheyplay.com was launched in 2007 by media industry professionals Ira Becker and Jon Davison, with the following mission: "Our singular goal is to provide useful insight and information within a wholly unbiased and independent environment, empowering parents to do what they do best: parent." The site features columns called "Ask gamer dad," and "In the family room," as well as a current listing of the top-selling games by platform, and down-to-earth descriptions of what parents need to know about the current games. They are sponsored by kid-friendly games like *George of the Jungle* and *We Ski*.

In response to the release of *GTA IV*, whattheyplay.com provided a comprehensive *GTA IV* parent's resource center. They interviewed kids about topics ranging from why they like to play *GTA* to discussions of how under-aged kids planned on getting a copy of the game. They also provided videos showing game content that parents might find objectionable organized by the Entertainment Software Rating Board (ESRB) content descriptors for the game: strong language, partial nudity, strong sexual content, blood, and intense violence.

Let's take some time here to detail the content that appears in a game like *Grand Theft Auto IV*. What kinds of things do kids hear and see when they play? I think this is a crucial part of the conversation about controversial issues in the media. Content like sex and violence, after all, can be portrayed in an infinite variety of ways. To really understand the issues, you need to know exactly what kids are seeing, and therefore learning about, when they play these games. We should pause for a moment here and acknowledge that parents could not so easily see this content without the Internet and without people who care about these issues providing the content to parents. So these are excellent examples of how media can provide information and community to parents in a way previously unseen.

What's in a Game?

Okay, so let's return to analyzing the specific content of *GTA IV*. For the rating of intense violence, we see characters punching and kicking each other and throwing flaming objects. Moving into the gun violence, we see the main character standing on the street shooting civilians and police officers while cursing his targets, calling them names, and making quips. In one scene he shoots someone point blank in the skull and blood spurts out, the man dies, and the main character curses the man. A promo for *GTA IV* jokes about going out on dates and shooting people, promising, "liquor, guns and fun." For the examples of drug and alcohol use, characters drink or snort cocaine and then kill pedestrians remarking that they didn't like the way the pedestrian was looking at them.

In terms of strong sexual content, *GTA IV* is more graphic than its predecessors. Past versions of *GTA* depicted sex by showing a car rocking from a distance accompanied by sound effects and sexual dialogue. In *GTA IV*, you see the characters' bodies through the car windows—for example, a man on top of a woman clearly having sex or a woman with her head in a man's lap. So, the depictions of sex, although they do not show total nudity, are becoming more explicit. Scenes also show women in thongs and pasties dancing in front of men while the men make crude comments.

According to whattheyplay.com, why do thirteen-year-olds say they like the *GTA* games? According to one young player: "Last week, I missed one homework and my teacher yelled at me. When I went home, I started playing [*Grand Theft Auto*] *Vice City*, and did a cheat code to get a tank. I ran over everybody. And I smashed a lot of cars and blew them up. Like, I was mad, and I turned happy afterwards."[3]

Very typically, many pooh-pooh the idea that games can affect players and speak in an insulting way about anyone who says otherwise. For example, a news article[4] covering the release of *GTA IV* stated, "Rockstar Games and its GTA franchise are a focal point for critics that fear violence in video games warps the minds of young players and turns them into real-world thugs or killers." Similarly, players are incensed by the notion that game content affects players. In reaction to the discussion of why teens like *GTA* on whattheyplay.com, players posted the following comments.[5] The comment title precedes each quote.

No problems: "I've grown up with the GTA games, and they are no problem what-so-ever! And these cases that have surfaced where a teenager has blamed GTA for him raping a girl, or shooting someone, is the fault of the parents, because they'd rather blame someone else for their kid's mess, and not look at themselves to see what caused the actions!"

Games will not effect [sic] the sane: "I'm 25 years old and have been with the GTA series since the very beginning. Despite all the fun I have causing mayhem in the digital world of GTA, never once did I get the feeling it was ok to do the things I do in the game world in the real world. It really comes down to a person's ability to keep fantasy separate from reality. The GTA games in no way encourage the behavior of it's [sic] characters."

This is about art: "You can find violent material on the very pages of the bible but they will never claim that the bible is influencing our youth negetivly [sic]. This is so hippicritical [sic] i need to stop writing immiediatly [sic] so i can punch a wall. You all need to do a lot more thinking. A 17 year old kid is smarter than you, and thats [sic] just pathetic."

I've read many comments over the years of game players who are angry with anyone who says their games may cause negative behavior. I think these comments are typical of what I've read and I think they merit deeper analysis. First, I understand the frustration of the players and I think it is based on a misunderstanding. The teenagers of the world (especially the boys) play violent video games and they are not morphing into a mob of thousands upon thousands of murderers. The research, however, clearly shows that video game violence exposure increases aggression. Where's the disconnect? The disconnect is primarily that the effects do not typically take the form that the players anticipate—namely, a game play session followed by murder. Keep in mind that psychologists do not measure murder as an outcome in the laboratory—for obvious reasons. What we do measure is aggression—someone harming someone else or believing that they are harming someone else. This can take many forms, including actions like insults, sabotage, or delivering blasts of noise that they believe can permanently damage hearing—the latter being an outcome my colleague Brad Bushman recently measured in his lab.

More on these issues shortly, but before I expand on those ideas, I want to address the comment that "this is about art." I think another frustration of the gaming community is that the creativity they admire is not given appropriate respect in the larger community. They are angry that outside the gaming community, the concept that a video game constitutes art is often laughed at. Let me give you an example. In the spring of 2008 I was a guest on a radio call-in show called *These Days* on KPBS in San Diego.

When someone compared the graphics of the latest video game to that of a blockbuster film, the host laughed. Later, a game developer called in and commented that when the host laughed, it hurt him. What happened? The host laughed again.

I felt bad for the caller. I'm not being sarcastic; I really did. Let me go on record as saying that I believe a video game can be art and it can be a major technological accomplishment that has value and that the creators can be proud of. But let's be fair here—scientific studies are also works of art, they also have value, and they are also conducted with extreme care and with the hope that they will be of value to the world at large. Rather than being dismissive of anyone's work, we can offer respectful critiques. That doesn't mean we must be coldly evaluative. We can have passion about our area of expertise, but it's important also to be open-minded and respectful.

Scholarship Versus Salesmanship

So, approaching this with an open mind, let's talk about the science behind the social psychology of the mass media—what goes into it and what value it has. I hope along the way that I can clear up some of the myths associated with media violence research and that I can communicate exactly why I believe this research is as valuable as it is—a fact that has sometimes been lost in the media coverage of the social psychological study of media violence. I also believe, as outlined in Chapter 1, that those who are trying to make a profit from media violence have a vested interest in promoting the notion that the science is all wrong. In the end, the little guy who buys the product and supports the wealthy industry execs becomes just a pawn in the game. That person's naïveté about the industry ends up being harmful to him. Think about it this way: when someone has something to sell you and that product is widely regarded by scholars to be harmful, whom should you believe, the scholars or the salesmen? Who is more likely to be using you?

Gamers aren't the only ones lining up to say that the results of media violence research are garbage. *USA Today* published an article[6] summarizing some of my research on the effects of exposure to violent video games. At the end of the article, presumably to be fair and balanced, they interviewed someone with an opposing viewpoint. Jonathan Katz—an outspoken critic of, well, media criticism—was quoted as saying, "If this study was right, there'd be hundreds of bodies lying around. People are pushing an agenda of hysteria on parents."

Okay, let me take these ideas in turn. "If this study was right, there'd be hundreds of bodies lying around." Again, here we see the idea that media violence researchers think that playing a violent video game or watching a violent movie will result in only one thing: murder—lots of murder! As for the "pushing an agenda of hysteria"—that's rhetoric. He's making the argument that if you are critical about media violence that means you are trying to make the unsuspecting citizens of America hysterical.

Unhealthy Diets Result in Real—If Not Dramatic—Results

Maybe an analogy would be useful here. Let's say that medical researchers find that fat consumption is related to heart problems. Let's say, for argument's sake, that the researchers had scientific proof that diets high in fat cause heart problems and this research was written up in *USA Today*. How would it sound if there were a health research critic who was quoted as saying, "If this study were right, people would be dropping dead in McDonald's restaurants all over the country. These doctors are pushing their agenda of health hysteria"? It's really a similar thing. People don't die right after eating cheesecake (thank you, God) or pork rinds or lard, but we understand those things are not heart healthy. What does it mean that they're not heart healthy? It means that the more fat you have in your diet, the greater is your risk of heart problems. Also, the less healthy foods in your diet, like fruit and vegetables, the greater your risk of heart problems.

The same is true for your media diet, and remember, we actually call it media consumption for a reason. You consume media. You take it in and it becomes a part of you. The more you see people hurting each other, disrespecting each other, and treating each other poorly, the more that makes its way into your consciousness. That's especially true with the way aggression is generally portrayed in the media—as cool, gratifying, fun, and without consequences. When my son was in the second grade, he saw one boy from his class beat up another boy in the bathroom at school. When he talked about it, his eyes filled with tears and he told me how bad it had made him feel to see that little boy get hurt. I gently explained that this is one reason why mom speaks out against violence in the media. Real aggression is not cool or fun or glamorous; it's a little boy getting hurt and his friends feeling terrible as they see it happen.

Jeanne Funk and her colleagues[7] understand the importance of children's feelings about violence—like my son's sadness at watching a friend get hurt—in the broad scheme of media violence research.

They were interested in discovering whether there was a relationship between feelings of empathy—like my son felt for his friend—and playing violent video games. They measured violence exposure—both real and in the media—empathy and attitudes toward violence, in fourth and fifth grade boys and girls. What they found was intriguing. Of the variables they studied, only video game violence exposure was associated with lower empathy. Watching violent movies and playing violent video games were both associated with stronger pro-violence attitudes. When Funk and her colleagues measured empathy, they asked questions like whether it bothered the child when other children got hurt. When they measured attitudes toward violence, they asked things like whether people with guns and knives are cool. The results of this study have many implications. The results certainly show that the more violent video games you play, the less likely you are to be concerned about other people getting hurt and the more likely you are to think that aggression is cool and appropriate. These results are also important because decreased empathy and increased positive attitudes about violence have been linked in previous research to aggressive behavior. Funk and her colleagues also discussed the notion that decreased empathy and increased pro-violence attitudes after media violence exposure also indicate desensitization. In other words, one may not realize one is being affected because negative reactions to media violence become blunted with increased exposure. We can relate this back to the discussion in Chapter 1: one reason people who are exposed to more media do not think it affects them might well be because increased exposure causes desensitization.

Sins of Commission and Sins of Omission

Let's not forget the other part of the diet analogy, though: the less good stuff you have in your diet, the greater your risk. The more you are watching harm and negativity in the media, the less you are watching anything that uplifts you—also, the less you are doing media-free activities like talking to your friends, playing sports, or drawing. Remember the reference to Dorothy and Jerome Singer's work in Chapter 2? They stress how important it is for children to engage in free play and that such play helps children build skills like managing emotions, delaying gratification, and getting along with others.[8] In fact, media scholars are beginning to talk about the media violence issue in terms of risk factor models. The more negativity and the less positivity in your media diet, the greater your risk for negative outcomes.

Put Down the Fry—Before you Die

When it comes to what we eat, we know what tastes good and we know what's good for us. We also know that what tastes good isn't always good for us. With this knowledge and understanding, we make our choices. To extend the metaphor, we're still arguing that French fries are healthy—that scientists are just alarmists and they want to mess up the fun we have eating French fries. The most controversial topics in media are relational—harming people, presenting an unbalanced view of sex and sexuality, encouraging racial and sexist stereotypes. These are issues that affect us all. They are social issues, not individual ones. That's what makes this everybody's business. My interest is in revealing that the emperor is unclothed. At the individual level and at the level of government and culture, we then make choices about what to do with that information.

Media Violence Myths—Another Kind of Big Bang Theory?

Before we move on, I want to revisit the myth that media violence exposure causes murder and if it doesn't, then it has no effect. This is just one of many myths about media violence that experts have written a bit about. In *The 11 Myths of Media Violence*, Potter defines a myth as something most people in the culture accept even though the logic is flawed or the evidence does not support it. His number one media violence myth is that people think media violence doesn't affect them, but it does affect others—this is the third person effect that we discussed in Chapter 1. The psychology of the third person effect is actually fascinating. If the result were not a naïveté that makes people vulnerable to being used and makes them more likely to be changed for the worse, I would sit around just being fascinated by it. I think the third person effect represents what Anna and Sigmund Freud would have called a defense mechanism—a way to protect ourselves from the uncomfortable knowledge that we are doing something that doesn't make sense. We defend our egos by thinking that we are invulnerable. There's no reason to defend what other people are doing. They can be as stupid or vulnerable as they want and it does not scare us into rejecting what we believe is true—that media violence can be harmful and that others are really vulnerable to its effects. So, we see what people report over and over again—that they think they are not vulnerable to media effects, but that other people are. For example, one study showed that the more violent the video games a person plays, the less likely that person is to think media violence has negative effects.[9] And interestingly, new research demonstrates that those who are most deeply engaged by video games, those who are absorbed and transported by them, also tend to be more aggressive.[10]

Other top experts have argued convincingly about media violence myths. In the book *Media Violence and Children*, Doug Gentile and Craig Anderson[11] outline video game violence research and summarize what scientists have found in this research. They review data from a variety of research designs, including meta-analyses—studies that summarize a large body of past published research—and draw conclusions from the studies. These experts report that the research clearly documents five main findings, as follows. Playing violent video games *(1)* increases the body's physical arousal (for example, heart rate and blood pressure), *(2)* increases aggressive thoughts (thoughts related to harming another person), *(3)* increases aggressive feelings (like hostility), *(4)* increases aggression (behavior intended to harm someone else), and *(5)* decreases helping.

The authors also take on the issue of industry critiques of research, saying that when research threatens the profits of big business,[12]

> there is a tendency for that industry to deny the threatening research and to mount campaigns designed to highlight the weaknesses, obfuscate the legitimate findings, and cast doubt on the quality of the research. The history of the tobacco industry's attempt to ridicule, deny, and obfuscate research linking smoking to lung cancer is the prototype of such efforts. The TV and movie industries have had considerable success in their 40-year campaign against the media violence research community. The same type of effort has now been mounted by the video game industry.

In another chapter of the same volume, Gentile and Sesma[13] outline *Seven Myths about Media Effects*: *(1)* media effects are simple and direct, *(2)* the effects of media violence are severe, *(3)* media effects are obvious, *(4)* violent media affect everyone in the same way, *(5)* causality means "necessary and sufficient," *(6)* causality means immediacy, and *(7)* effects must be "big" to be important.

Let me highlight and comment on some of these myths. Let's take simple, direct, severe, obvious, and immediate and put them together for a moment. These reflect some of the quotes from real people I mentioned earlier in this chapter. People conceptualize media violence effects as turning kids immediately into murderers or as resulting in piles of bodies lying in the street. We seem to think only in extremes—that if I see the neighbor's kid playing *Grand Theft Auto* and he doesn't turn on the spot and shoot another child, that media violence has no effect on children. This is, very thankfully, not the way the human mind works.

There are, of course, natural restraints against murder. There are social sanctions ranging from disapproval to the death penalty. The great American psychologist B. F. Skinner said that his parents used to hold up the idea of prison as a warning to keep him on good behavior. That reminds me of how my husband—a psychology professor—enjoys joking in a twisted way with our son that if he's really bad, he's going to get sent to "juvy." But aside from my family's rather warped sense of humor, it's perfectly true that we understand that murder is the ultimate crime and we therefore know there are extreme social sanctions against it. And in the animal kingdom, animals will fight to defend their interests, but there is a strong tendency to prefer fighting *for* something as opposed to fighting to the death. Naturally, this preserves the species and so it is adaptive.

So, please, can we dispense with the notion that playing a violent video game or watching a violent movie will result in the person who is exposed morphing immediately into a robotic death machine? Careful now! Don't swing wildly back to the other extreme. This doesn't mean that media violence has no effects on real aggression. It does. These effects are documented over and over by scientists. It's just that you should understand the effects are subtle (at least more subtle than always and immediately going postal on the nearest human) and long term. They build over time, and the outcomes can take many forms such as harassing a colleague at work, spreading rumors about a roommate, or getting in a fist fight after drinking too much. Make no mistake, watching more media violence does predict whether you will end up in jail for violent crime. It predicts whether you will beat your spouse. The negative consequences of media violence exposure are definitely there; they just play themselves out in ways that are more subtle than many people apparently expect them to be.

Also important to understand is the idea of "necessary and sufficient." If you've taken a course in logic, you may recall these two words as tools of the trade. Basically, what we mean here when we talk about necessary and sufficient is this: (1) everybody who is aggressive wasn't provoked by violent media, and (2) if only violent media were involved, that probably wouldn't be enough to provoke the aggression. It's an important point, so I'll draw some lines under it: media violence isn't the only cause or even the main cause of violence. Media violence exposure is part of the grand scheme in a person's life. It tends to teach people that violence is an acceptable, socially sanctioned way to solve conflict. It reshapes the brain and makes aggression a more likely outcome. It takes the place of other, more adaptive solutions to life's conflicts. It alters social thinking, for example, to characterize some people as more acceptable targets of violence. Seeing violence on the screen teaches complex ideas about social interactions—about how we should treat other people. Now, let's take a closer look at the science used to investigate media violence effects.

Analyzing the Quality of the Science of Media Psychology

Anyone who has gone to college (or primary school, for that matter) has had an education on the fundamentals of science. Let's revisit that education in the context of studying media effects. The most basic premise of science is that it is a fundamental system of logic, designed to answer hypothetical questions while minimizing bias. To perform a scientific investigation, we form a hypothesis—usually based on a broader theory—and then we collect data to see if there is support or evidence for it. All things being equal, if the premise is true, it should be supported by the research. If it is not true, it should not gain support. Over time, if scientists conduct many investigations, a body of evidence emerges that suggests whether the ideas and relationships we study really seem to hold up.

Let me give you several examples and you can see what you think. There are studies, for instance, that demonstrate that children whose school environments are noisy (such as happens with schools in the vicinity of airports) have more difficulty concentrating on their work than students in schools without noise problems. Now, does that mean that children whose schools are near airports are dumb and will never amount to anything? Or is it that they are poor kids and their upbringing is actually causing their school problems? Maybe their parents are to blame because they let them go to school near an airport, therefore making them bad parents? No, those comments are far afield from the actual findings or are outright misinterpretations of the findings. It does, however, mean that, all things being equal, it's harder to concentrate on schoolwork when it's noisy. In the laboratory, scientists simulate such real-world situations by giving people tasks to work on with or without distracting noise levels and measuring their performance. Let's say, as is the case, the scientists discover in their laboratories that noise impairs performance and that these results are reported in the media. What would you think if people got mad about these results, said the scientists were quacks and that they did not believe the findings, got mad about scientists ganging up on noise when there are so many other bad things happening in the world? Well, you see where I'm going with this. Those things actually happen as a reaction to media violence research. My point: one has to be critical of other people's observations about science just as one has to be critical about science itself, or news media, or any other form of authority.

Speaking of education, I was given the gift of an excellent education, and for this reason I feel an obligation to tell the public what I have learned, whether it is controversial or not. I was among the first generation of my very large family to go to college. My education was almost entirely funded by scholarships from University of Missouri-Columbia and the state of Missouri —a fact that I am very aware of and grateful for. While I had to work hard and make the grades, my state government and university supported my education. When I was a sophomore in college, I began working with Craig Anderson, who later directed my dissertation. I consider Craig the consummate social scientist, well versed in everything from research methods, design, and statistics to broad scientific theory. My parents never went to college, but I was trained at the Ph.D. level by one of the finest social scientific minds in the country. I guess America really is the land of opportunity. In that context, it is my firm belief that I owe the larger community the benefits of that education.

I have joked before in print that I have a Ph.D., and I'm not afraid to use it. That joke is essentially true. I understand social science—I understand how the media works and how media messages affect people, and I consider it a fundamental part of my life's work to translate science in the public interest. Whatever those in the media industry may believe, it is not my mission in life to be a killjoy and denigrate video games and people who like them. I like nonviolent video games. I know several people who work for the game industry who are very likable. I am not on a vendetta. But I do have a personal mission to translate science in the public interest; to do anything less would be to fail to give back what I have been given so freely by my state and country.

I teach the history of psychology, and every semester my students write biographies of psychologists. The biography paper assignment is structured so that students present the psychologist's life and career contributions and end the paper with an integrative approach, analyzing how the life experiences and personality of the individual informed the career. This is why I relate my own background, personality, and views along the way in this book. Teaching the history of psychology gives me a broad perspective on the human enterprise that is science. I think the view of any science is incomplete without this comprehensive, human approach because the enterprise of science is made up of scholars operating within the bounds of their own internal mission statements.

Now that you know something of my background and my personal mission as a scientist, let's get into the details of some of the media violence research. I want to point out why I think it is such high-quality research that merits your consideration as you make media choices. Next, I'd like to describe one of the most remarkable research programs in the entire discipline of modern psychology. I am not blowing wind up your collective skirt, gentle readers; you would be hard pressed to find a body of work in the entire discipline that lives up to these standards. Settle in and let me tell you all about it.

Yale child psychologist Leonard Eron began this project circa 1960 with the premise that effective child psychologists should involve themselves in the community. He wanted to investigate the causes of childhood aggression and he began auspiciously by interviewing every third grader (856 to be exact) in Columbia County, New York. He also interviewed 80 percent of their mothers and fathers.[14] Leonard Eron, who died in 2007, was a scientist whose work was a shining example of science at its best. First, it began with a genuine desire to work hard to help children, and it progressed with an unparalleled degree of everything that makes science good: high standards, methods of research that make sense and are uncompromising, and, at the end of the day, findings that matter to a lot of people.

This project that Leonard Eron began evolved into a one of the longest running projects of its kind in the history of psychology—spanning over forty years and known collectively as the Columbia County Longitudinal Study.[15] A longitudinal study is one that follows participants over time, collecting information at different points in time. Along the way, a number of scientists joined Eron on this project, most notably his close colleague L. Rowell Huesmann, now at the University of Michigan at Ann Arbor Institute for Social Research.[16,17]

After the initial interviews with the parents and children in 1960, there were subsequent interviews when the participants were nineteen, thirty, and forty-eight, as well as interviews with 551 of the participants' own children. Let me insert here that if you are a social scientist all these statistics about the Columbia County Longitudinal Study are not only impressive—they may actually inspire the need for a fainting couch. Researchers, as a group, are gluttons for punishment. We enjoy things like design, methodology, and statistics that, at least according to the many students I've known, are quite distasteful to others outside the research world. Some historians of psychology[18] speculate that one reason the modern science of psychology took off in Germany was that Germans are an exacting people—people who enjoy big heaping loads of tedious work. (I myself am of largely German descent, and may I say I love big heaping loads of tedious work?) The simplest research project is frankly a nightmare to most people, as countless students have told me over the years. Ninety-nine percent of all humans who have ever lived (and I am totally making these numbers up) want nothing to do with the amount of work the most typical research project takes. But the Columbia County Longitudinal Study—that one required superhuman skills and commitment from the researchers.

So, after all of that painstaking work, what did Eron, Huesmann, and their colleagues find? They found that the violent television the kids viewed when they were eight caused them to be violent later in life. For the sake of detail, let's look more closely at some of their data analysis. They grouped participants by their scores on preference for violent TV (high, medium, and low violence preference) and for real-life aggressive behavior (high, medium, and low aggressive behavior). What they discovered was that regardless of how aggressive they were as third graders, those who watched more violent TV as third graders were reliably the young adults (18- and 19-year-olds) who were the most aggressive. They were also able to ascertain that it was indeed the violence viewing that caused the aggression—in other words, it was not simply that kids who like to watch violence also are aggressive but that the exposure to media violence caused them to be aggressive later in life. They were able to ascertain this causal connection using advanced statistical modeling techniques. The methods and analyses were sophisticated and powerful. Furthermore, the scientists did an effective job at translating their high-level science for public consumption. Though sometimes the scientists who are smart at the very complex tasks necessary for high-quality research aren't the strongest at explaining it to laypersons, this was not the case for Huesmann and Eron and their colleagues. It was stellar science all the way through, from execution to translation.

Huesmann and Eron's team has also spent decades elaborating on exactly why and how media violence exposure causes increases in aggression. They have shown definitively that aggressive behavior is, in part, learned and that an important part of that learning is how viewing aggression changes how you think. It quite literally restructures your brain and how you understand the world.

What reaction did the Columbia County Longitudinal Study receive? Rowell Huesmann and Eric Dubow tell the story best, describing their colleague Leonard Eron's life work in the *American Psychologist* in 2008:[19]

> The 1970 follow-up was part of the U.S. Surgeon General's initiative on the effects of television, and Eron's conclusion from that follow-up, that media violence causes aggression, was published in the *American Psychologist*.... It led to a storm of controversy. Critiques and countercritiques were written.
>
> Mass media interests promoted opposition to the conclusion. Believing strongly in the importance of the public policy role for psychologists, Eron spoke about his work repeatedly in public forums, on radio and TV shows, and in testimony before Congress. His firm but polite demeanor under fire convinced many skeptics of the truth of his conclusions. After hearing Eron's testimony, U.S. Surgeon General Jesse L. Steinfeld testified in March 1972 before the U.S. Senate Commerce Committee that "it is clear to me that the causal relationship between [exposure to] televised violence and antisocial behavior is sufficient to warrant appropriate and immediate remedial action. There comes a time when the data are sufficient to justify action. That time has come."

Huesmann and Eron and their colleagues continued to conduct key studies over the years, including the Cross National Television and Aggression Study. In this version, they began with six- to ten-year-old kids who grew up in the American Midwest and in Finland, Poland, and Israel in the 1970s and 1980s. These participants were first and third graders during the initial interviewing stage. The researchers interviewed them as elementary schoolchildren three times at one-year intervals. Then they caught up with them again fifteen years later when they were young adults. They found that there were correlations between childhood television violence viewing and adult aggression in all the countries. They also found the causal effect of being a heavy TV violence viewer as a child and adult aggression in all the countries except Australia. Huesmann[20] reports:

> The boys and girls who were in the top 25% in TV violence viewing at age 6 to 10 behave significantly more violently 15 years later. They are more likely to shove and throw things at their spouses. They are more likely to shove, punch, beat, and choke other people. They are more likely to commit crimes and traffic offenses. They are seriously

more aggressive than those who were not watching a lot of TV violence when they were children!

In his book *The Eleven Myths of Media Violence*, James Potter argues that many private citizens and political leaders have believed for a long time that media violence causes harm. This stance is certainly underlined by reviewing some of the now almost fifty years of research produced by Huesmann and Eron and their colleagues, as well as the work of many other fine scholars. One problem, Potter believes, is that those who are concerned simply do not know what to do to solve the problem. Potter cites an impressive series of government-sponsored hearings over the years designed to discuss the problem of media violence. But, he says, what happens after the hearing is over? No specific, powerful, global changes take place and years later we simply end up repeating the process all over again. In fact, Potter argues that when it comes to the public debate over media violence, we have been stalled at essentially the same place for over fifty years!

Experts Agree: Violence Breeds Violence

Recently a group of the top media violence experts were asked to come together and author a paper summarizing the current consensus among media violence experts. These scholars concurred with Potter that there is general agreement in the scientific community that media violence causes aggression. In fact, these scholars[21] concluded that "the scientific debate over whether media violence increases aggression is essentially over." They reported on the many methods of research used over all the most popular genres of media (TV, movies, video games, etc.)—studies that repeatedly document the same essential message—violence breeds violence.

We already discussed one important research methodology—the longitudinal studies on children's violent TV exposure. Another key type of study that has greatly contributed to our knowledge of media violence effects are the experiments showing that short-term exposure to media violence increases aggression relative to people not exposed to media violence. To be able to appreciate the power of this design, you don't need a Ph.D. in psychology, just an understanding of good logic. Good science is really just good logic. Think about a classic experimental design— there is a treatment group and a control group. For example, let's imagine the treatment group takes a diet pill and the control group takes a placebo (a pill with no medicinal properties). Now let's say there is a box full of pill bottles—half diet pills and half placebos, and the bottles and pills all look alike. Participants are randomly handed a pill bottle. If, at the end of the testing period, the people who took the diet pills lost more weight than the people who took the placebos, logic suggests the diet pills probably cause weight loss. See what I mean? It's just logic. The easiest explanation for the differences between groups is that they took different pills.

Okay, now let's apply this same logic to a basic experiment on media violence. Take 200 people and show half a violent film clip and the other half a nonviolent film clip, and then measure their aggression. If the group who saw the violent film clip are more aggressive, then logic suggests it was probably what they saw in the film that caused them to be more aggressive. When you look at the simplicity and strength of a design like this, it is hard to imagine how people could disagree with the basic premise of what scientists have found. Many studies with strong designs—like the long-itudinal studies and experiments described here and more—show that media violence exposure causes aggression. I think that evidence is pretty definitive and that science (again, logic) is one of the best tools we have to try to help us make sense of a complex world.

Examples are always helpful, so let's look at the particulars of some of the media violence experiments. University of Missouri social psychologist Bruce Bartholow and his colleagues[22] asked ninety-two college males to play either *Unreal Tournament* (a violent game in which the player's job is mostly to shoot whoever comes in his path) or *Myst* (a nonviolent game in which players explore and solve puzzles). They told the participants that the study was designed to test how playing video games affects your ability to mentally and physically react quickly and to make decisions. Then they all played a computer game in which a blip appears on the screen and they see how fast they can react by pressing a button. If they were the fastest, they got to punish their opponent by blasting him with an obnoxious noise—they chose how loud and how long the noise blast would be. If they lost, they were the ones who got to hear the noise blast. What Bartholow and his colleagues found was that these college guys punished their opponents more if they'd just been shooting people on a video game screen than if they'd just been playing a game that involved thinking and exploring. The message: practice violence on the video game screen and you will punish a real person more in your real life. Playing at harming someone increases the chances that you would *really* hurt someone. Fantasy creates reality.

Now, in this study, as typically happens in research, the participants really weren't harming anyone—they just thought they were. An actor showed up in the lab and pretended to be the opponent, but he really wasn't forced to take the punishment. What matters, of course, is that the guys thought they were punishing another guy. In fact, any of the guys who said they didn't think anyone was really getting hurt were not included in the data analysis.

Since I've mentioned my dissertation,[23] let me tell you a little bit about it. Craig Anderson and I conducted two studies. In the first study, we were interested in whether playing violent video games predicted real-life aggression. So we tested over 200 college students and discovered that this was the case—the more violent video games you played, the more likely you were to have threatened someone or hit someone, either a schoolmate or a teacher, for example. Playing more violent video games in real life also predicted other kinds of delinquency such as cheating and lying, and it predicted poorer school performance. These relationships were stronger for people with aggressive personalities and for males.

So the first study took a snapshot of the way violent video game players differ from others. But to isolate whether the video game violence causes the aggression, a scientist needs to do a design that will measure that cause, so we designed an experiment to do just that. We wanted to pick a violent game and a nonviolent game and see whether players were more aggressive after playing the violent game. First, we made sure the two games we used were rated by a separate group of students as equally exciting, fast paced, and so on, but different in violent content. Based on these pretests, we selected *Myst* and *Wolfenstein 3D* and randomly assigned male and female students to play one or the other. Those who played the violent game had more aggressive thoughts than those who played the nonviolent game, as measured by a cognitive reaction time task—a test designed basically to measure what thoughts are active in the brain. We measured aggressive behavior using a competitive task, like the one I described above that Bruce Bartholow and his colleagues used. People who'd played the violent video game responded with more aggression toward an opponent than those who had played the nonviolent game. Taken together, these two studies show that those who choose to play violent video games also tend to be more aggressive, and that playing a violent video game causes players to be more aggressive and to think more aggressive thoughts.

Berkowitz and Geen[24] demonstrated how lessons learned in the mass media about violence are evoked and acted upon by viewers. In their study, male participants watched either an aggressive scene in which the aggression was justified, an aggressive scene in which aggression was less justified, or an exciting but nonaggressive control film. Participants were then given an opportunity to administer punishing shocks to an accomplice. For some of the participants, the name Kirk associated the potential victim of the participant's aggression with the aggressive film character. Results indicated that viewing justified aggression increased aggressive behavior. Also, if the victim had the same name as the actor in the aggressive film (Kirk Douglas), he also received more punishment. The latter finding showed that an insubstantive cue like a name can evoke aggression when connected with media violence. So here we see that trivial things associated with a violent film, like the character's name, can trigger aggressive responses. Furthermore, if in the world of fantasy aggression is justified, we take that as real information and act more aggressively because of it.

What Exactly Are We Learning from Violent Media?

We've seen that the science shows that when people are exposed to violence in the media, they are more aggressive than others who weren't exposed to that content. We've seen that you can predict with accuracy that if you play more violent video games in real life, you are more aggressive. But what exactly are we learning? There are many ways we are changed by watching violence that is condoned, encouraged, and/or glamorized in the media. Bear in mind that while we may conceptualize the learning of aggression from media as the sign of a low society, in an ironic way it is actually a sign of what astute social learners we are. When we play a video game in which it is cool to blow people away or pummel them to death with a golf club (as in *Grand Theft Auto*) we are learning that the "right people" around us support violence. Young, hip guys who program video games think this type of violence is cool, hip, and exciting. How could violence really be bad if a swanky, professional piece of media like the *Grand Theft Auto* series is produced by the big dogs and finds its way to shelves in clean, shiny stores around the world? We're not dumb when we learn violence from media; we're merely learning a complex social lesson that we are being sold. What would be smarter is if we would understand the whole context of how media is produced and marketed and make more evolved choices about how to spend our time. Now let's examine another study that took a different approach to studying the outcomes of media violence exposure.

> The only thing necessary for the triumph of evil is for good men to do nothing.
>
> —Edmund Burke

Aggression isn't the only possible negative effect of exposing oneself to media violence. For example, media violence exposure might blunt the tendency to help other people. Brad Bushman and Craig Anderson[25] wondered how exposure to video game violence might influence the way people react when they witness a real-life argument between two people. Three hundred twenty college men and women were in the laboratory participating in a study in which they had played either a violent or a nonviolent video game. The researchers had a surprise in store for their participants: they arranged for a fight to (apparently) take place within earshot of the students. In a clever prediction, they thought the people who'd just played a violent game would be less likely to intervene to help the person getting hurt right outside their door. They were right: those who'd just played the violent game were less likely to help and those who did help took longer to do so than those who had played the nonviolent game. They also asked the people in the study to make a judgment as to how serious they thought the fight was and found some interesting results. The people who'd just played the violent game thought the fight was less serious than the other participants did. Furthermore, the researchers found that people who played violent video games regularly were also less likely to help and thought the fight was less serious than those who played fewer violent video games by their own choice. So, the implications of this study are that there are immediate effects of playing a violent video game, and there are also long-term effects such that playing violent video games can make people less helpful and less sensitive to fights happening around them in real life.

In a second study, Bushman and Anderson investigated the effect of watching a violent movie on adult moviegoers' responses to a woman in need of help. An accomplice of the researchers with a bandaged foot dropped her crutches just outside a movie theater and was struggling to pick them up. Moviegoers who had just seen a violent film were 26 percent slower to help her than moviegoers who had just seen a nonviolent film. But what if people who choose to see violent films are just less helpful than those who choose to see nonviolent films? The researchers took this into account, too. The accomplice flipped a coin to decide whether to stage the crutch-dropping scene before or after the movie. There were no differences in helping before the movie based on movie type. In other words, these data suggest that it is not that less helpful people choose violent movies, but rather it was watching violence that caused the moviegoers to be less helpful.

Media Violence on the Brain

Because people find it hard to believe that media violence has a real effect on people, it is helpful to look at some of the brain research. Even skeptics would have a hard time explaining the very real changes in the brain that take place after media violence exposure and the consequences of those changes documented by the research. Bruce Bartholow, Brad Bushman and Marc Sestir[26] conducted a series of studies that tell a clear and important story about what happens in the brain as a consequence of media violence exposure and why it matters. Again, many people criticize media violence research either in ignorance or in order to manipulate the public for their own purposes. But consider what a great set of studies these are scientifically and you will realize it's easy to offer a kind of lazy criticism, but it's difficult to produce this kind of truly high-quality science.

Bartholow, Bushman, and Sestir identified young men as heavy or light players of violent video games and investigated whether there were differences in how these men's brains reacted to violence. They found that the brains of violent video game players worked differently from brains exposed to less video game violence. Specifically violent video game players showed reduced sensitivity when looking at real violence. This blunted brain response is called desensitization—meaning that those with this response are less sensitive to the suffering of others. (We discussed Jeanne Funk's work on desensitization in children earlier.) Bartholow and colleagues cleverly ruled out a number of alternative explanations for these findings. For example, the men did not show desensitization to negative, nonviolent images (for example, a baby with a deformity). So, it wasn't the negative quality of the images that violent video game players showed a blunted reaction to. Violent video game players were less sensitive specifically to other people getting hurt. Furthermore, these studies showed that when the men were given a chance to attack someone else in the lab, the heavy violent video game players were more aggressive than the light violent video game players. Bartholow and colleagues also tested whether this response was due to the men's having a prior aggressive personality and found that it was not; it appears to be the game content that accounted for the differences in both aggressive behavior and in desensitization. To sum up this important set of studies, I'd say it tells us that exposing yourself to higher levels of media violence causes your brain to change so that it is less sensitive to other people's suffering and that you are then more willing to inflict harm yourself.

There are other interesting brain studies that support what Bartholow, Bushman, and Sestir found. One of the first relevant studies was published by the British journal *Nature*.[27] The doctors who authored that study found that when we play video games, the brain releases a pleasure chemical called dopamine. This suggests a number of things. For one, it suggests that when we perpetrate violence on the video game screen it is rewarded by a very pleasurable release of endorphins. Players learn that hurting other people is fun and rewarding—it feels very good. These data further suggest that playing video games can be physically addicting. The authors note that dopamine release is implicated in behaviors involving learning, reinforcement, attention, and skills that integrate senses and movements. Another way of saying that is that video games are very powerful teachers. Game developers seek to get players in the zone where they are working hard and learning, but where they also feel motivated toward reaching their goals and getting the high that comes from being successful in the game.

I've heard game developers speak about this and I know they are very aware of the psychology behind what creates this kind of gaming experience. And I think that's great if the game content isn't antisocial. I think if players really understood that their brains are literally changing for the worse when they play violent video games instead of flying into an angry state of denial, they might realize that this is not at all in their own best interest. The research shows that you can tell a teenager that smoking is bad for him and he won't really care. But tell him that smoking makes him look un-cool or makes his breath bad and he will care. You know, sometimes people don't want other people to look out for their heath and happiness. Sometimes people just want to smoke their cigarettes or eat their unhealthy diets or fill their hours with unhealthy media and that is their choice. It remains an irony, though, that the people who care about these young people—the people who have their best interests in mind are the ones whom they reject while the people who are using them for profit are the ones they defend. Sometimes I wonder if there is any way to break through this very powerful hold the profiteers have on these kids.

And they *are* kids. The video game industry will tell you all day long that the average gamer is thirty-three years old. That is one of those cases where there are lies, damn lies, and statistics. Yes, there are some thirty-something gamers out there, and gaming is on the rise among young adults. Proportionally speaking, however, kids and teens are still the biggest group of avid gamers. Eight- to seventeen-year-olds are much more likely to be gamers than any other ten-year age grouping, and most kids and teens play video games.[28] Since studies show that most popular games are violent, that means kids and teens are regularly exposed to video game violence.

Okay, back to the brain research. A study funded by the Mind Science Foundation (www.mindscience.org) investigated how children's brains respond when the kids are watching violent versus nonviolent TV.[29] The scientists reported that watching TV violence recruits a network of brain regions involved in the regulation of emotion, arousal and attention, episodic memory encoding and retrieval, and motor programming. This pattern of brain activations may explain the behavioral effects observed in many studies, especially the finding that children who are frequent viewers of TV violence are more likely to behave aggressively. Such extensive viewing may result in a large number of aggressive scripts stored in long-term memory in the posterior cingulate, which facilitates rapid recall of aggressive scenes that serve as a guide for overt social behavior.

Furthermore, the researchers explained that although the children were consciously aware that the TV violence they watched was not "real," their brains reacted as if it were real. When it comes to seeing violence, our brains react as if we are undergoing threat. We don't distinguish in that way between fantasy and reality.

Reel-to-Real

Again, we're so attracted to media not because stories on TV, in books, movies, or video games are "real" in the sense of nonfiction but because they have a reality to us in the sense of being meaningful. Why do swarms of kids and adults alike flock to their local bookstore when a new *Harry Potter* book comes out? Do they stand there waiting in line for the latest installment in the story because they love stories that aren't real? No—that's dumb. They love the story of *Harry Potter* because he is real to them. Yes, they know he's not sitting in a castle somewhere in England. Yes, they know people can't really shoot lightning bolts out of a magic wand. (If we could, I would do nothing else.) But J. K. Rowling is one of the richest women in the world because she's made characters and situations that are so human and meaningful to us that we choose to hold them in our mind's eye as real, even though part of us knows they are not real in the mundane sense. I guarantee you, for many people in the world, Harry Potter is more real than their own next-door neighbor.

Let me give you a couple of examples from my own life. Sometimes when life presents me with a challenge, I think of how Professor Dumbledore said to Harry Potter—okay, sorry— nerd alert! Anyway, I was saying, I think of how Professor Dumbledore said to Harry Potter, "Dark and difficult times lie ahead. Soon we must all face the choice between what is right and what is easy." Or I think of a time when Harry's schoolmates shunned him unfairly and how the truth redeemed him in the end. These are inspirations to me because of the real ideas I take away from fiction. The author of a book or a movie or a game paints us a picture of possibilities. What if you were in a situation where your peers did not believe you? How should you act? Could you be brave like Harry Potter? How do young people who are dating feel about each other and treat each other? Is it socially acceptable to cheat on your girlfriend? To hit her? Is it okay to talk trash about your best friend behind her back? All of these scenarios are the social psychology of real life that we've seen played out before our eyes on small screens, big screens, and pages of books and magazines all of our lives. We are always learning about the nuances of social situations—romantic relationships, interacting with your boss or co-workers, feeling lonely or ugly—from watching many, many stories produced and packaged for us by the media.

More Mirror Neurons

I mentioned research on mirror neurons earlier, but I want to revisit the topic and relate it to media violence. One of the most fascinating scholarly papers on the subject of media violence that I have ever read came not from a psychologist or a communications Ph.D. but from a philosopher. In *Media Violence, Imitation, and Freedom of Speech,* philosopher Susan Hurley says that we think of imitation as childish, but in fact imitation is a relatively complex skill and one that is important for our survival. Imitation requires getting inside the mind of someone else and is a fundamental mechanism in building complex social systems.

Psychologists have studied the importance of imitation in human development. The great American psychologist William James discussed the importance of what he called "ideomotor theory," the idea that "every representation of movement awakes to some degree the movement it represents."[30] Media violence theories include the presence of this kind of instigation to physical imitation. In terms of media and learning, "watching an action sequence speeds up your own performance of the same sequence, even if you cannot explicitly distinguish and recognize that sequence."[31] When a child watches his mom bake a cake or when we as adults watch a chef prepare a meal on television, it is actually part of the process of learning how to do the task through imitation. If the model is rewarded for the behavior, we learn that lesson as well. In our mediated culture (a culture in which we watch social behavior taking place on screens), this might mean seeing TV chef Rachael Ray get a magazine deal or watching her have dinner with a member of Aerosmith on one of her shows. (There's a complex social message for you: Great cooks get to have dinner with Aerosmith. Insert mental guitar riff here!)

A fascinating set of research studies has demonstrated that we unconsciously imitate those around us, but that we are not aware of it. Psychologists like Chartrand and Bargh[32] have shown that if we are in the room with a "foot shaker" or a "face rubber" we'll shake our foot or rub our face more as well, but we won't be aware of it. The "chameleon effect" is their finding that we unconsciously and passively imitate the behaviors of those around us. When asked about their imitation of the witnessed behaviors, participants in the study claimed they hadn't even noticed the behaviors in question. This work reminds me of the paper by Nisbett and Wilson I discussed in Chapter 1, in which they demonstrated—among other things—that you can give a person a hint to solve a problem and you can show that she used the hint, but that she will be unaware of it and would even deny it if asked.

As mentioned earlier, neuroscientists have uncovered a brain mechanism for this type of social imitation called "mirror neurons."[33,34] Recently, scientists have explained how what we see is pretty dang literally *mirrored* in our minds for the purpose of helping us learn to imitate it. The brain responds very similarly whether you are doing something or watching someone else do it. This makes a great deal of sense since imitation is adaptive—it's one crucial way we learn. Here's where Susan Hurley makes an important connection. She wonders if we can't help but mirror in our minds what we witness, and if witnessing violence in the media increases violent behavior, then how can media violence be protected by freedom of speech? Doesn't that come under the category of yelling fire in a crowded theater? Liberal societies, she argues, protect freedom, so long as it doesn't infringe on others' rights by causing harm.

Very recently, top aggression theorist Leonard Berkowitz[35] has emphasized the importance of understanding the role of automaticity in aggression. Berkowitz notes that "many impulsive actions, particularly antisocial ones, are due to failures of restraint after they were initiated involuntarily."[36] It's important to note that Berkowitz also thinks that controlled psychological processes, like teaching aggressive ideas or priming aggressive schemas, are also important links in the chain between media violence exposure and aggression. But he argues that situational cues, such as media violence, that are associated with aggression and negativity can involuntarily initiate or heighten aggressive responses. Regarding mirror neurons, Berkowitz writes, "It is even possible that neuropsychological mechanisms, such as the operation of the mirror neurons in the brain, contribute to this susceptibility to observed violence by creating an inclination to imitate what was just witnessed."[37]

Okay, now I'm starting to get excited because we're coming back around to one of the major points I want to make in this book. When it comes to media exposure, we are powerfully affected but at the same time either unaware of it, or even consciously antagonistic to the idea. This is simultaneously so frustrating and yet so fascinating to me.

Let's talk a bit more about some of the ideas I introduced in Chapter 1. Let's revisit why we think we are not affected by what we experience via the media, even though the research documents that we so clearly are affected. You know, it strikes me that we have here the reason that Sigmund Freud is the best-known psychologist in history. We can criticize Freud on any number of grounds, ranging from his overemphasis on sex as a cause of psychopathology, to his inability to tolerate dissent of any sort from his colleagues. But one main reason we can't stop talking about Freud is because of what he taught us about the unconscious mind. Freud used Gustav Fechner's analogy that the human psyche is like an iceberg—a lot more of it is under the water (i.e., unconscious) than is above the water (i.e., conscious). We fool ourselves with the notion that the mind is completely conscious—that we are completely aware of our own motivations when we absolutely are not.

Since we are so patently unaware of our own unawareness, you can't ask us whether we are affected by media violence and expect an answer that contains anything resembling accuracy. We don't realize either that we are affected or how much we are affected. In the end, that makes us very vulnerable to being shaped by the media. That we "choose" to spend so much of our "free time" pointing our eyeballs at media messages (irony emphatically intended) gives this idea unparalleled importance and meaning for us as a society and as individuals.

With the case of media violence, again we see how our fantasies become reality. Our fantasy life—the time we spend watching fictional stories in the media—causes very real changes in who we are and what we do. And since we are unconscious of these changes, we often become media apologists—passionately defending those who manipulate us. Based on logic and evidence, the "debate" over media violence should be over. That we still discuss it as a controversial issue is actually revealing of the powerful psychology at work behind the scenes.

Four

SEEING THROUGH AND SEEING BEYOND MEDIA VISIONS OF RACE AND GENDER

Most of what we know, or think we know, we have never personally experienced. We live in a world erected by stories. Stories socialize us into roles of gender, age, class, vocation, and lifestyle, and offer models of conformity or targets for rebellion. They weave the seamless web of our cultural environment. Our stories used to be hand crafted, home made, community inspired. Now they are mostly mass produced and policy driven, the result of a complex manufacturing and marketing process we know as the mass media. This situation calls for a new diagnosis and a new prescription.[1] (Gerbner, 1999)

— George Gerbner

We may not realize it, but very often we learn about other people through what we see in the mass media. This is especially true when the other people we're talking about are different from ourselves and we have little face-to-face contact with members of their group. Who believes—or would want to admit—that he or she learns about other people and ideas primarily through watching TV and movies and playing video games? Nobody, right? And that is part of the problem. As described in Chapter 1, when we fear or reject the influence of mass media, we make ourselves vulnerable to being directly used or manipulated. In the case of media stereotypes—of race, sex, age, sexual orientation and other social categories—we open ourselves to seeing others through the eyes of the media instead of through our own eyes.

So, what's wrong with learning through the media? Learning through the media is not all bad. Sometimes mass media stories can be informative, even inspirational. Think of a show, reporter, or other source that you trust. It might be *Sesame Street* or Tom Brokaw, *All Things Considered,* or *Scientific American Frontiers with Alan Alda.* For example, I subscribe to a National Public Radio podcast called *Driveway Moments.* NPR characterizes *Driveway Moments* as stories that audience members found so riveting, they kept listening to the story even if they had to sit in their driveways to finish. One of these *Driveway Moments* is from NPR science correspondent Robert Krulwich. Krulwich's report *Going Binocular: Susan's First Snowfall* describes how Susan—a visually impaired woman who had never seen the world in three dimensions (3D)—underwent a treatment that miraculously gave her binocular vision for the first time in her life. Through the interview, Susan relates that snowstorms had always looked more like distant white sheets than like individual flakes dancing around her. I am mesmerized listening to her describe being overwhelmed with the joy of seeing the big flakes of a snow shower falling lazily around her for the first time.

The NPR story of Susan's first 3D experience of a snowfall is an example of mass media communicating social information well. I have never experienced what Susan did; I didn't know about her condition or its treatment or what it would be like to go from 2D to 3D vision. But after listening to the story, I feel like I understand something about the essence of that experience from afar. I've picked up information about a group of people—those with visual impairments—and I've learned something about their struggles and triumphs through NPR's telling of this woman's story. I've also learned more about perception and medical science.

But what about the times when an information source is not so trustworthy? One fundamental lesson of media psychology that we have to understand is that we are not directly experiencing other people through the media. Rather, we are being given a prepackaged, mass produced vision and that vision can be very much influenced by media producers' desire for profit above other motives.[2] Producers may have hidden agendas. They may simply tell a story for the shock value of it in the hope of getting ratings. The producers themselves may help create a story so they can report it and gain an audience for their advertisers. Or perhaps those who produce the story have a personal interest in telling a story a particular way.

Part of understanding the social information you hear in a media story is to understand who is telling the story and why. As an extreme example, a film in which the stars smoke may have been funded in part by a tobacco company. A TV show that shows the negative health consequences of smoking may have been funded in part by the government or a health organization, or by a producer who wants to educate people about the health risks of smoking.

Seeing Is Believing

I can't go on without saying how very slick this actually is and how powerful it is, especially to more naïve and less educated viewers. When they see a person smoking in a film, they pretty much digest uncritically the agenda of the show's producers. There are many ways in which this is accomplished: by using young, healthy looking, attractive stars; by creating a sense of consequence-free fun using music, dancing, lighting, setting, and any number of other methods. You digest a vision of how life is without questioning it. Another example is often seeing young, attractive, thin actors and actresses eating high-calorie foods in the media. For example, think about your favorite ads for various fast food restaurants. Have you ever noticed that the actors and actresses who pretend to frequent fast food restaurants in those ads are quite often thin and attractive. Such visions are very misleading because they send unconscious messages: eat whatever you want, and still be thin! By implication, if you are not thin, why not because it is so easy? We see pretty blatant examples of thin beauties eating high calorie (and high profit) junk food consistently in the media. Can you think of any?

Let Me Tell You About Your Kind: Images of Race in the Mass Media

Think about the stories that are told in mass media about members of diverse racial groups. The almost exclusive portrayal of groups by outsiders and groups in power is problematic from the outset. How would Americans, for example, be represented differently if portrayed by other Americans versus being portrayed by Asians, Arabs, or even by a subgroup of Americans such as the religious right? Should men be the ones to tell most women's stories? If they are, what are the consequences? Would any of us want someone outside our group to tell most of its stories, especially with the motive of making money from the stories? There is also the danger of the teller skewing the stories in order to degrade the group and thus "keep them in their place"—their place being lower on the social hierarchy than that of the wealthy White men who run the companies that produce these images.

How does a mass-produced, mass-marketed image bias or alter our social understanding about members of different groups? In this chapter, I want to focus on this understanding specifically as it relates to major social groups, so I will focus on gender and race representations in the media. Let me borrow an example from Clint Wilson, Felix Gutierrez, and Lena Chao, the authors of the book *Racism, Sexism and the Media*.[3] They ask us to think about what we know about Native Americans and where we got that information. Unless you are a Native American, or have other direct knowledge, you almost certainly took much of your information from the mass media: Clint Eastwood or John Wayne movies, Disney's *Pocohontas*, and TV news magazine stories about Native Americans, for example. Well, we may not think about it, but when we do this we are learning about Native Americans mostly through the eyes of a select group of White males, which is very different from learning about them from Native Americans themselves. The news media tend to cover Native Americans in one of two ways: as what the authors call "zoo stories" or "problem people stories." Zoo stories are more or less caricatures of Native American culture—like Tonto saying "How!" Problem people stories are those that focus on Native Americans as alcoholics or as impotent drains on society.

Also problematic is the potential harm that negative stereotypes in the media have on the way the targets of the stereotypes view themselves. According to Linda Holtzman,[4] author of *Media Messages: What Film, Television and Popular Music Teach Us about Race, Class, Gender and Sexual Orientation*, Latino men have been variously ignored by the media or characterized as largely poor, uneducated, or buffoons. This type of media image sends the message that other people have a negative view of your group. Portrayals of African Americans in the media have often involved problems with misinformation and distortion. For example, in the film *Mississippi Burning*, the heroes of the film were White. The director claimed that if the heroes had been African American, this would have been unacceptable to predominantly White audiences of the 1980s. According to Holtzman, early films were overtly, even outrageously, racist, such as the 1905 film, *The Wooing and Wedding of a Coon*. Films continued to show blatant stereotypes of African Americans, which evolved from hateful images to images of happy slaves and servants. After World War II, the portrayal of African Americans transitioned into more dignified, yet non-threatening roles, such as the part of Sidney Poitier in *Guess Who's Coming to Dinner*. In the 1960s and 1970s, there was an era of "Blaxploitation" films such as *Shaft*. In the 1980s and 1990s, more complex black characters emerged, and black actors, actresses, producers, and directors gained wide-spread popularity. While there have been advancements in the role of African Americans in the media, there are still issues including stereotyping, unequal representation, and submission to the White culture. When we see representations of people in the mass media, we form or add to our schemas, which are expectations—either about our own group (the psych term for this is "ingroup") or about groups to which we do not belong ("outgroups"). Schemas are a type of mind-set that can evolve into pre-judgments or stereotypes.

Racial and Gender Stereotyping in Video Games

Because it is important to understand how young people learn infor-mation about other racial groups and their own through the lens of mass media, my colleagues and I[5] investigated how video game char-acters represent different racial groups. We chose two types of formats to analyze: video game magazines and video game covers. Both of these provided still images—scenes depicting video game characters from the top games—to analyze. The magazines we analyzed included *Game Informer*, *GamePro*, and *Electronic Gaming Monthly*, which are three of the top ten best-selling magazines among teens. By the way, did you know that *Game Informer* and *GamePro* have more subscribers than *Maxim* or *Rolling Stone*? I didn't.

When you analyze hundreds of images, you start to see the trends in how different people are characterized. I think that a big picture perspective is very telling. Like the examples cited above, the people who write and produce video games are predominantly White males, so characterizations of women and non-Whites are largely from the perspective of outgroup members. Our analysis of video game maga-zine images revealed some intriguing trends in how men of different races were portrayed. Men were very violent on the whole, with

African American (73%) and Hispanic (80%) men proportionately a bit more likely to be portrayed as violent than White men (66%). Deeper analysis was even more revealing. White men were the largest group (26% as compared to 14% of African American men) who were portrayed in ways that glamorize aggression. No Asians were shown this way. While 30 percent of African American men were portrayed playing a sport, only 8 percent of White men were, and no Hispanic or Asian men were. And while a third of Asian men were shown using computers and technology, as were 14 percent of White men, only 3 percent of African American men were portrayed this way. Past research has shown that there are three central traits to the negative African American stereotype: lack of intelligence, athleticism, and rhythm. These findings highlight two of those three central stereotype characteristics.

Representing

Let's talk a bit more about representation and why it's important. Representation means that members of different races, sexes, and other social groups should be portrayed proportionally in the media—in a way that is roughly similar to their numbers in the larger social group they represent (like the U.S. population or the U.S. military). Individual television shows, movies, or games need not be representative of the larger population because individual story lines may focus on a particular group—like a movie that tells a story about Latinas. That is why one looks for representation as a larger trend, such as in a genre like TV sitcoms or commercials or best-selling men's magazines.

One of the first scholars to study the influence of mass media on culture, George Gerbner, was widely known for his analysis of television known as the Cultural Indicators Project (www.disinfo.com). Gerbner—who was a Hungarian refugee—often focused attention on how White males in what he called the "prime of life" were the most typical TV characters. He also noted other discrepancies in representation, such as the fact that men outnumber women three to one in prime-time television. In violent scenes, men are most often the aggressors and women and non-Whites are disproportionately likely to be the victims of aggression. Gerbner also recognized that men are more likely to be media executives and producers, game developers, and even narrators.

We can ask how well a certain group like women or men of color were represented in a genre. Then we can ask whether that representation was respectful—whether it showed positive or realistic and nuanced portrayals. When you underrepresent a group as a trend within a genre, you are telling a subtle story about race, gender, sexual orientation, and other traits. You are saying these people don't matter as much, they are not "regular" or "normal" people—that they are not the people we want to tell stories about and get to know, for example.

Beyond Representation, There Is Characterization

Scholars call the stories we tell about a person a *characterization* or *portrayal*. I think these are informative and appropriate terms. Characterization suggests that you are sketching the character or moral value of a person. Portrayal implies that you are framing the person—telling that person's story your way—so both terms work well. Not to confuse, but we can also use the word *represent* to mean characterize or portray. Represent can mean that a character acts as an image of other characters like him. This is similar to the idea that one character can be a stand-in for other characters of the same race, sex, age, or other demographic, which is of course why representation is important.

In our investigation of video game covers, we found several characterizations of different racial groups. African American men were again clearly stereotyped. For example, we defined "thug" as someone who engaged in criminal behavior absent clear and present danger and "vigilante" as a criminal response to a threat. While 23 percent of African American men were portrayed as thugs, only 3 percent of White men were. In a reversal, no non-Whites were portrayed as vigilantes, while 3 percent of Whites were. Nineteen percent of Whites wore protective armor, while no African Americans did. Seventy-five percent of Asian men were martial artists, compared to 6 percent and 5 percent of White and African American men, respectively. Thirty-two percent of African American men were portrayed as athletes, compared to 5 percent of White men. While 7 percent of White male video game characters were soldiers, not a single African American, Hispanic, or Asian man was portrayed this way, which is in stark contrast to the 33 percent of the U.S. military who are non-White. These characterizations tell a story about African American men. The story is that African American men are likely to be either thugs or athletes, not soldiers. The image from *Grand Theft Auto: San Andreas* included in Figure 4-1 is representative of that characterization of African American men as violent street criminals.

FIGURE 4.1. Our research on portrayals of African American men in video games reveals that they are disproportionately represented as thugs and criminals and dangerous aggressors, and as athletes, while they are less likely to be portrayed as soldiers or as using computers. [Screen shot from *Grand Theft Auto: San Andreas*—from Take Two Interactive and Rockstar Games.]

Seeing Stereotypes Changes How You Think

These negative characterizations engender negative effects. In an experiment, my colleagues and I[6] exposed White participants to video games with White and African American male characters and then asked them to respond as quickly as possible to violent objects (ex., a sword) and nonviolent objects (ex., a cell phone) flashed on a screen. Results showed that participants responded faster to the violent objects after seeing African American male video game characters and faster to the nonviolent objects after seeing White male video game characters. These results show that the negative stereotype of African American men as violent was brought to mind by the African American male video game characters. This was true regardless of whether the game was violent or not. Just the presence of an African American male video game character *primed* (brought to mind) the concept of violence.

Digesting Images of Socially Constructed Stereotypes

I thought it was crucial to unpack these video game images for a number of reasons. Media imagery is a source of powerful social storytelling and one that we've just begun to understand. Visual imagery plays an important role in socialization, specifically in how we extract and apply meaning from everyday experience, and therefore in how we construct social realities. I like the way Ostman[7] put it: "Visual communication contains a trove of emotionally-laden, non-logical connotations" that become part of the viewer's social schemas. And Cowan[8] said: "Given the popular culture's devotion to visual media, the socialization process may be influenced strongly by exposure to visual materials." The old saying is "a picture is worth a thousand words" and I think this is true when it comes to learning about people from the images of mass media. It's amazing the amount of nuanced social information that can be portrayed in an image. Not only do we remember images better than words, but we also can get away with telling a story about social groups (women, African American men) with a picture when we couldn't get away with saying the same thing with words. My research has shown[9] that exposure to negative stereotypes of Black men in the media causes negative reactions that are applied to other Black men. On the other hand, it has also shown that exposure to positive exemplars of Black men, such as Barack Obama and Martin Luther King Junior, causes positive reactions that are applied to other Black men as well. This research is discussed more fully in Chapter 7.

How Fantasy Images Become Our Realities

A basic premise of this book is that fantasies such as those we see in the media actually become our realities in a number of ways. Media violence— as we saw in Chapter 3—breeds real life aggression. It is also true that exposure to stereotypes in the media breeds stereotypical thinking. Let's look more deeply at one of the reasons this is true by delving into what I believe is a fundamentally important—but under-studied—piece of research for media psychologists.

Morgan Slusher and Craig Anderson[10] explored the extent to which people distinguish between their own real experiences with stereotypes and times when they just imagined stereotypes. In one study, the authors found that when people are asked to imagine members of groups such as lawyers or clergymen, they tend to imagine them as their social stereotypes. For example, when imagining a lawyer shopping for a car, one imagines a wealthy man shopping for a Mercedes rather than a guy in jeans shopping for a used pickup truck. In a second study, the researchers told male and female college students that they were going to participate in a study of visual imagery to test their visual imagination skills. Participants imagined scenes that were either stereotypical or not stereotypical and they were also given open-ended situations in which they could generate stereotypes or not. Findings indicated that participants weren't able to distinguish between stereotypes they were exposed to and stereotypes they just imagined. Slusher and Anderson[11] put it like this:

> When people imagine a picture, they come to believe that they have actually seen that picture more often. We suggest that when people imagine other people, particularly those who belong to an identifiable social group, they incorporate their stereotypes into their imaginations. As a result, people may come to believe that they have seen this "picture" more often (i.e., the picture of an individual fitting their own stereotype). If this occurs, people are providing their own *imaginal confirmation* of their previously established stereotypes.

Imaginal confirmation: that means we may actually confuse *seeing* an African American man behave like a criminal and *imagining* it. Isn't that amazing? This is another way of saying that we confirm our own stereotypes—and without even knowing it. The participants in the study failed at "reality monitoring," at knowing when they had really experienced a stereotype or when they had just imagined it. Now, when you apply this to how an African American man is represented in the mass media, you can easily see that we would confuse seeing a real person behave stereotypically and seeing just an image of it on a video game cover, for example. We're not likely to sufficiently differentiate between seeing a thuggish African American man in *Grand Theft Auto* with having seen a real person like this on the street. In an important sense, our minds treat media imagery like this is as if it were real. Therefore, when you degrade someone in the media, you are degrading the real members of that person's social group. Our brains don't fully recognize the difference.

Recall, too, the research suggesting that when we are transported by fictional stories, we are more easily persuaded by their content. This transportation theory, I think, can also be used to explain the persuasive power of mass media images. When you get lost in a story, you become uncritical of the persuasive messages embedded in the story, accepting them involuntarily.[12] Persuasive messages can be verbal, such as a description of a character who holds racist views, but they can also be communicated through an image, such as when an African American man in a video game is portrayed as a street criminal. Since we don't differentiate between stereotypes we've just imagined and those we've seen confirmed in real life,[13] then surely we don't differentiate between real people who confirm a stereotype and fictional characters who do. Again we see how media characters portrayed in a stereotypical manner persuade us that the stereotype is true.

(Dis)like and (Dis)respect (Fiske, Xu, Cuddy, & Glick, 1999)

Let's examine further why the particular representations of African American men described above lead to negative stereotypical thinking. For one thing, creating this vision of the African American man as a member of the "dangerous minority" becomes an iconic representation of what it means to be an African American man. You've told a story about what "these people" are like. Just imagining it makes you think you have seen it in real life. We don't make the fantasy-reality distinction we believe we do. Thus we've learned about other people through mass media story-telling. Once again, crucial here is the fact that we most likely do so without realizing it. In fact, if asked we'd be likely to deny it.

Patricia Devine and her colleagues[14,15] have shown that racial stereo-typing is implicit—in other words, often done automatically or without conscious awareness—and that even people who don't endorse racial stereotypes are aware of what those culturally held stereotypes are. Since media consumption, as discussed earlier, is the main waking activity of the human race right now, I think it's safe to say that most of our stories about race and gender come from the media. Isn't that an astounding notion? Most of our "encounters" with people who are different from us involve our watching produced video on a screen. If specific sources of media, such as video games, are consistently pre-senting stereotypical views of women and non-Whites, the public should become conscious of this and then act on that knowledge by calling for change from the industry.

Stereotyping Theory: The Importance of Warmth and Competence

Susan Fiske, Peter Glick, and their colleagues have worked for many years to help us understand stereotypical thinking and its effects.[16,17,18] These scientists explain that the content of stereotypes falls into two basic domains: warmth and competence. For example, the mentally retarded are regarded as warm (likable and good intentioned) but incompetent (unable to compete with us). A major conclusion from this research is that perceived competence follows from social status and perceived warmth follows from the degree to which you feel you compete with a person.[19]

Members of any given group can be high or low on warmth and high or low on competence and this determines how we feel about members of that group; it determines whether we are prejudiced against them. For example, several samples of students and nonstudents were interviewed and asked what groups are the targets of stereotypical thinking. Results showed that African Americans were the group thought to be the most likely targets of stereotyping; they were mentioned, in fact, by a full 74 percent of respondents, whereas the next most common group that people thought were stereotyped were Hispanics, mentioned by only 45 percent of the sample. Further questioning revealed more detail about the nature of stereotypes. "Rich Blacks" fell into a category of relative competence, but relative low warmth—forming the stereotype that group members have high status but are relatively disliked. Fiske, Glick, and colleagues say this group evokes "envious prejudice"—jealousy and resentment that comes from feelings of injustice but a begrudging acceptance of competence. Also in this "envious prejudice" group were Asians, Jews, and feminists. The authors note that less successful people in otherwise dominant groups—such as poor Whites—are perhaps more likely to feel this type of envious prejudice.

In contrast, "paternalistic stereotypes" (paternal means fatherly) are applied to groups not likely to compete for resources or otherwise threaten the ingroup. Examples of warm but incompetent groups are housewives and the elderly. Another group is what these researchers call the "low-low" group—those low in competence and warmth such as welfare recipients. These groups come closest to generating what the scientists call the "pure antipathy" of "contemptuous prejudice." People feel the following prejudicial emotions toward these groups: anger, contempt, disgust, hate, and resentment. People in the "low-low" group are thought to be an unfair drain on society. Groups that fell into this category included poor African Americans, poor Whites, and migrant workers.[20]

When we look at how groups are represented in the media, it's important to see how they fit in with these types of stereotypes and evoked prejudices. As Glick, Fiske, and colleagues note, attitudes toward African Americans differ greatly depending on whether people stereotype them as wealthy or poor, for example. In our analysis of video game characters, we see that the African American males were evocative of a very specific stereotype—the "dangerous minority," the criminal or thug. This stereotypical person is not warm or likable, and not competent in the sense of successful in socially sanctioned ways. This figure is also a drain on society as a criminal element that is a threat to others. Thus, the stereotypes of African American men as they are represented in video games are particularly likely to evoke the constellation of emotions cited above—anger, contempt, disgust, hate, and resentment. Anger, of course, is associated with aggression and one outcome of these feelings of antipathy and dislike is aggression against the stereotyped group. Aggression can take many forms, from outright physical violence to much more subtle forms of discrimination and derogation.

Scholars have noted that one reason for racial stereotyping in the mass media is that producers want to make their messages clear and often have a short time to do that. So they resort to stereotypes to make a point quickly and to establish characters. Of course, the "concern is that those stereotypic, snapshot depictions present young people with a social reality. Even if a program is judged by children to be fictional (or even scripted and rehearsed), it may still be perceived as socially realistic."[21]

I'm not a successful African American man, but I am a professional woman. That means I fall into that same category as a potential target of envious prejudice, so I understand the feeling. As an example of the behaviors this can evoke, consider the following study by Jennifer Berdahl called *The Sexual Harassment of Uppity Women.*[22] Berdahl hypothesized that sexual harassment is not primarily a crime of passion but rather a crime of aggression motivated by a desire to inflict harm. If it were a crime of passion, so to speak, men would be more likely to sexually harass traditional women—women who would fit Glick and Fiske's warm but incompetent group. If, however, men harass women to inflict punishment, then men should be more likely to harass so-called uppity women—feminists, successful professionals, and women who believe in equality between the sexes. She found that women who had more instrumental personalities—meaning they were typified by the traditionally male qualities of "getting the job done"—had experienced more sexual harassment (such as sexist jokes and sexual advances) than more traditional, less threatening feminine women. So, belonging to a stereotyped group can lead to real harm.

Muslim and Middle Eastern Stereotypes in the Media

Enny Das and her colleagues[23] noticed that the news media have lately associated terrorism with Muslims in general rather than with Muslim extremists. They wondered what the ramifications would be. Das and her colleagues found that exposure to news coverage about terrorism increased death-related thoughts and also increased agreement with a news article that suggested problems with integrating Muslims into society. They also found that prejudice against Arabs went up after exposure to terrorism news for Europeans, but not for Arabs. These researchers suggest that terror management theory offers a theoretical basis for understanding these results. For example, they found that people with higher self-esteem reacted differently than those with lower self-esteem when reminded of death. For individuals with high self-esteem, their levels of prejudice were low whether they had seen news about terrorism or a news story that didn't involve terrorism. But for those with low self-esteem, prejudice against Arabs rose after seeing the terrorism news report relative to the control news report. Again, evoking the specter of one's own mortality can increase protectionist sentiments for some. Therefore, reporters should make clear the distinction between Muslims in general and Muslim extremists. Another important factor is the audience; if they are only processing peripherally or not making critical distinctions themselves, this will alter their perceptions.

In a related set of investigations, researchers from the University of Michigan's Aggression Research Group studied the effects of exposure of American youth to images of Middle Eastern violence in the media.[24] They found that exposure to perceived acts of violence in the mass media was related to increased prejudice against the target groups. Furthermore, these scientists found that identification with a particular group (Arabs or Israelis) predicted more negative stereotypes about the opposing group.

Media Representations and Social Power

So far we have touched upon the issue of social power, but now I'd like to focus on it in more detail—to talk about the social hierarchy of various groups within our culture; how that hierarchy relates to stereotyping, prejudice, and discrimination; and where media representations fit in. Social power is also called hegemony. Sociologist R. W. Connell[25] writes about hegemonic masculinity and emphasized femininity. Hegemonic masculinity includes a very specific vision of masculinity that is purported to be dominant in the culture. The vision of the dominant male in our culture is a man who is White, heterosexual, young, strong, and Christian. Because this view is one of male dominance, women are always construed as subordinant and subservient to these men—there is no hegemonic femininity. Connell is careful to stress that this is a socially constructed ideal and that in reality most men don't fit the mythic ideal (like John Wayne, for example). Speaking of myth, enter the media, which fit in in a very interesting way. Media visions of men and women serve not to report reality but to reflect and support the cultural mythology of hegemonic masculinity. As Connell[26] puts it, although

"few men are Bogarts or Stallones, many collaborate in sustaining those images."

And as Slusher and Anderson so skillfully showed us, we don't differentiate well at all between the myths we hold in our mind's eye and what we take to be a real view—in this case, of the sexes. And in fact, either through ignorance or malicious intent, big media can sell us an image of people—be it the hegemonic male or the "dangerous" African American man—that we accept as part of our reality, not realizing how this reality was constructed for us or the degree to which it contains myths.

(Mr. and) Miss Representation

Ambivalent Sexism Theory[27] also accepts the notion that men are dominant in our culture but with the awareness that there are in fact mixed (ambivalent) feelings about both men and women that society recognizes. These mixed stereotypes are that men are "bad but bold" and women are "wonderful but weak." Stereotypes about men take two forms: hostility toward men (e.g., men are sexual predators) and benevolence toward men (e.g., men are more willing to put themselves in dangerous situations for others). Ambivalence toward women takes two forms referred to as benevolent sexism (for example, a kind of paternalistic care for the "weaker sex") and hostile sexism (e.g., negative feelings toward women who challenge men, such as feminists, or women who "use their feminine wiles").

You may recognize that these clearly relate to the aforementioned view that encapsulated stereotypical notions as relating to two general dimensions: warmth and competence. Women are warm—they are more likable than men and men are often seen as arrogant and hostile. But men are dominant because they are instrumental. Their social power is then legitimized because it becomes inevitable—they have the competence needed for success in the culturally important arenas. Women are likable, but likability doesn't get the job done and it doesn't put you on the top of the status hierarchy.

Other theories of prejudice also support the idea that the inherent right to power and privilege of the dominant social group maintains the status quo of the current social hierarchy. For example, research by John Jost, Mazarin Banaji,[28] and others supports System Justification Theory—the idea that there is a general motive to support the social hierarchy, the status quo. Paradoxically, this motive is often stronger for those who are lower on the social totem pole and is partially responsible for people in disadvantaged groups feeling inferior. Interestingly, in the light of the unconscious nature of many of the effects discussed here, justification of the social status quo is most readily observable at nonconscious levels of awareness.

The Consequences of Social Inequality

What are the ramifications of these types of social beliefs? Data from an international sample,[29] representing sixteen nations, documented an inverse relationship between ambivalent sexism and the United Nations (UN) indices of gender inequality. These UN indices of inequality included women's representation in high-status jobs in both business and government, and other measures such as life expectancy, literacy rates, educational attainment, and standard of living. In other words, to the extent that we accept the notion of men as "bad but bold" and women as "wonderful but weak," we support real, material gender inequality. This translates worldwide into seeing women as less likely to attain career and educational goals at the level that men do.

Relating this back to media representations, we can see that it is important that such imagery does not project the "bad but bold" and "wonderful but weak" gender mythology because to the extent that it does, it will support social inequality. And, as we have seen, even those most likely to be negatively affected by such mythologies often are unaware of many important aspects of the situation. They are unaware that mythologies in the media affect them. They are unaware that they are motivated to justify the status quo of their own social inferiority.

Media Representations of Gender

Television and the Macho Man Image

Erica Scharrer[30,31] defines hyper-masculinity and hyper-femininity in ways that that are consistent with the theories described above. Hyper-masculine men think aggression is "manly" and have hardened attitudes toward sexuality. Hyper-feminine women are submissive to and dependent upon men and display emphasized (hetero)sexuality. Scharrer exposed college men to *The Sopranos*—a show that has both violence and a theme of hyper-masculinity as well as to a nonviolent show and a violent show without a hyper-masculine theme. She found that seeing the *Sopranos* caused its young, male viewers to be relatively more likely to endorse the hyper-masculine beliefs that violence is manly and thrilling.

While being powerful has its appeal, glamorizing violence is far from universally beneficial to its male viewers. In fact, research tells a much different story. Aggressiveness is negatively correlated with intelligence across the life span: if you are more aggressive, you are generally less intelligent. TV violence viewing is also predictive of the likelihood that you will go to jail for a violent crime.[32]

Another important factor is the extent to which viewers identify with or want to be like the characters they watch. This in and of itself implies something fascinating about reality and fantasy—to want to be like a fictional character he or she must have a certain reality for you. Longitudinal studies have shown that when a child feels similar to an aggressive character on television, he or she is more likely to imitate that aggression later in life.[33] Furthermore, Dara Greenwood[34] found that when young women idealized (wanted to be like) female action heroes such as *Buffy the Vampire Slayer*, they were more likely to feel and behave aggressively.

Viewing Masculinity, Femininity, and Male-Female Relations Through the Lens of Video Games

Erica Scharrer studied how men and women are portrayed in the advertisements of three top-selling video game magazines. She found that males outnumbered females three to one and that males were depicted as muscular and females as sexy. Fifty-five percent of the ads contained violence. Tracy Dietz, in an earlier study of women in video games,[35] found that females were mostly absent from games, but when they were depicted, it was most likely as weak characters needing rescue by the male hero. This characterization, of course, still exists in video games. Mario is still trying to rescue the Princess from the evil Bowser. However, the latest research shows that characterizations of females have changed quite a bit.

Kathryn Phillips Thill and I[36] found that most females (roughly 60% for each characterization) in the top-selling video game magazines were portrayed as sex objects and as visions of beauty. At the same time, the great majority of men (over 80%) were portrayed as powerful aggressors. Furthermore, by what we believe is a conservative estimate, about a third of the men were portrayed as hyper-masculine. We used Scharrer's definition of hyper-masculine and rated characters as such only if they had particularly outsized muscles and fairly extreme emphasized masculinity (ex., chiseled features and stubble). Interestingly, about 40 percent of female characters were both sexy and aggressive, which is a departure from what Dietz had found nine years earlier. What we see in these characterizations is that the depictions of males and females in video games are the kinds of stylized myths about men and women that we discussed above. Men are powerful aggressors. Women's sexuality is emphasized: they are sex objects and thus their importance as serving men's needs is emphasized. This juxtaposition puts us right back to the theories of sexism we discussed. Powerful masculinity is hegemonic. Femininity is stylized, objectified, and subordinated.

Giving "Glamour Shot" a Double Meaning

One of the first things that attracted my attention about video game magazines was that their images of men seemed to highly glamorize violence. This is problematic because, as the National Television Violence Study (NTVS)[37] demonstrated, glamorizing violence makes violence more attractive and thus more likely. The NTVS also noted that television sanitizes violence, depicts it with unrealistic consequences, and often pairs violence with humor. These are antisocial lessons about violence. I noticed that often these violent men in video game magazines were just standing there with their weapons as if to say, "violence is cool." So we specifically looked for this type of characterization—times when video game characters were not fighting and not using their weapons. They were just standing around doing what I call "posing" with weapons. I also like to think of it as the "aggressive glamour shot."

When you look at this juxtaposition of the female sex object and the male violent hero, we see brought to life for young people blatant examples of a sexist social hierarchy. These characterizations are exactly what the theorists described above were writing about when they expressed concerns for how sexism is socialized and what the consequences of a sexist socialization are.

Now, we wondered, to what extent are these blatantly sexist characterizations just being transmitted to avid gamers? Do youth in general know about these sex-role stereotypes? So Kathryn and I asked eighteen-year-olds about their mental images of male and female video game characters. These were male and female teenagers who were not, as a group, avid gamers. I was actually surprised how much the results of this very open-ended questioning mirrored the images of characters that we had studied. How did our teenagers describe the typical male video game character? The five most common characterizations, in order, were as follows, starting with the most common answer: powerful (ex., "strong"), aggressive (ex., "violent," "deadly"), hostile attitude (ex., "mean," "cocky," "belligerent"), athlete, and thug (ex., "gangsta"). The single most common term used to describe a male video game character was "muscular." For female characters, the teens noted these common characteristics: provocative dress (ex., "tight clothes," "naked"), curvaceous figure (ex., "big boobs"), thin (ex., "skinny"), sexual (ex., "hooker," "slutty," "sexy"), and aggressive (ex., "likes to kill.") The single most common term used to describe a female video game character was "big boobs."

So, we've seen that among video game characters, there are pretty overt racial and sex-role stereotypes. For example, in one study, my colleagues[38] and I discovered that there were only two female main characters out of twenty video games analyzed: one was African American, the other Israeli. We also analyzed which characters were most likely to be the targets of violence. Of the human male targets, 25 percent were Middle Eastern. Thus, women were grossly underrepresented as heroes, and Middle Easterners were grossly overrepresented as targets of violence. This may well send the message that Middle Easterners are the "kinds of people" whom it is socially acceptable to harm.

Do Blatant Sex-Role Stereotypes Promote Real Harm?

What are the implications of exposure to images that are so blatantly stereotypical?

What effect does viewing these stereotypes have on young men and women? It follows that exposure to the pervasive imagery of men as powerful, mean, and violent and women as degraded objects to be used and subjugated has implications for harmful treatment of women in real-life situations.

My colleagues Brian Brown, Michael Collins, and I[39] investigated these issues. We started by choosing stereotypical images of male and female video game characters that this earlier research had revealed were typical representations in the culture. We selected representative images of women and men from top-selling video games including *Grand Theft Auto: Vice City, Grand Theft Auto: San Andreas, Dead or Alive Xtreme Beach Volleyball 2, BMX XXX, Saint's Row, Resident Evil,* and *Gears of War.* (See Figures 4-2A and 4-2B for examples of actual images used in the study.)

Now, as we have discussed previously, in an experiment one uses at least two groups for comparison—the experimental group and a control group. In the experimental group, participants saw the stereotypical video game content. We wanted to select a control group of images that would present *both* men and women in roles that were realistic and high in social status and power. We therefore chose real pictures of men and women who were current U.S. congresspersons. The hope was that we were presenting a vision of men and women as competent and powerful in positive ways.

(a)   (b)

FIGURES 4.2A AND 4.2B. Examples of sex role stereotyped (L) images from video games and of professional men and women (R) used in Dill, Brown, and Collins (2008). The image on the left is a screen shot from *BMX XXX* (2002, Acclaim Entertainment). On the right is Senator Mary Landrieu (D-LA)—www.landrieusenate.gov. After viewing stereotypical images like the one on the left, young men were more tolerant of sexual harassment compared to those who saw the professional, respectful images.

Participants either saw a ten-minute video presentation of the video game images or the images of congresspersons.

We wanted to measure the differential effects of this exposure on a real-world outcome in which women experience harm because of their gender. We decided to study sexual harassment because it is so commonly experienced and because, as described above, it is not a sexual crime but a crime intended to harm the victims (as the "uppity" women study demonstrated). Would stereotype exposure lead to greater support of harassment of women? Would men react differently from women to these images? To find answers to these questions, we thought it was important to use a realistic example of harassment, so we chose the author Naomi Wolf's personal account of her experience as a young college student being sexually harassed by her male professor (excerpted from *The Silent Treatment* by Naomi Wolf—from NewYorkMetro.com). One reason we chose this story is because we believed it was not on either extreme (ex., a story of a rape or of a mild flirtation). Thus we thought that perceptions of the story could vary fairly widely. All participants read this story and then were asked some probing questions about their views. For example, they were asked to judge, if the story is true, whether this means the professor is guilty of sexual harassment and then how harshly he should be punished for his behavior. Further, they rated the extent to which they blamed the female student for the professor's behavior and then how deeply they felt the experience affected her, how seriously she should be taken, and how sorry they felt for her. Taken together, all these judgments indicate the participant's sensitivity toward and tolerance of sexual harassment.

The results were very interesting. While men and those who had viewed the video game characters were more tolerant of sexual harassment, further differences emerged. We found a significant three-to-one contrast. Do you remember the game from children's TV in which the characters sang, "three of these things are not like the other"? That's what a three-to-one contrast shows—that one group responded differently from the other three. In this case, what we found was that the men who saw the stereotypical images of men (as powerful) and women (as sex objects) behaved differently from the other three groups. They were significantly more tolerant of sexual harassment than any other group. So seeing stereotypes of men as powerful and dominant and women as demeaned and objectified caused these men to be less likely to see an event like this as even being sexual harassment. Further, this group reported that they would be more lenient on the perpetrator of sexual harassment. This has implications for male bosses who receive complaints from female employees; if they are more exposed to these media stereotypes of gender, this study suggests that they would be less helpful to their female subordinant and potentially cause her harm by failing to appropriately punish the transgressor.

Are Stereotypes in the Media "Just Harmless Entertainment"?

Scientists at the University of Maryland's Center for Children, Relationships and Culture[40] wondered what young people thought about the idea that stereotypes in the media are "just harmless entertainment." They showed students stereotypical video game content such as women as sex objects and violent men. Male adolescents were more likely to view both violence and gender stereotypes as harmless entertainment, though they did disapprove more of the stereotypical content. Also, people who played more video games—mostly males—were the least likely to think that exposure to violence and stereotypes in video games could actually change people's behavior. This was a general finding as well: most of the adolescents didn't think people were affected by exposure to media violence or media stereotypes. The more someone uses media with negative content, the more they are likely to say that the content does not affect them. Again, we see what is either naïve or self-protective thinking. In other words, either those who use more media are less informed about its effects or more likely to rationalize an increased use that at some level they know is harmful.

Let's Hope Your Boss Doesn't Watch Jerry Springer

Sensationalistic talk shows such as *The Jerry Springer Show* are now common in our media culture. We have probably all laughed at the extreme guests on some of these shows. But does viewing this kind of content cause harm, or is it harmless fun? A team of researchers[41] studied how watching promiscuous women on the *Jerry Springer Show* affected viewers. Participants saw a clip from the Springer show, either featuring a promiscuous or a nonpromiscuous woman. Later in the study, they read a sexual harassment scenario. They were asked to rate this unrelated woman in the sexual harassment story as to how promiscuous they thought she was. Results showed that those who had seen the promiscuous women on the Springer show applied this stereotype to the unrelated woman who had been sexually harassed. In other words, being exposed to stereotypical, degrading images in the media of promiscuous women affected how people rated other, unrelated women. It taught stereotypical thinking—in this case "women are just like that." In this particular case, the viewers of the stereotypical content also believed that the sexual harassment victim had experienced less trauma and that she was more to blame for her own harassment. In the end, what we learn from this once again is that stereotypes in the media do really matter. They are not, in fact, "just harmless entertainment." They change our view of the world around us.

Teaching Degradation Through the Media

Pornography research has stressed the idea that when it comes to sexual video material, it is not explicit sexual content that is harmful, but it is degradation that matters. When women are depicted in pornography in degraded and submissive roles, viewers become less supportive of equality between the sexes and more lenient in assigning punishment to a rapist.

Media degradation of women can also reinforce the ideas that women are sex objects and/or sexually promiscuous and can undermine reactions of empathy to real women.

Researchers from the University of Massachusetts[42] invited participants to take part in two short studies: a censorship study and a study about legal decision making. In fact, this was all part of one investigation: the researchers were interested in how seeing degraded women would influence participants' views on rape. The scientists constructed a twenty-two-minute video compilation of scenes from the movies *9½ Weeks* and *Showgirls* that was rated to degrade women. They defined degradation as depicting women as objects to be exploited and manipulated sexually. The film clips they used included a striptease and a scene with a blindfolded woman. These scenes contained male dominance and power and female availability and submission, and also emphasized male—but not female—sexual gratification. First, participants watched either the derogatory scenes or a control video from an animation festival. Next, in what they thought was the legal decision-making study, they read a magazine account of either a date rape or a stranger rape. Results showed that the men who had seen the degrading media images of women showed significantly different reactions to the date rape account. These men were more likely to say that the victim of the date rape enjoyed it and that she secretly got what she wanted. Again, we see that men can learn lessons about women through exposure to media stereotypes.

It's important to note that these movie scenes did not even contain violence against women, but they still supported what are called "rape myths"—these are false stereotypes, cultural beliefs—about rape, such as the notion that women deserve rape or that they secretly want to be raped.

More on Media, Rape Myths, and Social Learning

In another study,[43] men and women were exposed to magazine advertisements containing either objectified or progressive images of women or containing no people at all (the control condition). Interestingly, men and women reacted differently to the objectified versus progressive women in the ads. Whereas seeing the derogatory images of women caused men to become more likely to endorse rape myths, it caused women in the experimental group to be less likely than control participants to support rape myths. The authors noted that incidence rates of rape were higher in states that had higher circulation rates of pornography and—in a seeming paradox—were higher in states where women's power and status were higher. The authors interpreted this as indicating a backlash against women's rise to social power in the form of violence against women. Again, we see that stereotyping in the media raises issues of status and power of men versus women in the real world.

In a classic study, Edward Donnerstein and Leonard Berkowitz[44] angered some men by giving them electric shocks; others were not shocked. Then the men saw a film. Some saw a neutral film, some saw a nonviolent, sexually explicit film. The most theoretically interesting conditions in the study involved two rape scenes. In one rape scene, the victim protested; in another version, she initially protested, but then appeared to enjoy the attack. This was the "rape myth" video—a rape scene that brought to life the idea that women secretly want to be raped. While the angered men tended to react aggressively in general, there were interesting differences in the behavior of the nonangered men, which varied depending on what type of film they had seen. Only the men who had seen the "rape myth" scene were more likely subsequently to be aggressive toward a real woman in the laboratory.

Once again, we see that people learn ideas in the media that can change their behavior. Media messages do matter. In fact, not only do they matter but they are powerful teachers. Again, when you take into consideration the power of the media coupled with the strong tendency of people to be ignorant of or to deny that power, there is a lot of room for harm. Here we see that so strongly because the harm we are talking about is aggression against women. Violence breeds violence. Degradation breeds degradation.

Music and Degradation

One more example: a group of researchers[45] conducted a national long-itudinal sample of over 1,400 teenagers. They were interested in whether listening to music with sexually degrading lyrics affected the teens' attitudes and behavior. The researchers selected sixteen artists whose music represented a variety of genres. They classified the sexual content of the lyrics on these artists' latest recordings. Here is one example of a sexually degrading lyric, from Ja Rule's *Living it Up*: "Half the ho's hate me, half them love me/ The ones that hate me/Only hate me 'cause they ain't fucked me/And they say I'm lucky/Do you think I've got time/To fuck all these ho's?" (By the way, have you noticed that if your kids are in the car with you, this is the song that will be blasting from the car next to you at a stoplight?) Results showed that teens who listened to the degrading music lyrics more often were more likely to initiate sexual intercourse or more advanced sexual behaviors during the two-year course of the study. Of course, such activity is related to sexually transmitted disease rates as well as teen pregnancy. These teens themselves had a tendency to see early sexual behavior as problematic and to wish they had waited longer to have sex.

Positive Images of Gender and Race in the Media

After that conversation, I imagine you are ready for some good news. I know I am. And there are, thankfully, positive examples of gender and race in the media. There are media messages that can influence us for the better. A film like *Akeelah and the Bee*, for example, shows the struggles of an African American girl to find her own positive voice and identity and to believe in herself. The depiction of Akeelah is respectful and nuanced. Viewers identify with the universal elements of her characterization. That underlines an important element in respectful characterization—telling stories with universal elements erases boundaries. It doesn't matter if Akeelah looks like you or comes from your neighborhood, you see her humanity. You understand what she's going through and you like her. Such characterization transcends social class and is unifying.

Since 2004, *Time* magazine has ranked the 100 most influential people in the world. The list is diverse and is based on the power of the person's influence—for better or worse. On the cover of the 2008 *Time 100* are men and women of many colors. Notable Americans include Oprah Winfrey and Barack Obama. Oprah is categorized among the "heros and pioneers," while Obama is on the "leaders and revolutionaries" list. Oprah, as a media pioneer and notable public servant, is surely one of the great examples of positive media images of African American women. She represents what can happen even against the odds and thus she is an inspiration.

Similarly, seeing Barack Obama through the eye of the camera has moved people across the country and around the world. Interestingly, he was ranked higher than John McCain, Hillary Clinton, and George W. Bush on *Time's* 2008 "leaders and revolutionaries" list. Obama's mother was white and his father Kenyan, so he is of mixed race. Like Oprah's story, Obama has taught us that media exposure to truly inspirational people of color can change things. Running on a message of change, Obama's rise to the top as the first African American president was helped by his media exposure.

Race and Gender in Kids' Media: Little Bill, Dora, and Kai-Lan

Let's turn to children's media and positive examples of gender and race. Aída Hurtado and Janelle Silva[46] discuss how we learn racial and gender identities through the media. The media teach us about who is in power, who is subjugated to that power, and what stereotypes are held about our ingroups and outgroups. They use the example of the show *Little Bill* as an ideal way to subtly teach positive, uplifting messages about diversity. The show was created by the famous actor and writer Bill Cosby, and is about a five-year-old boy's adventures. Calling their approach critical multiculturalism, Hurtado and Silva talk about how *Little Bill* takes on issues of diversity honestly and gently, by going with *Little Bill* as he navigates situations that deal with identity and simply by watching him interact with his family and friends. This type of critical multiculturalism challenges traditional media mythologies about social power. Through positive stories, *Little Bill* breaks cultural stereotypes (such as those about intellectual competence and gender roles) and supports the acquisition by viewers of a positive, private sense of "me-ness." As the authors put it:[47]

> *Little Bill*'s core mission is to communicate that African American communities are not violent, chaotic places full of dysfunction, populated by people who only speak Black English and dress like gangster rappers. The series also highlights the importance and diversity of African American culture, history, and social relations, going beyond the stereotypes usually shown in children's media. The world that Little Bill lives in is peaceful, filled with love and gentleness.

Nickelodeon's *Dora the Explorer* is a show with a Latina main character that has enjoyed immense commercial success, garnering little fans of diverse racial backgrounds. The show *Dora the Explorer*, as I see it, tries to do a number of positive things including encouraging kids to interact with what they see on the screen and teaching them about a Latina as well as her culture and language. Dora also has a healthy physical appearance, unlike your typical skinny princess. I have a preschool-aged daughter who is a big fan of Dora, so I have had lots of exposure to the spunky little chica and her best friend Boots the monkey. I have noticed that toddlers find her mesmerizing and that costumes depicting Dora are among the few non-Princess outfits for preschool girls that show up at Halloween.

While I don't know of a scientific study of the positive effects of watching Dora (let me add that to my "to do" list), I can tell you about my experience. My family and I often go to a local restaurant that has a largely Spanish-speaking staff. The people who work there are wonderfully kind; they often take time to talk and joke with us. One day a man at the restaurant asked my son how he was in Spanish, to which my three-year-old daughter replied, "Muy bien." Now, my son has always been great with language and he is a real people person, and I have chuckled to myself to see the little guy saying "Feliz navidad" and other Spanish phrases in this restaurant. But I was really blown away when my quiet little girl came out with a Spanish phrase. I knew that Dora had been her teacher. Some Spanish language had become natural to her. We've even used some Spanish around the house, like calling stars "estrellas" (Dora is in the habit of chasing stars) when we read a book my daughter has about stars.

Dora is an adventurer (*una exploradora*) and a positive influence on the whole. You may know that Dora now has a cousin with his own show: Diego of *Go, Diego, Go*. Diego rescues animals and teaches Spanish as well, and I would rank him among TV's positive multicultural influences for kids. I do have a concern about Diego, though. I have wondered whether he was created because the producers felt that they could not have a show for children with a little girl as the hero and just leave her as the sole hero of that universe. Maybe they didn't think little boys would buy Dora toys.

The reason all of this bothers me is that I grew up as girls so often do, with heroes in the media who were mostly boys. I made do. I imagine that might be what boys and girls of color do as well. I read myself into the characters I loved, and decided in my own mind that they *could* have been like me. They *could* have been girls. I loved to read Donald Sobol's mysteries about *Encyclopedia Brown, Boy Detective* when I was little and imagine solving little mysteries around my neighborhood. I also read *The Great Brain* series by John Fitzgerald, about the hilarious adventures of a little boy in rural, turn-of-the-century Utah. Just between you and me, I remember that my classmates in grade school noticed me reading the *Great Brain* books and thought it would be funny if they started calling me "the great brain"—so they did. Well, it could have been worse! But my point is: why couldn't little boys be expected to idolize Dora?

Aside from my questions about why Dora needed to be joined by Diego, and the obvious point that Dora is incredibly lucrative (if she were human, she and Boots would each have their own mansions), as I said, I still do think they are positive influences on kids. And there are other positive influences. Any time a show or game depicts a child respectfully and as a person rather than a stereotype, that is a good representation. Programs where boys and girls of different races interact positively are important for children to see as well. When this happens, it is an example of what social psychologists call the "extended contact hypothesis." Namely, when we see people like us interacting with other sorts of people—most especially those we have little experience with—we learn positive lessons. We learn that people from our group can be friends with people from other groups. This makes us both more accepting and more likely to really interact with different sorts of people in our real lives.

Nick Jr. has a new show similar to Dora but exploring Chinese language and culture. It is called *Ni Hao, Kai-Lan*, which means Hello, Kai-Lan. Kai-Lan Chow is a five-year-old Chinese American girl who speaks Mandarin. Her grandfather Ye Ye teaches her about Chinese customs. While the *New York Times*[48] described Dora as a "geography nut" and "problem solver," it called Kai-Lan a "peacemaker" and "amateur therapist" based on her habit of helping her friends deal with their emotions. Given that Asian characters have been called "invisible" because of their gross underrepresentation in the media, having a Chinese female heroine of a children's show is good. Just having more respectful representations of Asians (I'm thinking something less extreme than Fu Manchu) is important. Kai-Lan with her language and culture lessons fits the bill.

Building a Healthier Media Culture for All

Respectful depictions and multicultural interactions in the media are very uplifting and healthy for all of us. When children from different backgrounds play well together on children's shows such as on *Sesame Street*, and when they are each presented as equally valid human beings, it sends important messages. It is the premise that was used in casting a group of racially diverse men and women for the TV series *Star Trek* in the 1960s. It's the reason—as mentioned earlier—Martin Luther King Jr. reportedly told actress Nichelle Nichols, who played Lt. Uhuru on the show, that she could not quit because she was a role model to so many African American girls. Just as degrading characterizations cause damage, respectful characterizations are powerfully good.

Let me leave you with what I think is a very fine example of representations of race and gender in the media. PBS's station WGBH in Boston, funded in part by the National Science Foundation and Arby's restaurants, produced a show that debuted in 2006 called *Fetch! with Ruff Ruffman*. The show—a reality game show hosted by comical cartoon dog Ruff

Ruffman— features a cast of real kids that changes each year. The twee-naged cast is half girls and half boys and is racially diverse. Furthermore, the kids look like real kids, in T-shirts, ponytails, jeans, and tennis shoes; there are no Hollywood wannabes there. Every week the kids are given a variety of challenges including taking quizzes, solving puzzles and problems of all sorts, and exploring different jobs. They have been asked to shovel manure on a farm, solve mysteries in a castle, do stand up comedy or forecast the weather on TV, make chocolates, and track animal scat and pitch makeshift tents in the wilderness. It is a competition, but the show also teaches cooperation. Here is part of the show's educational philosophy from www.pbskids.org/fetch:

> FETCH! shows that reality programs can help kids learn how to tackle problems, overcome fears, brainstorm, and collaborate. Reality programs allow viewers to see that real expertise often takes time to develop and that learning is about the journey, not the destination. And, rather than be an impetus for anti-social behavior, they can create a positive environment for modeling pro-social skills and resolving conflicts between kids.

The show also encourages what it calls "habits of mind"—problem-solving tools including "curiosity, perseverance, risk-taking and creative and critical thinking."[49] "Fetch! with Ruff Ruffman web site on pbskid-s.org," With other shows using stereotypes as a lazy storytelling strategy, being mean-spirited and sometimes antisocial, a show that encourages growth in so many ways is absolutely amazing. It does what all shows should do regarding social categories like race and sex—it simply lets people be real people and it encourages these real kids to grow in healthy, challenging ways. I wish more programs were created with the kind of consciousness that PBS's *Fetch! with Ruff Ruffman* has.

When media producers treat race and gender respectfully—when they treat *people* respectfully—they can do some good rather than simply using their audience for all they think we're worth.

> Racially prejudicial stereotyping is debilitative in a society, especially one as diverse as the United States. Not only does the stereotyping work against the groups' recognizing and understanding the common humanity of all people, it also provides succeeding generations of all racial groups – White and non-White – with distorted self-images. The coupling of biased portrayals with the social and psychological

power of mass entertainment threatens the maturation of American society into a model of multicultural tolerance and unity (Wilson et al., 2003) (p. 134).

At this time in history, our nation is becoming more culturally diverse. We have witnessed the election of the country's first African American president and we have seen positive reactions to Obama's election both here and around the world. We know that so many have been inspired by President Obama and his family and embrace the progress they represent. Now more than ever we need to be aware of the power of mass media images of gender and race – both for the bad and for the good – in the process of socialization. Media producers will give us respectful representations of diverse groups if we as an audience decide that we will accept no less. How well we understand and address media representations of race and gender will have consequences on the future of our evolving society.

Five

ISSUES IN MEDIA AND SOCIAL
LEARNING: RAP MUSIC, BEAUTY AND
DOMESTIC VIOLENCE

We humans are like no other species. We are highly skilled creatures who adapt to physical and social environments and who survive and thrive despite our physical vulnerabilities. We accomplish these feats largely due to outstanding mental abilities. I know, sitting around the Christmas tree watching as someone tries to assemble a toy or even get the toy out of the box, "outstanding mental abilities" isn't the first phrase that comes to mind, but it's true. Our intelligence allows us to make complex judgments and choices, many of which are social—for example, attributions about the intentions of people from outside our social group or skills that help us gain power and control over others. All of this used to be accomplished through face-to-face interactions within communities.

Right now we are at an unprecedented moment in the social history of the human race because very many of our "social interactions" occur via the mass media. Think for a minute about a group of monkeys—they live in a social group, maintaining the social order. Some monkeys are at the top of their hierarchies, enjoying the privileges that come with this high social status—mating with the best female monkeys, for example. Monkeys don't watch other monkeys on TV and compare themselves. Male monkeys don't feel inadequate because they compare their bodies to the bodies of monkeys on TV or the Internet who are amazing physical specimens. Their mates don't wish they had the bodies of these super-monkeys. Monkeys don't see extreme deviant behavior of other monkeys from across the country or around the world. Young monkeys don't meet predatory monkeys on the Internet.

Okay, enough monkey business. All of this was to make the point that humans are unique communicators by definition. When you add technologies from our recent history, like television and newspapers, that changes how we communicate. When you add the very recent changes in communication such as social networking sites, You Tube, text messaging, and more global television access and news coverage reaching audiences at lightning speed, you change the fundamental landscape of human communication in such a way that no one can really predict the ramifications.

We live in an era where a *Saturday Night Live* skit can alter a politician's public standing. A You Tube video can be broadcast on television and reported on in newspapers and magazines, ultimately altering perceptions of people and events worldwide—either legitimately or illegitimately. Strangely, since most of our waking time is spent with mass media, we are actually learning more social information from staring at screens than from staring into the eyes of real people in our lives.

This chapter explores some specific, real-world examples of how we learn complex social information through the mass media. There is an infinite array of examples to explore—it's an interesting exercise to generate your own list. In this chapter, the focus will be on topics that are based on or specifically related to my own research and expertise. Topics include how people learn about domestic violence through the mass media, the power of the "beauty myth," and social characterizations in rap music lyrics.

Domestic Violence Media Coverage: How Books, TV and Magazines Have Influenced How We Understand and Address Domestic Violence

Domestic violence did not begin in the 1970s, but public consciousness of the issue did emerge in a very real way in that decade. In 1974, Englishwoman Erin Pizzey published *Scream Quietly or the Neighbours Will Hear.* On the cover were pictures of physically abused women, beaten and bruised. *Scream Quietly* brought public attention to domestic violence, which at that time was more likely to be called wife beating, wife battering, or wife abuse. Erin Pizzey also opened the first shelter for victims of domestic violence in a London suburb in 1971. Around the same time

Woman House, the first battered women's shelter in the United States, opened its doors and what became known as the shelter movement began.

From the perspective of a social psychological approach to mass media, notice that the issue was defined and understood in certain ways and not in others, which has implications. Using the terms "wife beating," "battering," or "abuse" defined domestic violence as men's aggression against women. Pizzey herself has taken issue with this definition throughout her career, writing and speaking about how her observations suggested that the women involved in abusive relationships were often also violent. She started a men's shelter as well, which she reported was closed due to underfunding. The issue of the gender of domestic violence victims continues to be debated, but most agree that women are considerably more likely to be targets of domestic violence than men, though no one would argue that there are indeed male victims of domestic violence. In fact, it may be simply that men's superior physical strength puts female victims of physical abuse more at risk for serious injury. But for our purposes, the point is that we largely understand domestic violence as a women's issue due to vivid media landmarks such as *Scream Quietly*. In this case, the public received a gross message about violence—husbands physically batter wives and this is an issue that needs to be addressed. More subtle and detailed messages can often be lost, misunderstood, or misconstrued.

Intentionally and unintentionally, both helpful and harmful media messages get sent and received. Messages about domestic violence are communicated in a variety of ways, ranging from news reports to more detailed accounts like those that appeared in Pizzey's book, to those from less serious outlets like entertainment magazines. What we choose to talk about and what we choose to ignore all contribute to public opinion about domestic violence. Part of the reason public opinion about domestic violence is important is that it shapes public policy, which, in turn shapes how the police respond to victims and influences financial support for shelters and other social services. Another reason mass media coverage of domestic violence is important is the teaching component. It is a way for people to better understand one aspect of relationships, to be aware of potential problems, and to know more effective ways of responding. This is important for current and future victims, for friends and family, and for members of the culture at large. More broadly, it is a way for us all to understand one aspect of the human condition.

Several months ago, I attended a yoga class sponsored by my local Women's Resource Center. After doing yoga together, the group of women sat down to a light lunch and we began socializing. A local woman, roughly my own age, had brought her mother to the event. The mother heard that I was a psychologist who had done some research on violence, which sparked a passionate soliloquy on domestic violence. She said she'd recently read a magazine article about an abused wife. She was emphatic that *she* would never have allowed her husband to beat her. If he tried, she would have left him immediately. What was wrong with these women who let themselves be abused? Metaphorically, my jaw dropped when I heard these opinions. Didn't this lady know that domestic violence situations are much more complicated than she was suggesting? Didn't she understand that there are many reasons women don't leave abusive situations? I told her I was fortunate to have never been a victim of domestic violence myself, but I understood that it was a complex picture. To blame the victims is really to do them a disservice—literally adding insult to injury.

Also at the table with us was my friend who was the director of the women's center. She had seen many women come to her doors to escape a violent, abusive situation. We tried to explain gently that the women who are victims of domestic violence are not unintelligent, masochistic, or really fundamentally different from any other woman. Abusive relationships are often characterized by a larger pattern of coercion. Abusive men control their partners' lives using strategies such as limiting their access to transportation and communication, thus keeping them isolated from friends and family and from the benefits of a social support system. An abuser can sabotage his partner's attempts to work or to get an education, thus keeping her financially dependent. A common tactic is for an abuser to criticize his partner, saying she is unattractive, unintelligent, or unworthy and lucky to have a man at all. If he thinks she might try to escape the situation, he uses other coercive tactics such as threatening to take the children or to harm or even kill her or the children. The terrible fact is, abusers do often harm or kill their ex-partners after the partner has left. They do continue to stalk or threaten the victim and to involve the children.

So victims of domestic violence are often not in a situation in which they can walk out the door so easily. As Evan Stark explains eloquently in his 2007 book *Coercive Control: How Men Entrap Women in Personal Life*, intimate abuse goes beyond the physical to psychological manipulation and coercion. In fact, victims report that the mental anguish they experience can be worse than the physical pain. Often the victim entered the relationship as a young woman and the abuse came on gradually. Part of the cycle of coercion is a pattern whereby the abuse starts slowly and is often followed by expressions of sorrow and vows never to repeat the abuse. Women want to believe this of the men they love and many do and get caught in the trap. It is a psychological bind. All of this makes it harder for police and other interested parties to understand the total situation and makes it more likely for the victim to be blamed.

One-third of American women report being physically or sexually abused by a husband or partner some time in their lives. Current estimates are that approximately 4 million women are abused each year. Reports have indicated that about 25 percent of females who go to the emergency room for treatment are the victims of domestic abuse. A third of teenagers say that they know someone who has been punched, kicked, slapped, choked, or otherwise physically hurt by her partner. (Visit loveisnotabuse.com for these and more facts about domestic and dating violence.) Given these statistics, I wondered at the time why this mother was so quick to blame the victims of domestic violence. Why, in this country where domestic violence is so commonplace, was it possible that women can have very little knowledge about these important issues?

To answer these questions, we need to go back and think about how people learn about socially relevant issues in our culture. How would one learn about spousal abuse or dating violence? Such information could be consciously taught in schools, in churches, or in the home, but not enough good information is being transmitted this way. I mentioned the Web site loveisnotabuse.com earlier. This is an example of how the Internet can be an excellent source of information and even activism about socially important issues such as domestic and dating violence. Fortunately, teenagers who are technologically savvy (technology natives, as we call them) are more likely than this older woman to know how to search effectively for information and resources on the Web. In cases like this, the Internet is an especially helpful resource because of the sensitive nature of the topic, and women and teenaged girls may feel embarrassed to admit that they want access to these resources. Searching the net is generally more private than finding other resources. Of course, an abusive husband might well limit his wife's access to the Internet as well, or might track the Web sites she uses if he himself is technologically savvy enough. Abusive boyfriends may similarly track cell phone call records or read their girlfriends' text messages as a way to manipulate and control their social interactions. But, again, technology can have real advantages in enabling people to find the latest and the most useful information.

How has the public learned about abusive relationships and what are the implications? To address this question, Kathryn Thill and I[1] investigated how popular American magazines have talked about domestic violence over a thirty-year period. As it turned out, this investigation became a multimedia story because the magazines covered issues and events that took place or were documented in other media such as on television. We began with 1974, the year *Scream Quietly or the Neighbours Will Hear* was published and also the year that the first battered women's shelter in America opened its doors, collecting all the American popular magazine articles on domestic violence that were published that year. Moving forward, we did the same for the years 1984, 1994, and 2004. We did this initially because we wanted to take a sample of articles that was both deep (every article published in every American magazine in that year) and broad (every ten years so as to cover potential changes over time).

As it turned out, selecting these years made historical sense as well because there were watershed events relevant to domestic violence or highly publicized news stories relevant to domestic violence that took place in each of the years 1974, 1984, 1994, and 2004. Relevant events in 1974 included the publication of *Scream Quietly* and the opening of the first American battered women's shelter; 1984 saw the broadcast of *The Burning Bed*, a film that sparked public conversation about domestic violence. In 1984, Congress passed the Family Violence Prevention and Services Act. In 1994, the world watched and listened to the trial of O. J. Simpson and heard about his past abusive relationship with murdered ex-wife Nicole Brown Simpson. That same year, President Bill Clinton signed into law the Violence against Women Act—the most far-reaching legislation in modern history concerning domestic violence. Later that same year, the world was drawn into another story of an abusive marriage—this time that of John and Lorena Bobbitt. In 2004, Scott Peterson was convicted of the murder of his wife Laci and their unborn child, and later that year President Bush signed the Unborn Victims of Violent Crime law. Sadly, domestic violence scholars have long identified pregnancy as a time when partner violence against women *increases* rather than decreases as one might have imagined.

In 1984, the made-for-television movie *The Burning Bed* garnered wide attention and critical acclaim. *The Burning Bed*, starring Farrah Fawcett, dramatized the true story of Francine Hughes, telling how she met and married Mickey Hughes and how Mickey repeatedly and brutally abused her. One reason the story was so compelling to the public is that one night, after Mickey beat, raped, threatened, and verbally abused her, Francine snapped. As Mickey lay passed out drunk, Francine poured gasoline over him, took their children out to the car, and came back in and lit Mickey and the bed aflame, killing him—thus the title *The Burning Bed*. Also fascinating to the public was the fact that Francine was acquitted of all charges in Mickey's death due to reasons of temporary insanity.

Here we have a true case of domestic violence, dramatized on television and discussed in magazines and other media outlets. This story provides an example in which there are layers of media coverage and discourse about an important social issue. Looking back, what can we learn about domestic violence from this public discourse? How did American magazines cover *The Burning Bed*? What we found for this case was broadly true of domestic violence coverage in American magazines across the thirty-year span we studied. When American magazines discuss domestic violence, they tend to do so in a way that is sensational or shallow or both. We found that many times these magazine articles about abusive husbands and abused wives simply retold the lurid and shocking details of episodes of assault or murder. While *The Burning Bed* involved dramatizing Francine's experiences of being beaten, it went beyond that in a way that was potentially helpful to other victims and in a way the magazine articles about the story did not.

American Magazines and a Serious Issue (no pun intended)

A deeper analysis of media coverage of *The Burning Bed* reveals a lot about the social psychology of mass media. Our analysis of all the American magazine articles related to domestic violence in the year 1984 showed that *The Burning Bed* sparked many of them. So far so good—we have a real-life story of domestic violence and a film adaptation that emphasized some important, realistic, and potentially helpful information. But, as mentioned earlier, when the magazines opened up discussions on this issue, instead of using it as an opportunity to help the many American victims of domestic violence or to prevent young women from entering abusive relationships, they mostly took the metaphoric low road and simply reported sensational stories of physical beatings designed to sell magazines by hooking readers with the promise of lurid descriptions.

Another mistake the magazines made was providing misleading information. For example, a typical approach at the time was to interview actress Farrah Fawcett about her role in the film. While there is nothing wrong with that approach in principle, what ended up happening is that the actress said some helpful and some misleading things about domestic violence. For example, Farrah said that during the abusive scenes in the movie she wanted to hit back and repeatedly asked herself why Francine stayed. Farrah is not a counselor or someone who is trained to understand how to best help victims. I say this not to offend Ms. Fawcett who, as I understand it, took the role in part because of her passionate feelings about domestic violence. Farrah's statement is not unlike the story of the mother asking why women stay. This is a legitimate question, but one that could be addressed much more effectively by giving expert advice based on the realities that so many women have endured. Sadly, the public would later learn that Farrah actually endured domestic abuse herself.

Of course, all magazine articles need not be informative. People are welcome to read magazine articles about the most popular toenail polish colors or play a video game in which a large chimpanzee throws barrels at things. (Monkeys throwing barrels = fun!) We can be as silly and frivolous as we want to be. The TV show *Seinfeld* billed itself as a show about absolutely nothing—not that there's anything wrong with that. Communications scholarship (specifically a "uses and gratifications" approach to media) identifies three reasons people read magazines: diversion, surveillance, and identity motives. The first two motives, diversion and surveillance, basically mean that people read magazines as a form of escapism (to relax and pass the time) and to learn information (keeping abreast of the latest issues of importance to people in broader society). The last motive is a more complex social motive and involves learning what others do and what they value and how we fit into that picture.

While it is legitimate for magazine articles to be frivolous, what about frivolous or misleading articles about a serious issue that is known to affect so many readers in ways that can be profoundly damaging? We know that two of the motives for reading magazine articles are to learn about issues that are important to people in our culture and to see how our own actions and feelings fit into the big picture of our society. So where does this put a frivolous or misleading article about a serious issue? It's one thing to write a silly escapist article about toenail polish, but what about domestic violence? I believe journalists have a greater responsibility when writing about a serious issue. Kathryn Thill and I found that many of the domestic violence articles sent the message that it is the woman's responsibility to "fix" "her" situation. Domestic violence is a woman's problem and it is up to women to solve it. This tends to take the responsibility off the perpetrators and tends to blame the victims. When the murder of Nicole Brown Simpson was reported by the press, battered women's shelters received record numbers of phone calls. Apparently, domestic violence victims realized that their abuse could end in murder. This is a good example of how public discourse about an issue through mass media can be an opportunity for education and real change. If the magazines and other outlets had taken this opportunity more seriously, they could have provided a very important service for their readers. They could have changed lives as well as interested their readers.

If most articles support the myth that abuse is the woman's problem and it is up to her to fix it, then readers may well come to believe it themselves as the belief is apparently widely accepted. If journalists believe it, and no one contradicts it, it must be true. Also, consensus dictates that if most victims can solve their own problems, I should be able to solve mine as well. Furthermore, the availability heuristic—the idea that the more easily we can think of certain examples, the more typical the examples are—comes into play. If the "typical" domestic violence story is for a woman to escape successfully and solve her own problem, then that must be what most women do.

Our research found a strong tendency for domestic violence coverage in American magazines to simply cover newsworthy events, such as the broadcast of *The Burning Bed*, the O.J. trial, and other cases of celebrity involvement with domestic abuse such as those involving James Brown, in either a shallow way or in a news report style that covers simple facts like the events in a trial. There were significantly fewer articles about domestic violence than about other important issues such as breast cancer and abortion. Underlining the celebrity story–driven trend, by far the most articles related to domestic violence were published in *People* magazine—a magazine whose mission indicates that it intends to write about people and not issues.

Remember that two of the three primary motives for reading magazines are largely social—to gather information about what people are talking about and to see how your life fits into the picture. Since domestic violence affects so many Americans, misinformation in magazine coverage does not satisfy the reader's intended motives in reading the magazine. In one article, for example, readers are misinformed that victims of domestic violence are secretly masochistic—a well-known myth. A woman reports that her husband dominated her from the day they met and she always *wanted* to be dominated by him. Social psychologists often cite people's desire to believe in a just world—if women are abused, they must deserve it because the world is a fair place. This myth certainly supports that belief, and by extension it hurts victims again. If it is their fault, why should we help?

For me, the most egregious example is an article in *Redbook* about actress Halle Berry called "Beauty and the Brave."[2] This story relies on a common myth about domestic violence—the Cinderella premise, which Evan Stark discusses in his book *Coercive Control*.[3] According to this Cinderella myth, men are either abusers or saviors, and women are spared from abuse only if fate delivers her a savior. "Beauty and the Brave" spins the tale that Halle Berry's savior is Atlanta Brave's baseball player David Justice. Through Justice's love, all of Berry's former problems with domestic abuse are solved. Of course, Berry later divorced Justice. And Cinderella stories do not help women tell the difference between these supposed abusers and saviors. They put a woman's well-being in the hands of fate and depict women as helpless and dependent. Berry, who is the first African American Oscar winner for best actress, is portrayed as merely a "beauty," saved by her "Brave" man. Psychologically, we may want to emulate Berry. We may think our views should mirror those advocated by the article. This type of fantasy may be more appealing than the grim reality of abuse.

So a story that is not supposed to be about an issue ends up presenting an issue in a misleading way. What could we have learned that would have been more helpful? Well, let's go back to the film *The Burning Bed*. I believe it actually did a good job of showing the pattern of coercive control described by Stark and other domestic violence experts. In *The Burning Bed*, Mickey tells Francine she can't go to college. He controls what she wears and whom she sees. He humiliates her by ordering her to make him dinner and then after she makes it, he throws it on the floor and shoves her face into the food, then demands that she clean it up. Francine wants to leave, but she worries how she will support the children. She does not have enough support from family members who often excuse Mickey's abusive treatment. When she tries to get away, Mickey comes and menaces the family. He repeatedly threatens to kill her and tells her she is no good. The film dramatized these ideas effectively. The magazines that discussed the film, unfortunately, did not take the opportunity to help readers further the public discourse started by the film. Ultimately, both the reality and the unreality portrayed by mass media influence how people think about a very real issue.

Fantasy and Reality—More Gray than Black and White

After *The Burning Bed* aired nationally, related news stories followed. Shelters received record numbers of calls, from both men and women wanting counseling about their domestic situations. There were reports of men beating their wives in response to the film. In Chicago, a battered wife watched *The Burning Bed* and then shot her husband.

Again, we go back to a central message of this book on the social psychology of the media. Stories in the media mean something real to the people who watch them. The social messages are complex and interact with the life experiences of the person watching. We have to stop thinking there are two separate notions, one called fantasy and one called reality, and that our processing of fictional stories does not affect this real thing we call life.

The Burning Bed was based on a true story, which has been shown in the social psychologists' laboratory to be more likely to incite aggression in the viewer. To make the point that this applies to fiction as well as nonfiction, let's consider a related, but purely fictional, film. Farrah Fawcett, who portrayed Francine Hughes in *The Burning Bed* to critical acclaim, also starred in the movie *Extremities*, the story of a woman who turns the tables on a rapist who humiliates and tortures her by humiliating and torturing him. One tagline for *Extremities* was the subtle "Alone and vulnerable. The perfect victim ... or so he thought." A less subtle tagline said, "What she did to survive is nothing compared to what she'll do to get even." (For more on *The Burning Bed* or *Extremities*, visit the Internet Movie Database at imdb.com).

BBC reporter Barry Norman interviewed Fawcett in 1986[4] at the time of the film's British release, questioning the potential danger of the film's plot, saying: "Any film story which treats women as objects to be brutalized should be handled with extreme care because the world, alas, has more than its share of lunatics and cretins who believe that's precisely how women should be treated." When Norman comments that Farrah's character's torture of the potential rapist makes her just about as bad as he is, Farrah replies, "I tried my best to get down there where you men hover sometimes.... [T]he only way I could see to vindicate myself was to do that ... the only way to make him feel as scared and degraded and inadequate as I had felt." She continued by describing personal experience with physical abuse and humiliation as her inspiration for playing the film role the way she did. When pressed on the point of whether the film might encourage bad men to copycat the crime in the film, she replied that she did not find the portrayal in any way encouraging of violence.

This interview raises a number of important issues. First, we see again an actress being asked to give expert opinion about rape. Being an actress does not bar you from being an expert on rape, but it certainly does not guarantee it either. The interview of the actress about the serious issues explored in the film raises intriguing issues. How does the public separate acting from reality? Is it totally separate? We've already seen that Farrah Fawcett has both personal experience and interest in women's issues and domestic violence. She reported herself that she used her own experience to play these roles. Again, are there really two things here—one clearly fantasy and one reality?

I think this line of reasoning invites one to look closer at portrayals and how viewers construe them. In a classic social psychological investigation of attribution—how we explain people's behaviors—psychologists Jones and Harris[5] asked participants to read aloud a speech either defending or criticizing the politics of Cuban dictator Fidel Castro. Other students were asked to judge whether each speaker's attitude was consistent with his or her speech. Remember, the students had no choice as to whether they were defending or criticizing Castro; they were simply asked to do it. Results indicated that the audience generally believed that the speakers endorsed the beliefs espoused by their speeches. This finding is an example of a very common social bias known as the fundamental attribution error—we assume people's internal attitudes are consistent with their behaviors. The fundamental attribution error is basically synonymous with the term "correspondence bias," which means we have a bias to think people's behavior matches (corresponds to) their attitudes.

I think we can apply this idea to acting, which of course is one of the main things we watch in all our free time spent staring into screens. We often assume an actor's behavior matches his internal beliefs and attitudes. So, if an actor often plays villains, we assume he is an evil sort of man in real life. When Farrah plays a victim who fights back, we assume she personally endorses her character's beliefs. This is meaningful for a number of reasons, some of which have been discussed in other contexts. For one thing, when people identify with aggressors, they are more likely to emulate them. When people think what they see on the screen is more realistic, they are also more likely to act like the actor in question. I make these points not to say that people should or should not emulate the character Francine Hughes but to underline the social psychology in action here. We most emphatically do not say to ourselves, "This is acting. It is not related to reality and it has no lessons I can apply in my life." We pretty much believe the exact opposite. In other words, the concept of media as pure fantasy is . . . well, pure fantasy.

Real Reality Media

We know that one-third of women will face domestic abuse in a lifetime. That's a staggering statistic. Given how many of us this issue affects, are there helpful media resources available? There are indeed. In fact, I've mentioned some already. We saw how *The Burning Bed* presented some realistic, important, and pretty novel information about domestic violence. Also, the Web site loveisnotabuse.com has some practical information, and there is a special emphasis on teens and dating violence, which is important for the prevention of domestic violence. How about magazines? Our study revealed just two articles, one from *Oprah's O Magazine*[6] called "She's Come Undone," and one from *Ladies' Home Journal*[7] called "Wife Beating," that were great resources. Those were too few given the dozens of articles published in those four years that broached the issue, yet failed to do it service.

Having said that, I want to describe the best magazine resource I have found on domestic violence. This magazine did not appear in the years we studied, and if it had, we would not have found it in our search because it is not available everywhere. Even so, happily it reaches many women who can benefit from it. The magazine is called *Diane* and it is published and distributed by the *Curves for Women* fitness centers. In the fall of 2006, *Diane* published an issue on the faces of domestic violence. The cover page showed images of sixty-three women who have survived domestic violence. As I read Abigail Esman's story, "If I Could Close My Eyes"[8] in the issue, I got chills—the good kind. Here was reality. There was no Cinderella story, no blaming the victim, no shallow coverage. Here was a story that explained clearly and directly things that are difficult to understand. What is the abuse really like? How could the beatings not be the worst part of the abuse?

> Four million American women a year are abused by their partners— one every 10 seconds. We've all seen ... the photographs of women made up to look bruised. But they don't tell the real story. The real story is not the blood or the bruises or the shattered bones. The real story is the part you cannot see. It is the part we feel long after we've ceased noticing that it hurts when he hits us. It's the fear, fear that follows us everywhere, rising and falling with the events of the day, looming over us, a black shadow ... that keeps our shoulders hunched as we try to become invisible, recoil from the blows, verbal or physical we know will come.

As to the question of how people end up in abusive relationships, I'll let Abigail tell it in her own words:

> The ascent of abuse is gradual. It begins very slightly and gets progressively hotter, so that by the time the bones are shattered in

your jaw and you are telling people stories of falling down stairs, it doesn't even seem all that bad.

And there is the question that we seem to always come back to: why do women stay with abusers? Again, Abigail has a way of speaking directly and with eloquence:

> In 1978, the prevailing view was still that battered women were masochists. But I wasn't a masochist. It was just that leaving seemed—and usually is—at least as dangerous as staying. There was the social stigma, the very real fear of retribution. Better, I thought, to endure the beatings—which, I was always certain, wouldn't happen . . . . I loved him even though he didn't exist outside my own imagination. I didn't understand that the man I loved was my own mirage . . . from one moment to the next he became a different person, a gentleman, a lover, holding me as if the beating had never happened. He even told me sometimes that it hadn't . . . now . . . I see that the man who once wept as he held his dying cat in his arms was the same man who had caused its death in the first place—and that this moment was the entirety and the whole of our life together.

Curves is a fitness center for women. As a member at a local *Curves*, I have noticed that *Diane* magazine has often been given away or sold for a dollar, so the magazine is accessible to many women. This special issue on domestic violence gave great practical advice and contacts. It listed companies that make special provisions to aid victims of domestic violence, tips for helping a daughter or a friend, and practical tips to help a woman cope

---

Practical Advice about Domestic Violence. Adapted from *Diane: The Curves Magazine*, Fall, 2006 special report on domestic violence.

Helping a daughter: Make sure you and your daughter have conversations about what makes a healthy relationship. Advise her to be wary and to talk to you if a boyfriend tells her what she should wear, gives her a cell phone and calls any time, or threatens violence during arguments.

Practical information for domestic abuse victims: pack a bag with important items and consider keeping it at a family member's house; create a code word that means you need the police and tell it to those you trust; in conflicts, try to get to a room you can lock or can leave from. If you have left: give a photograph of the abuser to your coworkers and children's principal and teachers, contact a domestic violence agency for advice on staying safe. Call 1-800-799-7233 for the *National Domestic Violence Hotline*.

To donate a cell phone to a survivor, go to www.ncadv.org/donate.

in an abusive situation (see above insert). Next, we consider images in the media and how they alter our perceptions.

Deconstructing the Social Construction of Un-reality Media

Picture in your mind's eye a woman in a swimsuit. Now picture what the average American woman looks like in a swimsuit. Do the images match? Which one can you do more easily? I'm guessing that if you are an average American, when you imagine a woman in a swimsuit you are more likely to visualize the type of woman we see in the media—young, very thin and beautiful, with big breasts. Why would this be the first image that comes to mind? One reason is the social psychological principle of the availability heuristic. This decision rule simply says that if it is easy to think of an example of something, it must be because that type of example is very common. Usually this type of rule of thumb serves us well. If I asked you to think of an average kitchen sink, you probably would think about sinks you see in your home and in the homes of your friends and family. Although you might also think of some you have seen on television and in magazines, you'd probably make a judgment that's pretty realistic in terms of being fairly representative of middle-class kitchen sinks. (I tried to think of an example of any everyday item that we don't see more often in the media than in real life. I don't know if I succeeded when I picked the kitchen sink, but the fact that it wasn't easy is interesting in and of itself.) But when we think of a woman in a swimsuit, our greater experience is probably with media fantasy than with reality. What does that mean from a social psychological perspective? Well, it means that if we apply the availability heuristic we will make the judgment that women in swimsuits do or should look like those women we see on TV, movies, magazines, and even videogames. There are repercussions to this way of thinking. For example, if women typically do or should look like the women we see on the screen or the page, then we use that as a standard when we judge real women. And of course, what we are talking about here is not the swimsuit but the body that wears it. For men, the result may be having higher expectations for the appearance of the women in their lives. For women, the result is almost certainly feelings of inadequacy, even guilt and shame, and the belief that we are failures as women, in a fundamental way.

Thinness in women is standard fare on television and this is not nearly as often the case for men on television. Studies have shown that exposure to mass media portrayals of the thin ideal increases psychological pain and feelings of inadequacy for women, and they increase the drive to buy products and services that promise to make women thinner. Even those we consider to be beauties are subject to this thin ideal. Miss America contestants and models, among others recognized for their beauty, have been shrinking across the decades. These women are now about 25 percent smaller than the average woman. When we are talking about the range of women's weights, 25 percent is a really significant difference—like the difference between 140 and 105 pounds, for instance. One hundred forty pounds is actually less than the average woman weights. But I have seen covers of tabloid exposés that reveal the "horrifying" fact that some young starlet now weighs 140 pounds. And we've probably all watched a beauty pageant in which even very tall women, as most pageant contestants are, weigh just over 100 pounds. Since social comparison is a natural psychological process, the conclusion for women is practically inescapable—we are in a game that is hyped as ultimately important, and we are doomed to fail.

If Using You Is Wrong, I Don't Wanna Be Right

It's easy to see that this situation sets the stage for a social dilemma. What do you do when you can profit from someone else's pain, especially when you know this pain is so fundamental that not only will it work but it is such a perfect trap that the pain and subsequent spending to relieve the pain seem virtually bottomless? It's clear what many businesses have done with these circumstances: they have profited from the pain of many, using imagery in the media to help create an unreachable ideal and thus a boundless source of revenue.

In Chapter 1, the section entitled "Darwin Didn't Anticipate Hollywood," I broached this topic. Basically, we are programmed to compare ourselves to relevant others (am I smart enough, pretty enough, healthy enough to attract a mate, for instance), but we are using the wrong comparison group. In *The Beauty Myth*,[9] Naomi Wolf talks of a plastic surgeon whose patients, he believed, all were highly attractive but felt universally unattractive because they compared themselves to models.

Kristen Harrison[10] discovered this when she studied television's ideal figure for women, which she found corresponded to women's size 10 breasts, on the same body as a size 2 waist and size 4 hips. You don't have to be a doctor to realize this figure basically does not occur in nature. In fact, breasts are largely made of fat, and real healthy bodies are much more proportional than this decidedly unreal 10–2–4 ideal. Why would your body fat disproportionately land on your chest? It doesn't make sense outside the world of plastic surgery. In fact, since all fatness is considered sinful in American culture, but since large breasts are simultaneously considered very attractive, and since breasts are mostly made of fat, I propose a new trend. Guys should go around saying, "Hey, baby, those breasts are fat!"—meaning it in a good way. I'm kidding of course, but one needs to keep a sense of humor about a phenomenon that causes almost universal unease to women. Studies typically reveal pathological rates of body dissatisfaction among American women. Often these rates are around 95 percent. Think about what that means. Really. Most American women are uneasy, distressed, or downright depressed about the way they look. Something that causes so much unhappiness is a real problem.

Now if the average American woman is a size 14, it's easy to understand the kind of social comparison that goes on. If you are a woman, I probably don't need to explain this to you. If you are a man, imagine this: you are much larger than the images you see everywhere. You are told you are not socially acceptable if you do not become smaller than you could reasonably be able to become. Where's the way out? Well, for Harrison's subjects, there were some clear answers. Exposure to the "curvaceously thin" media ideal predicted desire for women to be more like this ideal and for men to desire women to be more like this ideal. Even though large breasts are considered attractive, Harrison found what she called a "mainstreaming" effect such that women with larger than ideal breasts wished for them to be smaller. These data suggest that media ideals warp our standards of beauty. Women and men who see this ideal are more likely to desire women to obtain this unnatural set of proportions. Sadly, what is not surprising is that both the men and women in this study who had greater exposure to the media ideal were more likely to believe women should have cosmetic procedures such as liposuction and breast augmentation surgery. The conclusion: what is natural is not socially acceptable due to a perversion of body image accomplished by mass media. This perversion serves the dual purpose of attracting attention (all advertisers want is consumers' eyeballs looking at their product because they know advertising sells) and creating the strong desire for women to spend money on their appearance.

Of course these images are compelling—imagery that is unreal in this way would have to be compelling. It's why cartoon women are often drawn with extreme proportions—pushing the limits makes a novel image and one that exaggerates desirable characteristics. If video game character Lara Croft were real, she couldn't do the athletic tricks she does in the game—she'd be lucky to be able to stand up with those huge breasts! And if Disney's Princess Jasmine were real, we'd probably find her alarming because her eyes are bigger than her waist. Exaggeration grabs our attention. For many women, this on-screen exaggeration leads to a real-life sense of inadequacy and obsession with trying to win an impossible game.

Imagery sells ideas. If we see an image, we believe it is a deep confirmation of the underlying truth being projected. McCluhan said:[11] "Most people find it difficult to understand purely verbal concepts. They suspect the ear; they don't trust it. In general, we feel more secure when things are visible, when we can 'see for ourselves.'" I think we put too much trust in what we see, and we do not adequately comprehend the extent to which media images are false—constructed precisely to entice and persuade. Actress Jamie Lee Curtis posed for *More* magazine with and without the now typical mass media enhancements—lighting, wardrobe, makeup, stylists, and photo retouching. In one shot, she stood in her underwear, in the other, she used all the tricks of the trade, and the differences were striking. The magazine was flooded with fan mail for Curtis in which readers described her as their hero and deeply enjoyed how normal she looked in the under-wear shot. Curtis showed the difference between fantasy and reality. She revealed the man behind the curtain.

Rejecting the pressure put on women by the unrealistic ideals and unhealthy values perpetuated by mass media, artist India Arie sings these lines in her song *Video:*[12] "I am not the average girl from your video, and I ain't built like no supermodel, but I learned to love myself unconditionally." She continues: "My mama said a lady ain't what she wears but, what she knows. But, I've drawn a conclusion, it's all an illusion, confusion's the name of the game . . . . This is a true confession of a life learned lesson I was sent here to share with y'all . . . . Go on and love yourself 'cuz everything's gonna be all right."

The Beauty Myth: Keeping It Real

Speaking of speaking out and keeping it real, no one has spoken with a more direct and honest voice on these issues than author Naomi Wolf. Her book *The Beauty Myth*[13] opened eyes to a new way of thinking about the image of women perpetuated in popular culture. The myth she reveals is that the media ideal of beauty is an attainable goal and that women should do what it takes to meet that goal. People have tried to explain away the beauty myth by saying it is only natural; it has always been this way; it is inevitable. Wolf provides data against all these arguments saying, among other things, that Darwin himself didn't argue that a culturally defined beauty won mates. She notes that there are societies in which men's culturally defined beauty is emphasized and those where women choose multiple partners. What a culture defines as beauty has in fact changed over time.

I would add that women who are too thin are not as likely to reproduce and support healthy offspring; a gaunt, starved model is hardly the blueprint for the ideal mother from Mother Nature's point of view. We should know this since this figure almost never occurs in nature. Furthermore, women who have had breast augmentation surgery often lose sensation in their breasts, so the argument that this false beauty "ideal" is sexy for women and desirable for them to attain does not meet basic standards of logic either. A friend recently commented that it has become very common for parents to give their daughters the "gift" of breast augmentation surgery for their high school graduations. It has become a norm, but is it really a gift?

Why dangle in front of women a carrot that they will never eat? One powerful reason is to sell them all the products they need for their unending journey. In the 2002 edition of *The Beauty Myth*, Wolf noted that profits from the diet, cosmetic, and cosmetic surgery industries totaled almost $55 billion a year and that the cosmetic surgery industry was the fastest growth sector of the U.S. economy. We used to sell the myth of the happy homemaker and we literally sold household products to women. Now with the working woman as the norm and with more power and rights, women are being sold on the need for "beautification." So the motive is economic as well as one of power. Women whose energies have been zapped by self-doubt and time spent buying and using beauty products and services are weaker.

Take a look at the photo of Jessica Simpson on the cover of *Rolling Stone* magazine (see Figure 5-1), presented as the ideal housewife. In this one image, we merge the old-fashioned myth of the housewife whose primary occupation was buying and using household products with the beauty myth's ideal woman who occupies herself with buying and using beautification products. It's a compelling image, isn't it?

Do you think girls "naturally" want to beautify? In my college classroom, I ask students to make a list of products or services commonly used to "beautify." They go from head to toe—from hair implants to nail polish, from hair color to ankle tattoos. If you've never done this, try it. First, do it for all the products and services you know are commonly used by people of your age and sex. Do it for the opposite sex. Do it for yourself. Think about what you would need to take with you if you were traveling in order to make yourself "presentable" according to our cultural definition.

And if you think this is over the top for young women, what about little girls? When my son Jason was in preschool, I remember reading a parenting

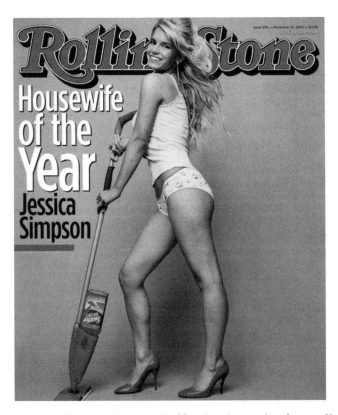

FIGURE 5.1. Jessica Simpson: Domestic Goddess. Iconic American beauty, Simpson is featured here as a mythic "ideal" woman, cleaning the house in hot pink stilettos and not much else. Like other starlets, she has been "accused" on the cover of tabloids of gaining weight—the ultimate crime when the "beauty myth" says the goal of womanhood is to fit a nearly impossible standard of appearance.

Web site that featured discussion groups. I happened upon a discussion group with parents of preschool girls commiserating that their daughters were worried about their looks. They were worried that they were fat or not pretty enough. Some said their daughters had not wanted to go to school because they feared being teased or rejected for their looks. I've seen data that most college women have been teased about their weight or appearance during childhood. When a three- or four-year-old girl is worried that she is fat or not pretty enough to go to school, we have to take a long, hard look at what messages we're feeding these kids.

As a college professor, I have the good fortune of working with young people and I continually learn from them. I ask them questions. I'm a social psychologist; I can't help myself! This past year, I asked my social psychology class what they would do differently socially if they could "get away with it." Some gave funny answers, saying they would sing everywhere they went, or that they would pop into other classrooms and shout out random words. That last one made me laugh. But do you know what the number one answer was, by far? They said they would not do their hair and makeup. Now these were anonymous answers, so I couldn't analyze my data by sex, but 60 percent of college students nowadays are women, and more than 60 percent of my psychology students are women. It's safe to say that the students reporting this were mostly women. Isn't that interesting? The thing these (mostly) young women want to break free from is "beautification."

Sometimes I have freshmen visualize spending a day as a member of the opposite sex. Part of the visualization is thinking about how it would be different to get ready in the morning. When I do this with a class and ask them about it, they say adamantly that it is much easier to be a young guy than to be a young woman. The guys say they would hate to have to "get ready" for the world like their female classmates have to every day. The women say that in this way, they wish they were guys. These eighteen-year-old girls are "beautifying" against their will and against their better judgments. They wish they could let it go, but they can't. Why can't they? It's a free country, as we like to say in the United States. We can do whatever we choose, right? So why don't we?

Well, time and time again in this book when I'm talking about how mass media change us, I go back to the word "unconscious." Our feelings of insecurity generated by mass media imagery are largely unconscious. They are also emotional. Ask a social psychologist and she'll tell you: you can't change an attitude that is based on emotions by using logic or rationality. It just won't happen. Again, there is a degree to which people do not realize they are even feeling these things or if they do realize it, they don't know why they are feeling them.

Again we see that unreality shapes reality. The "beauties" we see in the media are completely unrealistic. Real people do not look like that, nor would it really be healthy for us to look like many of these media models. But these unreal images are pervasive and they change dramatically how most women feel about themselves.

And it is no longer limited to women. Businesses are learning that women are not the only ones whose insecurities can be exploited for profit. On men's magazine covers we see the emerging pressure toward having the "six pack" abdominal muscles. For men, muscles—especially toned abs—are desirable. Eating disorders in men are now on the rise.

Women, Minorities and Rap Music

It's not only images of beauty that have power over people's lives. There are other kinds of negative characterizations. Psychologist Melinda Burgess, sociologist Beth Wright, and I studied images of women in rap music.[14] We asked college students to describe how men refer to women in rap songs. The top three responses were ho or whore (80% of respondents), bitch (60%), and slut (about 30%). When asked to think aloud about what rappers most often rap about, they said (in order) sex, drugs, money, women, and violence. These visions of rap music lyrics actually match up pretty well with what people who have analyzed the content of the songs themselves have found. This study will be discussed in greater detail in Chapter 7.

Scholars who have studied rap have uncovered some other interesting information. For example, my students thought the primary audience for rap music was African American men. It's not. It's young, white suburban kids. People sometimes say that rap music is African American self-expression. Jennifer Lena, a music scholar from Vanderbilt, actually found that in the beginning rap lyrics spoke of the neighborhood and of independent artistry.[15] However, when the mostly White-owned and -managed big conglomerates started to produce most American rap music, the lyrics turned to topics like sex, drugs, crime, and violence against women. Interestingly, when I asked my students if they thought these types of lyrics could be a negative influence on listeners, they overwhelmingly said yes.

I can hear it now: when a media scholar is critical of content—even of blatant content that degrades minority women—people don't like it. Young people find their identity in their music and they don't like it criticized because criticizing the music is then taken as criticizing the listener. Ironically though, it will be mostly young White men who will not like hearing that it is unacceptable for African American rappers to call African American women whores, sluts, and bitches.

Recently I worked with an African American female high school student, supervising a research project. This bright, capable young woman told me a story that I can't forget because I think it is representative of the problem presented here. She told me that her very little brother started to listen to rap lyrics. One day her brother approached her and asked her, "Are you a ho?" She was struck by his honesty. He'd heard it in the lyrics and he really wanted to understand, was his sister a ho? By extension are all African American women and girls—or all women and girls—hos? Often if we listen to our kids, we can learn something about the culture in which we are raising them.

Real. Good.

Just as glossy magazine pictures of gaunt female models or men with ripped muscles change the way people think and act, so too, thankfully, do the positive messages. I quoted India Arie's lyrics earlier. She has also sung about the beauty of being brown. Messages like that can be revolutionary too. They have true power that can change lives for the better. There is a classic social psych study that showed when you are in a group and there is pressure on you to confirm, having just one "dissenter"—one person who agrees with you and goes against the crowd—makes conformity drop noticeably. So it is with media myths. One voice that questions unhealthy media messages can help draw out other people who yearn for more true reality in media. When we question and think and support each other, we move out from under the thumb of big business and dirty politics and we move in the direction of real freedom.

Section Three

THE SOCIAL PSYCHOLOGY OF MEDIA

INFLUENCE

Six

ADVERTISING, CONSUMERISM, AND

HEALTH

One of the most influential psychologists in history, John B. Watson, was a radical behaviorist. Behaviorism holds that people and animals learn through basic, observable principles such as by associating one experience with another or by learning through the consequences of actions. For example, Pavlov trained his dog to drool when hearing the sound of a bell because a dinner bell always sounded when dinner was served. B. F. Skinner trained animals to play the piano and to play ping pong—even to guide missiles for the U.S. military—by manipulating the consequences of their behavior. Famously, J. B. Watson taught "little Albert"—a toddler—to fear white, fluffy things. How? He gave Albert a white, fluffy toy or animal and then made a scary sound, which caused Albert to cry. After that treatment, just seeing the toy or animal would make little Albert cry.

What else did Watson, famous for warping the mind of a toddler, contribute to psychology? Basically, he found a way to make the rest of us pretty neurotic too because he was one of the first psychologists to actively influence advertising. It's an interesting story, actually. John B. Watson had a pretty warped childhood himself. His father, from whom he later became estranged, was a drinker and a carouser. His mother was "insufferably religious";[1] and his nanny instilled in him a lifelong fear of the dark by telling him the devil was in the dark and might come and take little John to hell. He had trouble dealing with his emotions and publicly endorsed an unsentimental method of parenting that favored shaking hands over hugs and kisses. His own children and grandchildren were apparently scarred by what many would consider an emotionally blunted upbringing, and his son William committed suicide. His scholarly career soared early, but was cut short when he had a first-marriage-ending affair with his graduate student Rosalie Raynor, who had assisted him in the "little Albert" research. Banished from academia, he reinvented himself and became an advertising executive, making four times his professorial salary.[2]

> Advertisers have programmed many of us into a shopping habit.[3]
> —James Potter

Apparently operating under the same ethical code implemented during his academic career, Watson recommended to advertisers that they could make a fortune by manipulating basic human motivations and emotions to their advantage, and often, of course, to the consumer's disadvantage. One of his basic ideas, used with gusto and impunity by advertisers today, was to convince people that their possessions were inferior and consequently that they needed new possessions. In other words, he helped create the modern consumer mentality: one does not buy an item out of need but out of a psychological desire to compare favorably to others' material possessions or out of a general neuroticism based on the notion that buying will satisfy deep motivations. That's where the social psychology meets the basic behaviorist psychology. Advertisers manipulate our desires, and often these desires are social, like the desires to be liked, to be attractive, or to do what everybody else is doing.

Let's take a look at an example of advertising using behaviorism with a social twist. Everyone knows that hot rod magazines often show what on the hood of the car? Right: a sexy woman in a bikini. Now this is crazy from any rational perspective. So why use bikini models in the ads? From a behaviorist perspective, the car is associated with the sexy woman. When you think of the car, it excites the kinds of feelings you get when thinking about the sexy woman. Using another learning principle, a guy shopping for a muscle car might now believe that if he buys one, it will attract a hot woman. So in a funny way, buying a car now becomes a more social decision, rather than a decision that is purely about transportation.

Since social motives are powerful and fundamental to human nature, ads often exploit social motivation. You buy mouthwash because you don't want to turn off co-workers or potential dates. You associate a fresh pot of coffee with a commercial featuring a warm, happy family. The coffee's brand and look now make you feel the pleasure associated with a warm, happy family, and you may buy that kind of coffee hoping unconsciously to draw that social situation to yourself. I suggest to my students that when you want to buy a product, do a very simple thing: think about what you get when you buy it. If you want to drink coffee and you like the taste of a certain brand, then buy it. But if you buy based on the mythology of the commercial, you are really not getting that when you buy. If you buy an expensive perfume based on an elegant ad, you probably want to ask yourself if you really like how it smells, if you can afford it, and if you even like wearing perfume at all. Companies sell sneakers by making commercials showing the wearer having fun with his friends. The message: these sneakers are fun! These sneakers will make you look cool to the kids at school! Again, you have to think through what you are getting as well as how you are being manipulated. Always be wary of the original plan John B. Watson suggested to advertising executives: make people think they need new stuff. Do you need another pair of sneakers, or has a company manipulated you to give your money to them?

Two Views on Material Things: Caretaking Versus Consuming

At a largely unconscious level, advertising sells values, like the value of acquiring new material possessions. My grandparents on my mom's side—Grandma and Grandpa Leonard—had a different point of view about how to handle your property. They were great believers that hard-earned belongings merited care and that what you cared for would and should last. They were proud that they knew how to take proper care of things; it meant that they were skilled, responsible, and not wasteful. They had a clock, for instance, that the whole family admired, and they kept it clean and in excellent working order. When they died my aunt inherited the clock as a prized possession. I grew up loving that clock—a beautiful and unique polished cherry wood mantel clock whose pendulum was a lovely blonde girl in a blue dress on a swing.

My Grandma Annie, dad's mom, had another perspective on the value of possessions. As Grandma Annie got on in years, she acquired the habit of marking her possessions with a family member's name. When my Uncle Tom asked her, "Mom, why does this thing have my name taped on the bottom?" Grandma would reply, "Because I'm leaving it to you when I die." This would cause eruptions of merriment all around because on my dad's side of the family, we are all, shall I say, delightfully irreverent?

But in all seriousness, I tell these family stories because we are encouraged by mass media to be a throwaway culture and I do not know how many people today grow up with the mentality of keeping and caring for possessions. The younger generations have grown up in a consumer-oriented society in which buying is akin to a sport and having "old" things is something of an embarrassment inasmuch as it indicates you are not well off enough to afford new ones. Another aspect of a throwaway society is that products themselves tend to be made to last only a short period of time, both satisfying and perpetuating the consumer culture.

Now, I'm not suggesting that I am not a product of the age in which I grew up. I think it's a big mistake to project the image that expertise makes me immune to the psychological mechanisms I study. It doesn't. I like to randomly blurt out confessions during my talks just so the audience doesn't think I'm peddling some myths of my own. Psychologists are human. My kids use plastic spoons right now, for example, because they have a tendency to take their yogurt and applesauce tubs in the back yard with our nice spoons and leave them in the grass so that daddy can run over them with the lawnmower. Thus we are contributing a quantity of plastic spoons to a landfill somewhere. Like everyone, life presents me with conflicting motives and I make choices. I'm not immune to the concepts I study, but I am a kind of freak about them. My little son, for example, could tell you all about commercials trying to sell you something from a very tender age. Everyone knows psychologists warp their children.

> I don't care where the eyeballs come from. I care about the
> eyeballs.
> —Andy Markowitz, director, Digital Marketing, Kraft Foods,
> speaking at an advertising summit[4]

If we were alien scientists whose job it was to understand Earthling behavior, I think we would wonder a lot about why Earthlings spend so much time staring into screens. Why do they spend more time watching other Earthlings pretending to do stuff instead of doing real stuff themselves? And why watch each other on video instead of live? Yep, I'm pretty sure I would shriek and gesture wildly with my tentacles at my fellow alien scientists trying to come up with a good theory for that one.

It's all very simple. Advertisers are well aware that the more our eyeballs look at their ads, the more money they make. Seeing an ad makes us more likely to buy the product, but we are mostly unaware that this is true. If you ask people, they will say that ads do not affect them, and yet we know they do. Ads are powerful. The psychology that hooks us in to devoting most of our free time to media is very powerful. The biggest reason we spend an incredible amount of time staring into screens and at other forms of mass media is because we are being manipulated by big business to do so.

Business manipulates us to get our money. This is a basic tenet of media education. It's so simple. We know it, I think, at a cognitive level. If you ask us to think about it, we could tell you that ads work—they sell products. The third person effect, though, protects our egos by making us believe that other people are manipulated—not us! Of course, that makes us more vulnerable to manipulation. We even defend the manipulators, becoming media apologists, not unlike a victim of abuse defending her abuser. What a perfect prescription for exploitation!

Advertising and Agenda Setting

Some argue that advertisers, and indeed all media, do not influence what we think as much as they tell us what to think about. This is called the agenda setting theory because media are said to set the agenda for viewers like a leader sets the agenda for a meeting. When an advertiser emphasizes a product or its attributes or a brand, this suggests what value it has and how other people view it. Sutherland and Galloway suggest that advertisers do more agenda setting than persuading. They write:

> Products that are advertised heavily have a status conferred upon
> them—i.e., they are felt by customers to be "the most popular"
> products. The media are assumed to carry that which is more
> important, more in demand, more notorious. Just as "the ordinary
> person" does not appear on TV, neither does "the ordinary product."
> The fact of something being included in the media is not seen by the
> reader or viewer as giving that thing status, but as strong presumptive
> evidence that the thing has status—otherwise it would not be in
> the media.[5]

We see in this explanation a social message that underlies repeated advertising of a product, value, or brand. Namely, other people must like it, want it, value it, and in some cases agree with the underlying values or messages. Indeed, consumers believe that advertised products are superior to products that aren't advertised. For example, a brand name clothing detergent is superior to a no-name brand. I think that when we impute social status onto ideas projected in an advertisement or in other forms of media, this presumes that the media have done more than set the agenda. They have persuaded us of the social status and worth of the product, habit, value, or other idea they communicated.

Advertisements do set an agenda. For example, the many commercials for hair removal products such as waxes, appliances, and creams for legs, face, and the so-called bikini area imply that women need to be hair-free in all of these areas, and that one will not be socially acceptable if one does not purchase such products or services. The products that are advertised most frequently are believed to be superior and to be used and liked by more people. A woman may digest different kinds of social messages from these ads such as which products a person of her age and social position should prefer and use. Again, I think this means that the ads have gone beyond setting an agenda to persuading consumers of a product's social value.

Levels of Manipulation

John B. Watson advised making people believe their things are inferior so they would buy new things. That is a blatant and intentional type of manipulation. You want people to believe something that both isn't true and isn't in their own best interest to believe. There are other forms of manipulation that cause intentional harm. For example, I sometimes notice advertisements that appear designed to shame women into feeling bad about themselves, thus motivating them to buy what the ad sells. Some ads present "before and after" photos of women and the "before" photo will give a more average size, such as size 12 or even 10. The "after" photo will give a very small size like a size 2. The message this sends very clearly to most of the viewers—since again, the average American woman is about a size 14—is that *their* size is considered fat. This is a very straightforward case of implied social comparison. It also implies that an appropriate goal would be for average American women to be quite small. This isn't realistic or even necessarily the most healthy goal.

Other manipulation that occurs via the mass media appears to me to be less intentional. This manipulation is less like a direct attack and more like collateral damage. If producers follow the general premise that they want to do whatever encourages people to tune in, then they create media that grab attention. These attention-grabbing elements may teach unintended lessons. For example, we regularly see highly attractive people in the media. Producers may have made that choice because highly attractive people—unsurprisingly—attract attention. It gives us pleasure to look at beautiful people. But then the media become filled with highly attractive people and people spend more time watching these attractive people. In the end, they see many highly attractive people in the media, and the availability heuristic tells them that it's because there are many highly attractive people around. I now have to adjust my views of my own looks to be less attractive than "all the people I see everyday." I now feel that my looks are inferior as a consequence of mass media doing everything they can to get my attention. It's not necessarily intentional, but it doesn't need to be intentional to have a major influence on people. And of course, sometimes it is intentional.

Something similar to what happens with physical appearance happens with material possessions and lifestyles. We define normal or desirable by what we view in the media. Mass media constructs a norm of consumerism. A T-shirt I once saw said, "Whoever dies with the most toys wins." People I see in magazines or on TV have many things, and I make the inference that I need to have them too in order to fit in or to outdo my neighbors. According to the book *Affluenza: The All-Consuming Epidemic*, the average American home in 1955 is equal in size to the average American *garage* in 2000. The advertisers push our buttons and we respond—one reason so many Americans today are in debt. Advertisers make people anxious and needy for products that promise to make them happy, popular, and attractive. Consumers spend money chasing this elusive dream of social currency, only to wind up very often in debt, thus creating more anxiety and stress.

Product Placements—Pretty Sneaky

Have you ever noticed people in a movie, television program, or even on the Internet using a product? Maybe they are drinking a Coke or smoking a Camel. In the TV show *Heroes*, for example, the character Hiro Nakamura mentions repeatedly that the car he and his friend Ando have rented is a Nissan Versa. These are called passive ads or product placements. These passive ads send subtle social messages: this movie star that I love smokes; therefore, smoking is cool. Or take another message: this perfect family created on the screen before me drinks Coke. I associate Coke with something warm and happy. If I drink Coke I will be like them and I will have the things that they have, including love and warmth. All of this is part of the same equation—behaviorism plus social psychology equals manipulation as well as the math that matters most: manipulation equals profits.

There is a set of values that says there is nothing wrong with this. America was founded on principles of freedom. Free enterprise and the free market are foundational to how we do business and why we are successful. That's one business perspective on values. What about a sociological, psychological, or even anthropological perspective? Respectively, these disciplines would ask the following: What makes a society strong? What makes people happiest and healthiest? What kind of culture will have a lasting positive impact on human history? In this context, I think any business approach that resembles manipulative profiteering is short-sighted and benefits only those who profit financially from it in the short term. Anyone who cares about humanity from a larger perspective—certainly including spiritual, philosophical, and ideological perspectives—should have problems with the negative, manipulative kind of marketing we see so often today.

Advertising Food and Fitness

Mass media do create some beautiful illusions. Earlier I mentioned the way thin, sexy stars eat high-calorie foods on camera, creating the illusion that we can all eat that way and look like they do. For me, one commercial takes this to the extreme to the extent that it's probably even making fun of itself. The ad I'm talking about is the one in which Paris Hilton washes a car in manner described by critics as resembling soft-core porn, and then bites into a huge Hardee's hamburger (see Figure 6-1A). We have to laugh when we see this ad—I don't think Paris or her girlfriends usually drive-through Hardee's for lunch. A parody ad by Accolo recruiting featured a man who looked more like he's had a few Hardee burgers in his time, the fictitious "Eugene" (see Figure 6-1B). If you look at the Paris Hilton ad and the parody ad side by side, you get a dose of fantasy versus reality. When you eat a high-fat diet, you generally get fat, but media create illusions that we easily swallow (pardon the pun.) We want to eat like Eugene and still look like Paris, so we're vulnerable to the fantasy that media producers sell us.

Media Illusions: Seeing Is Believing

But there is also a more innocent level here. Since our brains weren't created to process media but to process real social information, I imagine if we see a beautiful person eating rich food and still looking thin, part of us believes it is true because seeing is believing. We're not built to discount what we see, to identify illusions. We're built to do just the opposite—to take in social information as just that. From an evolutionary or biological perspective we

FIGURES 6.1A AND 6.1B.   A Hardee's commercial described by some critics as soft-core porn, in which Paris Hilton washes herself and a car and then eats a Hardee's hamburger in as sexual a way as humanly possible (top). Below, in a parody ad, "Eugene" eats the same hamburger with more realistic results on his figure.

are *supposed* to believe what we see, not doubt it. Our thinking makes perfect sense if you look at it that way. We shouldn't feel bad, but we should, given that most of what we see now is fantasy and not reality, get smart about it so we are not as vulnerable to other people's agendas.

The Cycle of Fat to Fit to Fat Again

On a road trip years ago, my husband Jay and I checked out a book on tape from the business section of our local library that promised to be about improving your communications skills. As we drove and listened to the tape, we soon became incredulous at what we were hearing. The author suggested that you should listen carefully to what other people say so that you can learn what is the most important thing in the world to them. Why? If you know what's most important to someone, you can exploit that information for your own gain!!! We realized some people are unscrupulous enough to try to exploit others, but we didn't know they would actually (1) admit it in public and (2) unashamedly publish a book telling everyone what an awesome idea it is.

It seems that advertisers often take a page out of that guy's book. They think about what we want most and manipulate those motives for all they are worth. It's no secret that people want to be attractive and that attractiveness is basically synonymous with thinness in our culture, especially for women. Thousands of American women were surveyed[6] about what they want most in life. Did they want world peace or a cure for cancer? Did they want money? More than any other goal, these women wanted to lose ten or fifteen pounds. For advertisers, the insecurity and impassioned motivation that makes losing a few pounds the favorite dream of so many means that the same people will spend billions annually trying to grab the illusive brass ring.

And it's clear that the brass ring isn't health; it's attractiveness. For example, people smoke cigarettes sometimes because they think it helps keep them thin and, of course, cigarette smoking is one of the single worst things you can do for your health. Attractiveness means feeling good about yourself, feeling that other people value you, want you, even envy you— that's what makes something that might sometimes masquerade as a health goal really a social goal. And at the heart, it's all about perception. I say often in my social psychology class that in my field what we're interested in is perception. If a plastic surgeon's patients feel inferior, that's what motivates them, not the relatively factual notion that they are already attractive. They are similar to the domestic violence victim whose husband tells her she is fat and ugly and useless, so she stays with him in part because she believes it. He has altered her reality like advertisers alter our realities.

In the 1920s, the boyish figure of the flapper dancer was stylish, and buxom women actually bound their breasts to better fit the fashion. Today, teenaged girls ask a surgeon to implant bags of saline under their breasts so that a society attracted to disproportionately large breasts will find them more attractive. Thinking about this rationally, surgically altering one's body to gain self-esteem is a pretty extreme move, but social motives are very powerful, and media help normalize this extreme behavior. With TV shows like *Extreme Makeover* showing how to transform an ugly duckling into a swan, viewers are enticed by the notion that they can transform themselves.

Extreme-ly Misguided

In a college class on gender in society, my colleague sociologist Beth Wright and I showed an episode of *Extreme Makeover* and discussed it with our students. In the episode, a young, perfectly healthy size 10 woman wanted to find love. The solution: *Extreme Makeover!* They showed her in her underwear pointing out all her "flaws." They gave her pretty extensive liposuction, reducing her to a size 2, and increased her breasts to C cups. She also had plastic surgery all over her face, sessions with a personal trainer, a makeover, new hairdo, and new clothes. Wow, apparently beauty is a lot of work! The "reveal" segment showed her family crying tears of joy over her new look coupled with a discussion of how she was now going to find a man.

Our class discussed the way the show gives the impression that anyone can become "a beauty" and concluded that the amount of work done to this young woman would cost many thousands of dollars. Therefore, this kind of transformation is actually available only to the wealthy or to those who make it on the show, thus highlighting the unreality of this type of "reality" TV. Our students also commented about the show's subtle manipulation technique of pathologizing a normal, healthy body. This young woman was not overweight, but she was scrutinized in her bra and panties, while a doctor pointed out all the areas where he could surgically remove fat from her body.

Next, the class watched a segment about a woman who had found her true love. He was a farmer who treated her gently and had even helped rescue her from home foreclosure. He was the salt of the earth. He loved her kids. He loved puppies. He was handy around the house. The problem: he was seriously lacking in the "hottie" department. Our class actually didn't agree that his looks were a problem. He looked like a regular guy to them—okay, his ears were a little big maybe, his teeth a little crooked, but no big deal. Well, this guy wanted to be his fiancée's dream man, so he underwent plastic surgery to have his "love handles" removed (his farmer body was perfectly healthy to start with), and his eyelids lifted, among other things, and endured personal training sessions in which he learned how to punch like a man (according to the show). He got veneers on his teeth, a new hairdo and new clothes. Our class concurred that at the end of all this he was not better off than when he started. He basically looked like a plastic soap opera star, I thought. Worst of all, arguably, were the veneers on his teeth. The class agreed that the show's producers had wanted the quick fix for their big reveal, and had sacrificed real dental work for awkward looking TV-ready veneers. Again, the media were selling cosmetic procedures while pathologizing "real people" looks, encouraging feelings of inadequacy in viewers, and promoting shallow appearance focus. The media were also selling the fantasy that attaining these results is easy and accessible. And in both cases, the goal was social—to attain love and admiration.

Advertisers certainly have tapped a vein of gold by harnessing this intense social motive to enhance one's physical appearance. Without being conscious of it, we have allowed advertisers and the mass media in general to set standards for our looks that both make us feel inadequate and neurotic and move us to spend a great deal of our money on an array of products that never take away the bad feelings.

Food and Fitness Marketing: Selling Fitness and Fatness

We all have guilty pleasures. I'll confess to one of mine: I am drawn to women's magazines at the grocery store checkout counter—the more mundane the better. I buy them for escapism and end up reading them as the wife and the mommy—but also as the media psychologist—that I am. I have noticed a trend on the magazine rack at the grocery store—one that I find so amusing it's almost charming. Have you ever noticed this? The covers of some women's magazines regularly feature both weight loss and decadent food. To show you what I mean, I searched for general "women's interest" magazines on Amazon.com and found a favorite "guilty pleasure" magazine of mine that is typically on sale at my grocery store. I had to laugh as I scanned through the recent covers of this magazine because the cover stories fit my expectations to a "t." All three of the available magazine covers showed this "fit but fat" pattern. One issue proclaimed: "Lose six pounds this week," but also, "Eat your way happy." Another cover promised, "Lose ten pounds this week," but also happily reported, "Christmas cookies cure depression" and offered recipes for, "8 delicious holiday muffins." The editors of the third apparently missed the humor of simultaneously advertising "Look perfect in jeans" and "Your body can be 10 years thinner" right next to images of Easter cakes and cookies running the entire span of the magazine cover. Next time you are at the grocery store checkout, scan the women's magazines. I'll bet you can find some examples like these.

Temptation Followed Closely by Shame . . . and More Buying

When the good Lord created us, it was not to eat in an environment where so many high-fat, high-calorie foods were so readily available. The Garden of Eden did not have a Kentucky Fried Chicken drive-through and a Krispy Kreme shop. (Probably a good thing, since we seem to have gotten into enough trouble with just the apples.) From what I understand, high-calorie foods taste good because in an environment where food is scarce, it is adaptive to store fat in the body. Fast forward to modern-day restaurants and grocery stores and it's not hard to see that it takes some restraint not to really pack on the body fat. Enter the advertisers whose job it is to manipulate and exploit our most fundamental desires and voilà: an all-time high for obesity rates.

I don't think our problem is a rational one. Most people know that it's better to eat fish and broccoli than burgers and fries—we just don't want to. And then late at night we are sitting on the sofa watching TV and a pizza commercial comes on. The pizza is steaming hot. The cheese is bubbly. Our hand is on the phone. Heck, the Domino's commercials even play the sound of the phone dialing to encourage you to take that last step. Do you know the sounds I'm talking about? If you can sing them out now, that's probably a sign that their advertising is effective. We probably don't think much about being manipulated. We don't say, "Dang that Domino's for trying to make me fat!" As I've said, we're pretty unconscious about how our emotions and motives are being manipulated for profit. If you're like my family, someone just says, "Pizza!" in a voice like Homer Simpson's and with eyes glazed over with culinary anticipation like Homer's—and picks up the phone.

Recently, Subway turned the tables on these types of advertisements by choosing to emphasize the consequences of overindulging in fast food. Have you seen the ad? A man and woman are at a drive-through ordering, but instead of naming food items, they name the way their bodies will look if they eat them. The man orders love handles and his wife wants thunder thighs and a "badonka donk" butt. Subway's ad line is, "When you get greasy fast food, what are you really getting?" Don't get me wrong—it's still manipulation, just manipulation toward something that is better for you.

There are products and services that honestly offer something useful or needed. The difference is all in the awareness—do you know that you are being manipulated and can you evaluate which products and services will promote your well-being and happiness and which won't? Can you look beyond the hype to what you are really getting and make a choice based on that? Beyond that are other issues such as whether you can afford what's being sold. Psychologists who study decision making know that good decisions involve both rational and emotional components. What's clear, though, is that an uninformed, unconscious decision is a lot less likely to serve you and more likely to serve the person getting your money.

Children and Food Advertising

Up until now we have been talking about the effects of advertising on adult consumers. In the past, children were considered off limits to advertisers, but no more. Kids, especially teenagers, are a highly sought-after target group for advertisers, because they tend to have a lot of disposable income—recently estimated at about $200 million annually.[7] In other words, if you don't have to pay the gas bill, you might spend your money buying a video game or driving through Taco Bell late at night. Kids, of course, are even less likely than adults to be critical of advertising. Research has actually shown that kids—especially those below about age seven or eight—can't always tell the difference between what is a commercial and what is not.

The esteemed medical journal, the *Lancet*, has been published since the early 1800s and has a high impact worldwide on important medical issues. The word "lancet" means a window to let in light as well as a kind of scalpel to cut out disease, and the journal's founder embraced both meanings of the word—shedding light on medical issues and removing disease from the system. In true *Lancet* style, the journal has taken a strong stand on the issue of food marketing to children,[8,9] reporting that the relatively recent movement to target children with advertising has damaged children's health – both in the United States and in Europe – for a number of reasons. Media marketing to children has contributed to the evolution of children from active and creative to passive consumer. The journal writers note decreased body image and decreased general emotional health, and increased aggression, obesity, and type 2 diabetes.

The advertisers are very conscious of their aggressive marketing strategies toward children. The *Lancet* reported that at a recent convention on marketing to kids called Kidscreen, organizers advertised that they wanted to help marketers find ways to "own" kids, to "own" their minds, and to create "lifelong consumers." Pulling no punches, the *Lancet* called these strategies exploitation and quoted a leading speaker at the Stop Commercial Exploitation of Children Summit who compared these aggressive marketers to pedophiles in their motivation to understand children.

Weighty Issues

Beyond the very basic notion that it is not okay to exploit children—or anyone—destroying their health for your own financial gain, both the United States and the European Union are recognizing the very recent explosion in obesity rates and linking the problem with, among other causes, unscrupulous marketing practices. The *Lancet* reported in July of 2008[10] that in twenty-three of twenty-seven European Union countries, more than half of the adult population was overweight or obese. In the United States, the Centers for Disease Control report that the incidence of overweight in children and adolescents increased three to four times in the past three decades, ranging from about 15 percent to 20 percent of American children today.[11] There are multiple causes of this epidemic, most notably the coincidence with marketing unhealthy foods to children coupled with the increase in sedentary lifestyles that is associated with the boom in watching mass media as the most commonplace pasttime. Research (and logic) links the sedentary lifestyle associated with mass media viewing with decreased health on a mass level. For example, an intensive longitudinal study in New Zealand[12] assessed 1,000 participants from birth to age twenty-six and found that those who watched more TV were more likely than those who watch less to be obese and to have poorer overall physical health and fitness.

Fantasies and Illusions Change Health Realities

Both the United States and the European Union have held meetings and made suggestions to food advertisers, with little effect.[13] In the United States in 2005, the Institute of Medicine recommended forming a presidential task force on childhood obesity prevention, but it was not done. Also in 2005, the Federal Trade Commission (FTC) held a workshop with the Department of Health and Human Services to "develop guidelines for the advertising and marketing of food, beverages and sedentary entertainment to children and youth."[14] The recommendation from the workshop was that the industry self-regulate and advertise responsibly. This is arguably asking the fox to guard the henhouse, but the officials wanted to give the industry a chance to do the right thing. What happened next? "Food and advertising industry representatives have resisted efforts to regulate advertising to children, which led to the establishment of a bipartisan congressional Task Force on Media and Childhood Obesity in March of 2007."[15]

Meanwhile, the Federal Trade Commission was investigating how all the top U.S. companies market and advertise food to children and adolescents. The FTC investigated the activities of forty-four companies in the year 2006—the year after self-regulation was suggested, and filed its report in July of 2008. According to the FTC report,[16] the advertisers spent $1.6 billion to reach children and adolescents in 2006. The top food products marketed to children and adolescents were carbonated beverages, quick-service restaurants (a.k.a. fast food), and breakfast foods. How did the advertisers and marketers win over the hearts and minds of American kids? One strategy is using beloved celebrities to endorse a product. Another strategy marketers used a lot was "cross-promotions." Cross-promotion means linking a food product with some other thing kids love, like a cartoon character, TV show, movie, or toy. Companies often used cross-promotions for breakfast foods, restaurant food, snacks, candy, and carbonated beverages.

Of course, we all know they do this. Especially if you have children at home, this phenomenon is part of your life. McDonald's associates the funny cartoon movie *Kung Fu Panda* with their chicken nuggets. *Superman Returns* and *Pirates of the Carribbean* were two big movies of 2006, and the advertisers used these films to promote everything from cereals and fruit snacks to carbonated beverages and lunch kits. They created "limited edition" frozen waffles, candies, cereals, and snacks using images of popular characters as a sales technique. (Limited edition waffles!? Are you supposed to bronze them and put them on the mantel?) Junk food was also advertised using "spokescharacters" such as cartoon M&M's with different personalities and colors. Of course, every fast-food restaurant has a kid's meal with toys, and these are often associated with the latest movie or hot toy item.

According to the FTC report, the food industry also used more high-tech advertising techniques to reach children, such as Web sites and text messages. For example, kids are sometimes enticed by product packaging to go online and play "free games," which are really advertisements. If you go to www.happymeal.com as of this writing, at the top of the page in smallish print, you will actually see the words, "Hey kids, this is advertising." A newer form of marketing to youth is so-called viral advertising. This is the digital version of word-of-mouth. Viral advertising might include a

Web site or a social networking site where kids are invited to send an e-card or a text message to their friend that promotes a product. Advertisers are excited about the notion of getting people to tell each other about their product. If it comes from a friend, it is more persuasive.

Athletes Advertising Junk Food

The FTC noted one common marketing strategy that really makes no sense: the use of athletes to advertise junk food. For example, BMX biker Dave Mirra advertises for Slim Jims—the beef jerky. By the way, in a true cross-media ad campaign, Dave Mirra's BMX video game includes a character named Slim Jim, accessible through a cheat code. McDonald's and Coke both paid large sums of money to sponsor the 2008 Summer Olympics in Beijing. Of course, Olympic-level athletes have special diets and I'm thinking these probably don't include lots of Big Macs, fries and Cokes. Well, maybe for the Sumo wrestlers.

A consistent theme in these marketing schemes is fantasy. Advertisers create an illusion. It's an illusion that top athletes eat junk food diets. It's an illusion that you can eat a junk food diet and stay fit and trim like the actors and celebrities in the ads. We see it and it looks so real, so appealing. We want to do it too—eat yummy high-calorie foods and still be healthy and slim as a celebrity or an Olympic athlete. But it is a fantasy and it is one that harshly shapes our realities.

Offering our kids a toy to encourage them to buy a fast-food kids meal may be a brilliant marketing strategy. It may make companies lots of money, but strategies like this are, in reality, making our kids fat and damaging their physical and psychological well-being. I understand, believe me. I have small children and they both recognized McDonald's Golden Arches as toddlers. They love to get toys in their Happy Meals. Fortunately for me, they both like to play more than eat. My daughter rarely touches French fries, even if they are on her plate. But that's less the result of good parenting than it is simply good fortune. I do have to consider these things and make choices about them. I consider how often my kids eat fast food. When they do, I steer them toward fruit side dishes and milk, and I am glad these are available. I talk to them about nutrition and health. Parents indeed have to make the choices. I think government and media and marketers have roles to play, too. When advertisers draw us in with illusions—and especially when they present these illusions to children who are less equipped to deal with them—they share some responsibility for the consequences.

An assumption of government in a modern, developed nation is that they have a responsibility to protect consumers. And prevention is much more powerful than cure, in many cases. That is probably why the governments of developed nations around the world are stepping in to try to get something done about advertising junk food to kids. They realize it is going to be much more effective if the advertisers stop peddling these illusions than it would be to reason with consumers or to tell them what foods are healthy. Advertising is so powerful that it has the effect of encouraging people to make decisions they know consciously are not in their best interests, like eating junk food. Media imagery is powerfully motivating, and governments everywhere are dealing with the effects and considering ways to get advertisers to be less manipulative.

A recent ad slogan for McDonald's Happy Meals said that a Happy Meal has a full day's supply of happy. Some residents of the Beatles' hometown of Liverpool, England, apparently disagree. London's *Daily Mail* reported in 2008 that the Liverpool town council met and decided to ban Happy Meals because they are contributing to childhood obesity. Locals offered their support, making the following comments:[17]

> "We consider it is high time that cash-hungry vultures like McDonald's are challenged over their marketing policies which are directly aimed at promoting unhealthy eating among children."

> "In most Happy Meals the toy is sold with a burger containing four or five tablespoons of sugar, along with high-calorie fries and milkshakes."

> "The most calorific Happy Meal—cheeseburger, small fries and chocolate milkshake—has 740 kcals, almost half of children's recommended daily allowance of 1600."

> "They know that most children won't want carrots and water but put them on the menu to stave off the criticism from health campaigners."

> "These fattening meals are being shamelessly promoted through free toys and it is clear that it is going to take legislation to combat the practice."

Yes, kids love toys, they love sugar, and they love fun. But no kid finds it fun to be fat, to feel unhealthy, or to be the object of ridicule from the other kids at school because of their weight.

And there are other reasons fast food sells, of course. Parents are busy. When mom and dad come home from working all day, it takes a lot of effort to make dinner and clean up and do all the other household tasks. It's easier for parents to feed the kids fast food, and it may also be harder for parents to resist their kids' demands when they are tired. The more government and the public demand it, the greater the chance that we'll have healthier choices for fast food. I think it is a step in the right direction that more fast-food restaurants are offering more healthy choices. If we continue to work toward improvement, I think we can, as consumers and as governments, ask for and receive food that is quick and easy to get, but more healthy. I spend a fair amount of time in airports, and I have noticed that there are consistently restaurants that offer fresh fruit, like bananas. It is very convenient to know that I'll be able to find a healthy snack at the airport. The more restaurants provide choices like this, especially in a closed system like an airport, the easier it is for consumers to find something healthy to eat.

Selling the Dream: Advertising Weight-Loss Products

Another issue in the cycle of advertising both fatness and fitness is the marketing of diet pills and other "quick fix" weight-loss products and services, such as fad dieting books and foods. Diet pills have been called hope in a bottle. When an advertiser sells diet pills, he is really selling the magic bullet that consumers dream will make them attractive and will win them love and affection. Thus diet pills and fad diets represent the intoxicating dream of the immediate gratification of a fervent desire.

The National Eating Disorder Information Center or NEDIC (www.nedic.ca) reports that 80 percent of women do not like their body shape and size, that 70 percent of women are chronically dieting, and that 76 percent of respondents to a survey considered themselves too fat although 45 percent of those were underweight according to a doctor's chart. Perhaps most shocking, one in ten women surveyed said they would abort a child if they knew it had a tendency to be fat. NEDIC notes that although the diet industry makes $32 billion annually, dieters have a 95 percent failure rate. That is, 95 percent of dieters regain all their lost weight in one to five years. Amid graphics promoting the celebration of "real woman" bodies, NEDIC's slogan proclaims: "It's not our bodies that need changing. It's our attitudes."[18]

In recent years, some diet pills and herbal supplements have even been linked to serious illness and death. And this is even in the context of a fair amount of public acknowledgment that diet pills do not work. For example, in a recent high-profile settlement, the Federal Trade Commission fined the makers of several top-selling diet pills a combined $25 million for making false or unsubstantiated claims of quick and dramatic weight loss.[19] Some even falsely claimed other health benefits such as decreased risk of Alzheimer's disease and cancer! Among those who paid fines for false advertisement were the makers of TrimSpa, Xenadrine, CortiSlim and One-A-Day Weight Smart. Consumer's Union[20] reiterated its stance that diet pills can have dangerous effects on health, including heart problems. They cited recent research that reported more than half of consumers think diet pills are safe and also erroneously believe that diet pills are regulated by the Food and Drug Administration (FDA). Diet pills are classified as supplements, like vitamins, so they are not regulated by the FDA.

We are indeed attracted to the quick fix, and marketers prey on this weakness. Sometimes diet pills are boxed, priced, and named like prescription drugs as a marketing effort to give them added credibility. Some are sold in fancy bottles to resemble boutique products. Recent research[21] analyzed how women's magazines in the United States and Korea address the issue of weight loss. Results showed that Korean women's magazines typically promote passive methods of weight loss such as diet pills, diet drinks, aromatherapy, and even so-called diet crèmes (how swanky!). The Korean magazines took on the Western ideal of beauty and thinness that has been constructed, in part, by those who wish to profit from it. The researchers concluded that women who read the magazines may learn that losing weight is easy, quick, effective, and painless. According to the magazines, all it takes is a pill, a drink, or a crème! The authors therefore called for government regulation of these messages and also encouraged the magazine publishers to take responsibility for these false messages.

Of course, as Naomi Wolf explained in the *Beauty Myth,*[22] women's magazines make money through their advertising, and much of that advertising is for beauty products. Sometimes what masquerades as a magazine article is really another advertisement. Have you ever noticed that many women's magazines have "articles" about which mascara to use, what products "work" best on different hair types, what are the hot makeup colors? If you haven't read one of these magazines, browse through one next time you are in the store. When I was younger, I used to wonder naïvely how they decided which products to mention. Now I understand that these are advertisements masquerading as articles. It actually goes further than this deception of ads-as-articles. For example, if an advertiser's company profits from breast augmentation surgery, this will influence whether the magazine runs a health article suggesting problems or concerns about this surgery.[23] Women may think they are buying entertainment, escapism, or even helpful hints. What they are really buying in many cases is essentially one big advertisement. Rather than leaving readers feeling relaxed or entertained, these types of magazines often leave them feeling inadequate or anxious and motivated to buy all kinds of products to "improve" their looks.

Public Service Announcements

Happily, ads *can* be used to improve our health and safety. Take for example, Public Service Announcements or PSAs. We've all seen PSAs such as the Smokey the Bear "only you can prevent forest fires" campaign or the U.S. Department of Agriculture's food pyramid Web site at mypyramid.gov. The nonprofit Ad Council (AdCouncil.org) uses professional advertisers to create ads, and mass media outlets donate time or space for the ads. In a recent study, marketing professor Magdalena Cismaru found that more effective PSAs factor in consumers' perceptions of how difficult it will be for them to make the life changes the PSA suggests.[24] For example, the U.S. Department of Health and Human Services launched the Small Step PSA (www.smallstep.gov) that suggests little things people can do to lose weight and improve their health. Some of the tips include switching from whole milk to skim, eating before grocery shopping, and eating only half of your dessert. The Ad Council also produced TV and magazine ads as part of the campaign. For example, one ad shows a man's love handles gradually getting smaller with these labels, "started shooting hoops with son," "eats healthier and skips desserts," and "considering changing name to Buff Daddy."

The Ad Council's own research found that 55 percent of American children agreed that they would rather watch TV or play video games than play outside and that 57 percent of parents said that getting their child to eat healthy food is a major battle.[25] To encourage activity in children, the Ad Council produced a PSA encouraging children to take the small step of getting up and playing for an hour a day. Some PSAs have focused on drugs such as the famous "Just Say No" to drugs PSA or the Ad Council's current anti-steroid campaign. Let's turn now to the ways big business markets drugs to the American consumer.

Prescription Drugs

TrimSpa and Happy Meals are one thing, you might be thinking, but advertising does not affect the serious world of prescription drugs. If you are blissfully unaware of the marketing of prescription drugs to consumers, I hope it is because you are healthy and not in the market for a prescription drug yourself.

In the 1960s, the FDA was given authority over advertising of prescription drugs. At that time, drugs ads were usually to be found in medical journals targeting doctors. In the late 1990s, drug advertising rules were loosened, and we began to see an explosion of what are called direct-to-consumer (DTC) ads, mostly on television and in popular magazines and on the Internet. A direct-to-consumer ad is basically a commercial for a prescription drug targeting everyday people instead of doctors or other medical professionals. These ads can appear on TV, on the Internet, or in magazines—in any everyday form of mass media.

We've all seen these DTC drug ads. An older man walks along the beach throwing a tennis ball to his golden retriever. A voice says, "Ask your doctor about" insert-drug-name-here. When I first saw these ads on TV, they really got my attention. Ask my husband! When I saw one, I would laugh out loud and proclaim, "But, it doesn't even say what the drug is used for!" I was amazed. Time after time, I heard the ad line, "Ask your doctor if 'Drug X' is right for you." I wondered aloud, would a patient really go into her doctor's office and ask earnestly, "Doctor, is 'Drug X' right for me?" Without even knowing what condition it treats? And is the patient happy when she learns that she could use some Plavix or saddened when she learns that Propecia is not right for her? It seemed crazy to me, but now I know that it works for the drug companies. DTC ads are profitable.

Again, these marketing practices raised eyebrows to the extent that the government had to get involved. In 2005, the Congressional Research Service published a report to Congress on DTC ads for prescription drugs.[26] The report indicated that the drug industry spent $3.2 billion on DTC ads in 2003, primarily for its top fifty drugs. The drug most advertised in DTC ads was the heartburn drug Nexium, also known as the "little purple pill." Wow. When you think about it, giving the consumer an oh-so-easy, cute name like "little purple pill" kind of implies the consumer is like a child who needs a very easy name in order to remember it. If it were true, should such people really be responsible for choosing their own drugs, one wonders. Other drugs on the most-DTC-advertised list included sleep aid Lunesta, cholesterol drug Crestor, and allergy drug Nasonex. I bet you recognized most of those names as I did, which shows the power of those ad dollars at work.

Drug companies say these ads encourage people to visit their doctors and to take a more active role in their treatment. Critics say the ads can be misleading. For example, according to the report, "In September 2004, Merck & Co. withdrew its anti-inflammatory medication Vioxx from the market because studies had shown an elevated heart-attack and stroke risk with prolonged use. Questions were raised at a November 2004 Senate Finance Committee hearing about whether earlier studies by the company and others had suggested this risk in Vioxx."[27]

Research has found that seeing DTC ads does influence consumer behavior. Consumers are more likely to talk with their doctors about the drugs and to ask for a prescription after seeing DTC ads. A 2002 study[28] found that DTC ads influenced not only the doctor's prescribing the drug in question but also the diagnosis of the condition implicated. The authors found a trend that the more the drug company spent on the DTC ad, the greater the payoff in prescriptions. They noted that this was more likely to work for some drugs—seasonal allergy meds, for instance—than for others. One concern is that increases in requests for prescription drugs causes tax increases and increased health care costs to employers. In other words, ads targeting consumers create demand for a specific drug.

Straight to the Heart of the Matter

Well, we know that advertisers will go a long way to get to the heart of the consumer, but this story, reported in the *Chicago Tribune*,[29] takes that sentiment to a whole new level. Ever resourceful, advertisers, it appears, are now marketing medical equipment like home heart defibrillators, making an estimated $50 million in profits from direct-to-consumer ads, up from $0 a decade before. The company Medtronic is marketing a device that shocks the heart, selling it directly to consumers for a heart-shocking $20,000 to $30,000. According to the *Chicago Tribune*:[30]

> In the campaign, dubbed "What's inside," a soft voice tells viewers they will find inside the device "10,000 more kisses . . . 200 more football wins," saying it will "always be there for you—close to your heart with the power to restart it in case of sudden cardiac arrest." Dr. Sidney Wolfe, head of consumer group Public Citizens' Health Research Group, said he considers the ad highly misleading. "This is trying to frighten people and you are going to have people who are scared and uniformed saying, 'Let's not take a chance.' "

Whether it is marketing junk food to children or marketing problematic diet pills or prescription meds to adults, the one thing these advertisers have in common is businesses profiting to the detriment of the consumer. If allowed, marketing like this can have an adverse effect on the physical and mental well-being of the country in general. Persuasive messages seek to define normative behavior and ideals such as the habit of asking your doctor for a drug you've seen advertised on TV. According to what we see in the media, losing weight is easy, and eating high-fat foods isn't fattening. We're unconscious and uncritical of the power of media to move us to watch more than we want, to induce us to buy more than we want, and to take over our free time in ways that do not enrich us or make us happy. When it comes to your health, it pays to be smart about advertising.

Seven

GET WITH THE PROGRAMMING: MEDIA

MESSAGES ABOUT WHO YOU ARE

> Advertisers program an uneasy self-consciousness into our
> minds so that we are on the lookout for products that will make
> us look, feel, and smell better.
>
> — W. James Potter[1]

How do you feel about yourself? Women, are you thin enough, sexy
enough, pretty enough? Men, are you concerned about your abs, your
baldness, your, um, size? These are common concerns in great part because
making us self-consciousness is profitable for media executives.

Social psychologists study how self-image and self-esteem are shaped by
the mass media messages that pervade our social worlds. Because far from
being just entertainment and far from not mattering at all, those screens
relentlessly feed you messages about your place in the world and how you
should feel about yourself. As Potter puts it, media "constantly program the
way we think about ourselves."[2] How right he is!

On the one side, we have the producers of mass media. Their overarching
goal is to get our attention so that we will be moved to buy their advertisers'
products. They want to matter to us deeply. They want our money; therefore they need us to care—to be magnetically attracted so that we point our
faces at their screens. On the other side, there we sit. We are drawn in by
their psychology, but we're largely unaware—or in denial—about how

much their messages have come to matter to us. They call us "consumers," and this is a term so commonplace that we have come to accept that perspective unquestioningly. Is that who we are? Consumers? Is our main function in life to use products that advertisers sell us, or are we something more?

Earlier I told you a story about a business expert who advised that the best way to get what you want out of a person is to find out what's most important to that person and exploit it for your own gain. One of the things we care most deeply about is our place in the social world. Are we good enough? Are we competitive for the most important resources in life—for example, winning a mate and an esteemed position in society? Clearly, mass media executives have tapped the self-worth goldmine over and over. It's because self-worth is such a basic human need that businesses so eagerly and successfully use it against us. If you shake our foundations you motivate us to do whatever it takes to set them right, and that, of course, includes spending money.

Does Size Matter? Or How to Make Men Neurotic

Speaking of self-esteem, what better way to hit men below the belt than to target them, well, below the belt? In a society where men are the dominant group, men's issues tend to get less attention, but let's do something a little different and start with an example of where mass media have harmed men by targeting their sense of self-worth. And as long as I'm talking about men, I might as well go right ahead and jump into a conversation about penises.

One of the most common types of SPAM e-mail messages are those promising to enhance penis size. If one were to take the frequency of such ads as social information, then one would assume they are generated due to a major problem many men have. Of course, if you've ever been bored enough, curious enough, or tired-of-working enough to actually read one of these ads, you know that the ads themselves are decidedly unsubtle in telling men they have a problem. Personally, I find it particularly amusing when an ad features a quote, supposedly from a real woman, enthusiastically claiming that whatever product the company is selling has rocked her world. (I visualize these quotes as actually being written by middle-aged men in cubicles.) Of course, this is a very straightforward example of applying basic learning theory to marketing. The message is that if a man buys the product, his sex life and his masculinity will rise to all new highs. Women will find him irresistible.

As we have seen, it is often the ads themselves that create a state of want or inadequacy. Researchers from Cal State and UCLA wanted to find some reality in this media-fueled culture where masculinity and power have been equated with having a large penis. The researchers write:[3] "The flourishing penis enlargement industry indicates that at least some men worry enough about penis size to spend money on costly products and on potentially risky surgery to boost their self-confidence."

Okay, here comes the great part. This research team—God love 'em—reports findings sure to provoke sighs of relief from many quarters. They tell the absolute truth about how big real men's penises are, and what real women actually think about penis size. I would add that an underlying assumption of this work must be that Mother Nature created the average man to be, so to speak, up for any task for which he was designed.

Let me be a part of what I consider a public service announcement and share their news. For your information everyone, the average erect penis is 5.3 inches long, with most men ranging from 4.6 to 6 inches. Other than porn stars (done with mirrors?) or Aerosmith's *Big Ten Inch Record*, less than 3 percent of men have erect penises that are 6.9 inches or longer. There you have it. As I say to my students, don't say I never taught you anything.

As for women's attitudes, the great majority of women were satisfied with their partner's penis size. Graciously, only 6 percent of women said their partner's penis was smaller than average. In fact, the women were significantly more satisfied (85%) with their partner's penis than the men themselves were (55%). What we can take away from this, I think, is that a cultural belief—generated in great part by mass media—has caused men to lose confidence and have a distorted view of their own bodies as well as their value as men. These negative and misleading portrayals have unnecessarily harmed men's views of themselves. This case in particular is interesting because the industry was able to take advantage of a general ignorance created when people treat basic sex education as a taboo topic. It's easier to create a mythology when the facts have become obscured.

Talking about adult sexuality is one thing, but now we move to a discussion of how marketers have targeted children's basic social motives to be valued and wanted by using sex to sell them things. In the last chapter, we discussed how governmental deregulation has allowed marketers to target children directly, to the detriment of their health. We've seen how fiercely they have taken to this task, how they sell high-calorie fast food meals with toys, create whole TV shows to sell toys, and pay athletes to market junk food. Now we move into another territory big business is using to make a profit from unsuspecting children: marketing sex and sexiness to them.

Ready or Not, Here They Come

Hey kids, are you ready to be sexy? That sounds dumb, doesn't it? But it represents the direction in which mass media are taking our children. Everywhere you look, marketers are selling sex and sexiness to younger and younger children. Now, I'm not a prude, and I don't have a problem with media content for adults that talks about sex and relationships. I'm guessing I probably don't even need to say that after just having an extended conversation about penises, but just in case. But seriously, *not* discussing those topics with adults would be unhealthy, in fact. No, it's not even sex that is the issue, but rather the *marketing* of sexiness to children that is unhealthy. Our kids—little girls in particular—are being sold the notion that they are supposed to be sexy.

The very ubiquity of this marketing strategy may have desensitized us to its inappropriateness, at least partially. So, let's take a look at this situation for what it is by starting with a premise I think we can all agree on: it is not healthy for children to be having sex. Sexuality, ideally, develops as a child grows to maturity. In a healthy environment, children are curious about relationships and about sex and have caring adults to support their development. What they see around them supports a natural unfolding of their understanding of sexuality. But that is what takes place ideally—in a *healthy* environment. How would you describe the cultural environment in which we are raising our children when it comes to sex?

Sharon Lamb and Lyn Mikel Brown, the authors of *Packaging Girlhood: Rescuing Our Daughters from Marketers' Schemes*, are experts on the subject. They very astutely explain how girls are sold very limited notions of what it means to be a girl. A little girl is told that she is supposed to want to be a pretty pink princess. I'm sure you are familiar with this, but if not, go to the toy department of your local big box store and find the aisle that is completely pink. This is supposedly the aisle that represents what little girls all want: Barbies, Bratz, and pink princesses all the time.

Media and marketers now sell even the littlest girls on the idea that a girl's identity is wrapped up in being "sexy." There are many ways that American girls get told that this is who they are or who they should be. If you read the slogans on T-shirts sold to girls, you get the idea of the very limited identity marketers are prescribing for them. Lamb and Brown[4] give examples of these prescribed "choices," including becoming a "professional drama queen," or a "pretty princess beauty queen," or "delicious." Girls are supposed to be "hot," "sexy," "divas," and "beauties." T-shirt slogans[5] quip: "Official cheer bunny: we're hip, we hop, we're always on top," or "Come to cutie summer camp—feel the nature," or "Recess flirt—meet by the swings when the bell rings," the latter with a picture of lips in the background.

Have you looked at kids' Halloween costumes lately? Lamb and Brown point out that it is common now to see little girls' costumes that are designed to be "sexy," or to present them as little "divas." Boys' identities, as suggested by their clothes and costumes, are also very restricted. Boys are sold as tough and aggressive or even violent. I walked into my son's preschool one Halloween when he was about three and I was struck with the false division between the sexes that I was seeing. There seemed to be two choices: princess or tough guy. Boys had superhero costumes with fake "six packs" and bulging biceps. They had gritting, angry *Hulk* teeth. Girls wore gossamer pink fabric with glittery tiaras and delicate slippers. The Halloween costumes I remember from childhood were much more diverse and also much more likely to be homemade. Therefore, they really were about choosing who you wanted to be and exercising your own creativity. This was, however, not nearly as profitable to businesses that sell Halloween costumes.

I am struck by the same heavy-handed prescription for gender roles whether it is in the toy aisles at the local big box store or in the drive-through at the fast-food restaurant. The girls' toy aisle is pink and Bratz-ified (yes, I made that word up). The boys' toy aisle is dark and full of ripped, muscular bodies, weaponry, and characters that fight and show off their muscles.

I've had conversations about this with my son since he was old enough to talk. I have asked him, "Jason, are there really two kinds of people in the world? Are girls really all princesses? Are boys really all aggressive?" I've told him over and over that his mom fits neither category. I wouldn't be attracted to a princess doll or a doll that shoots people. And I've noticed that Jason gets interested and involved when we have these kinds of conversations. For example, at about age five, he came home from a friend's house claiming that he was just playing a video game, "but it wasn't a 'violent video game,' mom." He made the quotation mark signs with his fingers when he said "violent video game." There's a kid who has his mother's number. But my point is that from my experience, kids appreciate it when their parents start a conversation about the kinds of things that really matter. Even if it doesn't all come out just right, it shows them that you care.

Is It Okay to Sell Little Girls' Panties That Say "Eye Candy"?

Diane Levin and Jean Kilbourne discuss selling little girls on sexuality in their book *So Sexy So Soon: The New Sexualized Childhood and What Parents Can Do to Protect Their Kids.*[6] These experts very clearly state that the problem is not that kids are learning about sex. The problem is that the media and marketers target children with sexualized images that are confusing and that undermine their healthy sexual development. Their book is filled with the real-life stories of parents and teachers who are struggling to deal with unprecedented situations, like the seven-year-old who asks what a "blow job" is or the five-year-old who is suspended from school for saying he wanted to "have sex" with one of his classmates. In a world where there is now a series of Barbie dolls who model lingerie, where there are T-shirts for toddler boys that say "pimp squad," and where "mainstream national chains . . . are selling padded bras and thong panties for young girls that feature cherries and slogans such as 'Wink-Wink' and 'Eye Candy,'[7] the problem is not sex, but the widespread practice of undermining children's healthy sexual development for money."

This raises the issue of where boys fall in this discussion. The experts say that in this environment boys learn early, even before they really know what sex is, that girls are sex objects. Girls are supposed to focus on their looks and try to please boys by looking sexy or "hot." When marketers send these messages to boys, they have already undercut boys' ability to have healthy, respectful relationships with girls. When a girl is an object rather than a person, one is pretty much as good as another.

Why Does Sexuality and Aggression Draw Kids' Attention?

Some answer criticism about selling girls a vision of themselves as sex objects with the reply that sex is natural and therefore any sexual content in the media is, by extension, only natural too. Again, it is not sex or sexuality that is unnatural, but it is targeting children with ideas they are not ready for and packaging sexuality as sexual objectification that are the issues. A big question that is necessary to understand in this debate is why children are attracted to these sexual messages. Why does selling kids with sex draw them in? According to the authors of *So Sexy So Soon*, developmental psychology has answers for these questions and they have to do with the way children think, feel, and react to the world around them. Any information that is unfamiliar and dramatic will grab a child's attention. Children are also drawn to concrete visual stimulation. Even if dramatic, sexy imagery or stories are somewhat scary to a small child, still she will be drawn in. She will focus on the concrete image that has been prepackaged for her rather than questioning it or putting it in context. For instance, when a child sees another child dressed sexually in an advertisement, the child probably doesn't understand that the girl in the ad is an actress who has been paid to pretend to be a certain way. The child certainly does not know that the entire ad was the idea of some executives who most likely were wealthy White men or that it was created to make someone money. Also, if the actress in the ad is smiling or having fun, the child looking at the ad will tend to take it at face value—that this is what the child in the ad wants and enjoys. And since children do not understand media messages as well as adults can, they will not naturally analyze and resist them in the way that would best protect them from other people's agendas.

Another reason I think that selling with sex works is that sex and belonging are basic needs. They get our attention because we are organisms designed first and foremost to survive and reproduce. These responses are adaptive and tend to sustain the species. What is not adaptive is when businesses exploit and twist our natural tendencies for their own financial gain.

Should Kindergarten Girls Wear the Same Clothes as Teens?

It used to be that clothes for kindergarten girls were different from clothes for teens, but this has changed. Marketers are now often selling the same styles to the five-year-olds as to the fifteen-year-olds. As authors Lamb and Brown rightly emphasize, big business is now selling our little girls on an idea called "girl power," which is patently not about real power. Is a nine-year-old in a camisole or a shirt that shows her belly powerful in any substantive sense? Today's girls are being sold "very limited choices about who they can be alongside continuous pleas for them to shop, primp, chat, and do the things girls are 'supposed to do.'"[8] While girls should be supported and encouraged to be real individuals, they are sold this fake image of who it's okay to be.

As with sugary breakfast foods, bubbly beverages, and candy, marketers sell a brand of sexuality to children knowing that it is not healthy for them, knowing it will make them anxious. They *hope* their targets become so anxious that they will be motivated to buy the products that will supposedly "fix" them.

"While products aimed at tween girls promise perfect faces and bodies, friends and boyfriends, the marketers and manufacturers don't have to confront the negative impact on girls: the confusion about sexuality and romantic relationships, the anxiety about weight and appearance, the struggle with popularity and fitting in. No, they leave that to you [the parent].... At a time when daughters could be developing skills, talents, and interests that will serve them well their whole life, they are being enticed into a dream of specialness through pop stardom and sexual objectivity that will derail other opportunities."[9]

Baby Needs a New Pair of Shoes—No, Really—Get That Poor Baby a New Pair of Shoes!

A new company is marketing "her first high heels." Yep, that's right. These are "high heels" for baby girls up to six months old. In an interview for MSNBC, a product developer responded to criticism of the baby high heels by saying that the shoes were for "fashion" and "fun" and for "the experience."[10] Thongs for kindergarteners and high heels for baby girls: now we really have seen everything.

The *Today Show* discussed the shoes (see Figure 7-1), noting that a press release from the company invoked *Sex and the City*, speculating that the

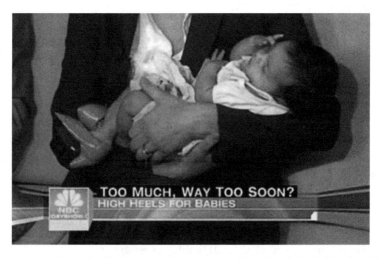

FIGURE 7.1. The *Today Show*'s Matt Lauer commented that these baby high heels might be a little too fashion forward, so to speak. Meredith Viera and Ann Curry said that some find the shoes offensive both because babies can't walk in them and because of what they suggest. Is it just me, or are these the same shoes Jessica Simpson wore with a camisole and panties on the cover of *Rolling Stone* (see Figure 5.1 in Chapter 5)?

characters on the show would no doubt approve of high heels for baby girls in colors like leopard, zebra, and hot pink satin. One blogger chimed in, "I wish the fashion industry would quit promoting adult like clothing and accessories for infants and toddlers. Doesn't anyone want to keep the little ones a normal dressed baby?" Another said, "I find them funny from a fashion and shoe lover's perspective but also a little disturbing that we are trying to create mini Carrie Bradshaw just a little too early. Shouldn't babies be wearing sweet bunny slippers or cheeky Robeezs?" *Today Show* host Matt Lauer quipped, "Thirty-five dollars for the heels; $45 to get the bustier with it."[11]

The hot pink baby stilettos are made out of squishy material and the heels scrunch up if baby tries to walk on them. If baby tries to walk on them . . . Hmmm. I remember my firstborn pulling himself up and walking while holding onto furniture at five or six months—an age deemed appropriate for baby girls to wear these shoes. You know what that reminds me of? *Packaging Girlhood* gently reminds us that clothes for girls should put first not only comfort but the extent to which the little girl can play, grow, and develop in what she is wearing. Even though the heels are squishy, it seems to me that they would just get in the way of a little girl trying to learn to walk. And it doesn't take a child development expert to see that the shoes are clearly for the amusement of the adults who buy them. No baby would *want* to wear funky puffy shoes with a weird squishy part under the heel. In that way it seems to me that putting these shoes on a baby is kind of like forcing your dog to wear a funny hat. The dog wants no part of it.

Sadly, in a few years these babies might just want to wear sexy clothes and sexy shoes because that's what the marketers are selling them. What they really want, of course, is not to be sexy but to be wanted and loved. The marketers just know how to exploit those basic human motives for profit. In *So Sexy So Soon*, Levin and Kilbourne tell the story of a normal seven-year-old girl crying in the bathtub because she thinks she is fat and not sexy enough. They tell the story of an eight-year-old girl's birthday slumber party in which the topic of conversation was how to get their mothers to buy them shirts that showed their bellies so that they could be sexy and get boys to like them. The little girls talked about the "cool" belly shirts they had seen in *Cosmo Girl* magazine and about trying to get around their parents by asking their grandparents to buy the belly shirts for them.

Need I even say that when you are seven or eight, it makes no sense for you to be sexy? Need I even say that the very fact that we now have a magazine called *Cosmo **Girl*** (which should be an oxymoron in the sense that they mean it) should be a wake-up call? It's not healthy. It's not developmentally appropriate. Children are not ready for sex, and wearing clothes that suggest they are is all wrong for them. It sends the message to little girls *and* to boys that they are objects to be used rather than people with unique ideas, talents, and dreams. This is yet another example of how media and marketers sell a false sense of liberation. Yes, we are free to dress any way we like, but dressing in a way that undermines your health and happiness is not my idea of freedom—quite the opposite. And our kids are not exercising freedom of choice when the choices we are given are very limited, pre-scribed, and undermine a child's healthy development.

Skankwear Is Everywhere

In her book *Stop Dressing Your Six-Year-Old Like a Skank*, comedian and mother Celia Rivenbark recalls an experience that's been shared by mothers of daughters across the country. Leaving behind softer, sweeter clothing designed for the littlest girls, Celia found herself staring down the racks of clothes designed for her now size 7 daughter and was seriously dismayed. It did not make sense to her that her six-year-old was now supposed to dress in the same clothes as an eighteen-year-old heading for college. She astutely noted that if, as these "choices" imply, you are supposed to dress your little daughter like a young woman going clubbing, then your daughter will miss the fun of being a child, among other things. When she told the store clerk that all these clothes looked like prostitute wear, she was told that all the moms say that. Like moms everywhere Celia is uncomfortable with little girls wearing shorts with the words JUICY or DELICIOUS across the rear end. She does not want to shop in a department she thinks should be called "L'il Skanks" or to buy the "little ladies of the night" look for a daughter who should be dressing for the monkeybars, not for the runway or the street corner. Here's how Celia put it: "I get it. Now that my kid is practically of child-bearing age (is six the new seventeen?) I must choose ... from t-shirts that scream things like BABY DOLL and JAIL BAIT not to mention a rather angry GIRLS RULE AND BOYS DROOL where an embroidered flower and buzzing bee should be. When did this happen? Who decided that my six year old should dress like a Vegas showgirl? And one with an abundance of anger issues at that?"[12]

My colleague sociologist Beth Wright and I have team-taught a course on gender in society. In this course, we have had our students form teams and go to different types of stores, looking for clothes for boys and girls of different ages. Our student reporters come back and tell the class about what they've seen. They show pictures of the clothes on the market today for children of various ages. I am struck by how these college students are really interested and concerned about what they are seeing. They, too, think the clothes designed even for the littlest girls look like they are made for prostitutes, and they don't like it that their little sisters have mostly bad options to choose from. My female college students have also been very honest and frank about how they navigated these issues themselves. The young women talk about feeling the pressure to wear what everyone is wearing while at the same time feeling uncomfortable with it. Some talk about coming to a point at which they decided they needed to present themselves in such a way that people would respect them rather than going for the oversexed pop star look. And the male college students are outspoken as well, talking about how they see that girls who dress with the oversexed look are attracting guys who want to use them, not guys who would care about them. And that's an excellent point, because this is not just about sex. It is about how males and females understand and relate to each other in all kinds of ways.

I've talked with moms of little girls and they too are distressed about the lack of good choices and the abundance of inappropriate items made available to them by marketers. Several of my friends and colleagues who are moms and grandmas of little girls have a problem with the clothes being offered to their girls. Moms have told me over and over about the conversations they have with their daughters in clothing store dressing rooms while overhearing other moms and daughters in nearby dressing rooms having the same conversations. Moms and dads have told me that they have taken to buying shorts from the boys' section for their little daughters because the ones in the girls' section are too short. Friends have said they order shirts and shorts for their little girls from classic catalogues like Land's End, which they consider one of the last bastions of non-skank wear for their little girls. When I hear this, I feel bad because I know not everyone can afford to order from a higher end catalogue. Along the same lines, less educated people may be more likely to accept what they are being offered as normal and healthy. Or they may know that they don't like what they see in the stores, but they may not have the skills and knowledge to understand what the effects of dressing their daughters in the typical oversexed-kitten girl wardrobe might be. And if they do, they may well feel powerless to change the system. And do you know what? Dressing your little girl should not be this hard! Marketers should not be allowed to undermine our parenting, let alone our children's health.

Fergie Teaches a Lesson in Pop Culture and Children

Now take a look at this image (see Figure 7-2). On May 20, 2008, singer Fergie appeared on NBC's *Today Show* doing a cover of Heart's "Barracuda." More to the point, she was wearing what appeared to be skin-tight plastic

FIGURE 7.2. Pop singer Fergie delivers sex-soaked performance of "Barracuda" in front of teen girls, moms, and little ones on NBC's *Today Show*. Critics called it inappropriate for children, but how different is it from the blatant sexuality American marketers sell children every day?

pants and was crawling, groaning, and gyrating her way through the number on a stage flanked by families with children. Fergie was criticized for this performance across the blogosphere. One blogger, noting that the Bratz dolls must have been one of Fergie's inspirations, had the following to say:[13]

> Most performers would stand on the *Today* show stage in Rockefeller Center, look out at the dozens of sweatshirted tourists holding signs, 8th graders on class trips, and families with small children who consider Al Roker's humor to be "spicy," and decide to tone down their act. After all, it is a morning show, and the kids are three feet away—maybe you should save your "suggestively stroking the middle-aged guitar player on my knees" bit for afternoon gigs. But not Fergie. She took one look in the embarrassed eyes of the kids at the end of the stage, and gave them exactly what they wanted: a 33-year-old pop singer on her hands and knees screeching and writhing mere inches from their faces, with only the thinnest layer of Lycra separating them.

Another (on video.msn.com) commented: "What a HOOKER! Even my husband thought she was a classless loser! Those parents should be tazed for letting their kids watch such horrible crap. Not to mention the cat woman hussie crawl and other assorted gyrations. What has this world come to??!! Jesus, please come quick!!!"

When I saw Fergie's performance, what struck me is that this image of an oversexed star playing to confused but curious children is really just holding a mirror up to our pop culture. What's the difference between selling little girls lingerie-clad Barbies or Bratz diva dolls and selling them an over-sexed Fergie on the *Today Show*? Only this time, the interesting thing was that we were confronted with the awkwardness and inappropriateness of the juxtaposition. We found ourselves *watching* children *watching* an oversexed media image. Look at the little blonde girl at the front of the stage and the little boy beside her looking down as Fergie crawls seductively in plastic pants inches away from them. Fix that image in your mind as a representation of what children have had thrust upon them in recent years.

The American Psychological Association Makes a Statement

The American Psychological Association (APA) is the largest association of psychologists in the world. Central to the APA's mission[14] is to use psychology in the public interest in order to advance public health and welfare. This means using psychological knowledge to benefit society and to improve people's lives.[15] In that spirit and with public concern over the issue increasing, in 2005 the APA established the Task Force on the Sexualization of Girls. Their charge was to report on the current psychological understanding of the influence of the sexualization of girls by mass media and popular culture. In their report, they were to make recommendations for everything from public awareness to new research and public policy.

What did the task force find? From TV and movies, to video games, the Internet, and magazines, they found a deep and pervasive sexualization of girls and women across virtually every popular form of media. Females were much more likely than males to be sexualized. The task force published a definition of sexualization, which included presenting a person's value as coming from his or her sexuality. According to the task force, a sexualized girl is an object of other people's agendas rather than an agent actively asserting her own will. When a girl is sexualized, others have imposed sexuality on her and narrowly defined a specific physical appearance she must attain and have equated it with sexiness.

What is the cost to girls and young women when the mass media and the broad culture represent them consistently as being valued for their appearance and their worth as sex objects? The APA Task Force reports clear and demonstrable damages that undercut both the physical and psychological well-being of girls and women. The sexualization of girls and women promotes eating disorders. Girls change the way they eat because of how media portray who they are supposed to be. Psychologically, exposure is associated with depression and low self-esteem. Girls and women feel badly about themselves because they compare themselves to this media image of who they are supposed to be, and they feel that they do not measure up. As a consequence of this narrow view of what it means for a girl or a woman to be a valued member of our culture, females experience greater self-image problems. They deal with emotional issues such as shame and anxiety. They deal with body shame. Finally, they develop an unhealthy sexual self-image. Being a psychologist, I could tell it to you in more detail from a scientific perspective, but it comes to this: we are making our girls and women sick by tolerating the pervasive misrepresentation of femininity in the mass media.

How Did It Get This Way?

I can't understate the importance of understanding that this is ultimately *not even about sex*. It is about money. Advertisers don't care about our sex lives; they care about getting their hands inside our wallets and purses. Simply put, in the current social order, it is advantageous for mass media to make us feel bad about ourselves so that we are motivated to spend money to fix what's "wrong" with us. Mass media are tapping into a bottomless pit of motivation because if we are always losing, we are always highly motivated to get on a winning path. For example, as noted media scholar Jean Kilbourne[16] so rightly points out, there are beauty standards set for women that are so high we are virtually all doomed to "fail." But that doesn't stop us from spending money trying not to fail. And nobody cares if this unending failure robs us of our self-worth, not to mention time, energy, and money.

As a college professor, I have worked with many young women over the years. I have talked with them and I have read their journals. I can tell you that there is a lot of pain out there and a lot of distorted self-images. If I were to make a list of what motivates me most strongly in my career, among the top motives would be the desire to help take away this deep pain so many are suffering. I think about how these young women's lives could be happier and healthier and how their attention could be more focused on the positive and I want to help them get there. I think about my own daughter, and I want to make it better for her, too.

You know, it didn't used to be this way, and it doesn't have to continue being this way. My friend Gary recently sent me a clipping from the May 24, 1951, edition of his hometown newspaper the *Taylorsville Times* of Taylorsville, North Carolina. It was an advertisement for a movie that featured a drawing of a sexy woman. Under the ad was a caption inserted by the newspaper staff, that read, "Children will neither understand or enjoy this picture…therefore we do not recommend it for them." I think this comment shows the extent to which we have gone backward from where we should be in helping our children navigate a world that includes mass media. The staff of the *Taylorsville Times* got it right. Children are not developed enough or experienced enough to understand this kind of content. It is not made for them and seeing it will likely confuse and potentially harm them. Today, not only has this basic message been lost, but people actually make this stuff for kids and not because they think they will enjoy it or even be able to cope with it, but because it will help the companies turn a profit.

Big Money Changed the Rules for the Little Guy

We can look back at U.S. history and see pretty easily how this happened. Historically, the U.S. government—through groups like the FCC and FTC (Federal Communications Commission and Federal Trade Commission)—has been in the practice of protecting children from harmful products and advertising. However, lobbyists for big media and marketing companies successfully moved the U.S. Congress to deregulate how they sell to children. Deregulation basically means fewer rules that restrict big companies. For our kids, that essentially means that the government bowed to the lobbyists and decided it was open season on selling to children. This "no rules" kind of environment put the fox in charge of the henhouse, with predictable results. Advertisers started meeting openly to discuss how best to target children. For example, they started the practice of making entire TV shows for kids that were just commercials to sell toys featured in the show, something that hadn't been possible under the previous rules. They began the cross-marketing strategies that are so prevalent now that we may have forgotten the days when they didn't exist. Cross-marketing, as discussed in the section on food marketing and children, involves selling a theme across products. For example, it's cross-marketing in action when your child's fast-food meal, breakfast cereal, fruit snacks, and school folder all sport the same TV star or characters from the latest movie.

"Telling Stories" about Other People

I grew up in the Midwest, but I've lived in the American South now for over a decade so I claim dual citizenship. Southerners have a delightful way of phrasing things, and since I love language, my ears perk up when I hear an interesting one. Southerners love indirection. If you are a liar, it wouldn't be neighborly to call you one, so we'll say something more charming. We'll say, for example, that you are "telling a story." So "telling a story" means lying. And if you are cheating, you are not "having an affair," you are "stepping out" on your spouse. I love that one! It sounds so quaint! But back to the quaint habit of "telling stories." This is a great characterization for media scholars because it captures so beautifully how the media can misrepresent people by the stories they tell about them.

Bad Rap

We've talked about how we form our personal identities as a consequence of who the media tell us we should be. Now let's look at a couple of examples that show how we form impressions of other people or groups through the mass media. Recently Melinda Burgess, Beth Wright, and I[17] investigated the "stories" rap music tells about women—especially African American women—and about African American men. One reason it is particularly important to study media representations of numerical minorities is that White people often live in rather segregated neighborhoods and don't always have much racially diverse contact. If you don't have many face-to-face interactions with people who are different from you, you may rely more heavily on the stories the mass media tell you about who members of other groups are.

Focusing on hardcore or "gangsta" rap, we asked college students what typical songs in this genre are about, what the typical video shows, what the rappers are like and what rappers say about women in the songs. It's a common mistake (an urban legend?) to believe that most people who listen to hardcore rap are African American. In fact, as the industry is well aware, their target audience is White—young White males specifically. Our sample of about 200 college students (75% White which is similar to the general U.S. population) also believed African American men are most likely to listen to hardcore rap. When I gave expert testimony to Congress in 2007, the big media executives (mostly older, White men) and rappers were there. The big media chief executive officers (CEOs) and rappers were aware of the idea that one thing that sells rap music to White suburban kids is the appeal of the "dangerous minority" Black stereotype. Whites want to vicariously enjoy a subculture that they see as cooler and edgier than theirs. Another thing that came out of the discussion was the argument that rap benefits the community that it comes from. Actually, research out of Vanderbilt University[18] documents that at its start, hip-hop and rap were evocative of the culture from which they emerged, and were also anti-corporate. It's only when the rich, White CEOs saw that rap was marketable (to White suburbanites) that rap content changed into the stereotypical violent and misogynistic brand that is now widely criticized.

Our study showed that our sample of college students believed strongly that the rappers and the industry benefit from rap music, not the community from which the music came. What did these college students think about rappers? In order of frequency, they described the typical rapper as a gangster, Black, a thug, rich, and disrespectful to women. Of the respondents who listed "Black" as a characteristic of rappers, 20 percent used a variation of the "n" word. What did they think rap songs were about? The most common responses were sex, drugs, women, and violence. These themes match up with research that has analyzed the content of top-selling rap songs. When asked how the rappers refer to women, the top answers were ho/whore, bitch, slut, "shawty," and sexy.

In general, this group of 200 college students thought that hardcore rap portrays African American women and men in very negative ways. They believe rap songs and videos characterize the men as dangerous, violent, criminal, disrespectful to women, and focused on money and acquiring things in a pretty stereotypical and tasteless way—flashy cars, prostitutes, and "bling," for instance. They think the genre shows a vision of Black women as sexualized and degraded. Let's take a closer look at the words they believe rappers call women: whore, bitch, slut, shawty, and sexy. First, shawty, if you haven't heard, is a derivative of shorty, which used to refer to a child but now is used as a term of affection for a friend or girlfriend. In mainstream culture, a bitch is an overbearing, mean woman. When you "bitch" about something, you are complaining. Talking about "bitches" in rap music, the word takes on a different meaning. It means someone you dominate and use. If you are "my bitch," you are my servant, sexual and otherwise. A group of "bitches" are the sex objects in the brood of a player or hustler. Whore/ho and slut are words that degrade female sexuality, making the argument that women's sexuality is dirty, promiscuous, and predatory.

Actually, you know what word perfectly describes the characterization of women in rap music? Rapacious. No, really. I love plays on words, but you have to admit, this one is pretty perfect. According to the Encarta World English dictionary, rapacious means "greedy and grasping, especially for money, and sometimes willing to use unscrupulous means to obtain what is desired." Though I take great delight in word play, I'm actually heading toward something deeper here. Characterizing a woman as your bitch and as a whore is sending out the message that women are rapacious. When you call someone a whore, you're putting out this degrading image of women as playing men for money and as using their sexuality to do it. Even your girlfriend, or a member of your promiscuous brood of women, is your "bitch." She does what you want, sexually and otherwise. As the APA Task Force on the Sexualization of Girls and Women rightly points out, when you make someone an object, you are saying she is really worthless in that she is to be used and then tossed aside. Any one of them will serve the purpose.

Bad Rap in Public Debate

Because rap music is controversial, it often inspires public debate. One particular image that widely provoked people was rapper Nelly's video for his song "Tip Drill." First, the title is basically crude street talk for a particular sex act. But it wasn't the explicit sexual content that garnered the attention; rather, it was an egregious act perpetrated in the video. If you haven't seen it, of course, you can watch it on YouTube. Black women in gold bikinis dance around a pool provocatively. Nelly walks up to a gyrating Black woman in a thong and swipes a credit card down her back side (see Figure 7-3). I think that image needs no further analysis than what I

FIGURE 7.3. Rapper Nelly swipes a credit card in a woman's backside in his video *Tip Drill*. African American women at Spelman College protested and *Essence* magazine launched a campaign called "Take Back the Music" partially in response to misogyny in rap music.

have already given. I'd just comment that this one moment is iconic of the way rap music is "telling stories" that tear down whole groups of people.

Students at Spelman College, a historically Black college for women, protested against the misogyny in videos like Nelly's. In 2005, *Essence Magazine*, marketed toward a predominantly African American audience, started a campaign called "Take Back the Music." Perhaps this was a case of the old saying that if it gets bad enough, it will finally have to get better. The visibility of the issue has called attention to it. When radio shock jock Don Imus called the Rutgers women's basketball team—a group of young champion athletes and scholars—"nappy headed hos," people defended his comments by saying this is the way Black women are treated in rap music. Bad and sad as it was, Imus's comments sparked the congressional hearing into the consequences of violent and misogynist rap music content.

The Imus incident demonstrates that when you demean people by how you portray them in the media, not only is this in and of itself an act of aggression, but it also encourages other people to hurt innocent members of the same demographic group. This rationale is what Melinda Burgess and I have elaborated on in our theory of media and aggressive degradation.[19] It is important that we understand that publishing degrading, stereotypical images of people in the media causes harm. This is what my colleagues[20] and I demonstrated in the study (discussed in Chapter 3) in which we compared the effects of exposure to progressive images of women with exposure to derogatory images. There we found that if men saw women portrayed in the media as sex objects, they became more tolerant of sexual harassment.

Progressive Imagery Uplifts, Degrading Imagery Tears Down, Or Up with Obama, Down with Thugs

We tested our theory of media and aggressive degradation again, this time examining the great difference exposure to positive imagery of African American men makes in contrast to the damage that can be done by negative, stereotypical images of these men. In this study,[21] young White men and women saw either positive or negative media images of African American men. The positive images were of highly esteemed African American figures Martin Luther King Jr. and Barack Obama. The negative images were stereotypical African American male video game characters whose portrayals were typical of negative stereotypes of Black men found in video games—powerful, violent thugs. Next, the college students were asked to give feedback about the Web site of an unknown political candidate. All the students saw the exact same Web site except that half of them saw an image of an African American man and the other half saw an image of a White man. These images were selected so that the men looked like respectable political candidates, each wearing a suit and speaking from a podium. The students believed they were rating how well the candidate's Web site worked for him, but along the way they rated their feelings toward the candidate himself. They also reported how likely they would be to vote for him, given the chance.

The results were striking. Those who had seen Barack Obama and Martin Luther King transferred that positivity onto an African American candidate, liking him more, rating him more highly, and being more likely to vote for him than their peers who rated a White candidate. But for those who had seen the stereotypical Black video game characters, the opposite was true. Evoking this image of the dangerous Black male thug caused college students to rate an unrelated African American candidate significantly lower than their peers rated a White candidate.

What does this mean? It means that if you put out a positive image of a group (women or African American men, for example), this tends to cause positive thinking about that group. You are giving an example that this group can be really good. In contrast, if you put out a negative picture (literally) of a group, this causes people to evaluate unrelated members of that group more poorly. How the media portray members of the group can help or harm other members of that same group. For all those who thought that what we watch on our screens doesn't matter, that media are just entertainment and no matter what we see, it changes nothing, this study demonstrates that is not true. How you portray someone—be it by race, gender, religion, or any factor—makes a difference for other members of that same group. The reason is that you are telling a story about what members of that group are like. This causes people to think in ways that are consistent with the stereotype or the image that you brought up with your representation.

Media Fantasies and Imaginal Confirmations

Remember that earlier we discussed a study by Slusher and Anderson[22] which showed that just imagining a stereotype made people believe that they had seen more instances of the stereotype in real life? This "imaginal confirmation" phenomenon applies to mass media imagery. These video game thugs are not real people. The game designers could have drawn them any way they wanted to—in either stereotypical or nonstereotypical ways. But seeing the fantasy images will tend to cause imaginal confirmation—the feeling that we've seen real people who are like this. That, in turn, will perpetuate negative stereotypes.

By the way, as discussed earlier, studies have shown that people generally believe that negative media content such as sexism or racism doesn't really matter because it is "just harmless entertainment." The results of our study on college students' perceptions about rap music run contrary to this popular belief. Our students strongly believed, as a group, that the kinds of images we see in rap music could be damaging. They believed the images could change people's attitudes and behaviors for the worse. That finding is pretty rare, and it gives me hope because it demonstrates that young people can be critical and thoughtful about the culture that surrounds them. It makes me feel good that if we do what experts, including the APA Task Force, recommend and make media literacy education part of our school curricula, then we can make a powerful move toward tolerance and toward understanding that one's identity is not a commodity someone else sells you. True freedom means making up your own mind about your self-worth and the value of those around you, not by buying what greedy corporations are trying to sell you.

Eight

THE SOCIAL PSYCHOLOGY OF

POLITICAL COVERAGE

On Friday June 13, 2008, I walked into a restaurant to eat dinner with my family. Glancing up at the plasma TV on the wall, I couldn't quite take in what I was seeing. Tim Russert, NBC News' Washington bureau chief and long-time moderator of *Meet the Press*, had collapsed at work and, at the age of fifty-eight and in the prime of his career, had died from a heart attack. What I felt was a visceral sense of loss, sadness, and the kind of wish to make it not true one feels upon learning of the sudden death of a friend or a cherished uncle.

What I felt might seem absurd, I know. Tim Russert and I had never met. Why should his death send me reeling? I think this is an example of what is good and human about mass media. As an excellent journalist, Tim made a difference in our lives because he provided us with a service that we couldn't do for ourselves. On *Meet the Press*, he was known for pressing politicians on the tough questions—on questions that mattered to us as everyday citizens. He forced the politicians to do their homework so they would have the answers Americans needed to hear. Through watching him do what he loved, the viewers felt they had come to know something of Tim Russert as a person, too. And that's why the relationship between Tim and his audience was not absurd, and why his death mattered to viewers like me.

Politics on the Screen—Deciding What's Fair and Balanced

What is political journalism? At its best, political coverage helps keep the general public informed of the most important issues and events happening in the country. And lest we forget, the press also shapes American politics. One example is that after the presidential election of 2008, the state of North Carolina was deemed too close to call for the Republicans or the Democrats. Eventually it was the Associated Press that analyzed the situation and publicly pronounced Obama the victor. Of course, on election day, the presidential candidates themselves watch the returns on television to find out who won and they act on that information. The electoral college does not vote until later, but we use the press as a source of election information. The American press is allowed access to government proceedings so that they can pass along relevant information to citizens. In countries without a free press, government, religious institutions, corporations, or other groups can control the information the press reports on either by omission or by misrepresentation. Of course, even with a free press, there is a manipulation that can and does occur. I'm a social psychologist, not a journalist, so I'm going to give you my vision of political coverage as a citizen and overlay that with what I think is important about it from a social psychological perspective. In analyzing the psychology behind political coverage, what we'll end up doing will be a valuable exercise in media literacy.

> A new form of "politics" is emerging, and in ways we haven't yet noticed. The living room has become a voting booth.
> Participation via television in Freedom Marches, in war, revolution, pollution, and other events is changing everything.[1]
> —Marshall McCluhan

It's not always easy to know what a so-called fair and balanced representation of a political story is. A "straight reporter" strives to present a story that covers "just the facts," without bias. She gives equal time to the relevant stakeholders. For example, a straight political reporter or program might attempt to interview both the Republican and Democratic candidate for office and ask them both the same questions. Beyond straight reporting there is also news analysis and commentary. Analysis and commentary, by definition, present judgments about events, ideas, and people in the news. If done well, news analysis offers something more than straight reporting. It offers an educated perspective on what's happening. Imagine, for instance, that you hear that Russia has invaded Georgia (the republic, not the state). What are you to make of this fact on your own? Unless you happen to be a historian or political scientist, you are probably at a loss to understand what this event means to you personally or to the world at large. Good political reporting goes beyond the role of a telegraph that transmits only the barest information by helping us make sense of the news.

Persuasion: Which Branch of the ELM Tree Will You Take?

Before we go any further, any conversation about the persuasive ability of the mass media would be incomplete without a review of one of the most important models of persuasion in social psychology: Petty and Caccioppo's Elaboration Likelihood Model of persuasion or ELM. I mentioned the ELM earlier, but want to go into more detail in this chapter. Basically, the ELM says that we can be persuaded either substantively or peripherally. If we really care about an issue, and we have the skill and the time to think about the relevant information, then we will take the ELM's Central Route to persuasion. Simply put, we'll process the arguments and make a reasoned decision based on the arguments. But, if we don't really care or don't have the resources (time, skill) to process the argument, we'll go the Peripheral Route. Since peripheral means "side" as in peripheral vision, this means we'll use less important aspects of the argument to make our decision. For example, if a speaker is attractive, well dressed, and charming, we'll more likely believe him regardless of the quality of his arguments. If we feel good—like at a political rally where we hear uplifting music, eat free food, and receive free gifts—we will be more likely to support the candidate.

With political content in the mass media, these sorts of shallow "look good" and "feel good" elements can be present, too. For example, let me make fun of myself by sharing with you a time when I took a walk down the peripheral path to persuasion. In 1992, I was twenty-two years old—a graduate student in my first semester of a social psychology Ph.D. program. I almost never watched TV during college or graduate school (no time). I also remember that I didn't have cable (no time, no money). But right before the presidential election, feeling an obligation to pay *some* attention to the election, I took a break from work by firing up the TV to watch political coverage. I happened to see what I could only term an "infomercial" for one of the presidential candidates. It featured "feel-good" shots of the candidate and his political promises—kind of a video version of kissing babies—feel-good music and warm fuzzy interviews. In short, it was very astutely and professionally produced to take advantage of the psychology of persuasion. I voted for that candidate and I have since believed that I was motivated quite a bit by that political "infomercial." I tell this story to underline that political media messages such as political ads are very powerful and can "get to us" even when we maybe should know better. They play on emotions by using many psychological techniques—camera angles, lighting, music, color schemes, jump cuts, and attractive spokes-people—to persuade the viewer.

The more media literate you are, the better the chances that your vote will represent what you really value as opposed to representing the hype often generated by mass media of all sorts. Does this matter? According to recent reports, more than a quarter of voters vote for a candidate who does not share their basic substantive beliefs. In a democracy you can vote for whomever you want to, whether that person agrees with you on substance or not. When it comes to mass media and politics, though, media hype can take precedence over substance. And it seems to me that, as important an adult decision as voting is, we should be raising a generation of future voters who at least know something about all of this.

> *Reality leaves a lot to the imagination.*
>
> —John Lennon

You know, politics may be the perfect topic to study if you want an understanding of the social psychology of the mass media. For starters, politics is serious business in that what politicians do matters to the people they govern. But political information is complex, and ordinary citizens mostly cannot learn about politics and government through firsthand experience. Enter the mass media where legitimate journalists try to do the service of supplying important information to their audiences. But in analyzing the events of the day, social psychology necessarily enters the picture. We see smart, successful people offering analysis and interpreta-tion—opinions—and we are swayed by those opinions. The media literacy knowledge needed to make the best decisions about all this political cov-erage really is quite high.

Thinking About What Goes On Behind the Scenes

Behind the scenes, pundits could be quite literally bought off by those who have financial interest in the politician or issue being covered. If not bought off, they may be influenced by other factors. For instance, networks may instruct teams of journalists to select the questions or issues that might generate the most emotional interest from viewers since their job is to keep an audience. Even reporters with good integrity can be influenced by the agenda of the commercial success of the network, magazine, or conglomerate they work for. On the other hand, there are factors that influence coverage for the good, such as independent awards and honors for journalistic integrity, and the ability of a report to be fact checked and analyzed by other news sources.

Political Coverage and Social Influence

Political coverage can shape how you think and about issues and candidates. For instance, if you read the headlines, you would infer that at a friend's party you should not yell out, "Recycling bin! Why bother!" When we hear so often about "going green," global warming, Al Gore's Nobel Prize, and so on, it tells us what behaviors are socially acceptable, especially for "people like us," however we construe that. There are other social cues we respond to in the media. Polls are a good example. If a candidate is ahead in the polls, that carries momentum because it puts consensus behind the candidate who is out front, inviting voters to jump on the winning bandwagon. Another example involves the social cues we receive from watching pundits discuss and debate in the media. News commentators often talk among themselves, and the reaction each commentator and each position provokes from the panel gives us social information. It suggests whether we'll be likely to be rewarded or punished socially for holding similar views. Furthermore, since one motivation for watching political coverage is keeping up with current information and common beliefs, we may adopt the perspective of a pundit we heard on television hoping it will play well around the proverbial water cooler the next day.

The Language of Persuasion

What factors might persuade us to adopt the perspective of a particular pundit we see on TV or on the Internet? One answer is how the pundit "frames" the issue. To frame something means to place it in perspective. For example, is a particular drop in the stock market a "blip," a "crash," or a "meltdown?" Are Democrats liberals or progressives? Are Republicans conservatives or right-wingers? Is gay marriage a political, religious, or financial issue, or none of the above? When you frame an issue, you are

SOCIAL PSYCHOLOGY OF POLITICAL COVERAGE   193

telling people what to think about it. From a social psychological perspective, reporting carries with it certain social inferences. For instance, if the press consistently reports on gay marriage, it sends the social message that gay marriage is an issue many people care about. That may or may not be true, but either way it causes you to think that if others care so much about it, maybe you should care about it too. This is a form of agenda setting as discussed in Chapter 6. The media set the agenda by defining what issues are important enough to talk about, and by inference, what most people are concerned about. This type of political agenda setting has been shown to be persuasive to viewers, influencing what they report caring the most about. Not to mention that it encourages you in general to conform to the opinions you see broadcast consistently. If four perspectives on gay marriage are typically discussed, you might choose one of those based on factors like your similarity to the people who hold the particular view in question. Of course, there are more than four ways to think about gay marriage, but particularly if you are only shallowly processing the messages broadcast (taking the peripheral route), it might pretty much seem like there are only four.

Let's take a deeper look at persuasive language. If I call the stock market drop a crisis, I am implying any number of things. For instance, I'm implying that there is cause for concern, that you may be hurt either now or in the future, and even that people who understand finance have judged that what occurred was a crisis. If it is the responsibility of journalists to inform the public on matters that are in their interest to know, then it can be very appropriate and responsible to call a particular event a financial crisis. Politicians are often the primary purveyors of persuasion and the press must navigate that minefield. On the other hand, if you as a news source call an event a crisis in order to increase your ratings or sales, then it's a very different situation. Then your coverage becomes like those sensational promos for local news that ask questions like, "Is our water supply toxic? We'll answer that at 11." Just as lobbyists for businesses manipulate politicians, businesses and politicians sometimes manipulate the press directly and intentionally. I make these points not for their own sake but in the context of a discussion of media literacy. If you don't know these things are possible, you're not able to read what you see nearly as well.

From our perspective as an audience, there is no magic filter that helps us see through the persuasive language. For example, think about the difference in framing when you use the terms "pro-choice" and "anti-choice" versus the terms "pro-abortion" and "anti-abortion" or "pro-life" and "anti-life." If you support *Roe v. Wade* are you for reproductive rights, a woman's right to choose, or a pro-abortion position? Which is most accurate? There is no litmus test for accurate political language. Beyond that, there is no single political reality out there. The inherent ambiguity of the topic allows ample room to manipulate perceptions. And probably we just accept whatever language we are used to hearing. There are also those who clearly use language in order to be provocative. For example, when conservative Alaska radio host Eddie Burke referred to organizers of the "Alaska Women Reject Palin" rally as "a bunch of socialist baby-killing maggots," he presumably knew that was inflammatory language. Some pundits offer extreme views and make inflammatory statements in order to get attention and thus boost ratings.

If your job were to write a headline about the news that a senator was sleeping with a woman other than his wife, what would you write? What would be fair? The same event can be labeled a scandal, a private matter, or irrelevant information by different news sources. The very fact that we believe it is our business to write or say *anything* about it is a judgment. There is a whole lot of gray area in determining what constitutes the public's need to know about a given story. What is for sure—at least to me as a social psychologist—is that the decisions that are made influence how the public understands the story and how they potentially act on the news.

Political Ads

During an election year, the public is exposed to many political advertisements and there has been debate about whether negative or positive ads are more effective. Greer and Greer[2] emphasize that people do not necessarily remember the content of an ad, but they remember their own mental construction of the content of the ad. For example, the researchers studied memory for both positive and negative radio ads about both Republicans and Democrats. They found that people remembered information in the positive ads relatively well. However, for the negative ads, people tended to fill in their own opinions without necessarily realizing that they were doing so. Emotional content is used in the media in order to get people's attention; however, as this study shows, it sometimes may backfire. This actually reminds me of a study by Brad Bushman and Colleen Phillips. They studied memory for products advertised during violent TV programming and found that, as the article's title puts it, "If the Television Program Bleeds, Memory for the Advertisement Recedes."[3] Watching violent programming decreases memory for the products advertised during these programs. The authors suggest that part of the reason for this is that violence can induce anger and anger management, both of which interfere with memory.

I would say that the same is true for political ads. I know that some attack ads make me angry!

Interestingly, these days one can avoid ads by using a service like TiVo. However, I have noticed that TV and Internet news sources actually cover and analyze the day's top political ads, making them harder to avoid. Sometimes, thankfully, political comedy shows lampoon the ads, helping us laugh off the anger they may produce. For example, during the Democratic primary race of 2008, Senator Hillary Clinton ran an ad suggesting that when the phone rings in the White House at 3 A.M., we need a president with the experience and judgment to respond to such a call. *Saturday Night Live* spoofed the Clinton ad, showing Senator Clinton answering the phone wearing curlers in her hair, night cream on her face, and a grandmotherly robe. In one such parody, President Obama phones Senator Clinton at 3 A.M. to ask her what he should do about the emergency.

The Colorful Language of Getting Elected

I remember discussions during the presidential primary of 2008 in which the press referred to Obama voters as the "latte-sipping" crowd and Clinton voters as the "beer drinking" crowd. Later, Republican vice-presidential nominee Governor Sarah Palin referred to herself as a "Hockey mom," and John King of CNN used the term when mapping out voter demographics. Terms like "hockey mom," "latte-sipping crowd," and the "boutique" voters versus the "Joe Six Pack" demographic are characterizations that alter perceptions. People like familiarity and consistency. Voters ask themselves, "Am I like the beer drinkers or the latte sippers? Which group is more socially powerful, acceptable, or impressive? Do people like me vote for this candidate?" and it potentially influences their views. In the election of 2008, Americans decided that rather than voting for the "maverick," they would choose the candidate who told them "Yes, we can!"

Front-Page News?

Another factor that influences perception revolves around which stories are covered and how much attention each story is given. "Front page news" literally means a story is important because it was placed on the front page of a newspaper, while a story that is "buried" is put toward the end of the newspaper section and might also be covered with less detail. Whether a story gets buried or gets presented as front page news is up to the journalists—the reporters, the editors, and other staffers at the newspaper. The same basic premise holds for television news shows that highlight the importance of certain news by making issues "top stories," or labeling them with a red banner that reads "breaking news." A red "breaking news" banner implies that this news is something you need to know about. This is another form of agenda setting.

In the final weeks leading up to the 2008 U.S. presidential election, a widely covered story involved the McCain campaign's objection to Barack Obama's use of the phrase "lipstick on a pig." Many reporters suggested that this lipstick story was a diversion from more substantive topics, and yet much time and energy was devoted to covering it. The choice to make this story "front page news" might have made a difference in how some citizens viewed the candidates, and thus potentially influenced the election.

As in other chapters, we see that because we are a media-saturated culture it is in our best interest to be media literate. Viewers should understand the many ways that political coverage frames the public debate. After all, what we're talking about here is the relationship between government leaders and citizens. Leaders will be elected, laws will be passed, and your tax money will be spent, so political coverage is relevant to everyone. Those who are ignorant of these issues make themselves vulnerable to manipulation.

Pointing out that journalists and how they cover stories have a lot of power to shape the way ordinary citizens think is not an indictment of journalism. To be sure, there seem to be a lot of persuasive pitches being offered in the world of political coverage. But recall that I started the chapter by celebrating Tim Russert's contribution to his audience and his country. The best journalists have to be both terribly smart and terribly articulate. Simultaneously, they must be informed and nuanced thinkers and be able to translate what they understand back into simple but strong language.

Florida, Florida, Florida

A case in point occurred on the night of the 2000 presidential election. The candidates were Al Gore and George W. Bush and no one realized at the time that the race would be as close as it was—so close, in fact, that there are still those who think that Gore actually won! Tim Russert, amid the confusion of an election night that would later turn into more of an election *month*, had the sharpness of mind to realize that the election would come down to the state of Florida. He scribbled electoral college math on a white board and finally erased it all and simply wrote "Florida, Florida, Florida." That white board is now in the Smithsonian Institution. Russert himself was named one of the 100 most influential people in the world by *Time Magazine* in 2008 and that "Florida, Florida, Florida" moment was named by *TV Guide* one of the 100 greatest moments in television history.

Great journalism takes an incredibly complex world and a mess of potential manipulations and sorts it out for the citizens it serves. And ideally, it does not end with the journalistic commentary, but begins there as the citizens use journalistic analysis to start their own conversations, their own political action and thinking. It takes a media literate audience to tell the difference between great journalism and, well, something else. Here's a case in point.

"Rush Limbaugh Is a Hole"

In 2008, a story broke about Senator John Edwards having an extramarital affair with his one-time videographer, Rielle Hunter. Edwards's wife Elizabeth had long been an esteemed public figure, in part due to her husband's earlier vice-presidential and presidential candidacies, her status as a lawyer and advocate, and her ongoing battle with cancer. This is how Rush Limbaugh responded to the news about the Edwards affair on his radio show:[4]

> We've been told that Elizabeth Edwards is smarter than John Edwards. That's part of the puff pieces on them that we've seen. Ergo. If Elizabeth Edwards is smarter than John Edwards, is it likely that she thinks she knows better than he does what his speeches ought to contain and what kind of things he ought to be doing strategy-wise in the campaign? . . . In other words, could it be that she doesn't shut up? . . . It just seems to me that Edwards might be attracted to a woman [background laughter] whose mouth did something other than talk.

Shortly thereafter on MSNBC's *Countdown with Keith Olbermann*, Keith called Rush out for these comments, saying:

> What better pre-pubescent dream of genital-waving dominance over all the women in the world than to blame the intelligence of a woman for her husband's infidelity? What a pure sentiment to share with the less-well-recompensed losers who comprise your audience than to dismiss their failures as husbands, as men, Rush, on the woman? I mean, . . . you wouldn't want an intelligent woman around you maybe to keep that dream job that you blew at ESPN so instead of sitting around in a radio studio making fun of a cancer victim somebody somewhere might still care about your opinion of the National Football League and permit you to be on television. Oh, no! Nothing worse than having an intelligent woman around, Rush. Rush Limbaugh is a hole!

Keith Olbermann was originally hired as a straight reporter by MSNBC, but, as his comments to Rush Limbaugh suggest, he changed his approach to include commentary and analysis, including Edward R. Murrow–inspired "special comment" segments. *Countdown with Keith Olbermann* is currently one of the most-watched news shows on the air and its special comment section was recently spoofed on *Saturday Night Live* where Olbermann was played by Ben Affleck. I offered the exchange about Elizabeth Edwards to bring up the notion that modern political coverage has expanded to make a place for voices who want to offer their open, unbridled opinions. Perhaps to some extent offering an opinion is more honest and less artificial than promising an unbiased report. But where is the line between reporting and analysis, analysis and punditry, punditry and propaganda, you might ask? From a media literacy standpoint, what's important is that ordinary citizens can generate informed opinions, not that we should all align on one "right answer." To further explore the various roles journalists can play in politics, I offer the following analysis in which Sam Boyd of the *American Prospect*[5] discusses where MSNBC's Rachel Maddow stands on the journalistic landscape:

> Maddow is not a Tim Russert or a Chris Matthews—an ostensibly nonpartisan interviewer who badgers politicians and policy-makers about contradictions in their records. Nor is she a Rush Limbaugh or a Glenn Beck—an attack dog who deals in calculated anger, bluster, and outrage. She's no mild-mannered liberal like Alan Colmes or a veteran observer like Wolf Blitzer or David Gregory. Maddow has broken the broadcasting mold . . . . She is liberal without apology or embarrassment, bases her authority on a deep comprehension of policy rather than the culture warrior's claim to authenticity, and does it all with a light, even slightly mocking, touch.

In late 2008, Bill O'Reilly of Fox vied with Keith Olbermann and Rachel Maddow of MSNBC for top ratings. These Fox and MSNBC anchors are seen as partisan for the right and left, respectively. Meanwhile, CNN offered *Campbell Brown: No Bias, No Bull* as straight talk without the partisan bias.

The Partisan Part of the Picture

There is some meaningful social psychology to explore behind the idea of partisan news coverage. When you tune in or log on, there is a choice in the perspective of the source where you find your political information. And modern news outlets seem aware of this, often commenting on each other's coverage. Some outlets are considered highly partisan. Whatever your political bent, all of this opens up a really exciting debate with some fascinating questions. What is the effect on viewers when programs or whole networks are seen as partisan? If networks or shows are partisan, have they taken their stance in order to increase their ratings? I don't claim to have all the answers, but just having the debate is an excellent exercise in media literacy.

For starters, social psychologists have long documented a basic tendency people have to divide the world into "us" versus "them"—called the ingroup and outgroup, respectively—and the consequences of those divisions. Studies show that even when we randomly assign people to two groups, you will like the members of your own random group more and you will give them more resources when you have the opportunity. It's kind of like extending your "me" bubble out so that you treat the people who are "yours" better. You favor them, you like what they say. There's a classic study in social psychology that showed the same quotation will be liked more if attributed to a favored political figure like Abraham Lincoln than if the same quotation is attributed to a less favored person. So even if a journalist from a show or network you think is on "the other side" said something sound, you might well reject it because you see it as negative or dumb just because it came from them. Research has also demonstrated a hostile media bias—the perception that media reports are biased against "your side."

Social psychology can help us dig deeper into what happens when news sources are seen as taking sides—either Republican or Democrat. The "us" versus "them" divide we find in news coverage is supported by sound social psychological theory. For one thing, we like people more who share our attitudes, including beliefs and values. If you take a group of people and measure their attitudes, you can reliably predict that they will like other people who share those attitudes. It doesn't matter if you do the measurement before they meet these other people or after, the phenomenon is robust. The total proportion of similarity you share with a person predicts your degree of liking for that person. It follows then, for news coverage, that if we like certain journalists, if we share a high degree of similarity with them, then we will want to watch their shows. We want to "spend time with them" so to speak because it will make us feel good and bolster our confidence in our own attitudes. One reason for this is that finding a journalist, show, or Web site that agrees with our perspective validates us. It shows that smart, successful people agree with us and that we therefore must have good judgment and a solid grip on reality, or at least that our conclusions are "normal."

It's also true that we find dissimilar attitudes repulsive; in other words, liking decreases to the degree that two people don't think the same way. So, not only might we seek out journalists who think like we do, but we are repelled by those who hold dissimilar attitudes, beliefs, and values. Some theorists think that the strong negative emotions produced by dissimilarity are evolutionary throwbacks to the time when humans were hunter-gatherers. Basically, it paid to focus on potential enemies in that attacking them, preemptively even, eliminated the possible harm they might unleash on you.

In *Seducing America: How Television Charms the Modern Voter*,[6] Roderick Hart argues that watching political coverage serves our emotional desires—among them, the desire to feel clever and important. Television helps us feel informed and also it wards off our fear of being obsolete—making us feel a part of the process in an intimate way. Hart also thinks that cynicism is the natural language of political coverage on television and so encourages political cynicism in viewers. He worries that watching political coverage deepens cynicism and substitutes for real involvement.

The bottom line for mass media outlets may well be their actual bottom line. In a media climate where networks look for "niche audiences"—special interest groups—what bigger news niche audiences could there be than Republicans and Democrats? So, it may be smart from a money-making perspective to supply sources of partisan reporting.

Tapping the Psychology of Party Affiliation

I have to say that I have often found it a distasteful premise that there are only two kinds of people in the world—Republicans and Democrats (okay, maybe three if you count Independents). Surely the world is more complex than that! Well, research tends to go against my sensibilities on this one. There is a strong body of evidence accumulating that there are reliable differences in a number of domains based on political party affiliation. Personality research indicates that liberals tend to prefer "flexibility over stability and progress over tradition."[7] There is also a growing body of research that supports the utility of the republican-democratic distinction, even at the physical level. See what you think.

Your Body Is Taking Sides

A group of political scientists[8] believe that a person's physical makeup can predict his or her party affiliation. These researchers showed scary pictures like spiders and maggots to self-described Republicans and Democrats. They measured skin sweat, which is a sign of the fight or flight response, and found that the Republicans had more pronounced startle responses than Democrats. Then they startled participants with loud noises and measured blinking—another startle response. They found that Republicans blinked more than Democrats in response to the noise. Those who startled more easily tended to have more conservative views on political hot-button issues such as the Iraq war and immigration.

The scientists concluded that people who are more sensitive to physical threats are also more sensitive to psychological threats and therefore take a more defensive, risk-averse stance on political issues. In an interview[9] about their research, the authors said that they were not trying to characterize conservative threat responses as better or worse than the those of liberals. One could argue that it is risky to ignore threat as easily as arguing that it is weak to be too frightened by threat. The broader characterization is that some people are more risk-focused and more risk-averse than others. If you have the perspective that something is risky, you may well react differently to it than someone who is not focused as much on the risk factor, but on other factors. For example, those who think about immigration in terms of risk will make different decisions from those who think about it in terms of social justice. Politicians can capitalize on this knowledge by evoking fear and suggesting that they are the only ones who can save you from disaster.

Manipulating Fear of Death Changes Political Positions

One study demonstrates that whatever your party affiliation, reminders of your own mortality can change how you view a candidate. Social psychologists Solomon, Greenberg, and Pyszczynski[10] and their colleagues have studied the influence of thinking about death on political outcomes. In one investigation, they had 100 participants think about television and another 100 think about the September 11, 2001, terrorist attacks; then the researchers asked them about their opinions of then President George W. Bush. When thinking of a neutral topic, the participants did not approve of Bush or his policies in Iraq, but in a dramatic reversal, thinking about 9/11 created very strong approval of Bush and his policies in Iraq. This group of researchers has also demonstrated that thinking about death caused increases in wanting to vote for Bush versus John Kerry in the 2004 presidential election. These scientists noted that as a matter of public record, it was a Bush campaign strategy to remind the public of the terror attacks of September 11 and the concept of domestic insecurity.

In their book *In the Wake of 9/11: The Psychology of Terror*, Pyszczynski, Solomon, and Greenberg use terror management theory to explain the pattern of reactions that results from thinking about your own death— that is, "mortality salience." Since we are the only animals who anticipate and are terrorized by the specter of our own deaths, we develop coping strategies to deal with this fear. Fear of death makes us more likely to cling to charismatic leaders who reinforce a worldview in which our great and right country wages an epic battle against "evildoers." These characterizations assuage our fears and bolster our self-esteem by making us feel part of something meaningful that is bigger and more enduring than we are. Furthermore, people with high self-esteem do not need to stomp down others in order to make themselves feel better. Aside from whether the candidate's positions make sense from a perspective of governing, they make sense from a psychological standpoint because such positions can win elections.

Another crucial aspect of the psychology of terror management theory is that by its nature it is not conscious. Here, we return to our theme of media manipulation without awareness. When a political strategy causes citizens to focus on death, they are not aware that their current feelings or arousal level have changed. In fact, the effect is stronger when tested after a time delay. I must underline, the theory is not that we look to the candidate who is rationally more capable of being a strong leader; rather, we look to the candidate who offers rhetoric that soothes our fears. As a case in point, President Bush's policies in Iraq were widely criticized by Republicans as well as Democrats and were mirrored in very low approval ratings by citizens. Arguably, poor leadership by President Bush made the world more vulnerable to terror, so it was not what he really offered the country that was appealing but rather the very astute use of rhetoric based on the psychology of fear. What is clearest to me as someone interested in advancing media literacy is that there is no doubt that politicians and journalists take advantage of this psychological information when wondering what will make their target audience respond most passionately.

Pushing the Hot Button: Emotion Versus Reason

Psychologists have long studied emotions and found that they are highly motivating. In fact, psychologists assume an inextricable link between emotion and motivation. Fear, as we have seen, is one of the most basic emotions and one that has been manipulated by the media and by politicians. Social psychologist Jack Brehm has studied the utility of emotions, citing, for example, the idea that anger motivates a response to the provocation while sadness may tend to motivate disengagement or withdrawal.

Research in political psychology has compared the relative influence of emotions versus knowledge in forming political opinion. Drew Westen of Emory University and his colleagues[11] were curious as to whether emotions or ideas would win out in voters' assessments of the Clinton-Lewinski scandal. This scandal revolved around a sexual relationship between then-President Clinton and a young White House intern, Monica Lewinski, and whether Clinton lied about it. The researchers measured people's emotional reactions to President Clinton, to the Democratic and Republican parties, and to affairs in general. Months later, the researchers asked the same people to make a factual assessment as to whether Clinton had met the criteria for impeachment set by the U.S. Constitution. Eighty-five percent of the time, they were able to predict how voters responded to the factual question from knowing how they felt about the issue. The scientists concluded that what voters *feel* and not the facts predict their political beliefs and actions.

You Can't Fight Feeling with Fact

Sometimes our attitudes are based primarily on facts—for example, if we choose which car to buy based solely on gas mileage. What the participants in the Clinton-Lewinsky study described above demonstrated was that they had emotion-based attitudes. Those who believed Clinton met the criteria for impeachment based their assessments not on knowledge of the criteria but on a dislike for Clinton. Social psychologists who study persuasion have long found in their research that you can't change an emotion-based attitude with facts. In fact, research actually shows that when you present facts that run contrary to people's feelings about a candidate, it actually motivates people to justify their endorsement of the candidate. That cognitive dissonance and justification, in turn, causes their original feelings to be even stronger.

In his book "The Political Brain: The Role of Emotion in Deciding the Fate of the Nation," Westen describes research in which he and his colleagues performed brain scans on Democrat and Republican partisans as they read contradictory statements attributed to John Kerry and George W. Bush just prior to the 2004 presidential election. The partisans were able to identify the contradictions in the opposing party's statements. However, when they read inconsistent statements from their own party's leader, they did not see the contradictions. Their brain scans showed that they went through a process of being threatened by the contradictory information, then attempting to regulate that emotion, then resolving the conflict. One of the main theses of the "Political Brain," is the notion that we think of people as rational decision makers when emotions are what is central to our decision-making processes. In other words, rather than being *rational*, it's perhaps more fitting to say that we are *rationalizers*. When we hear something threatening, we rationalize and we are not aware we are doing it. By now, I hope this sounds familiar to you.

Emotions Have a Place in Decisions

All of this is not to say that emotions have no legitimate role in decision making. Psychologists who study emotional intelligence find that, contrary to the accepted position that the best decisions are purely rational, the decisions that are objectively stronger tend to balance emotion and rationality. For example, if you chose to buy a car by making a list of all the "facts"—the crash test reports, gas mileage, and so on—this would not at all guarantee that you would be choosing the car that is best for you. However, persuasive media coverage seeks to manipulate the power of emotions to influence decision making. For example, associating a candidate with someone undesirable—even in the most shallow way—can change citizens' views of the candidate in part because they are processing in a peripheral way. Smear ads are an attempt to associate the candidate in a very basic way with whatever evokes a negative emotional response, while positive ads tend to evoke greater feelings of engagement with constituents. Videos of candidates hanging out with voters, bowling and drinking beer, are intended to capitalize on the finding that voters prefer what is familiar to them and to trust candidates who are familiar or "like me." Though it is a tenuous notion that a candidate for president is ever very much like the average voter (or whether, indeed, they should be), staffers know that this is a profitable illusion because it presses all the right emotional buttons.

Hey Good-Lookin', Let's Talk Politics!

Speaking of the psychology of form over substance, perhaps nowhere is that more evident than when one analyzes the power of physical attractiveness to win the hearts and minds of people. Attraction theory says that we like people who make us feel good. Of course, there are lots of ways people can make you feel good, including the aforementioned shared attitudes, but physical attractiveness is a particularly potent motivator. This argument actually works both for candidates and for the journalists who cover them.

For example, CNN's Anderson Cooper made *People Magazine's* 2005 list of "sexiest men alive." The female reporters and anchors on Fox News have also raised commentary due to their conspicuous brand of physical attractiveness. Some have called them the "news babes," "anchorettes," and "foxy ladies" while wondering aloud at their collective degree of blondeness. Believe it or not, researchers have studied blondeness on TV and found that it is much more common than in the real world, probably due to its association with youth and attractiveness. Though the physical attractiveness of the Fox "news babes" surely helps garner an audience, it has called into question their credibility. There is a difference between someone who seems to represent the stereotype "babe" and someone—for example, like MSNBC's Nora O'Donnell—who is attractive but whose appearance is professional. Research has shown that when it comes to physical attractiveness, people differentiate between "attitude prototypes" like "the babe"— empty headed and shallow—and competent, attractive professional women like Nora O'Donnell or Maria Shriver. While attractiveness in general is an asset, it can become a liability when it is presented in such a way that it undermines the respectability and credibility of the source.

To continue our discussion of the power of physical attractiveness in politics, let us turn to a historic example, the 1960 Nixon-Kennedy presidential debates. These contests marked the first televised presidential debates in U.S. history. Perhaps because of the newness of televising debates, Nixon did not take his physical appearance as seriously as would a modern candidate. He was recovering from an illness and had lost twenty pounds, and he refused the offer of makeup. Some said he was pasty, sweaty, and surly looking, and that he had a five o'clock shadow. Kennedy, on the other hand, looked tanned, healthy, and confident. Kennedy, of course, had Nixon beaten by a long shot in both the handsome and the charming categories. Because of all this, those who listened to the first debate on the radio judged Nixon the winner, whereas those who watched the debate on television (which, remember, was a new thing) judged Kennedy to have won.

All of this may be hard to imagine in an era when there is so much visibility for politicians. Pictures and videos of modern candidates are ubiquitous. If you want to hear or see a particular comment from a particular day, there are many sources readily available. For example, if I want to see any part of the first presidential debate of 2008 between McCain and Obama, I know I can go to YouTube and any number of other sites and find that video. I can save the debate coverage on my DVR and burn it to a disk. I can search on endless blogs and Web sites, or through magazines or even on TiVo or my iPod and watch videos of the event itself and of discussions and commentaries on the event—even those from ordinary citizens. In terms of media coverage of politics, it is a completely different world from the one pre-1960.

In Politics as in Romance, Looks Matter

Although we like to say that looks do not matter, years of social psychological research documents just the opposite. For example, research has shown that college students matched up on dates want to see their date again only if the date is physically attractive; other features such as shared interests are irrelevant. Also well documented by research, people generally believe that "what is beautiful is good." In other words, if a person is good-looking we attribute a whole host of other positive characteristics to him ranging from the belief that he has great social skills and is fun to be around to having great intelligence and even great character! Simply put, when we see good-looking outsides, we infer that the person is also better inside.

What are the consequences of mass media's role in politics vis-à-vis attractiveness and other physical characteristics of candidates? In October of 1992, *Time Magazine*'s cover featured the top three presidential candidates of that year: George H. W. Bush, Bill Clinton, and Ross Perot. The image contrasted the relatively handsome, strong appearances of Clinton and Bush with a silly, big-eared image of Perot. Not only did the cover mock his big ears but also his height since Clinton and Bush were nose to nose, while Perot's head poked up between the two, dwarfed by comparison. The cover became an iconic representation of Perot as physically inferior to Clinton and Bush. In fact, this joke at the expense of Perot's height represents a political reality: there has been a relationship between height of (male) presidential candidates and their electability, with the taller candidate winning about two-thirds of the time.

In a skit on *Saturday Night Live*[12] Ross Perot, played by comedian Dana Carvey, made fun of the notion that his physical appearance was an important issue:

> I got funny ears—fine! Okay? So, let's have a debate on my ears, okay, is that what you want? Okay, here's the deal on my ears—large oversized lobes, filled with wax and covered with thousands of spiky hairs! Are you happy? You happy? You got your lead story? You go do your story on that—I'm gonna talk about real issues.

Now, Myth #665: that I'm short. Let-let's just run with that premise for a minute. I-I-I find it fascinating that everybody's going bonkers about my height, when this country's going down the tubes like crack through a goose! Now, let's just, let's just accept your premise that I'm short! Do you call 5″-5′ short? 'Cause that's what I am, see? Do you realize that if 68% of the women in this country took a shower with me, they'd be looking up at me? Now, if that's short, then fine, go write your midget article while I save this country from ruin, okay? Case closed.

Today, media-savvy political staffers make efforts to present their candidates' physical appearance to its best advantage. In the televised presidential debates of 2004, care was taken to remove John Kerry's height advantage over George W. Bush. (Kerry is 6′4″, while Bush is 5′11″). John McCain, skin cancer survivor, reportedly spent $5,000 a year on makeup during the 2008 presidential campaign. Of course, sometimes fussing over your looks gets attention as well, as was the case when the media reported that Senator John Edwards spent $400 on a haircut and mockingly dubbed the senator "the Breck girl" for primping over his hair. And Republican vice-presidential nominee Sarah Palin was widely criticized for spending over $150,000 on clothes for herself and her family at high-end stores in the midst of one of the worst financial crises in American history—a story that may well have lost votes for the ticket.

The Role of Political Comedy in Public Discourse

Rage Against the McCain

In late September, 2008, less than two months before the presidential election, John McCain called comedian David Letterman personally to cancel the appearance he was scheduled to make that very evening on *The Late Show*.[13] He told Dave that, due to the financial crisis, he needed to suspend his campaign and return to Washington. McCain didn't immediately return to Washington, but stayed in New York and recorded an interview with Katie Couric. Dave discovered this and played an internal news feed showing McCain having his makeup applied for the Couric interview while Letterman quipped, "Hey John, you need a ride to the airport?" Letterman continued to go after McCain: "Ladies and gentlemen, this is starting to smell. That's not the John McCain I know. It makes me think something has gone wrong with the campaign.... This is not the way a tested hero behaves. Somebody's putting something in his Metamucil."[14]

In the days that followed, again very close to the election, Letterman took every opportunity to fire away at McCain, noting, for example, that the road to the White House runs through his (Letterman's) show. He devoted some top ten lists to the McCain campaign[15] such as, "Top ten questions people are asking the John McCain campaign," which included: "Do you still think the fundamentals of our economy are strong, genius?" And the top ten messages left on Sarah Palin's answering machine: "McCain again; do you remember where I parked the Straight Talk Express?" and "Hi, Katie Couric here. Have you thought of a Supreme Court case yet?" (The latter referred to an interview in which Governor Palin was asked to name a Supreme Court decision besides *Roe v. Wade* and could not.) The *Late Show* even presented special segments called, "A message from Sarah Palin," in which they spliced together debate footage to make sentences the governor had never said such as, "Oh, man, it's so obvious that I'm not ready to be vice president." And "I have no experience. John McCain should get rid of me." On the other side of party lines, Letterman had done past top ten lists about Obama such as the "Top Ten Ways to Mispronounce Barack Obama," which included "Bahama Mama," and "Dalai Lama."

Seriously Funny: Political Comedy Blurs the Line Between News and Entertainment

But comedy is just entertainment, right? Comedians have no real role in politics or public policy. Actually, major figures like Letterman and Jay Leno, Jon Stewart, and Stephen Colbert have strong followings, and when they slash a political figure with rapier wit, they can draw blood. There is a growing body of scholarly research that demonstrates very real political effects of political comedy. For example, when a political comedian mocks a candidate, the candidate's ratings show declines.

Politicians have made news by announcing their candidacies on political comedy shows. For example, Senator John Edwards announced his presidential candidacy on *The Daily Show* and McCain announced on *The Late Show with David Letterman*. An appearance on the top comedy shows is now a must for presidential candidates and when well timed can create a bump in their poll numbers. A study conducted in California found evidence for the "Colbert bump"—a month after an appearance on *The Colbert Report*, candidates got significantly higher campaign contributions than those who had not appeared on the show. Such appearances also give Americans a chance to see the candidate in a different light, interacting with a host that the viewers have come to like and trust.

In the world of political comedy, one show stands out as a unique and endlessly intriguing case study in the social psychology of political coverage. I'm talking about *The Daily Show with Jon Stewart. The Daily Show*, billed as "fake news" and claiming no journalistic responsibility, has a regular audience of around a million and a half viewers. The audience of political comedy shows like *The Daily* Show and its spin-off *The Colbert Report* tend to be relatively young and educated. These programs assume a working knowledge of current popular culture including people, events, and language. Since pop culture is, to a great extent, youth culture, it makes sense that younger viewers would learn more political information from political comedy shows than viewers who are older. If young people are more familiar with popular culture references and language, they should be able to understand, process, and remember the information presented better than older viewers.

Research has shown a relationship between watching *The Daily Show* and *Politically Incorrect with Bill Maher* and increased political knowledge, especially for younger viewers.[16] In 2007, the *New York Times*[17] reported that a survey by the Pew Center for the People and the Press revealed that those who were most knowledgeable about current events were likely to be viewers of *The Daily Show* and *The Colbert Report* whereas those who knew the least were likely to watch *Fox News* or local TV news. Scholarly research has also shown that more highly educated people learn more from political comedy shows than do less educated people. This is partly because more highly educated people have a greater knowledge base to build on and they also have stronger skills for processing that information.

For example, on October 2, 2008, the day of the vice-presidential debate between Senator Joe Biden and Governor Sarah Palin, Stephen Colbert of *The Colbert Report* began with this verbal headline, "Tonight: A debate between candidates for the most powerful office in the land: Dick Cheney's." You have to know enough and be sharp enough to construct social meaning from a statement like that. To really get the joke, you have to be aware of at least some of Dick Cheney's moves as vice president and be generally aware that Cheney tried to redefine and expand the role of the vice presidency. The joke probably gets funnier the more specific examples of Cheney's behavior you are familiar with and the degree to which you yourself question the political machinations of the Cheney vice presidency.

Faking It, or Faking Faking It? Or Is That Even the Right Question?

In interviews, Jon Stewart has claimed that *The Daily Show* is only in the business of telling jokes, that they don't have journalistic responsibilities and that they have no agenda of political influence. On the other hand, Lizz Winstead, co-creator of *The Daily Show*, told NPR that it is the satirist's job to be skeptical of politicians who have amassed power and to keep them in check with humor. *Newsweek* named Jon Stewart one of the twenty-five most influential voices in the 2004 presidential election. An Emmy and Peabody Award winner, *The Daily Show* has also won journalistic awards such as the Television Critics Award for outstanding achievement in news and information.

Now this is where I, as a social psychologist studying media influence, rub my hands together in glee. It's not because I want to reveal the sinister agenda of *The Daily Show*, *The Colbert Report*, or *Saturday Night Live*. Not at all! In fact, I'm a big fan of all of them. No, I get excited because this is one of the most brilliantly complex media literacy debates that we could have. We can start by asking what the intentions are of the host and writers. We can also talk about the idea that, regardless of intention, shows like these exert a real influence on political thought and action in our country. But I agree with political rhetoric scholar Aaron McKain[18] who says that it's not a simple black and white issue of whether *The Daily Show* is real or fake news. Instead, the intellectual exercise involves talking about how these new political comedies differ from other forms of news and what the implications of those differences are. For example, we tend to categorize network news as serious business, but a recent content analysis showed that traditional network news is relatively short on substance, emphasizing instead political "hoopla and hype."[19] Could there, in fact, be a reversal so that "real" news is more "fake" than the supposedly fake news? I can just imagine Jon Stewart delighting in the question, cupping his chin in his hands, grinning and asking, "Is fair foul and foul fair?"

PBS's Bill Moyers interviewed Jon Stewart in 2003 and 2007[20] to explore Stewart's views on political journalism and the place of *The Daily Show* in the journalistic landscape. Stewart explained that in the days of the Nixon-Kennedy debates, the media had the upper hand over politicians, but now the politicians have the upper hand. According to Stewart, the twenty-four-hour cable news networks "don't have time for journalism,"[21] and so end up just reading what the government feeds them. Others have noted that big media simply point their cameras at government and the big newsmakers and report what they are being given, rather than thoughtfully seeking out news on their own. Stewart goes on to describe what is essentially a kind of journalistic freedom that *The Daily Show* has, saying that they do not have to pretend to be objective.

Authenticity Matters

Now some may find a lack of pretense about objectivity to be an indictment of *The Daily Show*, but I think it speaks to one of the show's greatest attractions: the feeling of authenticity Stewart and his team capture. Interestingly, *Comedy Central* used the tagline, "Something approximating election news with something approximating honesty" on their *Daily Show/ Colbert Report* "Indecision 2008" Web site. When you think about it, it's a very weird thing—from a social perspective—to listen to straight reporters and wonder how they think or feel about what they're talking about. Reporters can seem robotic, cold, and distant when they are robbed of the power to interpret, analyze, and react to what they are reporting. Contrast this with Jon Stewart watching a news video with his audience and then looking horrified and yelling expletives at the video. He's modeling for the audience an opinion and a feeling about the rhetoric we all face on a daily basis.

Whether you agree with the specific opinion or not, it feels real while "real" news often feels fake. I think we want our journalists to react with human authenticity. After all, great reporters know the people they cover, they understand economics and government and politics better than we do as ordinary citizens. For one thing, it's their job to understand those things. For another, they had to be pretty smart—and by that I mean both book smart and people smart—to get a gig on TV. So we look at our screens at these smart, capable people and we wonder what they really think and that sucks the authenticity out of the transaction between journalist and audience. No wonder people find Jon Stewart so attractive.

The authenticity factor is part of what makes the top pundits attractive to their audiences. To be fair, it's probably what draws some people to more extreme perspectives like those of Rush Limbaugh as well. Even if we don't like what he's saying, we must admit that he appears to mean it. Although people have criticized the growing number of people—especially young, educated people—who get their news from political comedy shows, in "a landscape in which 'real' news is becoming increasingly harder to identify or define,"[22] I think it is actually an astute social judgment to choose a source that offers authenticity. Given the level of media literacy needed to even begin to sort through the complexities of political coverage, one element of the authenticity we seek is the honest voice of someone who can help us figure it all out. This excerpt from the Bill Moyers's interview of Jon Stewart addresses that issue:

> *Moyers*: "I do not know whether you are practicing an old form of parody and satire . . . or a new form of journalism.
>
> *Stewart*: Well then, that either speaks to the sad state of comedy or the sad state of news. I can't figure out which one. I think, honestly, we're practicing a new form of desperation where we just are so inundated with mixed messages from the media and from politicians that we're [the writers and cast of the show] just trying to sort it out for ourselves.[23]

I was in South America giving a presentation when Governor Palin was announced as Senator McCain's running mate in the 2008 presidential election. Not knowing who Governor Palin was, I missed the political comedy coverage that I usually watch at home. When I turned on CNN and discovered an international version of *The Daily Show*, I literally said aloud in my hotel room, "Thank God, some real coverage!" Then I laughed at myself because the statement sounded ridiculous. But I meant it. Since research has shown that *The Daily Show* offers as much substance as network news, maybe I'm not so crazy after all (or at least not for that reason.)

That's Funny: Analyzing Political Humor

Okay, now for some psychological analysis of political comedy. Some psychologists believe that when we laugh, we are releasing tension. While "real" news may increase our stress over serious topics like war, terrorism, and economic crises, "fake" news gives us a chance to release tension through laughter. Even if we're laughing at the absurdly bad way politicians sometimes take on serious issues, at least we're laughing. Furthermore, since humor is emotional, it has a special power to change attitudes beyond the power of the facts. When you mock someone, you get away with an attack by covering it with humor, hence the term "rapier wit"—a humorous attack that cuts like a blade. Such rapier wit is also powerful because—as we've seen—attitudes that are based on emotions are resistant to change through factual argumentation but are open to change through emotion-based persuasion. In addition, since humor accesses our emotional system and emotional information is easier to remember, that means we're more likely to remember what we see on a political comedy show than on a traditional news report. This may be one reason those studies show greater political knowledge among viewers of political comedy. Another reason is that it's far easier to remember something presented in an interesting way than something presented in a boring way.

At a McCain rally in the fall of 2008, an audience member told McCain that she didn't trust Obama and thought he was an Arab. McCain replied that Obama was not an Arab, that he was a decent family man and not to be feared. *Saturday Night Live* parodied the event by having a disoriented and messy-haired "Crazy McCain Rally Lady" interrupt *Weekend Update*, only to be talked down by anchors Seth Meyers and Amy Poehler. Crazy McCain Rally Lady made accusations such as "he converts with terriers" instead of "consorts with terrorists," and that she thought he was "muslin" instead of a Muslim. She also feared that he was half Egyptian and would turn the White House into a pyramid. On *The Daily Show*, Aasif Mandvey and John Stewart had a tongue-in-cheek discussion about the notion that one can be both an Arab and a decent man. The notion of Obama being a Muslim was a scare tactic used throughout the campaign. The satiric news coverage both mocked ignorance and raised the serious notion of fear of foreigners, especially Arabs and Muslims.

Political Comedy and Election 2008 Coverage

I'm writing in the days surrounding the 2008 presidential election, and it couldn't be a more perfect time to talk about the social psychology of political comedy. For one thing, this is a new world of political coverage that we live in. YouTube, offering twenty-four-hour accessibility to politics, media coverage, and public commentary is pretty much brand new. It didn't exist as we know it today in previous presidential elections. Blogging as we know it today is also brand new, too, in the grand scheme of things. The rise of cable over local and network news is another new phenomenon. And when you add all the issues I have already raised about how to interpret all this information that is available to us, it makes one's head spin. One way many people get some perspective on politics, in addition to some well-needed laughs, is by turning to political comedy.

Looking back on this election, I think one of the main things people will remember about what we saw in the media will be Tina Fey's spot-on parody of Republican vice-presidential nominee Governor Sarah Palin on *Saturday Night Live*. *SNL* is famous for its impressions of journalists and politicians like Darrell Hammond's amazing imitations of figures like President Bill Clinton and *Hardball's* Chris Matthews. In the fall of 2008, as fate would have it, the very talented Fey—longtime "co-anchor" of *SNL's* news spoof "Weekend Update"—also happened to resemble the Republican vice-presidential candidate. Fey parodied Palin's speeches, debate performances, and some interviews by Katie Couric that had been widely criticized in the media. When CNN's Wolf Blitzer and John King discussed the Fey impersonation,[24] Blitzer commented that he couldn't remember another time when *SNL* relied so heavily on direct quotes from the candidate to get laughs. King reported that behind the scenes, even Palin's own campaign staffers believed the Katie Couric interviews were disastrous. Of course, on the other side of the debate, one reason the Palin impressions were popular was because the candidate herself had developed a passionate following.

Videos of the Couric interviews and the Fey impersonation circulated on sites like YouTube and attracted millions of viewers. This example also highlights cross-coverage, when one news source discusses another—even a comedy source. Other examples of cross-coverage include *Hardball's* "Sideshow," segment where *SNL* skits are often chuckled over by Chris Matthews and his guests. The fact that "real" news sources regularly cover political comedy sketches speaks to their broad influence and appeal. So popular were the *SNL* political comedy skits during the 2008 election, that NBC launched a new show called *SNL: Weekend Update* that played on Thursday nights during the last month of the 2008 presidential campaign.

Make no mistake, *SNL's* political skits are very powerful. The staffers who work for the campaigns must watch the skits and try to diffuse negative characterizations. Because of the nature of humor, as we've discussed, portraying a candidate as an idiot in a political comedy skit can be much more damning than to question the candidate's intelligence or qualifications in a straight news story. Whereas one can attack a journalist's straight reporting or commentary, it doesn't play well to be affronted by a skit that is "all in fun." The McCain campaign tried to characterize Palin's disastrous interviews as "gotcha" journalism, but there was little they could say about the Tina Fey impersonation. In fact, the governor actually said she'd only *watched* the Fey impression but did not *listen* to it, probably at least in part so that she would not be asked to comment on the content.

SNL continued their brilliant parody with a spoof on the Biden-Palin vice-presidential debate. During the actual debate, when Palin and Biden shook hands, Palin could be overheard asking Senator Biden if she could

FIGURE 8.1. Jason Sudeikis of *SNL* mocked the inherent contradiction of Senator Biden's stance in the vice-presidential debate that he both considered John McCain a personal friend and found him unfit for office. Sudeikis spoofed Biden's position, saying, "Okay, let's be frank. John McCain—and again, this is a man I'd take a bullet for—is bad at his job, and mentally unstable."

call him "Joe." In the *SNL* parody of that debate, Palin asks Biden the same question and, when he answers in the affirmative, responds, "Okay, because I practiced a couple zingers where I call you Joe." In the debate, Senator Biden (see Figure 8-1) said he considered rival John McCain a personal friend, but he waged repeated attacks against the Republican presidential nominee. Jason Sudeikis, spoofing Biden,[25] said, "I love John McCain. He's one of my dearest friends. But, at the same time, he's also dangerously unbalanced . . . As my mother would say, 'God love him,' but he's a raging maniac."

The Power of Parody and Satire

Our modern mass media versions of political comedy stand on the strong shoulders of literary satirists. In 1729, Jonathan Swift published *A Modest Proposal: For Preventing the Children of Poor People in Ireland from Being a Burden to Their Parents or Country, and for Making Them Beneficial to the Public*, long considered one of the greatest examples of political satire in history. The crux of Swift's *Modest Proposal* is to attack the poverty problem in Ireland by encouraging poor Irish to sell their babies to the rich for food. In so doing it mocks political decision making and the attitudes of the day. Swift's *Modest Proposal* is a masterpiece because it brilliantly employs rhetoric to provoke an emotional response in the reader and thereby fuel political attitude change. For example, it provokes ire against Irish land-lords and pity for the poor, leaving readers in a trap that the author so expertly set. How can they disagree with his perspective when put in such a way?

Today's political comedy, such as the parody interviews on *The Daily Show* and *The Colbert Report* are in that same rhetorical tradition. When Colbert interviews a gay man with dark, provocative questions and offers him reasons to "go straight," he is doing a parody of news interviews while trying to make a point that there is folly in extreme social positions. Of course, *The Colbert Report* is one giant parody because Colbert's approach is to say the opposite of what he means while mimicking "his mentor" Bill O'Reilly. When a caricature artist draws a person's likeness, she amplifies individual characteristics. In the same way, the satire and parody done by political comedy shows identify legitimate points of concern through exaggeration.

In the midst of the parody and satire, Jon Stewart throws in a new brand of political interviews. Recently, he interviewed former prime minister of England, Tony Blair. The *London Guardian* covered the interview, noting that the "format of his [Stewart's] influential show allows him to sting with mockery and false chumminess."[26] The *Guardian* noticed that Stewart alternated between penetrating questions and diffusing the tension with humor. The *Guardian* also commented on the role of what they term our "satirical news show" in the landscape of American political coverage: "Perhaps it says something good about *The Daily Show*—or bad about the rest of the American television news media—that anyone might ever have expected a comedy talk show to penetrate deeply into a topic such as Blair's motivations for going to war in Iraq."[27]

Political Cartoons

Another historical precursor to the modern *SNL* skit or YouTube video is the editorial cartoon. Political cartoons are still around, though they have much more competition today with the aforementioned sources of political comedy. Let's take a look at a recent political cartoon and you can compare it to some of the other forms of political comedy we've been discussing (see Figure 8-2).

Without words (other than the candidates' name tags), this cartoon sends some pretty strong messages. Governor Palin looks vacuous, Senator McCain appears cranky, and the doctors seem concerned about the physical and mental stability of the pair. What a telling political state-ment! The facial expressions send some interesting social messages about

Chattanooga Times Free Press Bennett

FIGURE 8.2. This political cartoon from the *Chattanooga Times Free Press* questions John McCain's health, Sarah Palin's intelligence, and the wisdom of voting for their ticket—all in a single frame. The facial expressions of the four figures tell an interesting story. (Clay Bennet Editorial Cartoon ©2008 Clay Bennett. Used with the permission of Clay Bennett and the Washington Post Writers Group in conjunction with the Cartoonist Group. All rights reserved.)

the personalities and attributes of the candidates as well as the concern of the doctors. And the biggest punch line is probably the female doctor's choice to examine Palin's head rather than her heart. Like other forms of political humor, I think one can "get away with" more in a drawing than with words. If a pundit had come out and said, "McCain is too old. Palin is too daft," there would have been criticism. But somehow drawing a scene gives it a kind of constructed social reality that it's much harder to question. And the emotion-provoking value of the satiric meaning is more powerful than would be the direct statements it implies. Similarly, in the *SNL* skit of the vice-presidential debate, Joe Biden points at Sarah Palin and expresses with exasperation how many times he wanted to call her a dummy. But candidates can't do that and even journalists are limited in what they can say. They have to parse words carefully. Political cartoons and comedy skits don't have those constraints.

In the *SNL* spoof of the vice-presidential debate, PBS's Gwen Ifill (played by Queen Latifah) asks Palin how she and McCain will solve the economic crisis by being mavericks, to which Palin replies, "Ya know, we're going to take every aspect of the crisis and look at it and then we're gonna ask ourselves, 'What would a maverick do in this situation?' And then, ya know, we'll do that."[28] The audience laughs and Ifill makes a face in response. What messages does that parody send that would be much more difficult to get away with and much less effective if spoken openly? See if you can generate a list.

Taken together, these points are actually right on target with a debate the American voters have been engaged in: namely, whether our leaders should be "just like us" or whether they should be smarter than the average citizen. A now classic study by psychologist Martin Seligman tracked political speeches of presidential candidates between 1948 and 1984 and found a trend toward preferring "anti-intellectual" candidates. John Kerry, for example, was chided for sounding like a professor. (Wow, I guess professors like me should be really offended!) George W. Bush was elected, in part, due to his ability to be perceived as an average guy. On the other hand, Barack Obama got elected, though seen as a very intelligent man. Perhaps he found the balance between projecting likeability and intelligence.

Citizen Participation and the New Forms of Media

I'd like to end this chapter by noting how very different the role of the audience is becoming with the availability of new forms of media. Videos on sites like *YouTube, Colbert Nation*, and *Saturday Night Live*'s main Web page can garner millions of views. Additionally, viewers can submit comments about the videos, or their own response videos. CNN has a regular segment called iReport which plays videos that ordinary citizens have recorded of themselves sharing their views. New media are much more of a two-way street than traditional media. They are also much more in the moment compared to older forms of media.

Blogs, another a relatively new form of popular media, had their moments in the 2008 election as well. A blog started by a college student living with his mother has been given credit for launching Sarah Palin's vice-presidential bid. Professional blog sites like HuffingtonPost.com are regularly quoted on the top news shows, and bloggers are invited as guests on TV news.

And there were funny and fresh moments in the campaign when people used new media very effectively to get attention. Viral videos, so named because they spread like viruses, garner millions upon millions of views on the Internet. For example, as of this writing, the Web site viralvideochart.com reported that the pro-Obama music video "Yes We Can" had garnered over eighteen and a half million viewers and over 100,000 comments online. And remember that one of the ways the Obama campaign first received enthusiastic national attention was through the phenomenon that was "Obama girl." Then later there was a video in which Obama girl "battled" Rudy Giuliani's "Giuliani girl." And who could forget the instance when Paris Hilton responded to being included negatively in a political ad by creating her own ad in which she articulated an energy plan that sounded amazingly cogent?

Political campaigns are also taking advantage of (especially younger) constituents' habit of text messaging. Obama informed his supporters first about his choice of running mate using text messaging or e-mail, whichever the voter chose. Obama's Web site included links to new media sources such as Facebook, Twitter, LinkedIn, and Glee. In the second chapter I mentioned that young people prefer text messaging over e-mail because they can reach their friends wherever they are. The Obama campaign took advantage of new media use and profited by sending text messages to individual supporters. This astute use of the new media probably helped Obama with record registration of new voters and with voter turnout, which helped him win the election.

New forms of media are evolving rapidly. No doubt in future elections candidates who understand how to use new media most astutely will continue to be at an advantage. Voters with higher media literacy levels will be at an advantage as well. In the next chapter, I will give suggestions for becoming more media literate. And because dissecting political coverage requires particularly sharp media literacy skills, I will return to this topic as an example.

Section Four

REDEFINING FREEDOM IN A
MEDIA-RICH LANDSCAPE

Nine

FROM THE PASSENGER'S SEAT TO THE DRIVER'S SEAT

> We deal in illusions, man. None of it is true. But you people sit
> there day after day, night after night, all ages, colors, creeds.
> We're all you know. You're beginning to believe the illusions
> we're spinning here. You're beginning to think that the tube is
> reality and that your own lives are unreal. You do whatever the
> tube tells you. You dress like the tube. You eat like the tube. You
> raise your children like the tube. You even think like the tube.
> This is mass madness—you maniacs! In God's name you people
> are the real thing, WE are the illusion.
> —Fictional anchorman Howard Beale in the film *Network*[1]

In America, we spend two-thirds of our waking lives plugged into mass media. Our children spend more time staring at screens than they spend in school. Throughout this book, we have seen many examples of how we are powerfully influenced by mass media and how we are often unaware of this influence. For example, college students transported into the world of a story believed false assertions embedded in that story such as the idea that exercise weakens the heart and lungs. And while their confidence in these new beliefs lagged at first, over time they forgot where they learned the false information and their confidence rose to normal levels.

Of course, the social influence of the mass media goes beyond learning factual information either rightly or wrongly. We are bombarded by images and attitudes, constantly learning and constantly being persuaded. Our view of race and gender roles is informed by the stories and images we see before us on screens and pages every day. Kids watch ads showing that top athletes eat junk food and young girls are sex objects. Magazines spin illusions about domestic violence that do not serve their many readers who need help with a truly overwhelming problem. Violence is glamorized and sanitized. When we are transported by the world of fiction, our attitudes and beliefs change to be more consistent with ideas and claims that take place within the story. We suspend our disbelief and in so doing we open ourselves up to absorbing involuntarily the belief system dramatized in the fictional world[2,3] and to acting on those beliefs and ideas. Many times what we see on the screen provokes a change or a response outside our awareness. This is how the fantasy world of media shapes our realities.

We believe that though others are affected by mass media, we are not. Furthermore, fans of a particular medium are the least likely to believe its negative content has harmful consequences. For example, males who play more violent video games are the least likely to believe these games have harmful effects[iv] despite decades of scientific research suggesting that exposure to media violence increases aggression, hostility, and aggressive thoughts in those exposed.[5] Reading romance novels has been shown to increase negative attitudes toward condom use.

But there are also studies showing the benefits of exposure to positive health information incorporated into dramatic story lines. A team of breast cancer experts served as consultants on a Spanish language *telenovela* designed to educate viewers about this disease.[6] A study conducted after the program was aired showed that viewers had developed greater knowledge about breast cancer and were more likely to take positive steps such as calling 1-800-4-Cancer for information. Furthermore, viewers who identified with the characters in the *telenovela* were more greatly affected than those who identified less with the characters. We are moved by what we experience in mass media. Sometimes we are moved in positive directions and sometimes in negative ones, but media engage us deeply and have great power to change us. As Marshall McCluhan said, "All media work us over completely."[7]

I opened this chapter with a quote from Paddy Chayefsky's multiple Oscar winning drama *Network*. The American Film Institute ranked *Network* among the 100 greatest American films, and the Library of

Congress selected it for preservation in the *National Registry of Films* of cultural, historical, or aesthetic importance.

Even if you haven't seen *Network*, you probably know about one of its most famous scenes. Anchorman Howard Beale has had an epiphany: he sees the folly of a television industry unconcerned with quality and substance but focused on banalities designed to boost ratings. He sees the audience as sheep, eating up whatever the industry serves them. Beale tells his audience: "I don't know what to do about the depression and the inflation and the Russians and the crime in the street. All I know is that first you've got to get mad. You've got to say, 'I'm a HUMAN BEING, Goddamnit! My life has VALUE!' So I want you to get up now. I want all of you to get up out of your chairs. I want you to get up right now and go to the window. Open it, and stick your head out, and yell: 'I'M AS MAD AS HELL, AND I'M NOT GOING TO TAKE THIS ANYMORE!' "[8]

Network was released in the 1970s, and like Marshall McCluhan's *The Medium is the Message*, published in the 1960s, it has an uncanny resonance today. One of the marks of a fine work of art is its universality. The classics in literature and film have this universality. The astonishing part here is how Chayefsky and McCluhan both managed to write about mass media in a way that would continue to endure even as media and technology have changed so rapidly. One reason I think they both accomplished this was that they spoke about the underlying psychology and the basic relationship between people and mass media. Not only are these elements that have endured but they are what's fundamentally important to understand when approaching any form of media.

Now, I want to underline what might appear to be an unintended irony here but is actually an intentional one. In this chapter, I am asking you to rethink your relationship with mass media. In doing that, I am invoking a film and a book—two forms of mass media. This is no mistake. Chayefsky's and McCluhan's thinking has influenced, excited, and energized me. In exposing myself to their thinking, I am changed, and I think it's for the better. This book is not about defining media messages as bad; it's about defining them as powerful, persuasive, and influential. It's also about taking a look at how much of your time on this planet you spend hooked into other people's messages and how much time you devote to doing your own thing. To paraphrase Howard Beale, it's your life that is real. I'm not going to ask you to go scream out your windows (though, go ahead if you want). I'm going to gently suggest that if your life ever flashes before your eyes, I don't think you will want to see endless images of yourself staring into screens. We're happier when we're playing basketball, talking with our friends, or doing something creative. We're happier when we're getting into something we love like playing the guitar, volunteering for a cause we believe in, throwing a Frisbee at the park, or walking the dog.

There are absolutely delights to be had through the mass media. There are films, shows, and songs that have moved me and taught me things. My husband and I watch *The Daily Show* and we pause it and talk about the issues it raises or laugh and chatter about how funny a joke was. Just recently, I was hanging out at the university talking with my friends Dale and Kathy who are English professors, and Kathy played a segment from *The Daily Show* for us from the show's Web site. It was mocking the notion raised in the 2008 presidential campaign that there are two Americas: "real America," and "fake America." We laughed and talked about the ideas raised by the political satire. I know political comedy shows have started many such conversations around the country.

Today's technological advances also increase the ease of media access. TV shows can play on laptops, iPods, and iPhones all over. And media can sometimes offer unique experiences. My family plays games on the Nintendo Wii together. I love watching my daughter Regan swing her virtual tennis racquet. My son Jason and I have bonded while playing *Guitar Hero* together. I was proud of him when, at age six, he used the practice mode to painstakingly get better and better at the game. I've played *Guitar Hero* in Italy in the living room of my friends Carlo and Ximena, and I imagine I'll remember that experience for a long time. In my classroom, I play an NPR podcast of an interview with scientist Robert Sapolsky called "Does Age Quash Our Spirit of Adventure?" that excites me every time I hear it. And every time I play it, I can't wait to hear what my students will say about it. I play another delightful podcast called "Darwin and the Floating Asparagus," which always makes my students laugh but also teaches some things about history and psychology that are harder to teach in other ways.

Media messages are not uniformly bad or troubling. Again, my message is that media are powerful, persuasive and influential and that we are passively staring into screens more often than actively living our own lives. Given that this is the case, I have some recommendations. These ideas are designed to move you, as a consumer of mass media, from the passenger's seat to the driver's seat. I focus on making you more in control and less vulnerable to influence. Use these as a starting point, and customize them to fit your situation.

Recommendations

Always Assume that When You Are Plugged In, the Media
Are Persuading You

Dispense with the notion that media are "just entertainment" and do not influence us. This shift in perspective may seem inconsequential, but I believe this seemingly small change has the potential to make a significant difference in your life. The ancient Greek philosopher Heraclitus said that the nature of a thing is to hide its nature. Television shows, movies, video games, and songs may seem trivial, but they are not. The percentage of our lives that mass media now take up should tell us all we need to know about media's power over us.

Limit Your Exposure

Throughout this book, we have seen how media influence us outside of our awareness. Media can evoke reactions that are automatic and unconscious. This may be one reason we do not seem to think that media affect us, but that they do affect others. Other times, we may be conscious of media's influence over us, but deny it because we need to reduce the discomfort of cognitive dissonance.

Given the psychology of media influence, it follows logically that one major way to reduce it is to limit our exposure. There are many ways to approach this goal. I will offer a few tips. I will follow the model of the Ad Council's "Small Step" approach, based on the research that suggests that recommendations are more effective when people have suggestions for little ways they can change, rather than goals that seem too large to be doable.[9,10] For example, you might start by keeping a log of what you watch and when. Add up your exposure in, say, a week's time and see where you are. Then make a plan. You can start with little changes. You might decide, for instance, that you will watch a half hour or an hour less of TV per night. As a side note, Americans are sleep deprived, and sleep deprivation is correlated with reduced immune functioning, reduced concentration, and even obesity. You might simply decide to turn the TV off an hour earlier and go to bed earlier. I bet if you do, you will feel better almost immediately. Or you might decide to do some regular chores or read a book in the hour before you go to bed.

For children, the American Academy of Pediatrics recommends no more than one or two hours of screen time per day. Experts believe that simply limiting screen time in society will have positive effects such as reducing aggression.[11] As we have seen, increased screen time is also associated with other health factors such as increased obesity and reduced attention span in children. Clearly, one of the best things you can do for your children's health is to reduce their overall screen time. Also, when parents talk with their children about what they are seeing on the screen, and they criticize violent content, children have less interest in media violence and less aggressive attitudes.

An organization formerly known as TV Turnoff Network, now called the Center for Screen Time Awareness (at screentime.org) sponsors a media turnoff week every year in an effort to promote health and awareness of media effects. I have participated in TV Turnoff Week in the past, working with local schools on the initiative. I remember two things most strongly from these experiences: *(1)* that youth initially had very little idea what to do with themselves without electronic screens, and *(2)* that after an initial period of complaining, the participants were amazed and how good they felt and wanted to turn off the screens more often. Isn't it telling that our youth are so plugged into the matrix of mass media that they honestly don't know what to do without it? The organizers even published lists of TV-free activities (wash the dog, fly a kite, climb a tree, etc.) to give kids an idea of where to start without media.

Russ Geen, the social psychologist whose work I discussed in the media violence chapter, was my husband Jay's advisor in graduate school. When Jay and I were first married, we rented an apartment on the second floor of Russ and Barbara Geen's house. After dinner, Jay and I would often walk around the neighborhood where Russ and Barbara lived, talking and admiring the big, old houses while getting some exercise. I remember that habit fondly because those walks were a pleasure.

Speaking of pleasurable walks, the Italians have a pleasurable habit of taking after-dinner walks. Italians are known for their arts and letters, for their cuisine—for high culture and high society in general. Whether it is cooking, fashion, or even conversation, Italians embrace *la dolce vita*—the sweet life. Whereas Americans have high alcoholism rates, Italians drink wine and aperitifs with dinner as a way of enjoying life. In America, we are concerned with becoming a society of couch potatoes. In Italy, there is the lovely tradition of the *passeggiata* or evening stroll. Every evening, between about 5 P.M. and 7 P.M., Italians take a little stroll and see their neighbors. Part of the point is to see and be seen and to *fare la bella figura*—or as the English say, to cut a dashing figure. It is a charming social event—to be outside on the sidewalks and in the public squares, to meet up with friends, to walk and talk. I have lovely memories of walking with my friends Carlo and Ximena in Rome, gazing out over the Spanish steps at dusk (of almost falling in the fountain at the foot of the Spanish steps—okay, that wasn't very "lovely" of me, but it *was* funny), and of walking in the neighborhood most closely associated with *la dolce vita*.

I mention the Italian habit of the *passeggiata* or "little stroll" to point out that some cultural habits are much more healthy and enriching—both societally and individually—than others. We have come to a point in America where media consumption IS life for many of us. While I think media use can be *part* of a healthy lifestyle, I question the intelligence of the imbalance we have allowed to creep into our lives. We also seem largely unaware that we have let media take us over. I suggest we start to question that and to add some balance to our lifestyles as a society. Of course, not all Americans are couch potatoes. Some lead interesting, active, engaged lives. But too many of us have slipped into an unhealthy imbalance. Not only does the imbalance make us less active, less interesting, and less likely to contribute anything of lasting value to society; it also opens us up to being manipulated by what we see when we stare into those screens. Habits like after-dinner walks make life richer, and they are healthier and more memorable than time spent staring into a screen. Whatever you enjoy, do that. It might be taking a run with your dog, playing cards with your neighbor, or doing crafts or gardening with your preschooler.

Another approach would be to make a plan to do a screen-free activity you really like once a week. For example, on Thursdays you will play basketball with some friends rather than watching TV or playing video games. You can make a list of the things you most enjoy doing and add one of those activities to your week. Or you can make a list of the new things you want to try or learn. Take a class in yoga or photography or whatever it is you've always wanted to learn. Do that once a week instead of watching TV. I bet that if you do, five years from now you will remember playing basketball with your friends or learning photography much more than you'd remember watching some extra TV. I bet you'll get more pleasure out of it too.

In *Finding Flow*, Csikszentmihalyi says that according to his research, it is not watching TV or even retiring that makes us happy, contrary to popular opinion. What makes us happy is engagement—doing something that consumes us and makes us feel alive. It's worth stopping for a moment to address why we choose screen time above those things that make us happier. As Csikszentmihalyi explains, his research finds that

> hobbies are about two and a half times more likely to produce a state
> of heightened enjoyment than TV does, and active games and sports

about three times more. Yet these same teenagers [in his studies] spend at least four times more of their free hours watching TV than doing hobbies or sports. Similar ratios are also true for adults. Why would we spend four times more time doing something that has less than half the chance of making us feel good?[12]

The answer, according to his data, is that the most enjoyable activities require some investment in time and energy to get started. It is easier to passively watch TV, even though we find it less enjoyable. And the more we watch, the less we enjoy it. Another motive for passive entertainment is to distract us from things that are causing us anxiety. The problem with that motive, he says, is that in the end we are still left with a sense of "listless dissatisfaction."[13] The fact that young people participating in TV Turnoff Week didn't expect how good they'd feel without media, I think, underlines what Csikszentmihalyi's research tells us: counterintuitively, spending more time with media does not make us happier; in fact, it makes us less happy and more discontent. I would suggest finding that sweet spot of media consumption that uplifts you rather than drags you down.

Make Smart Choices About Which Media You Use

With mass media, there is good and bad to be had. The research documented in this book suggests content to avoid. Use ratings and content descriptors to help you make choices. You can also look for sources that are critically acclaimed. For example, I mentioned the American Film Institute's list of the 100 greatest films (available at AFI.com). The AFI also has lists for other film genres, like the 100 greatest comedy films. Like the classics in literature, great films can be influential in a positive way. If you are interested, you can read more about the arguments behind the film or about cinematic techniques used to produce it. That way, you are more actively engaged with what you are watching.

Speaking of the classics in literature, I recommend that you read more and watch less. Reading a book before bedtime might be a habit you'd enjoy developing. There are so many engaging and enriching choices out there. Try the classics. There are multiple sources that list great books to read. Modern Library polled readers and developed lists of the 100 Best Novels and the 100 Best Non-Fiction books in the English language published since 1900. You can find these lists and more online at http://www.randomhouse.com/modernlibrary/100best.html. Teachersfirst.com lists the best books for children and youth compiled by the National

Education Association. And why not join a book club so that you can not only read a good book but also discuss it with a group of intellectually stimulating people?

Another recommendation I have is that when you are watching TV, choose what you are going to watch in advance rather than surfing the channels. This can help you keep track of your viewing time, which will make it easier to manage how much you watch. A DVR service like TiVo can help with this. Watching prerecorded shows will allow you to fast-forward through commercials, thus avoiding those direct attempts at influence. Skipping commercials or segments that don't interest you can also help reduce your TV time. When you choose shows to watch in advance, you are also better able to tailor your viewing to your interests. For example, I love to do creative projects around the house. I watch home and garden shows for inspiration and ideas, recognizing that those shows are sponsored by businesses that sell home improvement products. One of my favorite shows right now is called *Look What I Did* on HGTV. I like the show because it features regular people who designed a creative project and who explain how they did it. To me, this is fascinating. Even aside from what I might do in my own house, I love to see other people create and enjoy that creation. I do know that all televised home and garden shows do not always portray projects realistically in terms of the time and cost involved. I like to shout out to my family things like, "It did not cost $8 to paint that room!" or "How did they find the perfect antique door, and so cheap? That's not realistic!" Call me goofy if you will, but my kids will grow up with an awareness of some of the fundamental ideas of media literacy.

Seek Alternative Viewpoints

It's easy to be swayed by a person you connect with in the media, or a perspective that you hear most commonly. Challenge yourself by seeking out alternative viewpoints. For example, after watching a presidential debate on television, compare how various news outlets scored who won the debate. Look at blogs online and newspaper articles. Talk to a variety of people about how they saw it. Resist the urge to see things only one way.

Approach Your Media Diet Like You Would Your Diet of Food

Watching films, playing games, and searching the Internet can enhance your life, but you have to be smart about it. Think about your media diet like you think about your diet of food. What you eat and how much you eat are factors in your long-term health and in how good you feel right now. If you eat lots of junk food, you are taking in too much of what is not healthy and not enough of what is healthy. You will feel worse and put yourself at risk for further problems. If you eat in moderation, and eat things that are good for you, you feel better and are at less risk for problems. The same is true for your media diet, and you have to make similar choices. Consuming the wrong things and consuming too much put you at risk for less healthy outcomes. These would include increased aggression, decreased empathy, impaired social and intellectual skills, and obesity.

When I was pregnant with my first child, a nurse at my obstetrician's office dutifully sat me down and played me a video that I since have referred to as the "propaganda video" for new moms. In this video, a young pregnant mother, surrounded by her well-behaved children, prepared a meal of steamed broccoli and plain, broiled chicken, to everyone's general delight. I call this the propaganda video jokingly because it was less helpful to the extent that it didn't seem realistic. Now, I did eat more broccoli and healthily prepared chicken and fish when I was pregnant with Jason, but I didn't eat them plain and I didn't have older children pretending they would eat them that way either. While I understand that the video was trying to make a good point, I think it's more helpful if we can meet parents (and everyone else) where they really are. I know, for example, that you are not going to watch *only* excellent films and TV shows, just like you are not going to eat *only* broccoli and tofu. That doesn't mean that you can't have a healthy, or even just a *healthier* media diet. I confess that sometimes I watch trash TV. A prime example would be that Japanese show where people run obstacle courses while announcers say things that would make fourteen-year-old boys guffaw. In the overall picture of my media diet, I guess shows like this would be like drinking a soda instead of water or eating cheese puffs instead of carrot sticks. It's okay to have some fat in the system, I think. But overall, to be healthier, you should reduce the overall intake and make what you do take in better. If you are what you eat, then you also are what you consume on screens.

Increase Your Media Literacy Skills

If you have read this book, then you have already increased your media literacy skills. There are other books, Web sites, and films that can help. You might start by visiting www.mediafamily.org, the Web site of the National Institute on Media and the Family. This site has many resources including columns and blogs, research information, media ratings information, and recommendations. There are also ideas for how you can get involved with efforts to increase media literacy in your own community.

There are also lots of activities you can do—by yourself, with friends or with your kids—to move from the passenger's seat to the driver's seat, increasing your control of your mass media diet and your understanding of how it influences you. While you watch, ask questions. Ask, "What ideas are they trying to sell me on? What assumptions are they making? What beliefs, values, or ideas does this program promote? Where do I agree and where do I disagree?"

You can talk with your kids about the media that target them. What are the characters like? What seems important to these characters? How are the characters the same and how are they different from the real people you know? What characters or brands do you see everywhere and why do you think this is? I talk to people a lot about mass media, and I often hear the idea that if you raise your kids right, they will be fine. I think that what we need to come to grips with is that in our current media-saturated culture, raising our kids right includes raising them to know something about media's power to influence us.

Your "Daily" Dose of Media Literacy

A fine example of media literacy education comes from James Trier, media scholar at the University of North Carolina at Chapel Hill.[14] Trier recommends using *The Daily Show with Jon Stewart* to teach critical media viewing. I'll summarize some of his recommendations for you. Trier's activities focus on the satire news update section of *The Daily Show*, which is Stewart's beginning monologue. An important media literacy lesson from the satiric news update is how *Daily Show* conventions differ from mainstream media conventions. Specifically, the mainstream media try to appear dispassionate, using sound bites about 10 seconds long that conform to specific criteria, such as being grammatically correct and without long pauses. *The Daily Show* breaks with these conventions. Furthermore, Stewart talks back to the speaker in the sound bites, using a technique called detournement or reversal of perspective to challenge or shift meaning. For example, Trier cites a *Daily Show* segment called "Progress Defined," which presents a series of quotes from President Bush about the Iraq war. The quotes begin in 2007 with Bush complaining that Congress is trying to block him just as the country is beginning to make progress in the war. Stewart talks back to Bush, noting that he thinks progress has just begun, then undercuts this by playing several past clips in which Bush says that we are making progress in the war, ending with Bush's infamous "mission accomplished" statement about the war in 2003.

There are many activities you could do from this starting point, either by yourself, with your children, or in a classroom with students of a range of ages. Trier recommends starting by asking why the video is funny. He also suggests beginning a class by defining detournement and then asking students to find other segments that use this technique. Later, he recommends comparing the same person or event as it is covered on a show like the *Nightly News with Brian Williams* to how it is covered on *The Daily Show*.

Can you think of other media literacy exercises that compare political comedy or satire to mainstream political coverage? The possibilities for this topic and others are endless. For example, you could analyze the reports from mainstream news media, looking for language that is persuasive one way or the other. Some claimed that mainstream media reported in a way that favored Obama over McCain in the 2008 presidential election. It would be profitable to discuss the notion of whether coverage that favors one candidate does so because of bias or because the facts are on the side of a particular candidate. Might coverage bias toward the candidate who is ahead in the polls in order to please viewers? What other reasons can you think of that reporting is or seems biased? Ask other questions such as who produces the show and what is the target audience. Search out trustworthy sources and find their perspective. For example, NPR does a show called *On the Media* that critiques media coverage.

Growing a Country of Media-Literate Citizens

One of the most important steps we can take to make broad change is to begin teaching media literacy skills in our schools. Some say there is no time to cover media literacy in schools. The end result is that American children spend most of their time with media, yet we have not addressed this by teaching them to be smart consumers of media. When we do that, we leave them vulnerable to influence at the hands of profiteers. We have seen examples of the weakness of this position. For example, the deregulation of advertising to children has had such negative effects that governments are feeling the urgent need to respond and make change. This is not a book about educational reform, but I assert that we do, in fact, have time to teach our children the things that will equip them best to be successful in life. It would be a mistake to miss the opportunity to teach them how to navigate the waters of the culture they are immersed in.

We're All Stakeholders

After giving expert testimony before Congress two times as a media psychologist, I was invited by the Organization for Economic Cooperation and Development (OECD) and the Korea Education and Research Information Service (KERIS) to come to South Korea and take part in an expert meeting. My role was to talk about how scientists and policy makers communicate. I was thrilled at the invitation. I was thrilled because the invitation meant going on an adventure halfway around the world and visiting South Korea for the first time. This was a promise that did not disappoint—the trip was both exciting and a sublime pleasure. But I was also thrilled because I had been asked to talk about something that I really care about that I don't think I'd ever been formally asked to talk about before. I had the opportunity to talk about communicating about science to different stakeholders. This was fun for me because what the topic addresses is basically the social psychology of social psychology!

I took the liberty of broadening my topic, not just to how scientists and policy makers communicate but to how four groups who have interest in understanding mass media research communicate. Those four groups are scientists, the public, policy makers, and business.

Communication is a real issue because these four groups speak different languages and have different motives. The four stakeholders also often have a poor understanding of each other, and when you don't understand someone, how can you communicate? In the *Eleven Myths of Media Violence*, James Potter[15] said that after over fifty years of public hearings about media violence, we have done little but spin our wheels over the issue. There continues to be concern and discussion, but to no real effect. I think a big part of why we find ourselves stuck, unable to make forward progress, is a lack of effective communication between the interested parties. Therefore I want to make some recommendations. To extend the driving metaphor, I want to recommend how we can get some traction and drive out of the rut we find ourselves in. In order to get there, I am going to get some help from an artist who knows something about science.

Earlier I recommended exposing yourself to different viewpoints in high-quality media. You really never know what you will discover when you take this advice. I find fascinating connections to my work everywhere. On a long airplane trip, I fired up my iPod and listened to *Things I Overheard While Talking to Myself*[16] by Alan Alda. In this book, the actor talks about the content of commencement addresses and other speeches he's given throughout his life. I thought I had been listening primarily for

FIGURE 9.1. The public, scientists and experts, policy makers and businesspeople are all stakeholders who have an interest in mass media and its influence. Scientists and other experts must learn how to communicate more effectively with all interested parties in order for their work to be most helpful. (With permission from Family Huddle (8421366): © Katrina Brown–Fotolia.com, VOTE (7502670): © Michael Flippo–Fotolia.com, Scientist (1468559): © Yuri Arcurs–Fotolia.com, Business (1538103): © Iryna Petrenko–Fotolia.com)

pleasure, but I stumbled upon something so intellectually imperative that I want to end my book discussing it.

Alan Alda is famous for playing Hawkeye Pierce in the TV show *M*A*S*H*, and I can hardly think of a character who was brought to life more brilliantly by an actor. In fact, as a side note, when I read some reviews of *Things I Overheard While Talking to Myself* on Amazon.com, one commentator opined that anyone over thirty *unconsciously* [emphasis added] believes Alan Alda IS Hawkeye Pierce! Well said.

In addition to making our collective fantasy of Hawkeye Pierce into a reality, for eleven years Alda hosted *Scientific American Frontiers*, in which he interviewed famous scientists about their discoveries. *Scientific American Frontiers* helped make science accessible to nonscientists. Alda's curiosity and enthusiasm were infectious, whether he was finding out what makes peppers hot or what happens when we dream. And his experience of helping scientists talk about their work with clarity informed his thinking both about science itself and about the need for better communication of science to the public.

This is the topic he discussed in a commencement address to young scientists and engineers at Cal Tech. In this speech, he explained why there is a real need to heal the breach that has developed between scientists and nonscientists. Alda compared art and science to the two hemispheres of the brain, suggesting that science has gotten a reputation as cold, while art is warm and human. People are more prone to rely on magical thinking than on scientific evidence. And people are confused if scientists disagree, often believing that science is an opinion and the scientific community just can't make up its mind. "We're in a culture that increasingly holds that science is just another belief. . . . We don't really get it that weighing evidence is different than taking on a belief."[17] And, he says, if the public doesn't understand how scientists think, that opens the door to call solid research junk science and dismiss it. If the public thinks science is just another opinion, then this labeling by politicians takes on a weight that is equal to the science.

As discussed earlier, Bushman and Anderson[18] presented a case that as scientific evidence for a link between media violence and aggression became stronger, the press began to report that the link was weaker. One reason for the flawed coverage was the misapplication of a journalistic principle of fairness. The press commonly presents a scientist and an industry representative as holding two equal sides of an argument, ignoring both the nature of science and the vested interest of the businessperson. As Alda so aptly put it, this reflects a deep lack of understanding that science is based on evidence rather than opinion. Another reason for the flawed coverage, according to the Bushman and Anderson, is that big companies that own newspapers and news magazines may also be in the business of selling violent media, such as video games and DVDs.

And what of the public's view of scientists? The American Academy for the Advancement of Science (AAAS) offered grants to filmmakers in order to encourage them to portray scientists as real people rather than stereotypes.[19] Why? Because the public forms their view of scientists from the mass media rather from real experience with scientists! And scientists in the mass media tend to fall into stereotypes such as the nerd, the cold fish, or the mad scientist. (And yes, I resemble some of those, but that's just a coincidence.) The AAAS simply wanted films to show scientists as real people, people who go fishing, have families, and are sometimes attractive—and that scientists can be women. This underlines what Alda said about science having the reputation of being cold and rather inhuman. The public mistrust distant, robotic scientists who speak from an ivory tower. That brand of science becomes a smug and incomprehensible opinion.

So how can we get the public to understand and value science? How can we get the public to see that scientists are human, often warm even? In his address to Cal Tech, Alda said that to open the channels of communication between scientists and the public, scientists must communicate their work in a way that causes people to fall in love with science. More specifically, in talking about research, scientists should lead people through the three stages of love defined as *(1)* lust, *(2)* infatuation, and *(3)* commitment.

"Lust for science?" I can hear you thinking. "What would that involve, exactly?" Lust for science is that stirring of excitement that comes when we hear about a scientific advance that amazes us. It makes us feel like we live in a world where science might just make us live longer or better. Our pulse quickens and the world feels fresh and exciting. To seduce an audience with a lust for science, Alda says, the attraction must happen right away. The scientist should begin by focusing on tone and body language. Be conversational and interesting in a way a lay audience can understand. Avoid slipping into lecture mode; watch your vocabulary. Show human warmth and feeling; use facial expression. If you speak with your authentic, human voice, the audience will get the sense that you are genuine human and not a god from Mount Olympus. Did you know that most professors never study teaching and most scientists never study how to communicate with the public? Isn't that amazing? I guess the accepted idea was that smart people would figure out by themselves how to communicate. But, of course, there are different ways of being smart. Some people are natural communicators, but great communication can and should be taught to scientists.

The next stage of falling in love with science is infatuation. Making a story emotional helps us remember it. Alda suggests that scientists frame their work as a detective story. Mysteries are dramatic. They involve blind alleys, ups and downs, and the desire for a breakthrough. It's important not to leave out the mistakes because they make the story more human.

I think that's so true. Scientists often don't publish the studies that don't work. We actually have a word for this: the file drawer problem; this means that studies that didn't show significant results end up in the file drawer rather than being published. But when we never talk about what didn't work, it seems that we are elite, flawless—again, inhuman. The audience doesn't know that this study they are hearing about is exciting to the scientist, in part because it worked! They may not know that lots of studies don't work. I can tell you that when you run your data and you see significant results—and remember, this is after much thought and work has gone into the process—when you see those numbers come up as you predicted, there is a palpable sense of awe and wonder, not to mention joy that you feel. Those are some of the human things that get lost when we just skip to the end. It makes something that was so hard seem so easy.

Finally, the last stage of falling in love with science happens when the scientist gets the audience to commit. Committing to a person means you have found real value in that individual. Committing to science, then, means you truly understand its value. Here Alda calls for simplicity and clarity of communication. He quotes Da Vinci who said that simplicity is the ultimate form of sophistication and Einstein who said that science should be explained so that a child could understand it. Perhaps my favorite line comes from physicist Richard Feinman, who said that if the scientist can't explain his work, he probably doesn't understand it himself. In my experience, that's often true.

Experts note that one reason public policy has not been better informed by the psychological literature on media is that interested parties like the press, the courts, and the general public do not understand basic scientific concepts such as how scientists understand cause and effect.[20] This problem was put into sharp relief for me when, the night before I testified before Congress in 2007, I was advised that politicians do not understand the scientific meaning of cause and effect. I was told that members of Congress treat research findings like poll data. Again, this frames scientific findings as a matter of opinion, rather than an understanding that scientific findings are based on evidence and not conjecture.

Humanizing Science

When scientists publish their data in journals, the communication follows prescribed standards that are impersonal. As Alda puts it, this is because the scientific community believes that the cult of personality should not rule. A fundamental principle of science is objectivity; therefore, subjective content such as personality and feelings are unwelcome in scientific communications. This is understandable because objectivity is an important and appropriate goal. But it is not the appropriate model for how scientists should communicate with those outside of the scientific community.

The public usually hears about scientific findings through the media. If the scientist gives an interview or testimony that is broadcast on television or the radio, for example, then the public gets to hear the scientist speak in her own words. Any time scientists communicate a message through the media, they should not speak in the same way as they would in a scientific journal. Here the scientist has the opportunity to do what Alda suggests: to speak with feeling, to put the personal back into the equation, and to speak with clarity so that a child, or at least a layman, can understand it. This is what I try to do when I speak about science. I give the facts, but I give them with feeling and in context. This is why I told you something about my life story, about where I come from and why I do what I do. It's why I let you see my goofy side along the way. I want you to know that scientists are also real people. We're parents, taking our kids to one more birthday party at Chuck E. Cheese, dreaming of the day they will go to college. Often we are really hard workers, in part because we believe that what we do matters. To the scientists out there who study mass media, I say that we have to work even harder. We have to concentrate on communicating our findings to the public in a way that is clearer and more engaging.

To the public, digesting scientific information, I assert that science is not just another opinion. Science is also not a cold, inhuman enterprise. Science means gathering evidence about what's true, as well as we can decipher the truth. It is not practiced by robots or heartless snobs. It is practiced by smart people who have a hunger for the truth. These are people who want to make the world a better place by finding answers that are worth knowing. And unlike the situation with business, scientists are not trying to get your money.

I want to thank you for taking this journey with me and for learning more about the social psychology of mass media. I hope you are primed to take greater control of your relationship with mass media. I also hope you understand better the science behind mass media's influence. You will get more pleasure out of life and you will be happier with the choices you made if you unplug more and actively do whatever engages you. You will also be happier and less vulnerable to other people's agendas if you are more educated about the media that take up so much of our time. According to *Finding Flow*, "it is how we choose what we do, and how we approach it, that will determine whether the sum of our days adds up to a formless blur, or to something resembling a work of art."[21] Life is short and it is precious. To put it metaphorically, up to now we have consented to ride shotgun while media drive us where they choose. It's time we hopped into the driver's seat and mapped out our own journey.

Notes

Chapter 1: Fantasy and Reality: A Primer on Media and Social Construction

1. Kilbourne, Jean. *Killing Us Softly 3*. Northampton, MA: Media Education Foundation, 2000.

2. House Committee on Energy and Commerce, Subcommittee on Commerce, Trade and Consumer Protection. *From Imus to Industry: The Business of Stereotyopes and Degrading Images*, September 25, 2007.

3. Brenick, A., A. Henning, M. Killen, A. O'Connor, and M. Collins. "Social Evaluations of Stereotypic Images in Videogames: Unfair, Legitimate, or 'Just Entertainment'?" *Youth and Society* 38, no. 4 (2007): 395–19.

4. "Poll Says Games Are Safe." 1999. Retrieved February 1, 2000, from http://pc.ign.com/articles/068/068231p1.html.

5. Glasser, Ira. "Television and the Construction of Reality." *Applied Social Psychology Annual* 8 (1988): 44–51.

6. Haney, Craig, and John Manzolatti. "Television Criminology: Network Illusions of Criminal Justice Realities." In *Readings on the Social Animal*, edited by E. Aronson. San Francisco: Freeman, 1980.

7. Appel, M., and T. Richter. "Persuasive Effects of Fictional Narratives Increase over Time." *Media Psychology* 10, no. 1 (2007): 113–34.

8. Green, Melanie C. "Linking Self and Others through Narrative." *Psychological Inquiry* 18, no. 2 (2007): 100–102.

9. Prentice, Deborah A., Richard J. Gerrig, Shelly Chaiken, and Yaacov Trope. "Exploring the Boundary between Fiction and Reality." In *Dual-Process Theories in Social Psychology*, 529–546. New York: Guilford Press, 1999.

10. Smith, Elaine, and Jessica Whiteside. "TV Sitcom So Transforms Use of English." *University of Toronto Magazine*, Spring, 2004, available at http://www.magazine.utoronto.ca/04spring/leadingedge.asp.

11. Deaux, K., and R. Hanna. "Courtship in the Personal Column: The Influence of Gender and Sexual Orientation." *Sex Roles* 11 (1984): 363–75.

12. Gutierres, S. E., D. T. Kenrick, and J. J. Partch. "Beauty, Dominance and the Mating Game: Contrast Effects in Self Assessment Reflect Gender Differences in Mate Selection." *Personality & Social Psychology Bulletin* 25, no. 9 (1999): 1126–34.

13. Gutierres et al., "Beauty, Dominance and the Mating Game," p. 1133.

14. Festinger, Leon, and J. Merrill Carlsmith. "Cognitive Consequences of Forced Compliance." *Journal of Abnormal and Social Psychology* 58 (1959): 203–10.

15. Gosling, P., M. Denizeau, and D. Oberle. "Denial of Responsibility: A New Mode of Dissonance Reduction." *Journal of Personality and Social Psychology* 90, no. 5 (2006): 722–33.

16. Kubey, Robert, Mihaly Csikszentmihalyi. "Television Addiction Is No Mere Metaphor." *Scientific American, Special Edition* 14, no. 1 (2004): 48–55.

17. Kubey et al., "Television Addiction," 48–55.

18. Bushman, Brad J., and Craig A. Anderson. "Media Violence and the American Public." *American Psychologist* 56, no. 6/7 (2001): 477.

19. Great thanks to an anonymous peer reviewer for suggesting this historical perspective on manipulation.

20. Bargh, John A., and Tanya L. Chartrand. "The Unbearable Automaticity of Being." *American Psychologist* 54, no. 7 (1999): 462.

21. Chartrand, Tanya L., and John A. Bargh. "The Chameleon Effect: The Perception-Behavior Link and Social Interaction." *Journal of Personality and Social Psychology* 76, no. 6 (1999): 893–910.

22. Prentice et al., "Exploring the Boundary."

23. Appel and Richter, "Persuasive Effects of Fictional Narratives."

24. Nisbett, R. E., and T. D. Wilson. "Telling More Than We Can Know: Verbal Reports on Mental Processes." *Psychological Review* 84, no. 3 (1977): 231–59.

25. Nisbett and Wilson, "Telling More Than We Can Know."

26. The course was taught by Craig Anderson.

27. Zimbardo quote from the Discovering Psychology film series—Constructing Social Realities—Annenberg Center for Public Broadcasting.

Chapter 2: Challenges and Opportunities of Growing Up in a Media-Saturated World

1. "Parent Center Bulletin: 7 Ways to Be a Better Parent." (2008), e-mail received January 28, 2008, from Parentcenter.com.

2. Singer, Dorothy G., Roberta Michnick Golinkoff, and Kathy Hirsh-Pasek. *Play = Learning: How Play Motivates and Enhances Children's Cognitive and Social-Emotional Growth.* New York: Oxford University Press, 2006.

3. McCluhan, Marshall, with Quentin Fiore and Jerome Agel. *The Medium Is the Message: An Inventory of Effects.* Corte Madera, CA: Ginko Press, 1967, p. 126.

4. Singer, Dorothy G., and Jerome L. Singer. *Imagination and Play in the Electronic Age.* Cambridge, MA: Harvard University Press, 2005.

5. *National Television Violence Study.* University of California, Santa Barbara, Center for Communication and Social Policy. 3 vols. Thousand Oaks, CA: Sage, 1998.

6. Media Awareness Network, "National Television Violence Study Year Three: 1996–97; Summary of Recommendations." *Report of the University of California, Santa Barbara Center for Communication and Social Policy Web site* (1996–1997), available at http://www.media-awareness.ca/english/resources/ research_documents/reports/violence/nat_tv_violence.cfm.

7. Cantor, Joanne. "The Media and Children's Fears, Anxieties, and Perceptions of Danger." In *Handbook of Children and the Media*, edited by Dorothy G. Singer and Jerome L. Singer, 207–21. Thousand Oaks, CA: Sage, 2001.

8. Gentile, Douglas A., and David Walsh. *Media-Quotient: National Survey of Family Media Habits, Knowledge, and Attitudes.* Minneapolis, MN: National Institute on Media and the Family, 1999.

9. Cantor, "The Media and Children's Fears."

10. Cantor, "The Media and Children's Fears."

11. Christakis, Dimitri A., and Frederick J. Zimmerman. "Television Viewing and Attention Deficits in Children." In *Pediatrics*, 114, no. 2 (2004), 511–12.

12. Christakis, Dimitri A., and Frederick J. Zimmerman. "Viewing Television before Age 3 Is Not the Same as Viewing Television at Age 5." In *Pediatrics*, 435–35, 2006.

13. Greenfield, Patricia, and Zheng Yan. "Children, Adolescents, and the Internet: A New Field of Inquiry in Developmental Psychology." *Developmental Psychology* 42, no. 3 (2006): 391–94.

14. Whitlock, Janis L., Jane L. Powers, and John Eckenrode. "The Virtual Cutting Edge: The Internet and Adolescent Self-Injury." *Developmental Psychology* 42, no. 3 (2006): 407–17.

15. Aronson, Elliot. *The Social Animal,* 9th ed. New York: Worth, 2004.

16. Potter, W. James. *Media Literacy.* Los Angeles: Sage, 2008.

17. Roberts, D., and U. Foehr. *Kids and Media in America.* Cambridge, UK: Cambridge University Press, 2004. See also the report of these data released by the Kaiser Family Foundation called *Generation M: Media in the Lives of 8–18 Year Olds,* available at http://www.kff.org/entmedia/ entmedia030905pkg.cfm.

18. Kubey, Roberttand Csikszentmihalyi, Mihaly. "Television Addiction Is No Mere Metaphor." *Scientific American, Special Edition* 14, no. 1 (2004): 48–55.

19. Csikszentmihalyi, Mihaly. *Finding Flow: The Psychology of Engagement with Everyday Life.* New York: Basic Books, 1998.

20. Randsford, Marc. "Average Person Spends More Time Using Media than Anything Else," *Ball State University Newsletter*, no. 9/23/2005 (2005), available at http://www.bsu.edu/news/article/0,1370,7273-850-36658,00.html.

21. McCluhan, *The Medium Is the Message*, p. 26.

22. Walsh, David, and Nat Bennett (Contributor). *Why Do They Act That Way? A Survival Guide to the Adolescent Brain for You and Your Teen.* New York: Free Press, 2005.

23. Brescoll, Victoria, and Marianne Lafrance. "The Correlates and Consequences of Newspaper Reports of Research on Sex Differences." *Psychological Science* 15, no. 8 (2004): 515–20.

24. Bushman, Brad J., and Craig A. Anderson. "Media Violence and the American Public." *American Psychologist* 56, no. 6/7 (2001): 477.

25. W. James Potter, Media Literacy, 2008.

26. Potter, *Media Literacy*, p. 20.

27. Ostrow, Nicole. "Sex on TV Linked to Teen Pregnancy in Survey of U.S. Teenagers," available at Bloomberg.com: Science, http://www.bloomberg.com/apps/news?pid=20601124&sid=a997bX.pjoWw&refer=science.

28. Walsh, David. "Mediawise Columns" (2008), available at http://www.media-family.org/mediawisecolumns/index.shtml. Some of Walsh's columns include "All Too Real: ADHD TV" and "MySpace for the Grade-School Set."

29. Lenhart, Amanda, Mary Madden, Alexandra Rankin Macgill, and Aaron Smith. "Teens and Social Media." *Pew Internet and American Life Project* (2007), available at http://www.pewinternet.org/PPF/r/230/report_display.asp.

Chapter 3: Media Violence: Scholarship Versus Salesmanship

1. "GTA 4 Karin Dilettante Hybrid Commercial." 2008, available at http://www.youtube.com/watch?v=Hnc0obe0NFk Grand Theft Auto 4 by Rockstar Games.

2. Parentingteens.com. "Violence & Video Games." Available at http://www.parentingteens.com/index/Parent+Forum/Parenting+Poll/Violence+and+ Video+ Games.

3. Retrieved May 9, 2008, from http://www.whattheyplay.com/features/why-do-young-teens-like-grand-theft-auto/. Quote from teen boy, par. 9.

4. AFP. "Cheers and Fears as Gta Iv Revs at the Starting Line." Available at http:// afp.google.com/article/ALeqM5h17OuUW4FyOuvSMki6LyvqYmbr5w, par. 4.

5. Retrieved May 9, 2008, from http://www.whattheyplay.com/features/why-do-young-teens-like-grand-theft-auto/.

6. Thomas, Karen. "Study Ties Aggression to Violence in Games." *USA Today*, May 10, 2000, 3D.

7. Funk, Jeanne B., Heidi Bechtoldt Baldacci, Tracie Pasold, and Jennifer Baumgardner. "Violence Exposure in Real-Life, Video Games, Television, Movies, and the Internet: Is There Desensitization?" *Journal of Adolescence* 27, no. 1 (2004): 23.

8. Singer, Dorothy G., Roberta Michnick Golinkoff, and Kathy Hirsh-Pasek. *Play = Learning: How Play Motivates and Enhances Children's Cognitive and Social-Emotional Growth*. New York: Oxford University Press, 2006.

9. Brenick, A., A. Henning, M. Killen, A. O'Connor, and M. Collins. "Social Evaluations of Stereotypic Images in Videogames: Unfair, Legitimate, or 'Just Entertainment'?" *Youth and Society* 38, no. 4 (2007): 395–419.

10. Funk, Jeanne B., and Christine M. Fox. "The Development of the Game Engagement Questionnaire: A Measure of Levels of Engagement in Videogame Playing." In *Meeting of the International Society for Research in Aggression.* Budapest, Hungary, 2008.

11. Gentile, Douglas, and Craig Anderson. "Violent Video Games: The Newest Media Violence Hazard." In *Media Violence and Children*, edited by Douglas Gentile. Westport, CT: Praeger, 2003.

12. Gentile and Anderson, "Violent Video Games," p. 147.

13. Gentile, Douglas, and A. Sesma. "Developmental Approaches to Understanding Media Effects on Individuals." In *Media Violence and Children*, edited by D. Gentile, 19–37. Westport, CT: Praeger, 2003.

14. Huesmann, Rowell, and Eric Dubow. "Leonard D. Eron (1920–2007)." *American Psychologist* 63, no. 2 (2008): 131–32.

15. Huesmann, L. Rowell, Leonard Eron, M. Lefkowitz, and Leopold Walder. "Television Violence and Aggression: The Causal Effect Remains." *American Psychologist* 28 (1973): 617–20.

16. Huesmann, L. Rowell, Jessica Moise-Titus, Cheryl-Lynn Podolski, and Leonard D. Eron. "Longitudinal Relations between Children's Exposure to TV Violence and Their Aggressive and Violent Behavior in Young Adulthood: 1977–1992." *Developmental Psychology* 39, no. 2 (2003): 201.

17. See also the Web site for the University of Michigan's aggression research program, available at http://www.rcgd.isr.umich.edu/aggr/.

18. Schultz, Duane, and Sydney Schultz. *A History of Modern Psychology.* Belmont, CA: Wadsworth/Thompson Learning, 2004.

19. Huesmann and Dubow. "Leonard D. Eron (1920–2007)."

20. Huesmann, L. Rowell. "Screen Violence and Real Violence: Understanding the Link." 2003, available at http://www.rcgd.isr.umich.edu/aggr/, p. 20.

21. Anderson, Craig A., Leonard Berkowitz, Edward Donnerstein, L. Rowell Huesmann, James D. Johnson, Daniel Linz, Neil M. Malamuth, and Ellen Wartella. "The Influence of Media Violence on Youth." *Psychological Science in the Public Interest* 4, no. 3 (2003): 81–110, p. 81.

22. Bartholow, Bruce D., Marc A. Sestir, and Edward B. Davis. "Correlates and Consequences of Exposure to Video Game Violence: Hostile Personality, Empathy, and Aggressive Behavior." *Personality and Social Psychology Bulletin* 31, no. 11 (2005): 1573–86.

23. Anderson, Craig A., and Karen E. Dill. "Video Games and Aggressive Thoughts, Feelings, and Behavior in the Laboratory and in Life." *Journal of Personality and Social Psychology* 78 (2000): 772–90.

24. Berkowitz, Leonard, and Russell G. Geen. "Stimulus Qualities of the Target of Aggression: A Further Study." *Journal of Personality and Social Psychology* 5, no. 3 (1967): 364–68.

25. Bushman, Anderson. "Comfortably Numb: Desensitizing Effects of Violent Media on Helping Others." *Psychological Science* 21, no. 3 (2009): 273–277.

26. Bartholow, Bruce D., Brad J. Bushman, and Marc A. Sestir. "Chronic Violent Video Game Exposure and Desensitization to Violence: Behavioral and Event-Related Brain Potential Data." *Journal of Experimental Social Psychology* 42, no. 4 (2006): 532–39.

27. Koepp, M. J., R. N. Gunn, A. D. Lawrence, V. J. Cunningham, A. Dagher, T. Jones, D. J. Brooks, C. J. Bench, and P. M. Grasby. "Evidence for Striatal Dopamine Release during a Video Game." *Nature* 393, no. 6682 (1998): 266.

28. Gentile, Saleem M., and Craig A. Anderson. "Public Policy and the Effects of Media Violence on Children." *Social Issues and Policy Review* 1 (2007): 15–61.

29. Murray, John P., Mario Liotti, Paul T. Ingmundson, Helen S. Mayberg, Pu Yonglin, Frank Zamarripa, Liu Yijun, Marty G. Woldorff, Gao Jia-Hong, and Peter T. Fox. "Children's Brain Activations While Viewing Televised Violence Revealed by Fmri." *Media Psychology* 8, no. 1 (2006): 25–37.

30. Hurley, Susan. "Imitation, Media Violence and Freedom of Speech." *Philosophical Studies* 117 (2004): 165–218, p. 170

31. Hurley, "Imitation, Media Violence and Freedom of Speech," p. 170.

32. Chartrand, Tanya L., and John A. Bargh. "The Chameleon Effect: The Perception-Behavior Link and Social Interaction." *Journal of Personality and Social Psychology* 76, no. 6 (1999): 893–910.

33. Giacomo Rizzolatti, and Destro Maddalena Fabbri. "Understanding Actions and the Intentions of Others: The Basic Neural Mechanism." *European Review* 15, no. 2 (2007): 209–22.

34. Nash, J. Madeleine. "The Gift of Mimicry." *Time*, January 29, 2007.

35. Berkowitz, Leonard. "On the Consideration of Automatic as Well as Controlled Psychological Processes in Aggression." *Aggressive Behavior* 34, no. 2 (2008): 117–29.

36. Berkowitz, "On the Consideration of Automatic as Well as Controlled Psychological Processes in Aggression," p. 117.

37. Berkowitz, "On the Consideration of Automatic as Well as Controlled Psychological Processes in Aggression," p. 124.

Chapter 4: Seeing Through and Seeing Beyond Media Visions of Race and Gender

1. Gerbner, G. "The Stories We Tell." *Peace Review* 11, no. 1 (1999): 9.

2. Gerbner, "The Stories We Tell," pp. 9–17.

3. Wilson, C. C., F. Gutierrez, and L. M. Chao. *Racism, Sexism and the Media: The Rise of Class Communication in Multicultural America*, 3rd ed. Thousand Oaks, CA: Sage, 2003, p. 327.

4. Holtzman, L. *Media Messages: What Film, Television and Popular Music Teach Us about Race, Class, Gender and Sexual Orientation*. New York: M. E. Sharpe, 2000.

5. Burgess, Melinda C. R., Karen E. Dill, S. Paul Stermer, Stephen R. Burgess, and Brian P. Brown. "Playing with Prejudice: The Prevalence and Consequences of Racial Stereotypes in Videogames." *Media Psychology* (Under review).

6. Burgess et al., *Playing with Prejudice*, under review.

7. Ostman, R. E. "Handbook of Visual Analysis." *Journalism and Mass Communication Quarterly* 79 (2002): 770.

8. Cowan, G. "Content Analysis of Visual Materials." In *Handbook for Conducting Research on Human Sexuality*, edited by M. W. Wiederman and B. E. Whitley. London: Lawrence Erlbaum, 2002, p. 345

9. Dill, Karen E., and Melinda C. R. Burgess. "Media Images as Positive and Negative Exemplars of Race: Evoking Obama or Videogame Characters Changes Outcomes for Black Men." (under review).

10. Slusher, M. P., and C. A. Anderson. "When Reality Monitoring Fails: The Role of Imagination in Stereotype Maintenance." *Journal of Personality and Social Psychology* 53, no. 4 (1987): 653–62.

11. Slusher and Anderson, "When Reality Monitoring Fails," p. 654.

12. Appel, M., and T. Richter. "Persuasive Effects of Fictional Narratives Increase over Time." *Media Psychology* 10, no. 1 (2007): 113–34.

13. Slusher and Anderson, "When Reality Monitoring Fails."

14. Amodio, David M., and Patricia G. Devine. "*Stereotyping and Evaluation in Implicit Race Bias: Evidence for Independent Constructs and Unique Effects on Behavior.*" *Journal of Personality and Social Psychology* 91, no.4 (2006): 652–61.

15. Devine, P. G., et al. "The Regulation of Explicit and Implicit Race Bias: The Role of Motivations to Respond without Prejudice." *Journal of Personality and Social Psychology* 82, no. 5 (2002): 835–48.

16. Glick, P., and S. T. Fiske. "The Ambivalent Sexism Inventory: Differentiating Hostile and Benevolent Sexism." *Journal of Personality and Social Psychology* 70, no. 3 (1996): 491–512.

17. Glick, P., et al. "Bad but Bold: Ambivalent Attitudes toward Men Predict Gender Inequality in 16 Nations." *Journal of Personality and Social Psychology* 86, no. 5 (2004): 713–28.

18. Fiske, S. T., et al. "A Model of (Often Mixed) Stereotype Content: Competence and Warmth Respectively Follow from Perceived Status and Competition." *Journal of Personality and Social Psychology* 82, no. 6 (2002): 878–902.

19. Fiske et al., "A Model of (Often Mixed) Stereotype Content."

20. Fiske et al., "A Model of (Often Mixed) Stereotype Content."

21. Pohan, C. A., and C. Mathison. "Television: Providing Powerful Multicultural Lessons Inside and Outside of School." *Multicultural Perspectives* 9, no. 1 (2007): 25.

22. Berdahl, J. L. "The Sexual Harassment of Uppity Women." *Journal of Applied Psychology* 92, no. 2 (2007): 425–37.

23. Das, E., B. J. Bushman, M. D. Bezemer, P. Kerkhof, and I. E. Vermeulen. "How Terrorism News Reports Increase Prejudice against Outgroups: A Terror Management Account." *Journal of Experimental Social Psychology* 45 (2009): 453–459.

24. Huesmann, L. Rowell, Eric F. Dubow, Paul Boxer, Jeremy Ginges, Violet Souweidane, Maureen O'Brien, Dominic Moceri, and Samantha Hallman. "Relations between Arab-American and Jewish-American Adolescents' Exposure to Media Depictions of Middle-Eastern Violence and Their Ethnic Stereotypes about the Violent Propensities of Ethnic Groups in America." *In Meeting of the International Society for Research in Aggression.* Budapest, Hungary, 2008.

25. Connell, R. W. *Gender and Power.* Stanford, CA: Stanford University Press, 1987.

26. Connell, *Gender and Power,* p. 185.

27. Glick, P., and S. T. Fiske. "An Ambivalent Alliance: Hostile and Benevolent Sexism as Complementary Justifications for Gender Inequality." *American Psychologist* 56, no. 2 (2001): 109–18.

28. Jost, J. T., M. R. Banaji, and B. A. Nosek. "A Decade of System Justification Theory: Accumulated Evidence of Conscious and Unconscious Bolstering of the Status Quo." *Political Psychology* 25, no. 6 (2004): 881–919.

29. Glick et al., "Bad but Bold."

30. Scharrer, E. "Hypermasculinity, Aggression, and Television Violence: An Experiment." *Media Psychology* 7, no. 4 (2005): 353.

31. Scharrer, E. "Tough Guys: The Portrayal of Hypermasculinity and Aggression in Televised Police Dramas." *Journal of Broadcasting and Electronic Media* 45, no. 4 (2001): 615.

32. Huesmann, L. R., et al. "Longitudinal Relations between Children's Exposure to TV Violence and Their Aggressive and Violent Behavior in Young Adulthood: 1977–1992." *Developmental Psychology* 39, no. 2 (2003): 201.

33. Huesmann et al. "Longitudinal Relations."

34. Greenwood, D. N. "Are Female Action Heroes Risky Role Models? Character Identification, Idealization and Viewer Aggression." *Sex Roles* 57 (2007): 725–32.

35. Dietz, T. L. "An Examination of Violence and Gender Role Portrayals in Video Games: Implications for Gender Socialization and Aggressive Behavior." *Sex Roles* 38 (1998): 425–42.

36. Dill, K. E., and K. P. Thill. "Video Game Characters and the Socialization of Gender Roles: Young People's Perceptions Mirror Sexist Media Depictions." *Sex Roles* 57 (2007): 851–64.

37. *National Television Violence Study.* Santa Barbara, CA: University of California, Santa Barbara, Center for Communication and Social Policy, 1998.

38. Dill, K. E., et al. "Violence, Sex, Age and Race in Popular Video Games: A Content Analysis." In *Featuring Females: Feminist Analyses of Media,* edited

by E. Cole and J. Henderson-Daniel. Washington, DC: American Psychological Association, 2005.

39. Dill, K. E., B. P. Brown, and M. A. Collins. "Effects of Media Stereotypes on Sexual Harassment Judgments and Rape Supportive Attitudes: Popular Video Game Characters, Gender, Violence and Power." *Journal of Experimental Social Psychology* 44 (2008): 1402–1408.

40. Brenick, A., et al. "Social Evaluations of Stereotypic Images in Videogames: Unfair, Legitimate, or 'Just Entertainment'?" *Youth and Society* 38, no. 4 (2007): 395–419.

41. Ferguson, T., et al. "Variation in the Application of the 'Promiscuous Female' Stereotype and the Nature of the Application Domain: Influences on Sexual Harassment Judgments after Exposure to the *Jerry Springer Show*." *Sex Roles* 52 (2005): 477–87.

42. Milburn, M. A., R. Mather, and S. D. Conrad. "The Effects of Viewing R-rated Movie Scenes that Objectify Women on Perceptions of Date Rape." *Sex Roles* 43 (2000): 645–64.

43. Lanis, K., and K. Covell. "Images of Women in Advertisements: Effects on Attitudes Related to Sexual Aggression." *Sex Roles* 32 (1995): 639–49.

44. Linz, D. G., E. Donnerstein, and S. Penrod. "Effects of Long-Term Exposure to Violent and Sexually Degrading Depictions of Women." *Journal of Personality and Social Psychology* 55, no. 5 (1988): 758.

45. Martino, S. C., et al. "Exposure to Degrading Versus Nondegrading Music Lyrics and Sexual Behavior among Youth." *Pediatrics* 118, no. 2 (2006): 782.

46. Hurtado, Aída, and Janelle M. Silva. "Creating New Social Identities in Children through Critical Multicultural Media: The Case of Little Bill." *New Directions for Child and Adolescent Development* 2008, no. 120 (2008): 17–30.

47. Hurtado and Silva, "Creating New Social Identities in Children," p. 25.

48. Hale, Mike. "A Pint-Size Peacemaker with a Lot to Teach." *New York Times*, February 7, 2008.

49. *Fetch! with Ruff Ruffman* Web site on pbskids.org. Available at http://pbskids.org/fetch/parentsteachers/program/edu_philosophy.html.

Chapter 5: Issues in Media and Social Learning: Rap Music, Beauty and Domestic Violence

1. Thill, Kathryn Phillips, and Karen E. Dill. "Domestic Violence in American Magazines." In *Violence against Women in Families and Relationships*, edited by Eve S. Buzawa and Evan Stark. Westport, CT: Greenwood Press, 2009.

2. Coppola, Vincent. "Beauty and the Brave." *Redbook* 183, no. 3 (1994): 46.

3. Stark, E. *Coercive Control: How Men Entrap Women in Personal Life*. New York: Oxford University Press, 2007.

4. TaggleElgate, "Farrah Fawcett BBC Film '86 *Extremities* Interview." 2007. Retrieved July 30, 2008 from http://www.youtube.com/watch?v=6LuX2vphPZw

5. Jones, Edward E., and Victor Harris. "The Attribution of Attitudes." *Journal of Experimental Social Psychology* 3 (1967): 1–24.

6. Ball, Aimee Lee. "She's Come Undone." *O, the Oprah Magazine* 5, no. 9 (2004): 300–30.

7. Durbin, Karen. "Wife Beating." *Ladies Home Journal*, June 1974.

8. Esman, A., "If I Could Close My Eyes," in *Diane: The Curves Magazine*. Emmaus, PA: Rodale, 2006.

9. Wolf, N., *The Beauty Myth: How Images of Beauty Are Used against Women*. New York: Harper Perennial, 2002.

10. Harrison, K. "Television Viewers' Ideal Body Proportions: The Case of the Curvaceously Thin Woman." *Sex Roles* 48 (2003): 255–64.

11. McCluhan, Marshall, with Quentin Fiore and Jerome Agel. *The Medium Is the Message: An Inventory of Effects*. Corte Madera, CA: Ginko Press, 1967, p. 117.

12. Arie, India. "Video." Song from the CD Acoustic Soul. March 27, 2001. Motown, Accession number B00005A1PR.

13. Wolf, *The Beauty Myth*.

14. Burgess, Melinda C. R., Karen E. Dill, and Beth A. Wright. "You're My Bitch: Crude and Degrading Treatment of Women in Hardcore Rap through the Eyes of the Predominantly White Target Audience." *Journal of Current Issues in Media and Telecommunications*, in press.

15. Lena, J. "Social Context and Musical Content of Rap Music, 1979–1995." *Social Forces* 85, no. 1 (2006): 479–95.

Chapter 6: Advertising, Consumerism, and Health

1. Schultz, Duane, and Sydney Schultz. *A History of Modern Psychology*. Belmont, CA: Wadsworth/Thompson Learning, 2004.

2. Schultz, Duane, and Sydney Schultz. *A History of Modern Psychology*. Belmont, CA: Wadsworth/Thompson Learning, 2004.

3. Potter, James. *The Eleven Myths of Media Violence*. Thousand Oaks, CA: Sage, 2002, p. 8.

4. Magazine Publishers of America. "Magazines 24/7, the Magazine Industry's Inaugural Digital Summit Debuts to a Sold-out Audience." Magazine Publishers of America, available at http://www.magazine.org/Press_Room/MPA_Press_Releases/14503.cfm.

5. Sutherland, Max, and John Galloway. "Role of Advertising: Persuasion or Agenda Setting?" *Journal of Advertising Research* 21, no. 5 (1981): 27.

6. Wolf, Naomi. *The Beauty Myth: How Images of Beauty Are Used against Women*. New York: Harper Perennial, 2002.

7. "Marketing Food to Children." *Lancet* 366, no. 9503 (2005): 2064.

8. "Selling to—and Selling Out—Children." *Lancet* 360, no. 9338 (2002): 959.

9. McLellan, Faith. "Marketing and Advertising: Harmful to Children's Health." *Lancet* 360 (2002): 1001.

10. Hyde, Rob. "Europe Battles with Obesity." *Lancet* 371, no. 9631 (2008): 2160.

11. Federal Trade Commission. "Marketing Food to Children and Adolescents: A Report to Congress." Washington, DC: Federal Trade Commission, 2008.

12. Hancox, Robert, Barry Milne, and Richie Poulton. "Association between Child and Adolescent Television Viewing and Adult Health: A Longitudinal Birth Cohort Study." *Lancet* 364, no. 9430 (2004): 257.

13. Rhodes, Ann. "Legislative Efforts to Combat Childhood Obesity." *Journal for Specialists in Pediatric Nursing* 13 (July 2008): 223.

14. Rhodes, "Legislative Efforts," p. 223.

15. Rhodes, "Legislative Efforts," p. 223.

16. Federal Trade Commission. "Marketing Food to Children and Adolescents."

17. "Liverpool Set to Ban McDonald's Happy Meals in a Bid to Cut Childhood Obesity." *Daily Mail*, 2008, available at http://www.dailymail.co.uk/news/article-517955/Liverpool-set-ban-McDonalds-Happy-Meals-bid-cut-childhood-obesity.html.

18. NEDIC. "Statistics." Available at http://www.nedic.ca/knowthefacts/statistics.shtml.

19. "Are Diet Pills Effective? Fat Chance." *Consumer Reports on Health* 19, no. 3 (2007): 3.

20. "Are Diet Pills Effective?" p. 3.

21. Minjeong, Kim, and Sharron Lennon. "Content Analysis of Diet Advertisements: A Cross-National Comparison of Korean and U.S. Women's Magazines." *Clothing and Textiles Research Journal* 24 (2006): 345–62.

22. Wolf, *The Beauty Myth.*

23. Wolf, *The Beauty Myth.*

24. Taylor, Peter Shawn. "Massaging the Message." *Canadian Business* 79, no. 7 (2006): 12.

25. "Ad Council Announces Collaboration to Combat Childhood Obesity: 'Coalition for Healthy Children.'" *AdCouncil.org* (July 13, 2005), available at http://adcouncil.org/newsDetail.aspx?id=34.

26. Vogt, Donna U. "Direct-to-Consumer Advertising of Prescription Drugs." Congressional Research Service, 2005. website: http//www.loc.gov/crsinfo/

27. Rhodes, "Legislative Efforts," p. 223.

28. Zachry, Woodie, Marvin Shepherd, Melvin Hinich, James Wilson, Carolyn Brown, and Kenneth Lawson. "Relationship between Direct-to-Consumer Advertising and Physician Diagnosing and Prescribing." *American Journal of Health System Pharmacists* 59 (2002): 42.

29. Jaspen, Bruce. "Medical Ads Aim Straight for the Heart." *Chicago Tribune*, January 23, 2007.

30. Jaspen, "Medical Ads Aim Straight for the Heart."

Chapter 7: Get with the Programming: Media Messages About Who You Are

1. Potter, W. James. *Media Literacy*. Los Angeles: Sage, 2008, 8.
2. Potter, *Media Literacy*, p. 8.
3. Lever, Janet, David A. Frederick, and Letitia Anne Peplau. "Does Size Matter? Men's and Women's Views on Penis Size across the Lifespan." *Psychology of Men and Masculinity* 7, no. 3 (2006): 129–43, 129.
4. Lamb, Sharon, and Lyn Mikel Brown. *Packaging Girlhood: Rescuing Our Daughters from Marketers' Schemes*. New York: St. Martin's Press, 2006, 16.
5. Lamb and Brown, *Packaging Girlhood*, pp. 26–27.
6. Levin, Diane, and Jean Kilbourne. *So Sexy So Soon: The New Sexualized Childhood and What Parents Can Do to Protect Their Kids*. New York: Ballantine, 2008, 226.
7. Levin and Kilbourne, *So Sexy So Soon*, p. 42.
8. Lamb and Brown, *Packaging Girlhood*, pp. 2–3.
9. Lamb and Brown, *Packaging Girlhood*, p. 6.
10. NBC News. "High Heels for Infants." Available at http://video.msn.com/video.aspx?mkt=en-us&vid=887008f3-1a01-4cb4-bb4b-151e70f90e10&fg=rss&from=05.
11. Celizic, Mike. "High Heels for Babies: Cute or Creepy?" 2008, available at http://www.msnbc.msn.com/id/26673132/?GT1=43001#storyContinued.
12. Rivenbark, Celia. *Stop Dressing Your Six-Year-Old like a Skank*. New York: St. Martin's Press, 2006, 28.
13. Gillett, Amelie. "Fergie Frightens Small Children." *The Week*, May 20, 2008.
14. The full mission statement of the APA is available at www.apa.org.
15. APS, the Association for Psychological Science, is another large organization for psychologists whose mission also includes advancing human welfare. More information is available at www.psychologicalscience.org.
16. Kilbourne, Jean, and M. Pipher. *Can't Buy My Love*. New York: Free Press, 2000.
17. Burgess, Melinda C. R., Karen E. Dill, and Beth A. Wright. "You're My Bitch: Crude and Degrading Treatment of Women in Hardcore Rap through the Eyes of the Predominantly White Target Audience." *Journal of Current Issues in Media and Telecommunications* (in press).
18. Lena, Jennifer. "Social Context and Musical Content of Rap Music, 1979–1995." *Social Forces* 85, no. 1 (2006): 479–95.
19. Dill, Karen E., and Melinda C. R. Burgess. "Towards a Theory of Media and Aggressive Degradation: Integrating the Literatures on Social Biases and Aggression in the Domain of Media Psychology." *Journal of Interdisciplinary Research* (in press).
20. Dill, Karen E., Brian P. Brown, and M. A. Collins. "Effects of Exposure to Sex-Stereotyped Video Game Characters on Tolerance of Sexual Harassment." *Journal of Experimental Social Psychology* 44 (2008): 1402–8.

21. Dill, Karen E., and Melinda C. R. Burgess. "Media Images as Positive and Negative Exemplars of Race: Evoking Obama or Videogame Characters Changes Outcomes for Black Men" (under review).

22. Slusher, Morgan P., and Craig A. Anderson. "When Reality Monitoring Fails: The Role of Imagination in Stereotype Maintenance." *Journal of Personality and Social Psychology* 52, no. 4 (1987): 653–62.

Chapter 8: The Social Psychology of Political Coverage

1. McCluhan, Marshall, with Quentin Fiore, and Jerome Agel. *The Medium Is the Message: An Inventory of Effects.* Corte Madera, CA: Ginko Press, 1967, p. 22.

2. Geer, John G., and James H. Geer. "Remembering Attack Ads: An Experimental Investigation of Radio." *Political Behavior* 25, no. 1 (2003): 69–95.

3. Bushman, Brad J., and Colleen M. Phillips. "If the Television Program Bleeds, Memory for the Advertisement Recedes." *Current Directions in Psychological Science* 10, no. 2 (2001): 43–47.

4. See the video clips of both Rush Limbaugh and Keith Olberman on YouTube by accessing the YouTube video title "Keith Olbermann Destroys Rush Limbaugh over Edwards Smear," available at http://www.youtube.com/watch?v=53Ef739Vlkg.

5. Boyd, Sam. "Channel Changer." *American Prospect*, September 24, 2008, available at http://www.prospect.org//cs/articles?article=channel_changer_08.

6. Hart, Roderick P. *Seducing America: How Television Charms the Modern Voter.* Thousand Oaks, CA: Sage, 1999.

7. Herbert, Ian. "This Is Your Brain on Politics." *APS Observer* 21, no. 8 (2008).

8. Oxley, Douglas R., Kevin B. Smith, John R. Alford, Matthew V. Hibbing, Jennifer L. Miller, Mario Scalora, Peter K. Hatemi, and John R. Hibbibg. "Political Attitudes Vary with Physiological Traits." *Science* 321, no. 5896 (2008): 1667–70.

9. Vedantam, Shankar. "Startle Response Linked to Politics." *Washington Post*, 2008, available at http://www.washingtonpost.com/wp-dyn/content/article/2008/09/18/AR2008091802265.html?hpid=topnews. September 19, 2008.

10. Solomon, Sheldon, Jeff Greenberg, and Tom Pyszczynski. "Fatal Attraction." *APS Observer online*, no. 10 2004, available at http://www.psychologicalscience.org/observer/getArticle.cfm?id=1660.

11. Herbert, "This Is Your Brain on Politics," p. 20.

12. "Saturday Night Live Transcripts." Available at http://snltranscripts.jt.org/92/92bperot.phtml.

13. "Letterman Reacts to John McCain Suspending Campaign." YouTube, 2008, available at http://www.youtube.com/watch?v=XjkCrfylq-E.

14. "Letterman Reacts."

15. "Late Show with David Letterman Top Ten." Available at http://www.cbs.com/latenight/lateshow/top_ten/index/php/20081006.phtml.

16. Cao, Xiaoxia. "Political Comedy Shows and Knowledge about Primary Campaigns: The Moderating Effects of Age and Education." *Mass Communication and Society* 11 (2008): 43–61.

17. Seelye, Katherine Q. "Best Informed Also View Fake News, Study Says." *New York Times*, April 16, 2007.

18. McKain, Aaron. "Not Necessarily Not the News: Gatekeeping, Remediation, and *The Daily Show*." *Journal of American Culture* 28, no. 4 (2005): 415–30.

19. Fox, Julia, Glory Koloen, and Volkan. Sahin. "No Joke: A Comparison of Substance in *The Daily Show* with Jon Stewart and Broadcast Network Television Coverage of the 2004 Presidential Election Campaign." *Journal of Broadcasting and Electronic Media* 51, no. 2 (2007): 15.

20. Trier, James. "*The Daily Show* with Jon Stewart, Part 1." *Journal of Adolescent and Adult Literacy* 51, no. 5 (2008): 424–27.

21. Trier, "*The Daily Show*," p. 427.

22. Trier, "*The Daily Show*," p. 427.

23. Trier, "*The Daily Show*," p. 426.

24. "CNN Laughs It Up over Sarah Palin Interview," 2008, available at http://www.youtube.com/watch?v=zeMypXCUWMw.

25. "Chris Matthews: *SNL* Goes after Biden and Palin," 2008, available at http://www.youtube.com/watch?v=9Ykh93bCQt8.

26. "Iraq, Bush and Cheering: Tony Blair on *The Daily Show* with Jon Stewart." *Guardian politics blog online*, 2008, available at http://www.guardian.co.uk/politics/blog/2008/sep/19/tony.blair.daily.show.jon.stewart.

27. "Iraq, Bush and Cheering."

28. NBC.com. "Vp Debate Open: Palin/Biden." *Saturday Night Live*, 2008, available at http://www.nbc.com/Saturday_Night_Live/video/clips/vp-debate-open-palin-biden/727421/.

Chapter 9: From the Passenger's Seat to the Driver's Seat

1. Lumet, Sidney. *Network*. Metro-Goldwyn-Mayer/United Artists, 1976.

2. Appel, Markus, and Tobias Richter. "Persuasive Effects of Fictional Narratives Increase over Time." *Media Psychology* 10, no. 1 (2007): 113–34.

3. Green, Melanie C. "Linking Self and Others through Narrative." *Psychological Inquiry* 18, no. 2 (2007): 100–02.

4. Brenick, A., A. Henning, M. Killen, A. O'Connor, and M. Collins. "Social Evaluations of Stereotypic Images in Videogames: Unfair, Legitimate, or 'Just Entertainment'?" *Youth and Society* 38, no. 4 (2007): 395–419.

5. Anderson, Craig A., Leonard Berkowitz, Edward Donnerstein, L. Rowell Huesmann, James D. Johnson, Daniel Linz, Neil M. Malamuth, and Ellen Wartella. "The Influence of Media Violence on Youth." *Psychological Science in the Public Interest* 4, no. 3 (2003): 81–110.

6. Wilkin, Holley W., Thomas W. Valente, Sheila Murphy, Michael J. Cody, Grace Huang, and Vicki Beck. "Does Entertainment-Education Work with Latinos in the United States? Identification and the Effects of a Telenovela Breast Cancer Storyline." *Journal of Health Communication* 12, no. 5 (2007): 455–69.

7. McCluhan, Marshall, with Quentin Fiore and Jerome Agel. *The Medium Is the Message: An Inventory of Effects.* Corte Madera, CA: Ginko Press, 1967, p. 26.

8. Lumet, *Network.*

9. Coalition for Healthy Children. "Ad Council Announces Collaboration to Combat Childhood Obesity." *AdCouncil.org,* July 13, 2005, available at http://adcouncil.org/newsDetail.aspx?id=34.

10. Taylor, Peter Shawn. "Massaging the Message." *Canadian Business* 79, no. 7 (2006): 12.

11. Gentile, Saleem M., and Craig A. Anderson. "Public Policy and the Effects of Media Violence on Children." *Social Issues and Policy Review* 1 (2007): 15–61.

12. Csikszentmihalyi, Mihaly. *Finding Flow: The Psychology of Engagement with Everyday Life.* New York: Basic Books, 1998, p. 67.

13. Csikszentmihalyi, *Finding Flow,* p. 65.

14. Trier, James. "*The Daily Show with Jon Stewart,* Part 2." *Journal of Adolescent and Adult Literacy* 51, no. 7 (2008): 600–05.

15. Potter, W. James. *The Eleven Myths of Media Violence.* Thousand Oaks, CA: Sage, 2002.

16. Alda, Alan. *Things I Overheard While Talking to Myself* [Audio Edition]. New York: Random House, 2007, chapter 14.

17. Alda, *Things I Overheard,* chapter 14.

18. Bushman, Brad J., and Craig A. Anderson. "Media Violence and the American Public." *American Psychologist* 56, no. 6/7 (2001): 477.

19. Kaplan, Karen. "Company Town; Scientists Say Movie Image Not a Pretty Picture; Film: Seeking to Counter Stereotypes, Group Offers Grants to Expose Student Filmmakers to Professionals in the Real World." *Los Angeles Times,* November 18, 1998, 5.

20. Gentile et al., "Public Policy and the Effects of Media Violence on Children."

21. Csikszentmihalyi, *Finding Flow,* p. 13.

Bibliography

AFP. "Cheers and Fears as GTA IV Revs at the Starting Line." http://afp.google.com/article/ALeqM5h17OuUW4FyOuvSMki6LyvqYmbr5w

Alda, Alan. *Things I Overheard While Talking to Myself* [Audio Edition]. New York: Random House, 2007.

Allen, Daniel. "You're Never Too Old for a Wii." *Nursing Older People* 19, no. 8 (2007): 8.

Allen, S. "Cholesterol: What Camp Are You In?" *Nutritional Perspectives: Journal of the Council on Nutrition* 29, no. 1 (2006): 23–7.

Alvy, Lisa M., and Sandra L. Calvert. "Food Marketing on Popular Children's Web Sites: A Content Analysis." *Journal of the American Dietetic Association* 108, no. 4 (2008): 710–13.

Amodio, David M., and Patricia G. Devine. "Stereotyping and Evaluation in Implicit Race Bias: Evidence for Independent Constructs and Unique Effects on Behavior." *Journal of Personality and Social Psychology* 91, no. 4 (2006): 652–61.

Amodio, David M., Patricia G. Devine, and Eddie Harmon-Jones. "Individual Differences in the Regulation of Intergroup Bias: The Role of Conflict Monitoring and Neural Signals for Control." *Journal of Personality and Social Psychology* 94, no. 1 (2008): 60–74.

Amodio, David M., John T. Jost, Sarah L. Master, and Cindy M. Yee. "Neurocognitive Correlates of Liberalism and Conservatism." *Nature Neuroscience* 10, no. 10 (2007): 1246–47.

Anderson, Craig A. "Effect of Violent Movies and Trait Hostility on Hostile Feelings and Aggressive Thoughts." *Aggressive Behavior* 23, no. 3 (1997): 161–78.

Anderson, Craig A. "An Update on the Effects of Playing Violent Video Games." *Journal of Adolescence* 27, no. 1 (2004): 113.

Anderson, Craig A., Arlin J. Benjamin Jr., and Bruce D. Bartholow. "Does the Gun Pull the Trigger?" *Psychological Science* 9, no. 4 (1998): 308.

Anderson, Craig A., Arlin J. Benjamin Jr., Philip K. Wood, and Angelica M. Bonacci. "Development and Testing of the Velicer Attitudes toward Violence Scale: Evidence for a Four-Factor Model." *Aggressive Behavior* 32, no. 2 (2006): 122–36.

Anderson, Craig A., Leonard Berkowitz, Edward Donnerstein, L. Rowell Huesmann, James D. Johnson, Daniel Linz, Neil M. Malamuth, and Ellen Wartella. "The Influence of Media Violence on Youth." *Psychological Science in the Public Interest* 4, no. 3 (2003): 81–110.

Anderson, Craig A., and Brad J. Bushman. "The Effects of Media Violence on Society." *Science* 295, no. 5564 (2002): 2377.

Anderson, Craig A., and Brad J. Bushman. "Effects of Violent Video Games on Aggressive Behavior, Aggressive Cognition, Aggressive Affect, Physiological Arousal, and Prosocial Behavior: A Meta-Analytic Review of the Scientific Literature." *Psychological Science* 12, no. 5 (2001): 353.

Anderson, Craig A., and Brad J. Bushman. "Human Aggression." *Annual Review of Psychology* 53, no. 1 (2002): 27.

Anderson, Craig A., and Brad J. Bushman. "Media Violence and the American Public Revisited." *American Psychologist* 57, no. 6/7 (2002): 448.

Anderson, Craig A., Nicholas L. Carnagey, and Janie Eubanks. "Exposure to Violent Media: The Effects of Songs with Violent Lyrics on Aggressive Thoughts and Feelings." *Journal of Personality and Social Psychology* 84, no. 5 (2003): 960–71.

Anderson, Craig A., and Karen E. Dill. "Video Games and Aggressive Thoughts, Feelings, and Behavior in the Laboratory and in Life." *Journal of Personality and Social Psychology* 78 (2000): 772–90.

Anderson, Craig A., Douglas A. Gentile, and Katherine E. Buckley. *Violent Video Game Effects on Children and Adolescents: Theory, Research, and Public Policy.* New York: Oxford University Press, 2007.

Anderson, Craig A., James J. Lindsay, and Brad J. Bushman. "Research in the Psychological Laboratory: Truth or Triviality?" *Current Directions in Psychological Science* 8, no. 1 (1999): 3–9.

Anderson, Craig A., and Christine R. Murphy. "Violent Video Games and Aggressive Behavior in Young Women." *Aggressive Behavior* 29, no. 5 (2003): 423–29.

Anderson, Daniel R., Jennings Bryant, John P. Murray, Michael Rich, Michael J. Rivkin, and Dolf Zillmann. "Brain Imaging—an Introduction to a New Approach to Studying Media Processes and Effects." *Media Psychology* 8, no. 1 (2006): 1–6.

Anderson, Kathryn B., Craig A. Anderson, Karen E. Dill, and William E. Deuser. "The Interactive Relations Between Trait Hostility and Pain." *Aggressive Behavior* 24, no. 3 (1998): 161–71.

Annys Shin. "FTC Chairman Set to Leave Post." *Washington Post,* 2008, D.1, February 29, 2008.

Anthony L. Mulac, Laura L. Jansma and Daniel G. Linz. "Men's Behavior toward Women after Viewing Sexually-Explicit Films: Degradation Makes a Difference." *Communication Monographs* 69, no. 4 (2002): 311.

"Appeals Court Affirms Order Requiring Seasilver Defendants to Pay Almost $120 Million in Diet Supplement Case." *Government Press Releases (USA)* 2008, Thursday, April 17, 2008.

Appel, Markus. "Fictional Narratives Cultivate Just-World Beliefs." *Journal of Communication* 58, no. 1 (2008): 62–83.

Appel, Markus, and Tobias Richter. "Persuasive Effects of Fictional Narratives Increase over Time." *Media Psychology* 10, no. 1 (2007): 113–34.

"Are Diet Pills Effective? Fat Chance." *Consumer Reports on Health* 19, no. 3 (2007): 3.

Arie, India. "Video." Song from the CD Acoustic Soul. March 27, 2001. Motown, Accession number B00005A1PR.

Armstrong, Edward G. "Devil Music and Gangsta Rap: A Comparison of Sexual Violence in Blues and Rap Lyrics." *Arkansas Review: A Journal of Delta Studies* 33, no. 3 (2002): 182.

Aronson, Elliot. *The Social Animal.* 9th ed. New York: Worth, 2004.

Aubrey, Jennifer Stevens. "Exposure to Sexually Objectifying Media and Body Self-Perceptions among College Women: An Examination of the Selective Exposure Hypothesis and the Role of Moderating Variables." *Sex Roles* 55, no. 3/4 (2006): 159–72.

Bachrach, Riva, L. Rowell Huesmann, and Rolf A. Peterson. "The Relation between Locus of Control and the Development of Moral Judgment." *Child Development* 48, no. 4 (1977): 1340–52.

Ball, Aimee Lee. "She's Come Undone." *O, The Oprah Magazine* 5, no. 9 (2004): 300–30.

Banner, David. "Mississippi." Umvd Labels, 2003.

Baran, Stanley J. *Introduction to Mass Communication: Media Literacy and Culture.* New York: McGraw-Hill, 2003.

Barbara, Muzzatti, and Agnoli Franca. "Gender and Mathematics: Attitudes and Stereotype Threat Susceptibility in Italian Children." *Developmental Psychology* 43, no. 3 (2007): 747.

Bargh, John A., and Tanya L. Chartrand. "The Unbearable Automaticity of Being." *American Psychologist* 54, no. 7 (1999): 462.

Bargh, John A., Mark Chen, and Lara Burrows. "Automaticity of Social Behavior: Direct Effects of Trait Construct and Stereotype Activation on Action." *Journal of Personality and Social Psychology* 71, no. 2 (1996): 230–44.

Bargh, John A., Paula Raymond, John B. Pryor, and Fritz Strack. "Attractiveness of the Underling: An Automatic Power-Sex Association and Its Consequences for Sexual Harassment and Aggression." *Journal of Personality and Social Psychology* 68, no. 5 (1995): 768–81.

Barlow, Dudley. "Violent Video Game Effects on Children and Adolescents: Theory, Research, and Public Policy." *Education Digest* 72, no. 6 (2007): 79–80.

Barner, Mark R. "Sex-Role Stereotyping in FCC-Mandated Children's Educational Television." *Journal of Broadcasting and Electronic Media* 43, no. 4 (1999): 551.

Barr-Anderson, Daheia J., Patricia Van Den Berg, Dianne Neumark-Sztainer, and Mary Story. "Characteristics Associated with Older Adolescents Who Have a Television in Their Bedrooms." *Pediatrics* 121, no. 4 (2008): 718–24.

Bartholow, Bruce D., and Craig A. Anderson. "Effects of Violent Video Games on Aggressive Behavior: Potential Sex Differences." *Journal of Experimental Social Psychology* 38, no. 3 (2002): 283.

Bartholow, Bruce D., Brad J. Bushman, and Marc A. Sestir. "Chronic Violent Video Game Exposure and Desensitization to Violence: Behavioral and Event-Related Brain Potential Data." *Journal of Experimental Social Psychology* 42, no. 4 (2006): 532–39.

Bartholow, Bruce D., Cheryl L. Dickter, and Marc A. Sestir. "Stereotype Activation and Control of Race Bias: Cognitive Control of Inhibition and Its Impairment by Alcohol." *Journal of Personality and Social Psychology* 90, no. 2 (2006): 272–87.

Bartholow, Bruce D., Karen E. Dill, Kathryn B. Anderson, and James J. Lindsay. "The Proliferation of Media Violence and Its Economic Underpinnings." In *Media Violence and Children: A Complete Guide for Parents and Professionals*, 1–18. Westport, CT: Praeger/Greenwood Publishing Group, 2003.

Bartholow, Bruce D., Marc A. Sestir, and Edward B. Davis. "Correlates and Consequences of Exposure to Video Game Violence: Hostile Personality, Empathy, and Aggressive Behavior." *Personality and Social Psychology Bulletin* 31, no. 11 (2005): 1573–86.

Basil, Michael D., Debra Z. Basil, and Caroline Schooler. "Cigarette Advertising to Counter New Year's Resolutions." *Journal of Health Communication* 5, no. 2 (2000): 161.

Batada, Ameena, Maia Dock Seitz, Margo G. Wootan, and Mary Story. "Nine out of 10 Food Advertisements Shown during Saturday Morning Children's Television Programming Are for Foods High in Fat, Sodium, or Added Sugars, or Low in Nutrients." *Journal of the American Dietetic Association* 108, no. 4 (2008): 673–78.

Baumeister, Roy F., Brad J. Bushman, and W. Keith Campbell. "Self-Esteem, Narcissism, and Aggression: Does Violence Result from Low Self-Esteem or from Threatened Egotism?" *Current Directions in Psychological Science* 9, no. 1 (2000): 26–29.

Beaver, E. D., S. R. Gold, and A. G. Prisco. "Priming Macho Attitudes and Emotions." *Journal of Interpersonal Violence* 7 (1992): 321–33.

Bellin, Harvey F., Dorothy G. Singer, Roberta Michnick Golinkoff, and Kathy Hirsh-Pasek. "My Magic Story Car: Video-Based Play Intervention to Strengthen Emergent Literacy of at-Risk Preschoolers." In *Play = Learning: How Play Motivates and Enhances Children's Cognitive and Social-Emotional Growth*, 101–23. New York: Oxford University Press, 2006.

Bellows, Laura, Jennifer Anderson, Susan Martin Gould, and Garry Auld. "Formative Research and Strategic Development of a Physical Activity Component to a Social Marketing Campaign for Obesity Prevention in Preschoolers." *Journal of Community Health* 33, no. 3 (2008): 169–78.

Berdahl, Jennifer L. "The Sexual Harassment of Uppity Women." *Journal of Applied Psychology* 92, no. 2 (2007): 425–37.

Berg, Eron M., and Louis G. Lippman. "Does Humor in Radio Advertising Affect Recognition of Novel Product Brand Names?" *Journal of General Psychology* 128, no. 2 (2001): 194.

Berkowitz, Leonard. "On the Consideration of Automatic as Well as Controlled Psychological Processes in Aggression." *Aggressive Behavior* 34, no. 2 (2008): 117–29.

Berkowitz, Leonard. "What I Meant to Say: Some Thoughts in Response to Pahlavan and Dodge." *Aggressive Behavior* 34, no. 2 (2008): 136–38.

Berkowitz, Leonard. "What Is Social Psychology Like These Days?" *PsycCRITIQUES* 49, no. 14 (2004).

Berkowitz, Leonard, and Russell G. Geen. "Stimulus Qualities of the Target of Aggression: A Further Study." *Journal of Personality and Social Psychology* 5, no. 3 (1967): 364–68.

Berkowitz, Leonard, and Eddie Harmon-Jones. "More Thoughts About Anger Determinants." *Emotion* 4, no. 2 (2004): 151–55.

Berkowitz, Leonard, and Eddie Harmon-Jones. "Toward an Understanding of the Determinants of Anger." *Emotion* 4, no. 2 (2004): 107–30.

Berkowitz, Leonard, Sheree M. Schrager, and Muriel A. Dunand. "Shared Suffering Can Mitigate Aversively-Generated Aggression: On the Role of the Target's Stimulus Characteristics." *Aggressive Behavior* 32, no. 1 (2006): 80–7.

Berns, Nancy. "Degendering the Problem and Gendering the Blame: Political Discourse on Women and Violence." *Gender and Society* 15, no. 2 (2001): 262–81.

Berns, Nancy. *Framing the Victim: Domestic Violence, Media and Social Problems.* New York: Aldine de Gruyter, 2004.

Berns, Nancy. "'My Problem and How I Solved It': Domestic Violence in Women's Magazines." *Sociological Quarterly* 40, no. 1 (1999): 85.

Berns, Nancy, and David Schweingruber. " 'When You're Involved, It's Just Different': Making Sense of Domestic Violence." *Violence against Women* 13, no. 3 (2007): 240–61.

Beth, Howard. "Sex, Lies and Stereotype?" *Joe Weider's Shape* 17, no. 8 (1998): 26.

Bettencourt, B. Ann, Karen E. Dill, Scott A. Greathouse, Kelly Charleton, and Amy Mulholland. "Evaluations of Ingroup and Outgroup Members: The Role of Category-Based Expectancy Violation." *Journal of Experimental Social Psychology* 33, no. 3 (1997): 244.

Bijvank, Marije Nije. "Violent Video Game Effects on Children and Adolescents: Theory, Research, and Public Policy." *Child and Adolescent Mental Health* 13, no. 2 (2008): 99–100.

Bless, Herbert, Norbert Schwarz, Galen V. Bodenhausen, and Lutz Thiel. "Personalized versus Generalized Benefits of Stereotype Disconfirmation: Trade-Offs in the evaluation of atypical exemplars and their social groups." *Journal of Experimental Social Psychology* 37, no. 5 (2001): 386.

Bloom, J., R. Hunker, K. McCombs, B. Raudenbush, and T. Wright. "Nintendo Wii Vs. Microsoft Xbox: Differential Effects on Mood, Physiology, Snacking Behavior, and Caloric Burn." *Appetite* 51, no. 2 (2008): 354–54.

Bodenhausen, Galen V., Norbert Schwarz, Herbert Bless, and Michaela Wanke. "Effects of Atypical Exemplars on Racial Beliefs: Enlightened Racism or Generalized Appraisals?" *Journal of Experimental Social Psychology* 31, no. 1 (1995): 48–63.

"Bogus Claims Cost Diet-Pill Makers." *Tufts University Health & Nutrition Letter* 25, no. 1 (2007): 3.

Bolls, Paul D., Annie Lang, and Robert F. Potter. "The Effects of Message Valence and Listener Arousal on Attention, Memory, and Facial

Muscular Responses to Radio Advertisements." *Communication Research* 28, no. 5 (2001): 627.

Boxer, Paul, Nancy G. Guerra, L. Rowell Huesmann, and Julie Morales. "Proximal Peer-Level Effects of a Small-Group Selected Prevention on Aggression in Elementary School Children: An Investigation of the Peer Contagion Hypothesis." *Journal of Abnormal Child Psychology* 33, no. 3 (2005): 325–38.

Boyd, Sam. "Channel Changer." *The American Prospect*, September 24, 2008. Available at http://www.prospect.org//cs/articles?article=channel_changer_08.

Bradley, W. Gorham. "News Media's Relationship with Stereotyping: The Linguistic Intergroup Bias in Response to Crime News." *Journal of Communication* 56, no. 2 (2006): 289.

Brenick, A., A. Henning, M. Killen, A. O'Connor, and M. Collins. "Social Evaluations of Stereotypic Images in Videogames: Unfair, Legitimate, or 'Just Entertainment'?" *Youth and Society* 38, no. 4 (2007): 395–419.

Brescoll, Victoria, and Marianne Lafrance. "The Correlates and Consequences of Newspaper Reports of Research on Sex Differences." *Psychological Science* 15, no. 8 (2004): 515–20.

Brescoll, Victoria L., and Eric Luis Uhlmann. "Can an Angry Woman Get Ahead? Status Conferral, Gender, and Expression of Emotion in the Workplace." *Psychological Science* 19, no. 3 (2008): 268–75.

Breslau, Karen, Robina Ricitiello, and Bob Jackson. "She Glitters, but Is She Really Gold?" *Newsweek* 144, no. 8 (2004): 31–31.

Breslau, Karen, Robina Riccitiello, and Bob Jackson. "Why We Watched." *Newsweek* 144, no. 21 (2004): 44–45.

Bricolo, Francesco, Douglas A. Gentile, Rachel L. Smelser, and Giovanni Serpelloni. "Use of the Computer and Internet among Italian Families: First National Study." *CyberPsychology and Behavior* 10, no. 6 (2007): 789–98.

Brock, Timothy C., and Melanie C. Green. "Domains of Persuasion: An Introduction." In *Persuasion: Psychological Insights and Perspectives*. 2nd ed., 1–15. Thousand Oaks, CA: Sage, 2005.

Brock, Timothy C., Jeffrey J. Strange, and Melanie C. Green. "Power beyond Reckoning: An Introduction to Narrative Impact." In *Narrative Impact: Social and Cognitive Foundations.*, 1–15. Mahwah, NJ: Lawrence Erlbaum, 2002.

Brown Givens, Sonja M., and Jennifer L. Monahan. "Priming Mammies, Jezebels, and Other Controlling Images: An Examination of the Influence of Mediated Stereotypes on Perceptions of an African American Woman." *Media Psychology* 7, no. 1 (2005): 87–106.

Browne, Beverly A. "Gender Stereotypes in Advertising on Children's Television in the 1990s: A Cross-National Analysis." *Journal of Advertising* 27, no. 1 (1998): 83.

Browne, Kari. "A Buried Statistic." *Ms.* 14, no. 3 (2004): 18–18.

Bruning, Fred. "Wife Beating—a Nation's Obsession." *Maclean's* 107, no. 30 (1994): 11.

Bryant, J. Alison, Ashley Sanders-Jackson, and Amber M. K. Smallwood. "Iming, Text Messaging, and Adolescent Social Networks." *Journal of Computer-Mediated Communication* 11, no. 2 (2006): 577–92.

Buchman, Debra D., and Jeanne B. Funk. "Video and Computer Games in the 90's: Children's Time Commitment & Game Preference." *Children Today* 24, no. 1 (1996): 12.

Buijzen, Moniek, Joris Schuurman, and Elise Bomhof. "Associations between Children's Television Advertising Exposure and Their Food Consumption Patterns: A Household DiarySurvey Study." *Appetite* 50, no. 2/3 (2008): 231–39.

"Bureau Of Consumer Protection Director Parnes Addresses 51st Annual Fdli & Fda Conference."*US Fed News Service, Including US State News*, March 26, 2008, http://www.proquest.com/ (accessed April 6, 2009).

Burgess, Melinda C. R., Karen E. Dill, S. Paul Stermer, Stephen R. Burgess, and Brian P. Brown. "Playing with Prejudice: The Prevalence and Consequences of Racial Stereotypes in Videogames." *Media Psychology* (Under review).

Burgess, Melinda C. R., Karen E. Dill, and Beth A. Wright. "You're My Bitch: Crude and Degrading Treatment of Women in Hardcore Rap through the Eyes of the Predominantly White Target Audience." In *Gender Roles*, edited J. H. Urlich and B. T. Cosell. Hauppauge, NY: NovaScience, 2009.

Burgess, Melinda C. R., Karen E. Dill, and Beth A. Wright. "You're My Bitch: Crude and Degrading Treatment of Women in Hardcore Rap through the Eyes of the Predominantly White Target Audience." *Journal of Current Issues in Media and Telecommunications*, in press.

Burt, Martha. "Cultural Myths and Supports for Rape." *Journal of Personality and Social Psychology* 38 (1980): 217–30.

Bushman, Brad J. "The Dynamics of Aggression." *Aggressive Behavior* 22, no. 5 (1996): 391–92.

Bushman, Brad J. "Effects of Warning and Information Labels on Attraction to Television Violence in Viewers of Different Ages." *Journal of Applied Social Psychology* 36, no. 9 (2006): 2073–8.

Bushman, Brad J. "Moderating Role of Trait Aggressiveness in the Effects of Violent Media on Aggression." *Journal of Personality and Social Psychology* 69, no. 5 (1995): 950–60.

Bushman, Brad J. "Some Consequences of the Media Linking Islam to Terrorism." In *Meeting of the International Society for Research in Aggression*. Budapest, Hungary, 2008.

Bushman, Brad J. "Targets of Violence and Aggression." *Aggressive Behavior* 18, no. 3 (1992): 249–51.

Bushman, Brad J. "That Was a Great Commercial, but What Were They Selling? Effects of Violence and Sex on Memory for Products in Television Commercials." *Journal of Applied Social Psychology* 37, no. 8 (2007): 1784–96.

Bushman, Brad J. "Violence and Sex in Television Programs Do Not Sell Products in Advertisements." *Psychological Science* 16, no. 9 (2005): 702–8.

Bushman, Brad J. "Violence in Video Games Desensitizes Players to Violence in the Real World." In *American Psychological Association*. San Francisco, CA, 2007.

Bushman, Brad J., and Craig A. Anderson. "Is It Time to Pull the Plug on the Hostile Versus Instrumental Aggression Dichotomy?" *Psychological Review* 108, no. 1 (2001): 273.

Bushman, Brad J., and Craig A. Anderson. "Measuring the Strength of the Effect of Violent Media on Aggression." *American Psychologist* 62, no. 3 (2007): 253–4.

Bushman, Brad J., and Craig A. Anderson. "Media Violence and the American Public." *American Psychologist* 56, no. 6/7 (2001): 477.

Bushman, Brad J., and Roy F. Baumeister. "Does Self-Love or Self-Hate Lead to Violence?" *Journal of Research in Personality* 36, no. 6 (2002): 543.

Bushman, Brad J., and Angelica M. Bonacci. "You've Got Mail: Using E-Mail to Examine the Effect of Prejudiced Attitudes on Discrimination against Arabs." *Journal of Experimental Social Psychology* 40, no. 6 (2004): 753–9.

Bushman, Brad J., Angelica M. Bonacci, William C. Pedersen, Eduardo A. Vasquez, and Norman Miller. "Chewing on It Can Chew You Up: Effects of Rumination on Triggered Displaced Aggression." *Journal of Personality and Social Psychology* 88, no. 6 (2005): 969–83.

Bushman, Brad J., Angelica M. Bonacci, Mirjam Van Dijk, and Roy F. Baumeister. "Narcissism, Sexual Refusal, and Aggression: Testing a Narcissistic Reactance Model of Sexual Coercion." *Journal of Personality and Social Psychology* 84, no. 5 (2003): 1027–40.

Bushman, Brad J., and Joanne Cantor. "Media Ratings for Violence and Sex." *American Psychologist* 58, no. 2 (2003): 130.

Bushman, Brad J., and Russell G. Geen. "Role of Cognitive and Emotional Mediators and Individual Differences in the Effects of Media Violence on Aggression." *Journal of Personality and Social Psychology* 58, no. 1 (1990): 156–63.

Bushman, Brad J., and Colleen M. Phillips. "If the Television Program Bleeds, Memory for the Advertisement Recedes." *Current Directions in Psychological Science* 10, no. 2 (2001): 43–47.

Bushman, Brad J., Colleen M. Phillips, and Roy F. Baumeister. "Do People Aggress to Improve Their Mood? Catharsis Beliefs, Affect Regulation Opportunity, and Aggressive Responding." *Journal of Personality and Social Psychology* 81, no. 1 (2001): 17–32.

Bushman, Brad J., Robert D. Ridge, Enny Das, Colin W. Key, and Gregory L. Busath. "When God Sanctions Killing: Effect of Scriptural Violence on Aggression." *Psychological Science* 18, no. 3 (2007): 204–7.

Bushman, Brad J., Angela D. Stack, and Roy F. Baumeister. "Catharsis, Aggression, and Persuasive Influence: Self-Fulfilling or Self-Defeating Prophecies?" *Journal of Personality and Social Psychology* 76, no. 3 (1999): 367–76.

Campo, Shelly, and Teresa Mastin. "Placing the Burden on the Individual: Overweight and Obesity in African American and Mainstream Women's Magazines." *Health Communication* 22, no. 3 (2007): 229–40.

Cao, Xiaoxia. "Political Comedy Shows and Knowledge about Primary Campaigns: The Moderating Effects of Age and Education." *Mass Communication and Society* 11 (2008): 43–61.

Caprara, G. V., V. Cinanni, G. D'Imperio, S. Passerini, P. Renzi, and G. Travaglia. "Indicators of Impulsive Aggression: Present Status of Research on Irritability and Emotional Susceptibility Scales." *Personality and Individual Differences* 6 (1985): 665–74.

Cara, B. Ebbeling, B. Pawlak Dorota, and S. Ludwig David. "Childhood Obesity: Public-Health Crisis, Common Sense Cure." *Lancet* 360, no. 9331 (2002): 473.

Carnagey, Nicholas L., and Craig A. Anderson. "Changes in Attitudes Towards War and Violence after September 11, 2001." *Aggressive Behavior* 33, no. 2 (2007): 118–29.

Carnagey, Nicholas L., and Craig A. Anderson. "The Effects of Reward and Punishment in Violent Video Games on Aggressive Affect, Cognition, and Behavior." *Psychological Science* 16, no. 11 (2005): 882–89.

Carnagey, Nicholas L., Craig A. Anderson, and Bruce D. Bartholow. "Media Violence and Social Neuroscience: New Questions and New Opportunities." *Current Directions in Psychological Science* 16, no. 4 (2007): 178–82.

Carnagey, Nicholas L., Craig A. Anderson, and Brad J. Bushman. "The Effect of Video Game Violence on Physiological Desensitization to Real-Life Violence." *Journal of Experimental Social Psychology* 43, no. 3 (2007): 489–96.

Carnaghi, Andrea, and Anne Maass. "In-Group and Out-Group Perspectives in the Use of Derogatory Group Labels." *Journal of Language and Social Psychology* 26, no. 2 (2007): 142–56.

Carr, Coeli. "You Can Read Her Like A ... Magazine." *Broadcasting and Cable*, January 24, 2005.

Cavender, Gray, Lisa Bond-Maupin, and Nancy C. Jurik. "The Construction of Gender in Reality Crime TV." *Gender and Society* 13, no. 5 (1999): 643–63.

Celio, Christine I., Kristine H. Luce, Susan W. Bryson, Andrew J. Winzelberg, Darby Cunning, Roxanne Rockwell, Angela A. Celio Doyle, Denise E. Wilfley, and C. Barr Taylor. "Use of Diet Pills and Other Dieting Aids in a College Population with High Weight and Shape Concerns." *International Journal of Eating Disorders* 39, no. 6: 492.

Celizic, Mike. "High Heels for Babies: Cute or Creepy?" 2008, available at http://www.msnbc.msn.com/id/26673132/?GT1=43001#storyContinued.

Chang, Chingching. "The Impacts of Emotion Elicited by Print Political Advertising on Candidate Evaluation." *Media Psychology* 3, no. 2 (2001): 91–118.

Chartrand, Tanya L., and John A. Bargh. "The Chameleon Effect: The Perception-Behavior Link and Social Interaction." *Journal of Personality and Social Psychology* 76, no. 6 (1999): 893–910.

Chatterjee, Ipsita. "Packaging of Identity and Identifiable Packages: A Study of Women-Commodity Negotiation through Product Packaging." *Gender, Place and Culture: A Journal of Feminist Geography* 14, no. 3 (2007): 293–316.

Chen, Serena, Annette Y. Lee-Chai, and John A. Bargh. "Relationship Orientation as a Moderator of the Effects of Social Power." *Journal of Personality and Social Psychology* 80, no. 2 (2001): 173–87.

Chidester, Phil. "May the Circle Stay Unbroken: Friends, the Presence of Absence, and the Rhetorical Reinforcement of Whiteness." *Critical Studies in Media Communication* 25, no. 2 (2008): 157–75.

"Child Obesity Seen as Fueled by Spanish Language TV Ads." *Ascribe Newswire: Health* (2008): 3.

"Chris Matthews: *SNL* Goes after Biden and Palin." 2008. http://www.youtube.com/watch?v=9Ykh93bCQt8.

Christakis, Dimitri A. "Can We Turn a Toxin into a Tonic? Toward 21st-Century Television Alchemy." *Pediatrics*, 120, no. 3 (2007), 647–8.

Christakis, Dimitri A., and Frederick J. Zimmerman. "Television Viewing and Attention Deficits in Children." In *Pediatrics*, 114, no. 2 (2004), 511–12.

Christakis, Dimitri A., and Frederick J. Zimmerman. "Viewing Television before Age 3 Is Not the Same as Viewing Television at Age 5." In *Pediatrics*, 118, no.1 (2006), 435–35.

Chuang, Shih-Chieh, and Hung-Ming Lin. "The Effect of Induced Positive and Negative Emotion and Openness-to-Feeling in Students' Consumer Decision Making." *Journal of Business and Psychology* 22, no. 1 (2007): 65–78.

Ciarrochi, Joseph, J. P. Forgas, and J. D. Mayer, eds. *Emotional Intelligence in Everyday Life.* 2nd ed. New York: Psychology Press, 2006.

Clark, A. E., and Y. Kashima. "Stereotype Maintenance in Communication: How Perceptions of Stereotype Sharedness Contribute to the Stereotype Content of Interpersonal Communication." *Australian Journal of Psychology* 55 (2003): 38.

"CNN Laughs It Up over Sarah Palin Interview." 2008. http://www.youtube.com/watch?v=zeMypXCUWMw.

"Chris Matthews: *SNL* Goes after Biden and Palin." 2008. http://www.youtube.com/watch?v=9Ykh93bCQt8.

Coleman, Lerita M., Lee Jussim, and Susan Hatter Kelley. "A Study of Stereotyping: Testing Three Models with a Sample of Blacks." *Journal of Black Psychology* 21, no. 4 (1995): 322–56.

"Commercializing Childhood." In *Multinational Monitor* 29, no. 1: 32–8: Corporate Accountability Research, 2008.

Connell, R. W. *Gender and Power.* Stanford, CA: Stanford University Press, 1987.

Coppola, Vincent. "Beauty and the Brave." *Redbook* 183, no. 3 (1994): 46.

Corns, C., and K. Metcalfe. "Risks Associated with Herbal Slimming Remedies." *Journal of the Royal Society for the Promotion of Health* 122 (2002): 213–19.

Cowan, G. "Content Analysis of Visual Materials." In *Handbook for Conducting Research on Human Sexuality*, edited by M. W. Wiederman and B. E. Whitley. London: Lawrence Erlbaum, 2002.

Cowley, Andrew D., and Gregory Minnaar. "Watch out for Wii Shoulder." In *British Medical Journal* 336, no. 7636 (2008):110.

Crawford, Mary, and Rhoda Unger. *Women and Gender: A Feminist Psychology.* 4th ed. New York: McGraw-Hill, 2004.

Csikszentmihalyi, Mihaly. *Finding Flow: The Psychology of Engagement with Everyday Life.* New York: Basic Books, 1998.

Cuddy, Amy J. C., Susan T. Fiske, and Peter Glick. "The Bias Map: Behaviors from Intergroup Affect and Stereotypes." *Journal of Personality and Social Psychology* 92, no. 4 (2007): 631–48.

Cuddy, Amy J. C., Susan T. Fiske, and Peter Glick. "When Professionals Become Mothers, Warmth Doesn't Cut the Ice." *Journal of Social Issues* 60, no. 4 (2004): 701–18. x

Dana, Mastro, Behm-Morawitz Elizabeth, and Ortiz Michelle. "The Cultivation of Social Perceptions of Latinos: A Mental Models Approach." *Media Psychology* 9, no. 2 (2007): 347.

Darby, A., P. Hay, J. Mond, B. Rodgers, and C. Owen. "Disordered Eating Behaviours and Cognitions in Young Women with Obesity: Relationship with Psychological Status." *International Journal of Obesity* (London) 31, no. 5 (2007): 876 (7 pages).

David, S. Ludwig, and L. Gortmaker Steven. "Programming Obesity in Childhood." *Lancet* 364, no. 9430 (2004): 226.

Deaux, K., and R. Hanna. "Courtship in the Personal Column: The Influence of Gender and Sexual Orientation." *Sex Roles* 11 (1984): 363–75.

Dellinger, Charlene A. "Review of Men, Masculinity, and the Media." *PsycCRITIQUES* 38, no. 8 (1993): 871.

Denise, Bortree. "Book Review: Girl Wide Web: Girls, the Internet and the Negotiation of Identity." *New Media Society* 8 (2006): 851–53.

Devi, Sharmila. "Progress on Childhood Obesity Patchy in the USA." *Lancet* 371, no. 9607 (2008): 105–06.

Devine, Patricia G. "Implicit Prejudice and Stereotyping: How Automatic Are They? Introduction to the Special Section." *Journal of Personality and Social Psychology* 81, no. 5 (2001): 757–59.

Devine, Patricia G. "Stereotyping and Prejudice: Their Automatic and Controlled Components." *Journal of Personality and Social Psychology* 56 (1989): 5–18.

Devine, Patricia G., and Andrew J. Elliot. "Are Racial Stereotypes Really Fading? The Princeton Trilogy Revisited." *Personality and Social Psychology Bulletin* 21, no. 11 (1995): 1139–50.

Devine, Patricia G., Margo J. Monteith, Julie R. Zuwerink, and Andrew J. Elliot. "Prejudice with and without Compunction." *Journal of Personality and Social Psychology* 60, no. 6 (1991): 817–30.

Devine, Patricia G., E. Ashby Plant, David M. Amodio, Eddie Harmon-Jones, and Stephanie L. Vance. "The Regulation of Explicit and Implicit Race Bias: The Role of Motivations to Respond without Prejudice." *Journal of Personality and Social Psychology* 82, no. 5 (2002): 835–48.

Dietz, Tracy L. "An Examination of Violence and Gender Role Portrayals in Video Games: Implications for Gender Socialization and Aggressive Behavior." *Sex Roles* 38 (1998): 425–42.

Difranza, Joseph R., and Robert J. Wellman. "Early Dating and Smoking Initiation: Some Thoughts about a Common Cause." *Addiction* 101, no. 12 (2006): 1682–83.

Dill, Jody C., and Craig A. Anderson. "Effects of Frustration Justification on Hostile Aggression." *Aggressive Behavior* 21, no. 5 (1995): 359–69.

Dill, Karen E. "Children at Play?" *Human Development* 48, no. 5 (2005): 315–22.

Dill, Karen E., Craig A. Anderson, and William E. Deuser. "Effects of Aggressive Personality on Social Expectations and Social Perceptions." *Journal of Research in Personality* 31, no. 2 (1997): 272–92.

Dill, Karen E., Brian P. Brown, and M. A. Collins. "Effects of Exposure to Sex-Stereotyped Video Game Characters on Tolerance of Sexual Harassment." *Journal of Experimental Social Psychology* 44 (2008): 1402–8.

Dill, Karen E., and Melinda C. R. Burgess. "Media Images as Positive and Negative Exemplars of Race:Evoking Obama or Videogame Characters Changes Outcomes for Black Men," under review.

Dill, Karen E., and Melinda C. R. Burgess. "Towards a Theory of Media and Aggressive Degradation: Integrating the Literatures on Social Biases and Aggression in the Domain of Media Psychology." *Journal of Interdisciplinary Research,* in press.

Dill, Karen E., and Jody C. Dill. "Video Game Violence: A Review of the Empirical Literature." *Aggression and Violent Behavior* 3, no. 4 (1998): 407–28.

Dill, Karen E., Douglas A. Gentile, William A. Richter, and Jody C. Dill. "Violence, Sex, Race, and Age in Popular Video Games: A Content Analysis." In *Featuring Females: Feminist Analyses of Media*, edited by Ellen Cole, and Jessica Henderson Daniel. 115–30. Washington, DC: American Psychological Association, 2005.

Dill, Karen E., and Kathryn P. Thill. "Video Game Characters and the Socialization of Gender Roles: Young People's Perceptions Mirror Sexist Media Depictions." *Sex Roles* 57, no. 11/12 (2007): 851–64.

Dixon, Travis L. "Black Criminals and White Officers: The Effects of Racially Misrepresenting Law Breakers and Law Defenders on Television News." *Media Psychology* 10, no. 2 (2007): 270.

Dixon, Travis L. and Cristina L. Azocar. "Priming Crime and Activating Blackness: Understanding the Psychological Impact of the

Overrepresentation of Blacks as Lawbreakers on Television News." *Journal of Communication* 57, no. 2 (2007): 229.

Donnerstein, Edward, and Leonard Berkowitz. "Victim Reactions in Aggressive Erotic Films as a Factor in Violence against Women." *Journal of Personality and Social Psychology* 41 (1981): 710–24.

"Dora to Help Libraries Celebrate Dia." *American Libraries* 39, no. 4 (2008): 14.

Douglas, Susan. "Blame It on Battered Women." *Progressive* 58, no. 8 (1994): 15.

Dunn, Katherine. "Truth Abuse." *New Republic* 211, no. 5 (1994): 16–18.

Durbin, Karen. "Wife Beating." *Ladies Home Journal*, June 1974.

Durham, M. G. "Girls, Media and the Negotiation of Sexuality: A Study of Race, Class, and Gender in Adolescent Peer Groups." In *The Production of Reality: Essays and Readings on Social Interaction.* 4th ed., edited by J. O'Brien. Thousand Oaks, CA: Sage, 2006.

Durkin, Kevin. "Television and Sex-Role Acquisition: II. Effects." *British Journal of Social Psychology* 24, no. 3 (1985): 191–210.

Duval, Laura Lawson, Janet B. Ruscher, Kathryn Welsh, and Sarah P. Catanese. "Bolstering and Undercutting Use of the Elderly Stereotype through Communication of Exemplars: The Role of Speaker Age and Exemplar Stereotypicality." *Basic and Applied Social Psychology* 22, no. 3 (2000): 137–46.

Eastwick, Paul, Alice Eagly, Peter Glick, Mary Johannesen-Schmidt, Susan Fiske, Ashley Blum, Thomas Eckes, Patricia Freiburger, Li-li Huang, Maria Fernandez, Anna Manganelli, Jolynn Pek, Yolanda Castro, Nuray Sakalli-Ugurlu, Iris Six-Materna, and Chiara Volpato. "Is Traditional Gender Ideology Associated with Sex-Typed Mate Preferences? A Test in Nine Nations." *Sex Roles* 54, no. 9/10 (2006): 603–14.

Elliot, Andrew J., and Patricia G. Devine. "On the Motivational Nature of Cognitive Dissonance: Dissonance as Psychological Discomfort." *Journal of Personality and Social Psychology* 67, no. 3 (1994): 382–94.

Emeagwali, N. Susan. "Financial Woes? Get Help!" *Techniques* 83, no. 3 (2008): 61.

Emily, Steel, and Vranica Suzanne. "FTC Tightens Food-Ad Focus; Agency Urges Companies Marketing to Children to Boost Self-Regulation." *Wall Street Journal* July 30, 2008, B.7.

Eron, Leonard D., and L. Rowell Huesmann. "The Relation of Prosocial Behavior to the Development of Aggression and Psychopathology." *Aggressive Behavior* 10, no. 3 (1984): 201–11.

Erynn Masi de, Casanova. "'No Ugly Women': Concepts of Race and Beauty among Adolescent Women in Ecuador." *Gender and Society* 18, no. 3 (2004): 287–308.

Esman, Abigail. "If I Could Close My Eyes." *Diane: The Curves Magazine,* Fall 2006.

Esman, Abigail. "Out of Control." *Diane: The Curves Magazine*, Fall 2006.

Eubank, Penny S. "Review of Narrative Impact: Social and Cognitive Foundations." *Journal of Language and Social Psychology* 22, no. 2 (2003): 238–43.

"Fake Drugs, Losing Battles." *University of California at Berkeley Wellness Letter* 22, no. 7 (2006): 8.

"Farrah Talks about Her Role of a Lifetime." *People Weekly*, 22 (August 1984): 109.

Federal Trade Commission. "Marketing Food to Children and Adolescents: A Report to Congress." Washington, DC: Federal Trade Commission, 2008.

Fejes, Fred J., and Steve Craig. "Masculinity as Fact: A Review of Empirical Mass Communication Research on Masculinity." In *Men, Masculinity, and the Media*, 9–22. Thousand Oaks, CA: Sage, 1992.

Ferguson, Christopher. "The Good, the Bad and the Ugly: A Meta-Analytic Review of Positive and Negative Effects of Violent Video Games." *Psychiatric Quarterly* 78, no. 4 (2007): 309–16.

Ferguson, T., J. Berlin, E. Noles, J. Johnson, W. Reed, and C. V. Spicer. "Variation in the Application of the 'Promiscuous Female' Stereotype and the Nature of the Application Domain: Influences on Sexual Harassment Judgments after Exposure to the Jerry Springer Show." *Sex Roles* 52 (2005): 477–87.

Festinger, Leon, and J. Merrill Carlsmith. "Cognitive Consequences of Forced Compliance." *Journal of Abnormal and Social Psychology* 58 (1959): 203–10.

"Fetch! With Ruff Ruffman Web Site on Pbskids.Org." Available at http://pbskids.org/fetch/parentsteachers/program/edu_philosophy.html.

Fiske, Susan T., Amy J. C. Cuddy, and Peter Glick. "Universal Dimensions of Social Cognition: Warmth and Competence." *Trends in Cognitive Sciences* 11, no. 2 (2007): 77–83.

Fiske, Susan T., Amy J. C. Cuddy, Peter Glick, and Jun Xu. "A Model of (Often Mixed) Stereotype Content: Competence and Warmth Respectively Follow from Perceived Status and Competition." *Journal of Personality and Social Psychology* 82, no. 6 (2002): 878–902.

Fiske, Susan T., and Peter Glick. "Ambivalence and Stereotypes Cause Sexual Harassment: A Theory with Implications for Organizational Change." *Journal of Social Issues* 51, no. 1 (1995): 97–115.

Fiske, Susan T., Jun Xu, Amy C. Cuddy, and Peter Glick. "(Dis)Respecting Versus (Dis)Liking: Status and Interdependence Predict Ambivalent Stereotypes of Competence and Warmth." *Journal of Social Issues* 55, no. 3 (1999): 473–73.

"4 Diet Pills Cited for Deceptive Marketing." *Environmental Nutrition* 30, no. 3 (2007): 3.

Fox, Julia, Glory Koloen, and Volkan Sahin. "No Joke: A Comparison of Substance in *The Daily Show with Jon Stewart* and Broadcast Network Television Coverage of the 2004 Presidential Election Campaign." *Journal of Broadcasting and Electronic Media* 51, no. 2 (2007): 15.

"FTC Chairman Kovacic Testifies on Commission's Fiscal 2009 Funding Request, Budget Justification." *US Fed News Service, Including US State News* (2008); HighBeam research, May 14, 2008, retrieved April 7, 2009 from http://www.highbeam.com/doc/1P3-1478829161.html.

"FTC Chairman Majoras Speaks at Antitrust Law Section Annual Meeting." *US Fed News Service, Including US State News* (2008). January 31, 2008; Targetednews.com, article Retrieved April 7, 2009 from http://www.targetednews.com/agency_news.php?a_id=2634.

Fujioka, Yuki,. "Television Portrayals and African-American Stereotypes: Examination of Television Effects When Direct Contact Is Lacking." *Journalism and Mass Communication Quarterly* 76, no. 1 (1999): 52.

Fuller, Lorraine. "WLBT News in the Deregulation Era: Modern Racism or Representative Picture?" *Journal of Black Studies* 35, no. 4 (2005): 262.

Funk, Jeanne, Robert Elliott, Heidi Bechtoldt, Tracie Pasold, and Areti Tsavoussis. "The Attitudes toward Violence Scale." *Journal of Interpersonal Violence* 18, no. 2 (2003): 186.

Funk, Jeanne, and Jill Hagan. "Children and Electronic Games: A Comparison of Parents' and Childrens' Perceptions Of." *Psychological Reports* 85, no. 3 (1999): 883.

Funk, Jeanne B., Heidi Bechtoldt Baldacci, Tracie Pasold, and Jennifer Baumgardner. "Violence Exposure in Real-Life, Video Games, Television, Movies, and the Internet: Is There Desensitization?" *Journal of Adolescence* 27, no. 1 (2004): 23.

Funk, Jeanne B., and Debra D. Buchman. "Children's Perceptions of Gender Differences in Social Approval for Playing Electronic Games." *Sex Roles* 35, no. 3/4 (1996): 219–31.

Funk, Jeanne B., Debra D. Buchman, and Julie N. Germann. "Preference for Violent Electronic Games, Self-Concept and Gender Differences in Young Children." *American Journal of Orthopsychiatry* 70, no. 2 (2000): 233–41.

Funk, Jeanne B., Debra D. Buchman, Jennifer Jenks, and Heidi Bechtoldt. "An Evidence-Based Approach to Examining the Impact of Playing Violent Video and Computer Games." *Simile* 2, no. 4 (2002).

Funk, Jeanne B., Debra D. Buchman, Jennifer Jenks, and Heidi Bechtoldt. "Playing Violent Video Games, Desensitization, and Moral Evaluation in Children." *Journal of Applied Developmental Psychology* 24, no. 4 (2003): 413.

Funk, Jeanne B., Margaret Chan, Jason Brouwer, and Kathleen Curtiss. "A Biopsychosocial Analysis of the Video Game-Playing Experience of Children and Adults in the United States." *Simile* 6, no. 3 (2006): 1.

Funk, Jeanne B., and Robert Elliott. "The Attitudes Towards Violence Scale." *Journal of Interpersonal Violence* 14, no. 11 (1999): 1123.

Funk, Jeanne B., Geysa Flores, Debra D. Buchman, and Julie N. Germann. "Rating Electronic Games." *Youth and Society* 30, no. 3 (1999): 283.

Funk, Jeanne B., and Christine M. Fox. "The Development of the Game Engagement Questionnaire: A Measure of Levels of Engagement in Videogame Playing." In *Meeting of the International Society for Research in Aggression*. Budapest, Hungary, 2008.

Funk, Jeanne B., Jill Hagan, Jackie Schimming, Wesley A. Bullock, Debra D. Buchman, and Melissa Myers. "Aggression and Psychopathology in Adolescents with a Preference for Violent Electronic Games." *Aggressive Behavior* 28, no. 2 (2002): 134–44.

Gamepolitics.com. "National Video Game Summit Agenda Details." Available at http://gamepolitics.com/2006/09/28/national-video-game-summit-agenda-details/.

Garry, Maryanne, Stefanie J. Sharman, Julie Feldman, G. Alan Marlatt, and Elizabeth F. Loftus. "Examining Memory for Heterosexual College Students' Sexual Experiences Using an Electronic Mail Diary." *Health Psychology* 21, no. 6 (2002): 629–34.

Geen, Russell, and Leonard Berkowitz. "Name-Mediated Aggressive Cue Properties." *Journal of Personality* 34, no. 3 (1966): 456–65.

Gentile, Douglas, and Craig Anderson. "Violent Video Games: The Newest Media Violence Hazard." In *Media Violence and Children*, edited by Douglas Gentile. Westport, CT: Praeger, 2003.

Gentile, Douglas, and A. Sesma. "Developmental Approaches to Understanding Media Effects on Individuals." In *Media Violence and Children*, edited by D. Gentile, 19–37. Westport, CT: Praeger, 2003.

Gentile, Douglas A. "Just What Are Sex and Gender, Anyway?" *Psychological Science* 4, no. 2 (1993): 120–22.

Gentile, Douglas A., and J. Ronald Gentile. "Violent Video Games as Exemplary Teachers: A Conceptual Analysis." *Journal of Youth and Adolescence* 37, no. 2 (2008): 127–41.

Gentile, Douglas A., Paul J. Lynch, Jennifer Ruh Linder, and David A. Walsh. "The Effects of Violent Video Game Habits on Adolescent Hostility, Aggressive Behaviors, and School Performance." *Journal of Adolescence* 27, no. 1 (2004): 5.

Gentile, Douglas A., Charles Oberg, Nancy E. Sherwood, Mary Story, David A. Walsh, and Marjorie Hogan. "Well-Child Visits in the Video Age: Pediatricians and the American Academy of Pediatrics' Guidelines for Children's Media Use." *Pediatrics* 114, no. 5 (2004): 1235–41.

Gentile, Douglas A., Muniba Saleem, and Craig A. Anderson. "Public Policy and the Effects of Media Violence on Children." *Social Issues and Policy Review,* in press.

Gentile, Douglas A., and David A. Walsh. "A Normative Study of Family Media Habits." *Journal of Applied Developmental Psychology* 23, no. 2 (2002):157.

Gerbner, George. "The Stories We Tell." *Peace Review* 11, no. 1 (1999): 9–17.

Gerbner, George, Larry Gross, Michael Morgan, Nancy Signorielli, Jennings Bryant, and Dolf Zillmann. "Growing up with Television: The Cultivation Perspective." In *Media Effects: Advances in Theory and Research*, 17–41. Hillsdale, NJ: Lawrence Erlbaum, 1994.

Gerbner, George, Larry Gross, Michael Morgan, Nancy Signorielli, James Shanahan, Jennings Bryant, and Dolf Zillmann. "Growing Up with Television: Cultivation Processes." In *Media Effects: Advances in Theory and Research.* 2nd ed., 43–67. Mahwah, NJ: Lawrence Erlbaum, 2002.

Gerrig, Richard J., and Deborah A. Prentice. "The Representation of Fictional Information." *Psychological Science* 2, no. 5 (1991): 336–40.

Gidycz, Christine A. Lindsay M. Orchowski Carrie R. King, and Cindy L. Rich. "Sexual Victimization and Health-Risk Behaviors." *Journal of Interpersonal Violence* 23, no. 6 (2008): 744.

Gillett, Amelie. "Fergie Frightens Small Children." *The Week*, May 20, 2008.

Glasser, Ira. "Television and the Construction of Reality." *Applied Social Psychology Annual* 8 (1988): 44–51.

Glick, Peter, and Susan T. Fiske. "The Ambivalence toward Men Inventory." *Psychology of Women Quarterly* 23, no. 3 (1999): 519.

Glick, Peter, and Susan T. Fiske. "An Ambivalent Alliance: Hostile and Benevolent Sexism as Complementary Justifications for Gender Inequality." *American Psychologist* 56, no. 2 (2001): 109–18.

Glick, Peter, and Susan T. Fiske. "Ambivalent Responses." *American Psychologist* 57, no. 6 (2002): 444–46.

Glick, Peter, and Susan T. Fiske. "The Ambivalent Sexism Inventory: Differentiating Hostile and Benevolent Sexism." *Journal of Personality and Social Psychology* 70, no. 3 (1996): 491–512.

Glick, Peter, Susan T. Fiske, Antonio Mladinic, Jose L. Saiz, Dominic Abrams, Barbara Masser, Bolanle Adetoun, Johnstone E. Osagie, Adebowale Akande, Amos Alao, Annetje Brunner, Tineke M. Willemsen, Kettie Chipeta, Benoit Dardenne, Ap Dijksterhuis, Daniel Wigboldus, Thomas Eckes, Iris Six-Materna, Francisca Expesito, and Miguel Moya. "Beyond Prejudice as Simple Antipathy: Hostile and Behavior and Benevolent Sexism across Cultures." *Journal of Personality & Social Psychology* 79, no. 5 (2000): 763–75.

Glick, Peter, Susan T. Fiske, and Scott Plous. "An Ambivalent Alliance: Hostile and Benevolent Sexism as Complementary Justifications for Gender Inequality." In *Understanding Prejudice and Discrimination*, 225–36. New York: McGraw-Hill, 2003.

Glick, Peter, Maria Lameiras, Susan T. Fiske, Thomas Eckes, Barbara Masser, Chiara Volpato, Anna Maria Manganelli, Jolynn C. X. Pek, Li-li Huang, Nuray Sakalli-Ugurlu, Yolanda Rodriguez Castro, Maria Luiza D'Avila Pereira, Tineke M. Willemsen, Annetje Brunner, Iris Six-Materna, and Robin Wells. "Bad but Bold: Ambivalent Attitudes toward Men Predict Gender Inequality in 16 Nations." *Journal of Personality and Social Psychology* 86, no. 5 (2004): 713–28.

Gloria Swindler, Boutte. Beyond the Illusion of Diversity: How Early Childhood Teachers Can Promote Social Justice." *Social Studies* 99, no. 4 (2008): 165.

Golinkoff, Roberta Michnik, Kathy Hirsh-Pasek, Dorothy G. Singer, and Roberta Michnick Golinkoff. "Why Play = Learning: A Challenge for Parents and Educators." In *Play = Learning: How Play Motivates and Enhances Children's Cognitive and Social-Emotional Growth*, 3–12. New York: Oxford University Press, 2006.

Gosling, P., M. Denizeau, and D. Oberle. "Denial of Responsibility: A New Mode of Dissonance Reduction." *Journal of Personality and Social Psychology* 90, no. 5 (2006): 722–33.

Graves, Lee, Gareth Stratton, N. D. Ridgers, and N. T. Cable. "Energy Expenditure in Adolescents Playing New Generation Computer Games." *British Medical Journal* 335, no. 7633 (2007): 1282–84.

Green, Melanie C. "Linking Self and Others through Narrative." *Psychological Inquiry* 18, no. 2 (2007): 100–02.

Green, Melanie C. "Transportation into Narrative Worlds: The Role of Prior Knowledge and Perceived Realism." *Discourse Processes* 38, no. 2 (2004): 247–66.

Green, Melanie C., and Timothy C. Brock. "Learning to Live Better from Entertainment." *PsycCRITIQUES* 49, no. 5 (2004).

Green, Melanie C., and Timothy C. Brock. "Persuasiveness of Narratives." In *Persuasion: Psychological Insights and Perspectives.* 2nd ed., 117–42. Thousand Oaks, CA: Sage, 2005.

Green, Melanie C., and Timothy C. Brock. "The Role of Transportation in the Persuasiveness of Public Narratives." *Journal of Personality and Social Psychology* 79, no. 5 (2000): 701–21.

Green, Melanie C., Timothy C. Brock, and Geoff F. Kaufman. "Understanding Media Enjoyment: The Role of Transportation into Narrative Worlds." *Communication Theory* 14, no. 4 (2004): 311–27.

Green, Melanie C., Timothy C. Brock, and Jeffrey J. Strange. "In the Mind's Eye: Transportation-Imagery Model of Narrative Persuasion." In *Narrative Impact: Social and Cognitive Foundations*, 315–41. Mahwah, NJ: Lawrence Erlbaum, 2002.

Green, Melanie C., Jennifer Garst, Timothy C. Brock, and Sungeun Chung. "Fact versus Fiction Labeling: Persuasion Parity Despite Heightened Scrutiny of Fact." *Media Psychology* 8, no. 3 (2006): 267–85.

Green, Melanie C., Jennifer Garst, Timothy C. Brock, and L. J. Shrum. "The Power of Fiction: Determinants and Boundaries." In *The Psychology of Entertainment Media: Blurring the Lines between Entertainment and Persuasion*, 161–76. Mahwah, NJ: Lawrence Erlbaum, 2004.

Green, Melanie C., and Neil Mulholland. "Resisting Social Influence." In *The Psychology of Harry Potter*, 299–310. Dallas, TX: BenBella Books, 2006.

Green, Melanie C., Abraham Tesser, Joanne V. Wood, and Diederik A. Stapel. "Transportation into Narrative Worlds: Implications for the Self." In *On Building, Defending and Regulating the Self: A Psychological Perspective*, 53–75. New York: Psychology Press, 2005.

Green, Thomas. "Tricksters and the Marketing of Breakfast Cereals." *Journal of Popular Culture* 40, no. 1 (2007): 49–68.

Greenfield, Patricia, and Zheng Yan. "Children, Adolescents, and the Internet: A New Field of Inquiry in Developmental Psychology." *Developmental Psychology* 42, no. 3 (2006): 391–94.

Greenwood, Dara N. "Are Female Action Heroes Risky Role Models? Character Identification, Idealization and Viewer Aggression." *Sex Roles* 57 (2007): 725–32.

Gross, Andrea. "A Question of Rape." *Ladies' Home Journal* 110, no. 11 (1993): 170.

Groves, Trish. "New Ideas Please." *British Medical Journal* 333, no. 7580 (2006): 1180–80.

"Gta 4 Karin Dilettante Hybrid Commercial." 2008. Video. Retrieved April 6, 2009 from http://www.youtube.com/watch?v=Hnc0obe0NFk.

Guerra, Nancy G., L. Rowell Huesmann, and Arnaldo Zelli. "Attributions for Social Failure and Adolescent Aggression." *Aggressive Behavior* 19, no. 6 (1993): 421–34.

Gutierres, S. E., D. T. Kenrick, and J. J. Partch. "Beauty, Dominance and the Mating Game: Contrast Effects in Self Assessment Reflect Gender Differences in Mate Selection." *Personality and Social Psychology Bulletin* 25, no. 9 (1999): 1126–34.

Hae-Kyong, Bang, and B. Reece Bonnie. "Minorities in Children's Television Commercials: New, Improved, and Stereotyped." *Journal of Consumer Affairs* 37, no. 1 (2003): 42.

Hale, Mike. "A Pint-Size Peacemaker with a Lot to Teach." *New York Times*, February 7, 2008.

Hall, Emma, and Ira Teinowitz. "Food Marketers Pledge No More Kids' Ads in the European Union." *Advertising Age* 78, no. 50 (2007): 2.

Hancox, Robert, J. Milne Barry, J. and Poulton Richie. "Association between Child and Adolescent Television Viewing and Adult Health: A Longitudinal Birth Cohort Study." *Lancet* 364, no. 9430 (2004): 257.

Haney, Craig, and John Manzolatti. "Television Criminology: Network Illusions of Criminal Justice Realities." In *Readings on the Social Animal*, edited by E. Aronson. San Francisco: Freeman, 1980.

Hargreaves, Duane A., and Marika Tiggemann. "Female 'Thin Ideal' Media Images and Boys' Attitudes toward Girls." *Sex Roles* 49, no. 9 (2003): 539–44.

Harman, Megan. "Sprouts with That?" *Canadian Business* 81, no. 6 (2008): 23.

Harmon-Jones, Eddie, and Patricia G. Devine. "Introduction to the Special Section on Social Neuroscience: Promise and Caveats."

Journal of Personality and Social Psychology 85, no. 4 (2003): 589–93.

Harrison, K. "Television Viewers' Ideal Body Proportions: The Case of the Curvaceously Thin Woman." *Sex Roles* 48 (2003): 255–64.

Harrison, Kristen. "Scope of Self: Toward a Model of Television's Effects on Self-Complexity in Adolescence." *Communication Theory* 16, no. 2 (2006): 251.

Harrison, Kristen, and Veronica Hefner. "Media Exposure, Current and Future Body Ideals, and Disordered Eating among Preadolescent Girls: A Longitudinal Panel Study." *Journal of Youth and Adolescence* 35, no. 2 (2006): 146.

Hart, Roderick P. *Seducing America: How Television Charms the Modern Voter.* Thousand Oaks, CA: Sage, 1999.

Hatoum, Ida Jodette, and Deborah Belle. "Mags and Abs: Media Consumption and Bodily Concerns in Men." *Sex Roles* 51, no. 7 (2004): 397–407.

Hayes, Sandy. "The Myspace Culture." *Voices from the Middle* 15, no. 2 (2007): 59–60.

Herbert, Ian. "This Is Your Brain on Politics." *APS Observer* 21, no. 8 (2008).

Hermelin, Francine G. "Women's Shelters: Demand Up, Donations Down." *Working Woman* 19, no. 11 (1994): 9.

Hewitt, Bill, and Maria Eftimiades. "The Other Nicole." *People* 42, no. 2 (1994): 36.

Hewitt, Bill, Lyndon Stambler, Ron Arias, Vickie Bane, Johnny Dodd, Champ Clark, and Frank Swertlow. "Can He Escape His Lies?" *People* 62, no. 15 (2004): 66–71.

HighBeam research, May 14, 2008, retrieved April 7, 2009 from http://www.highbeam.com/doc/1P3-1478829161.html.

Hoffnung, Michele. "Half the Human Experience: The Psychology of Women." *Sex Roles* 51, no. 7/8 (2004): 493–94.

Holtzman, Linda. *Media Messages: What Film, Television and Popular Music Teach Us about Race, Class, Gender and Sexual Orientation.* New York: M. E. Sharpe, 2000.

House Committee on Energy and Commerce, Subcommittee on Commerce, Trade and Consumer Protection. *From Imus to Industry: The Business of Stereotyopes and Degrading Images,* September 25, 2007.

Huesmann, L. Rowell. "An Information Processing Model for the Development of Aggression." *Aggressive Behavior* 14, no. 1 (1988): 13–24.

Huesmann, L. Rowell. "No Simple Relation." *Psychological Inquiry* 8, no. 3 (1997): 200.

Huesmann, L. Rowell. "Screen Violence and Real Violence: Understanding the Link," 2003, available at http://www.rcgd.isr.umich.edu/aggr/.

Huesmann, L. Rowell, Eric F. Dubow, Paul Boxer, Jeremy Ginges, Violet Souweidane, Maureen O'Brien, Dominic Moceri, and Samantha Hallman. "Relations between Arab-American and Jewish-American Adolescents' Exposure to Media Depictions of Middle-Eastern Violence and Their Ethnic Stereotypes about the Violent Propensities of Ethnic Groups in America." In *Meeting of the International Society for Research in Aggression*. Budapest, Hungary, 2008.

Huesmann, L. Rowell, Leonard Eron, M. Lefkowitz, and Leopold Walder. "Television Violence and Aggression: The Causal Effect Remains." *American Psychologist* 28 (1973): 617–20.

Huesmann, L. Rowell, and Leonard D. Eron. "Cognitive Processes and the Persistence of Aggressive Behavior." *Aggressive Behavior* 10, no. 3 (1984): 243–51.

Huesmann, L. Rowell, and Leonard D. Eron. "Individual Differences and the Trait of Aggression." *European Journal of Personality* 3, no. 2 (1989): 95–106.

Huesmann, L. Rowell, Leonard D. Eron, and Eric F. Dubow. "Childhood Predictors of Adult Criminality: Are All Risk Factors Reflected in Childhood Aggressiveness?" *Criminal Behaviour and Mental Health* 12, no. 3 (2002): 185.

Huesmann, L. Rowell, and Nancy G. Guerra. "Children's Normative Beliefs about Aggression and Aggressive Behavior." *Journal of Personality and Social Psychology* 72, no. 2 (1997): 408–19.

Huesmann, L. Rowell, and Jessica Moise. "Media Violence: A Demonstrated Public Health Threat to Children." *Harvard Mental Health Letter* 12, no. 12 (1996): 5.

Huesmann, L. Rowell, Jessica Moise-Titus, Cheryl-Lynn Podolski, and Leonard D. Eron. "Longitudinal Relations between Children's Exposure to TV Violence and Their Aggressive and Violent Behavior in Young Adulthood: 1977–1992." *Developmental Psychology* 39, no. 2 (2003): 201.

Huesmann, L. Rowell, and Laramie D. Taylor. "The Role of Media Violence in Violent Behavior." *Annual Review of Public Health* 27, no. 1 (2006): 393–415.

Huesmann, Rowell, and Eric Dubow. "Leonard D. Eron (1920–2007)." *American Psychologist* 63, no. 2 (2008): 131–2.

Hugenberg, Kurt, Galen V. Bodenhausen, and Melissa McLain. "Framing Discrimination: Effects of Inclusion versus Exclusion Mind-Sets on Stereotypic Judgments." *Journal of Personality and Social Psychology* 91, no. 6 (2006): 1020–31.

Hurley, Susan. "Imitation, Media Violence and Freedom of Speech." *Philosophical Studies* 117 (2004): 165–218.

Hurtado, Aída, and Janelle M. Silva. "Creating New Social Identities in Children through Critical Multicultural Media: The Case of Little Bill." *New Directions for Child and Adolescent Development* 2008, no. 120 (2008): 17–30.

Huston, Aletha C., Mildred M. Alvarez, Raymond Montemayor, Gerald R. Adams, and Thomas P. Gullotta. "The Socialization Context of Gender Role Development in Early Adolescence." In *From Childhood to Adolescence: A Transitional Period?* 156–79. Thousand Oaks, CA: Sage, 1990.

Hyde, Janet. *Half the Human Experience.* New York: Houghton Mifflin, 2006.

Hyde, Rob. "Europe Battles with Obesity." *Lancet* 371, no. 9631 (2008): 2160–61.

"Imus Apologizes for Controversial Comments about Rutgers Players." 2007, available at http://www.wnbc.com/news/11537229/detail.html?dl=mainclick.

"Iraq, Bush and Cheering: Tony Blair on *The Daily Show with Jon Stewart.*" *Guardian politics blog online,* 2008, available at http://www.guardian.co.uk/politics/blog/2008/sep/19/tony.blair.daily.show.jon.stewart.

Isen, Alice M. "An Influence of Positive Affect on Decision Making in Complex Situations: Theoretical Issues with Practical Implications." *Journal of Consumer Psychology* 11, no. 2 (2001): 75–85.

Jackson, L. A., L. A. Sullivan, and C. N. Hodge. "Stereotype Effects on Attributions, Predictions, and Evaluations: No Two Social Judgments Are Quite Alike." *Journal of Personality and Social Psychology* 65, no. 1 (1993): 69–84.

Jane D. Brown, Carol J. Pardun. "Little in Common: Racial and Gender Differences in Adolescents' Television Diets." *Journal of Broadcasting & Electronic* 48, no. 2 (2004): 266.

Jansma, Laura L., Daniel Linz , Anthony Mulac and, Dorothy J. Imrich "Men's Interactions with Women after Viewing Sexually Explicit Films: Does Degradation Make a Difference?" *Communication Monographs* 64, no. 1 (1997): 1.

Jargon, Julie. "Groups Urge Limits on Food Ads for Kids." *Wall Street Journal—Eastern Edition* 251, no. 62 (2008): A12.

Jaspen, Bruce. "Medical Ads Aim Straight for the Heart." *Chicago Tribune,* January 23 2007.

Jean, Martin. "The Food Industry and Health." *Lancet* 368, no. 9546 (2006): 1490.

Jennifer M Jones, Susan Bennett, Marion P. Olmsted, Margaret L. Lawson, and Gary Rodin. "Disordered Eating Attitudes and Behaviours in Teenaged Girls: A School-Based Study." *Canadian Medical Association Journal* 165, no. 5 (2001): 547.

Johansson, Thomas, and Nils Hammar, "Hegemonic Masculinity and Pornography: Young People's Attitudes toward and Relations to Pornography." *Journal of Men's Studies* 15, no. 1 (2007): 57.

John, R. Wilke. "FTC Head to Step Down, Is Seen Taking P&G Post." *Wall Street Journal,* February 28 2008, A.4.

Johnson, Brian D. "The Male Myth." *Maclean's* 107, no. 5 (1994): 38.

Johnson, James D., Brad J. Bushman, and John F. Dovidio. "Support for Harmful Treatment and Reduction of Empathy toward Blacks: Remnants of Stereotype Activation Involving Hurricane Katrina and L'il Kim." *Journal of Experimental Social Psychology* 44 (2008): 1506–13.

Jonathan, Watts. "Japan's Fatal Obsession with Bodyweight." *Lancet* 360, no. 9329 (2002): 318.

Jones, Edward E., and Victor Harris. "The Attribution of Attitudes." *Journal of Experimental Social Psychology* 3 (1967): 1–24.

Joseph, E. Uscinski. "Too Close to Call? Uncertainty and Bias in Election-Night Reporting." *Social Science Quarterly* 88, no. 1 (2007): 51.

Jost, John. "The End of Ideology." *American Psychologist* 61, no. 7 (2006): 651–70.

Jost, John T. "Coda: After 'The End of Ideology.'" *American Psychologist* 62, no. 9 (2007): 1078–79.

Jost, John T., Mahzarin R. Banaji, and Brian A. Nosek. "A Decade of System Justification Theory: Accumulated Evidence of Conscious and Unconscious Bolstering of the Status Quo." *Political Psychology* 25, no. 6 (2004): 881–919.

Jussim, L. "Social Perception and Social Reality: A Reflection-Construction Model." *Psychological Review* 98, no. 1 (1991): 54–73.

Jussim, Lee, Lerita M. Coleman, and Lauren Lerch. "The Nature of Stereotypes: A Comparison and Integration of Three Theories." *Journal of Personality and Social Psychology* 52, no. 3 (1987): 536–46.

Jussim, Lee, Christopher J. Fleming, and Cortney Kohberger. "The Nature of Stereotypes II: A Multiple-Process Model of Evaluations." *Journal of Applied Social Psychology* 26, no. 4 (1996): 283–312.

Kaplan, David A., and Ellen Ladowsky. "Bobbitt Fever." *Newsweek* 123, no. 4 (1994): 52.

Kaplan, Karen. "Company Town; Scientists Say Movie Image Not a Pretty Picture; Film: Seeking to Counter Stereotypes, Group Offers Grants to

Expose Student Filmmakers to Professionals in the Real World." *Los Angeles Times,* November 18 1998, 5.

Karasawa, Minoru, Nobuko Asal, and Yoshiko Tanabe. "Stereotypes as Shared Beliefs: Effects of Group Identity on Dyadic Conversations." *Group Processes and Intergroup Relations* 10, no. 4 (2007): 515–32.

Karlen, Neal. "Copycat Assault." *Newsweek,* October 22, 1984.

"Keith Olbermann Destroys Rush Limbaugh over Edwards Smear." YouTube, 2008. Retrieved April 7, 2009 http://www.youtube.com/watch?v=53Ef739Vlkg.

Kernahan, Cyndi, Bruce D. Bartholow, and B. Ann Bettencourt. "Effects of Category-Based Expectancy Violation on Affect-Related Evaluations: Toward a Comprehensive Model." *Basic and Applied Social Psychology* 22, no. 2 (2000): 85–100.

Keyes, Allison. "Political Humor's Hysterical History." 2008, available at http://www.npr.org/templates/story/story.php?storyId=95413835.

Kilbourne, Jean. *Killing Us Softly 3*: Northampton, MA Media Education Foundation, 2000.

Kilbourne, J., and M. Pipher. *Can't Buy My Love.* New York: Free Press, 2000.

King, Lorraine, and Andrew J. Hill. "Magazine Adverts for Healthy and Less Healthy Foods: Effects on Recall but Not Hunger or Food Choice by Pre-Adolescent Children." *Appetite* 51, no. 1 (2008): 194–97.

Koepp, M. J., R. N. Gunn, A. D. Lawrence, V. J. Cunningham, A. Dagher, T. Jones, D. J. Brooks, C. J. Bench, and P. M. Grasby. "Evidence for Striatal Dopamine Release during a Video Game." *Nature* 393, no. 6682 (1998): 266.

Konijn, Elly A., Marije Nije Bijvank, and Brad J. Bushman. "I Wish I Were a Warrior: The Role of Wishful Identification in the Effects of Violent Video Games on Aggression in Adolescent Boys." *Developmental Psychology* 43, no. 4 (2007): 1038–44.

Konijn, Elly A., and Brad J. Bushman. "World Leaders as Movie Characters? Perceptions of George W. Bush, Tony Blair, Osama Bin Laden, and Saddam Hussein." *Media Psychology* 9, no. 1 (2007): 157–77.

Konrath, Sara, Brad J. Bushman, and W. Keith Campbell. "Attenuating the Link between Threatened Egotism and Aggression." *Psychological Science* 17, no. 11 (2006): 995–1001.

Krohn, Franklin B., and Frances L. Suazo. "Contemporary Urban Music: Controversial Messages in Hip-Hop and Rap Lyrics." *ETC: A Review of General Semantics,* Summer 1995, 139–54.

Kruger, Justin, Nicholas Epley, Jason Parker, and Zhi-Wen Ng. "Egocentrism over E-Mail: Can We Communicate as Well as We Think?" *Journal of Personality and Social Psychology* 89, no. 6 (2005): 925–36.

Kubey, Roberttand Csikszentmihalyi, Mihaly. "Television Addiction Is No Mere Metaphor." *Scientific American*, Special Edition 14, no. 1 (2004): 48–55.

Kwak, Hyokjin, George M. Zinkhan, and Joseph R. Dominick. "The Moderating Role of Gender and Compulsive Buying Tendencies in the Cultivation Effects of TV Show and TV Advertising: A Cross Cultural Study between the United States and South Korea." *Media Psychology* 4, no. 1 (2002): 77–111.

Labbe, Colleen P., and Rosanne W. Fortner. "Perceptions of the Concerned Reader: An Analysis of the Subscribers of E/the Environmental Magazine." *Journal of Environmental Education* 32, no. 3 (2001): 41–6.

Lakin, Jessica L., Valerie E. Jefferis, Clara Michelle Cheng, and Tanya L. Chartrand. "The Chameleon Effect as Social Glue: Evidence for the Evolutionary Significance of Nonconscious Mimicry." *Journal of Nonverbal Behavior* 27, no. 3 (2003): 145.

Lamb, Sharon, and Lyn Mikel Brown. *Packaging Girlhood: Rescuing Our Daughters from Marketers' Schemes*. New York: St. Martin's Press, 2006.

Lanis, Kyra, and Katherine Covell. "Images of Women in Advertisements: Effects on Attitudes Related to Sexual Aggression." *Sex Roles* 32 (1995): 639–49.

Larson, Mary Strom. "Gender, Race, and Aggression in Television Commercials that Feature Children." *Sex Roles* 48, no. 1 (2003): 67.

"Late Show with David Letterman Top Ten." Available at http://www.cbs.com/latenight/lateshow/top_ten/index/php/20081006.phtml.

Lemmens, Jeroen S., and Brad J. Bushman. "The Appeal of Violent Video Games to Lower Educated Aggressive Adolescent Boys from Two Countries." *CyberPsychology and Behavior* 9, no. 5 (2006): 638–41.

Lena, Jennifer. "Social Context and Musical Content of Rap Music, 1979–1995." *Social Forces* 85, no. 1 (2006): 479–95.

Lenhart, Amanda, Mary Madden, Alexandra Rankin Macgill, and Aaron Smith. "Teens and Social Media." *Pew Internet and American Life Project*, 2007, available at http://www.pewinternet.org/PPF/r/230/report_display.asp.

"Letterman Reacts to John Mccain Suspending Campaign." YouTube, 2008, http://www.youtube.com/watch?v=XjkCrfylq-E.

Lever, Janet, David A. Frederick, and Letitia Anne Peplau. "Does Size Matter? Men's and Women's Views on Penis Size across the Lifespan." *Psychology of Men and Masculinity* 7, no. 3 (2006): 129–43.

Levin, Diane, and Jean Kilbourne. *So Sexy So Soon: The New Sexualized Childhood and What Parents Can Do to Protect Their Kids.* New York: Ballantine, 2008.

Lindner, Katharina. "Images of Women in General Interest and Fashion Magazine Advertisements from 1955 to 2002." *Sex Roles* 51, no. 7/8 (2004): 409–21.

Linebarger, Deborah, L. and Walker Dale. "Infants' and Toddlers' Television Viewing and Language Outcomes." *American Behavioral Scientist* 48 (2005): 624–45.

Linz, Daniel G., Edward Donnerstein, and Steven Penrod. "Effects of Long-Term Exposure to Violent and Sexually Degrading Depictions of Women." *Journal of Personality and Social Psychology* 55, no. 5 (1988): 758.

Lipsyte, Robert. "OJ Syndrome." *American Health* 13, no. 7 (1994): 50–51.

"Liverpool Set to Ban McDonald's Happy Meals in a Bid to Cut Childhood Obesity." *Daily Mail* 2008, http://www.dailymail.co.uk/news/article-517955/Liverpool-set-ban-McDonalds-Happy-Meals-bid-cut-childhood-obesity.html.

Loseke, Donileen R., and Joel Best. " 'Violence' Is 'Violence' . . . Or Is It: The Social Construction of 'Wife Abuse' and Public Policy." In *Images of Issues: Typifying Contemporary Social Problems*, 191–206. Hawthorne, NY: Aldine de Gruyter, 1989.

Lumet, Sidney. *Network.* Metro-Goldwyn-Mayer/United Artists, 1976.

Lyons, Anthony, and Yoshihisa Kashima. "How Are Stereotypes Maintained through Communication? The Influence of Stereotype Sharedness." *Journal of Personality and Social Psychology* 85, no. 6 (2003): 989–1005.

Maass, Ann, Mara Cadinu, Gaia Guarnieri, and AnnaLisa Grasselli. "Sexual Harassment under Social Identity Threat: The Computer Harassment Paradigm." *Journal of Personality and Social Psychology* 85 (2003): 853–70.

Macrae, C. Neil, Galen V. Bodenhausen, Alan B. Milne, Luigi Castelli, Hadyn Ellis, and Neil Macrae. "On Disregarding Deviants: Exemplar Typicality and Person Perception." In *Validation in Psychology: Research Perspectives*, 59–90. New Brunswick, NJ: Transaction, 2001.

Macrae, C. Neil, Galen V. Bodenhausen, Alan B. Milne, Luigi Castelli, Astrid M. Schloerscheidt, and Sasha Greco. "On Activating Exemplars." *Journal of Experimental Social Psychology* 34, no. 4 (1998): 330.

Madell, Dominic E., and Steven J. Muncer. "Control over Social Interactions: An Important Reason for Young People's Use of the Internet and Mobile Phones for Communication?" *CyberPsychology and Behavior* 10, no. 1 (2007): 137–40.

Magazine, O. "The O Media Kit." Harpo Productions, available at www.OMediakit.com/r5/home.asp.

Magill, M. Elizabeth. "Temporary Accidents?" *Michigan Law Review* 106, no. 6 (2008): 1021.

Maher, Jill K., Kenneth C. Herbst, Nancy M. Childs and Seth Finn. "Racial Stereotypes in Children's Television Commercials." *Journal of Advertising Research* 48, no. 1 (2008): 80.

Malkin, Amy R., and Kimberlie Wornian. "Women and Weight: Gendered Messages on Magazine Covers." *Sex Roles* 40, no. 7/8 (1999): 647–55.

"Marketing Food to Children." *Lancet* 366, no. 9503 (2005): 2064.

Marr, Kendra. "Children Targets of $1.6 Billion in Food Ads; FTC Discloses 2006 Spending in First-Ever Report." *Washington Post,* July 30 2008, D.1.

Martin, Andrew. "Nickelodeon to Limit Use of Characters on Junk Foods." *New York Times* 156, no. 54038 (2007): C3.

Martino, Steven C., Rebecca L. Collins, Marc N. Elliott, Amy Strachman, David E. Kanhouse, and Sandra H. Berry. "Exposure to Degrading versus Nondegrading Music Lyrics and Sexual Behavior among Youth." *Pediatrics* 118, no. 2 (2006): 782.

Mastro, Dana E., and Maria A. Kopacz. "Media Representations of Race, Prototypicality, and Policy Reasoning: An Application of Self-Categorization Theory." *Journal of Broadcasting & Electronic Media* 50, no. 2 (2006): 305.

Mastro, Dana E., and Susannah R. Stern. "Representations of Race in Television Commercials: A Content Analysis of Prime-Time Advertising." *Journal of Broadcasting & Electronic Media* 47, no. 4 (2003): 638.

Mastro, Dana E., Ron Tamborini, and Craig R. Hullett. "Linking Media to Prototype Activation and Subsequent Celebrity Attraction: An Application of Self-Categorization Theory." *Communication Research* 32, no. 3 (2005): 323–48.

Matthews, Anne E. "Children and Obesity: A Pan-European Project Examining the Role of Food Marketing." *European Journal of Public Health* 18, no. 1 (2008): 7–11.

McCluhan, Marshall, with Quentin Fiore and Jerome Agel. *The Medium Is the Message: An Inventory of Effects.* Corte Madera, CA: Ginko Press, 1967.

McFedries, Paul. "Game On." *IEEE Spectrum* 44, no. 2 (2007): 72.

McKain, Aaron. "Not Necessarily Not the News: Gatekeeping, Remediation, and *The Daily Show*." *Journal of American Culture* 28, no. 4 (2005): 415–30.

McKenna, Katelyn Y. A., and John A. Bargh. "Coming Out in the Age of the Internet: Identity 'Demarginalization' through Virtual Group Participation." *Journal of Personality and Social Psychology* 75, no. 3 (1998): 681–94.

McLellan, Faith. "Marketing and Advertising: Harmful to Children's Health." *Lancet* 360 (2002): 1001.

McNulty, F. "Murder Was Her Last Resort." *Redbook* no. 198 (November 1984).

Media Awarenes Network, "National Television Violence Study Year Three: 1996–97; Summary of Recommendations." *Report of the University of California, Santa Barbara, Center for Communication and Social Policy Web site* (1996–1997), available at http://www.media-awareness.ca/english/resources/research_documents/reports/violence/nat_tv_violence.cfm.

Microsoft. *Encarta World English Dictionary*. 1999.

Milburn, M. A., R. Mather, and S. D. Conrad. "The Effects of Viewing R-Rated Movie Scenes that Objectify Women on Perceptions of Date Rape." *Sex Roles* 43 (2000): 645–64.

Miller-Young, Mireille. "Hip Hop Honeys and Da Hustlaz: Black Sexualities in the New Hip Hop Pornography." *Meridians: Feminism, Race and Transnationalism* 8, no. 1 (2008): 261–92.

Minjeong, Kim, and J. Lennon Sharron. "Content Analysis of Diet Advertisements: A Cross-National Comparison of Korean and U.S. Women's Magazines." *Clothing and Textiles Research Journal* 24 (2006): 345–62.

Mohan, Anne Marie. "Diet Pill Package Gets Glamorous." *Packaging Digest* 43, no. 3 (2006): 52–54.

Monahan, Jennifer L., Sheila T. Murphy, and R. B. Zajonc. "Subliminal Mere Exposure: Specific, General, and Diffuse Effects." *Psychological Science* 11, no. 6 (2000): 462–66.

Moore, Elizabeth S., Hiram E. Fitzgerald, Vasiliki Mousouli, and H. Dele Davies. "Food Marketing Goes Online: A Content Analysis of Web Sites for Children." In *Obesity in Childhood and Adolescence*, Vol. 2: *Understanding Development and Prevention*, 93–115. Westport, CT: Praeger/Greenwood Publishing Group, 2008.

Moore, Trudy S. "O.J. Simpson's Case Brings New Focus on Abuse of Women." *Jet* 86, no. 11 (1994): 14.

Morrison, Margaret A., Dean M. Krugman, and Pumsoon Park. "Under the Radar: Smokeless Tobacco Advertising in Magazines with Substantial Youth Readership." *American Journal of Public Health* 98, no. 3 (2008): 543–48.

MPA. "Magazines 24/7, the Magazine Industry's Inaugural Digital Summit, Debuts to a Sold-out Audience." Magazine Publishers of America, available at http://www.magazine.org/Press_Room/MPA_Press_Releases/14503.cfm.

Murnen, Sarah K., Linda Smolak, J. Andrew Mills, and Lindsey Good. "Thin, Sexy Women and Strong, Muscular Men: Grade-School Children's Responses to Objectified Images of Women and Men." *Sex Roles* 49, no. 9 (2003): 427–37.

Murnen, S. K., C. Wright, and G. Kaluzny. "If Boys Will Be Boys, then Girls Will Be Victims? A Meta-Analytic Review of the Research that Relates Masculine Ideology to Sexual Aggression." *Sex Roles* 46 (2007): 359–75.

Murray, John P., Mario Liotti, Paul T. Ingmundson, Helen S. Mayberg, Pu Yonglin, Frank Zamarripa, Liu Yijun, Marty G. Woldorff, Gao Jia-Hong, and Peter T. Fox. "Children's Brain Activations While Viewing Televised Violence Revealed by Fmri." *Media Psychology* 8, no. 1 (2006): 25–37.

Nalini, Ambady, Shih Margaret, Kim Amy, and L. Pittinsky Todd. "Stereotype Susceptibility in Children: Effects of Identity Activation on Quantitative Performance." *Psychological Science* 12, no. 5 (2001): 385.

Namuth, Tessa. "When Did He Stop Beating His Wife?" *Newsweek* 123, no. 26 (1994): 21.

Nash, Madeleine J. "The Gift of Mimicry." *Time*, January 29, 2007.

National Institute on Media and the Family NIMF. "Mediawise Video Game Report Card." 2002, http://www.mediafamily. org/research/report_vgrc_2002-2.shtml.

National Institute on Media and the Family NIMF. "Research Update: Do Children's Brains See the Difference between Fantasy and Reality?" *MediaWise Enewsletter*, May 21, 2008, available at http://www. mediafamily.org/enews/05_23_2008_2.shtml?utm_source=enews5_21_08_research& utm_medium=enews5_21_08_research.

National Television Violence Study, Vol. 2. Thousand Oaks, CA: Sage, 1998.

National Television Violence Study, Vol. 3. Thousand Oaks, CA: Sage, 1998.

NBC.com. "Vp Debate Open: Palin/Biden." In *Saturday Night Live*, 2008, http://www.hulu.com/watch/37730/saturday-night-live-vp-debate-open-palin–biden.

Nedic. "Statistics." Available at http://www.nedic.ca/knowthefacts/statistics. shtml.

Nelly. "Da Derrty Versions." Umvd Labels, 2003.

Nemeth, Mary, and William Lowther. "Hot Off the Presses." *Maclean's* 107, no.4 (1994): 66.

Nestle, Marion. "Food Industry and Health: Mostly Promises, Little Action." *Lancet* 368, no. 9535 (2006): 564.

Newnham, David. "Outside In." *Nursing Standard* 22, no. 22 (2008): 26–27.

News, NBC. "High Heels for Infants." Available at http://video.msn.com/video.aspx?mkt=en-us&vid=887008f3-1a01-4cb4-bb4b-151e70f90e10&fg=rss&from=05.

Nisbett, R. E., and Lee Ross. *Human Inference: Strategies and Shortcomings of Social Judgment.* Upper Saddle River, NJ: Prentice Hall, 1985.

Nisbett, R. E., and T. D. Wilson. "Telling More Than We Can Know: Verbal Reports on Mental Processes." *Psychological Review* 84, no. 3 (1977): 231–59.

"Oceans Apart; Mergers and Dominant Firms." *Economist* 387, no. 8578 (2008): 89.

O'Connor, Lisa A., Jeanne Brooks-Gunn, and Julia Graber. "Black and White Girls' Racial Preferences in Media and Peer Choices and the Role of Socialization for Black Girls." *Journal of Family Psychology* 14, no. 3 (2000): 510.

Ostman, R. E. "Handbook of Visual Analysis." *Journalism and Mass Communication Quarterly* 79 (2002): 769–70.

Ostrov, Jamie M., Douglas A. Gentile, and Nicki R. Crick. "Media Exposure, Aggression and Prosocial Behavior during Early Childhood: A Longitudinal Study." *Social Development* 15, no. 4 (2006): 612–27.

Oxley, Douglas R., Kevin B. Smith, John R. Alford, Matthew V. Hibbing, Jennifer L. Miller, Mario Scalora, Peter K. Hatemi, and John R. Hibbing. "Political Attitudes Vary with Physiological Traits." *Science* 321, no. 5896 (2008): 1667–70.

"Parent Center Bulletin: 7 Ways to Be a Better Parent." 2008. E-mail bulletin, January 28, 2008,

Parentingteens.com. "Violence & Video Games." Available at http://www.parentingteens.com/index/Parent+Forum/Parenting+Poll/Violence+and+Video+Games.

Patten, Scott B. "'Diet Pills' and Major Depression in the Canadian Population." *Canadian Journal of Psychiatry/La Revue canadienne de psychiatrie* 46, no. 5: 438.

Payne, Gregg A., et al. "Uses and Gratifications Motives as Indicators of Magazine Readership." *Journalism Quarterly* 65, no. 4 (1988): 909.

Perry, Stephen D. "Commercial Humor Enhancement of Program Enjoyment: Gender and Program Appeal as Mitigating Factors." *Mass Communication and Society* 4, no. 1 (2001): 103.

Persky, Susan, and Jim Blascovich. "Immersive Virtual Environments versus Traditional Platforms: Effects of Violent and Nonviolent Video Game Play." *Media Psychology* 10, no. 1 (2007): 135–56.

Pewterbaugh, Mike. "Supplements Bulk Up Spot Market." *Response* 13, no. 3 (2004): 38.

Pingree, Suzanne. "Does Television Change Sex Role Stereotyping?" *PsycCRITIQUES* 33, no. 8 (1988): 713–14.

Pinto, Mary Beth. "On the Nature and Properties of Appeals Used in Direct-to-Consumer Advertising of Prescriptions." *Psychological Reports* 86, no. 2 (2000): 597.

Pohan, Cathy A., and Carla Mathison. "Television: Providing Powerful Multicultural Lessons Inside and Outside of School." *Multicultural Perspectives* 9, no. 1 (2007): 19–25.

"Poll Says Games Are Safe." 1999. http://pc.ign.com/articles/068/068231p1.html.

Posavac, Heidi D., Steven S. Posavac, and Emil J. Posavac. "Exposure to Media Images of Female Attractiveness and Concern with Body Weight among Young Women." *Sex Roles* 38, no. 3 (1998): 187–201.

Postmes, Tom, Russell Spears, and Martin Lea. "Intergroup Differentiation in Computer-Mediated Communication: Effects of Depersonalization." *Group Dynamics: Theory, Research, and Practice* 6, no. 1 (2002): 3–16.

Potter, W. James. *The Eleven Myths of Media Violence.* Thousand Oaks, CA: Sage, 2002.

Potter, W. James. *Media Literacy.* Los Angeles: Sage, 2008.

Powell, Kimberly, A. and Abels Lori. "Sex-Roles Stereotypes in TV Programs Aimed at the Preschool Audience: An Analysis of *Teletubbies* and *Barney & Friends.*" *Women and Language* 25, no. 2 (2002): 14.

Prentice, Deborah A., Richard J. Gerrig, Shelly Chaiken, and Yaacov Trope. "Exploring the Boundary between Fiction and Reality." In *Dual-Process Theories in Social Psychology*, 529–46. New York: Guilford Press, 1999.

Randolph, Laura B. "Battered Women." *Ebony* 49, no. 11 (1994): 112.

Randsford, Marc. "Average Person Spends More Time Using Media than Anything Else." *Ball State University Newsletter*, no. 9/23/2005 (2005), available at http://www.bsu.edu/news/article/0,1370,7273–850-36658,00. html.

Rhodes, Ann. "Legislative Efforts to Combat Childhood Obesity." *Journal for Specialists in Pediatric Nursing* 13, no. July (2008): 223–25.

Richard, Siegesmund. "On the Persistence of Memory: The Legacy of Visual African-American Stereotypes." *Studies in Art Education* 48, no. 3 (2007): 323.

Rivenbark, Celia. *Stop Dressing Your Six-Year-Old Like a Skank*. New York: St. Martin's Press, 2006, 28.

Rizzolatti, Giacomo and Destro Maddalena Fabbri. "Understanding Actions and the Intentions of Others: The Basic Neural Mechanism." *European Review* 15, no. 2 (2007): 209–22.

Roberts, D., and U. Foehr. *Kids and Media in America*. Cambridge, UK: Cambridge University Press, 2004.

Roberts, Donald F., and Christine M. Bachen. "Mass Communication Effects." *Annual Review of Psychology* 32 (1981): 307–56.

Robinson, Tom, and Caitlin Anderson. "Older Characters in Children's Animated Television Programs: A Content Analysis of Their Portrayal." *Journal of Broadcasting & Electronic Media* 50, no. 2 (2006): 287.

Roerig, James L., James E. Mitchell, Martina de Zwaan, Stephan A. Wonderlich, Shehzad Kamran, Sara Engbloom, Melissa Burgard, and Kathryn Lancaster. "The Eating Disorders Medicine Cabinet Revisited: A Clinician's Guide to Appetite Suppressants and Diuretics." *International Journal of Eating Disorders* 33, no. 4 (2003): 443.

Russo, Ann. "Framing the Victim: Domestic Violence, Media, and Social Problems." *Violence against Women* 12, no. 1 (2006): 116–19.

Sandiford, Kay, and Alan Burgess. "Shattered Night." *Good Housekeeping*, February 1984.

Saturday Night Live Transcripts. Available at http://snltranscripts.jt.org/92/92bperot.phtml.

Schultz, Astrid, and Franz Machilek. "Who Owns a Personal Home Page? A Discussion of Sampling Problems and a Strategy Based on a Search Engine." *Swiss Journal of Psychology* 62, no. 2 (2003): 121–29.

Scharrer, Erica. "From Wise to Foolish: The Portrayal of the Sitcom Father, 1950s–1990s." *Journal of Broadcasting and Electronic Media* 45, no. 1 (2001): 23.

Scharrer, Erica. "Hypermasculinity, Aggression, and Television Violence: An Experiment." *Media Psychology* 7, no. 4 (2005): 353.

Scharrer, Erica. "'I Noticed More Violence': The Effects of a Media Literacy Program on Critical Attitudes toward Media Violence." *Journal of Mass Media Ethics* 21, no. 1 (2006): 69.

Scharrer, Erica. "Making a Case for Media Literacy in the Curriculum: Outcomes and Assessment." *Journal of Adolescent and Adult Literacy* 46, no. 4 (2002): 354.

Scharrer, Erica. "Review, "The Politics of Force: Media and the Construction of Police Brutality, by Regina G. Lawrence. Berkeley: University of California Press, 2000. 279 Pp. $17.95 (Soft)." *Journal of Communication* 52, no. 2 (2002): 483.

Scharrer, Erica "The Politics of Force: Media and the Construction of Police Brutality. By Regina G. Lawrence. Berkeley: University of California Press, 2000. 279 pp. $17.95 (soft)." Journal of Communication 52, no. 2 (June 1, 2002): 483. http://www.proquest.com/ (accessed April 7, 2009).

Scharrer, Erica. "Third-Person Perception and Television Violence: The Role of Out-Group Stereotyping in Perceptions of Susceptibility to Effects." *Communication Research* 29, no. 6 (2002): 681.

Scharrer, Erica. "Tough Guys: The Portrayal of Hypermasculinity and Aggression in Televised Police Dramas." *Journal of Broadcasting and Electronic Media* 45, no. 4 (2001): 615.

Scharrer, Erica. "Virtual Violence: Gender and Aggression in Video Game Advertisements." *Mass Communication and Society* 7 (2004): 393–412.

Scharrer, Erica, Andrea Bergstrom, Angela Paradise, and Qianqing Ren. "Laughing to Keep from Crying: Humor and Aggression in Television Commercial Content." *Journal of Broadcasting and Electronic Media* 50, no. 4 (2006): 615.

Scharrer, Erica, and Ron Leone. "First-Person Shooters and the Third-Person Effect." *Human Communication Research* 34, no. 2 (2008): 210.

Scharrer, Erica, Lisa M. Weidman, and Kimberly L. Bissell. "Pointing the Finger of Blame: News Media Coverage of Popular-Culture Culpability." *Journalism and Communication Monographs* 5, no. 2 (2003): 47.

Schultz, Duane, and Sydney Schultz. *A History of Modern Psychology*. Belmont California: Wadsworth/Thompson Learning, 2004.

Sechrist, Gretchen B., and Charles Stangor. "Perceived Consensus Influences Intergroup Behavior and Stereotype Accessibility." *Journal of Personality and Social Psychology* 80, no. 4 (2001): 645–54.

Seelye, Katherine Q. "Best Informed Also View Fake News, Study Says." *New York Times*, April 16, 2007.

Seligmann, Jean, and Farai Chideya. "Bobbitts: Temporary Insanity." *Newsweek* 123, no. 5 (1994): 54.

"Selling to—and Selling Out—Children." *Lancet* 360, no. 9338 (2002): 959.

"Sen. Brownback Comments on FTC Report Studying Food Marketing Tactics." *US Fed News Service, Including US State News* (2008); Senator Sam Brownback's web site: http://brownback.senate.gov/pressapp/record.cfm?id=301523 Accessed April 7, 2009.

Sharma, Andrew. "Recall of Television Commercials as a Function of Viewing Context: The Impact of Program-Commercial Congruity on Commercial Messages." *Journal of General Psychology* 127, no. 4 (2000): 383.

Sharpley-Whiting, Tracy D. *Pimps Up, Ho's Down: Hip Hop's Hold on Young Black Women.* New York: NYU Press, 2008.

Shavitt, Sharon, Ashok K. Lalwani, Jing Zhang, and Carlos J. Torelli. "The Horizontal/Vertical Distinction in Cross-Cultural Consumer Research." *Journal of Consumer Psychology* 16, no. 4 (2006): 325–42.

Sherman, Brian R. "The Age Shift." *Industrial Engineer* 39, no. 10 (2007): 40–44.

Signorielli, Nancy. "Aging on Television: Messages Relating to Gender, Race, and Occupation in Prime Time." *Journal of Broadcasting & Electronic Media* 48, no. 2 (2004): 279.

Signorielli, Nancy, George Gerbner, and Michael Morgan. "Violence on Television: The Cultural Indicators Project." *Journal of Broadcasting and Electronic Media* 39, no. 2 (1995): 278–83.

Simpson, David. "The State of the Art and the Science of Persuasion." *PsycCRITIQUES* 50, no. 28 (2005).

Singer, Dorothy G., Roberta Michnick Golinkoff, and Kathy Hirsh-Pasek. *Play = Learning: How Play Motivates and Enhances Children's Cognitive and Social-Emotional Growth.* New York: Oxford University Press, 2006.

Singer, Dorothy G., and Jerome L. Singer. *Imagination and Play in the Electronic Age.* Cambridge, MA: Harvard University Press, 2005.

Singer, Jerome L., and Dorothy G. Singer. "Preschoolers' Imaginative Play as Precursor of Narrative Consciousness." *Imagination, Cognition and Personality* 25, no. 2 (2006): 97–117.

Slusher, Morgan P., and Craig A. Anderson. "When Reality Monitoring Fails: The Role of Imagination in Stereotype Maintenance." *Journal of Personality and Social Psychology* 52, no. 4 (1987): 653–62.

Smith, Anita, and Kipling D. Williams. "R U There? Ostracism by Cell Phone Text Messages." *Group Dynamics: Theory, Research, and Practice* 8, no. 4 (2004): 291–301.

Smith, Elaine, and Jessica Whiteside. "TV Sitcom So Transforms Use of English." *University of Toronto Magazine*, Spring, 2004, available at http://www.magazine.utoronto.ca/04spring/leadingedge.asp.

Smolowe, Jill, and Ann Blackman. "When Violence Hits Home." *Time* 144, no. 1 (1994): 18.

Solomon, Sheldon, Jeff Greenberg, and Tom Pyszczynski. "Fatal Attraction." *APS Observer online*, no. 10 (2004), available at http://www.psychologicalscience.org/observer/getArticle.cfm?id=1660.

Souweidane, Violet, and Rowell Huesmann. "The Influence of American Urban Culture on the Development of Normative Beliefs about Aggression." *American Journal of Community Psychology* 27, no. 2 (1999): 239.

Spence, J. T., R. Helmreich, and J. Stapp. "A Short Version of the Attitudes towards Women Scale (ATS)." *Bulletin of the Psychonomic Society* 2 (1973): 219–20.

Spencer, Margaret Beale. "Lessons Learned and Opportunities Ignored since *Brown V. Board of Education*: Youth Development and the Myth of a Color-Blind Society." *Educational Researcher* 37, no. 5 (2008): 253.

Spitzer, Brenda L., Katherine A. Henderson, and Marilyn T. Zivian. "Gender Differences in Population versus Media Body Sizes: A Comparison over Four Decades." *Sex Roles* 40, no. 7 (1999): 545–65.

Stangor, Charles, Gretchen B. Sechrist, John T. Jost, Joseph P. Forgas, and Kipling D. Williams. "Social Influence and Intergroup Beliefs: The Role of Perceived Social Consensus." In *Social Influence: Direct and Indirect Processes*, 235–52. New York: Psychology Press, 2001.

Stanley, T. L. "Geniuses in Diapers." *Brandweek* 48, no. 37 (2007): 32.

Stanten, Michele. "Weight Loss in a Bottle." *Prevention* 55, no. 5 (2003): 83–5.

Stark, Evan. *Coercive Control: How Men Entrap Women in Personal Life.* New York: Oxford University Press, 2007.

Stein, Harry. "Separation Anxiety." *Men's Health* 8, no. 8 (1993): 28.

Steinke, Jocelyn, Maria Knight Lapinski, Nikki Crocker, Aletta Zietsman-Thomas, Yaschica Williams, Stepanie Higdon Evergreen, and Sarvani Kuchibhotla. "Assessing Media Influences on Middle School-Aged Children's Perceptions of Women in Science Using the Draw-a-Scientist Test (DAST)." *Science Communication* 29, no. 1 (2007): 35–64.

Strasburger, V. C., and B. J Wilson. *Children, Adolescents and the Media.* Thousand Oaks, CA: Sage, 2002.

Subrahmanyam, Kaveri, David Smahel, and Patricia Greenfield. "Connecting Developmental Constructions to the Internet: Identity Presentation and Sexual Exploration in Online Teen Chat Rooms." *Developmental Psychology* 42, no. 3 (2006): 395–406.

Susan, Linn, and Courtney L. Novosat. "Calories for Sale: Food Marketing to Children in the Twenty-First Century." *The* annals of the American Academy of Political and Social Science, 2008, 615, 133–5.

Swim, J., E. Borgida, G. Maruyama, and D. Myers. "Joan Mckay versus John Mckay: Do Gender Stereotypes Bias Evaluations?" In *Psychological Bulletin* 105, no. 5 (1989): 409–29. TaggleElgate. "Farrah Fawcett BBC Film '86 *Extremities* Interview." 2007. Retrieved July 30, 2008 from http://www.youtube.com/watch?v=6LuX2vphPZw.

Tan, Alexis, Yuki Fujioka and Gerdean Tan. "Television Use, Stereotypes of African Americans and Opinions on Affirmative Action: An Affective Model of Policy Reasoning." *Communication Monographs* 67, no. 4 (2000): 362.

Tanis, Martin, and Tom Postmes. "Cues to Identity in Online Dyads: Effects of Interpersonal versus Intragroup Perceptions on Performance." *Group Dynamics: Theory, Research, and Practice* 12, no. 2 (2008): 96–111.

Tanner, Andrea, Sonya Duhe, Alexandra Evans, and Marge Condrasky. "Using Student-Produced Media to Promote Healthy Eating: A Pilot Study on the Effects of a Media and Nutrition Intervention." *Science Communication* 30, no. 1 (2008): 108–25.

Taylor, Susan L. "Owning Your Life." *Essence* 25, no. 5 (1994): 65.

Thakkar, Rupin R., Michelle M. Garrison, and Dimitri A. Christakis. "A Systematic Review for the Effects of Television Viewing by Infants and Preschoolers." *Pediatrics* 118, no. 5 (2006): 2025–31.

Thill, Kathryn Phillips, and Karen E. Dill. "American Magazine Coverage of Domestic Violence: Reflecting on 30 Years of the Public Dialogue about Intimate Abuse." In *Violence against Women in Families and Relationships*, edited by Eve S. Buzawa and Evan Stark. Westport, CT: Greenwood Press, 2008.

Thomas, Karen. "Study Ties Aggression to Violence in Games." *USA Today*, May 10, 2000, 3D.

Thompson, Darcy A., and Dimitri A. Christakis. "The Association between Television Viewing and Irregular Sleep Schedules among Children Less Than 3 Years of Age." *Pediatrics* 116, no. 4 (2005): 851–56.

"Thought for Food." *Lancet* 362, no. 9396 (2003): 1593.

Time. "The World's Most Influential People—the 2008 Time 100." Available at http://www.time.com/time/specials/2007/0,28757, 1733748,00.html.

Treadway, Molly, and Michael McCloskey. "Effects of Racial Stereotypes on Eyewitness Performance: Implications of the Real and the Rumoured Allport and Postman Studies." *Applied Cognitive Psychology* 3, no. 1 (1989): 53–63.

Treise, Debbie, and Michael F. Weigold. "AIDS Public Service Announcements: Effects of Fear and Repetition on Predictors of Condom Use." *Health Marketing Quarterly* 18, no. 3/4 (2001): 39.

Trier, James. "*The Daily Show with Jon Stewart*, Part 1." *Journal of Adolescent and Adult Literacy* 51, no. 5 (2008): 424–27.

Trier, James. "*The Daily Show with Jon Stewart*, Part 2." *Journal of Adolescent and Adult Literacy* 51, no. 7 (2008): 600–05.

Unkelbach, Christian, Joseph P. Forgas, and Thomas F. Denson. "The Turban Effect: The Influence of Muslim Headgear and Induced Affect on Aggressive Responses Using the Shooter Bias Paradigm." *Journal of Experimental Social Psychology,* in press.

Urso, Nicole. "Los Angeles Times Delves into Dr. Diet Pill Controversy." *Response* 13, no. 11 (2005): 9.

Uslaner, Eric M. "Social Capital, Television, and the "Mean World": Trust, Optimism, and Civic Participation." *Political Psychology* 19, no. 3 (1998): 441–67.

U.S. Census Bureau. "State and County Quick Facts." Available at http://quickfacts.census.gov/qfd/states.00000.html.

U.S. Census Bureau. United States Census 2000. Available at http://www.census.gov/main/www/cen2000.html.

van den Eijnden, Regina J. J. M., Gert-Jan Meerkerk, Ad A. Vermulst, Renske Spijkerman, and Rutger C. M. E. Engels. "Online Communication, Compulsive Internet Use, and Psychosocial Well-Being among Adolescents: A Longitudinal Study." *Developmental Psychology* 44, no. 3 (2008): 655–65.

Vanessa, Bush. "Primetime Blues: African Americans on Network Television." *The Booklist* 97, no. 9/10 (2001): 896.

Varney, Wendy. "Bang! Bang! Ka-Ching! War Profits from the Toy Box." *Social Alternatives* 21, no. 2 (2002): 41–45.

Vedantam, Shankar. "Startle Response Linked to Politics." *Washington Post,* 2008, available at http://www.washingtonpost.com/wp-dyn/content/article/2008/09/18/AR2008091802265.html?hpid=topnews. September 19, 2008.

Ventis, W. Larry, Garrett Higbee, and Susan A. Murdock. "Using Humor in Systematic Desensitization to Reduce Fear." *Journal of General Psychology* 128, no. 2 (2001): 241.

Vogel, David L., Douglas A. Gentile, and Scott A. Kaplan. "The Influence of Television on Willingness to Seek Therapy." *Journal of Clinical Psychology* 64, no. 3 (2008): 276-95.

Vogt, Donna U. "Direct-to-Consumer Advertising of Prescription Drugs." Congressional Research Service, 2005. Web site: http://www.loc.gov/crsinfo/ Order code RL32853.

Walsh, David. *Dr. Dave's Cyberhood.* New York: Simon and Schuster, 2001.

Walsh, David. "Mediawise Columns." 2008, available at http://www.mediafamily.org/mediawisecolumns/index.shtml.

Walsh, David. *Selling Out America's Children: How America Puts Profits before Values—and What Parents Can Do,* Minneapolis, MN: Fairview Press, 1994.

Walsh, David, and Nat Bennett (Contributor). *Why Do They Act That Way? A Survival Guide to the Adolescent Brain for You and Your Teen.* New York: Free Press, 2005.

Walsh, David A., and Douglas A. Gentile. "A Validity Test of Movie, Television and Video-Game Ratings." *Pediatrics* 107, no. 6 (2001): 1302.

Ward, Monique L., Ann Merriwether, and Allison Caruthers. "Breasts Are for Men: Media, Masculinity Ideologies, and Men's Beliefs about Women's Bodies." *Sex Roles* 55, no. 9/10 (2006): 703–14.

Wartella, Ellen A., Elizabeth A. Vandewater, and J. Rideout Victoria. "Introduction: Electronic Media Use in the Lives of Infants, Toddlers, and Preschoolers." *American Behavioral Scientist* 48 (2005): 501–4.

Watkins, Lucy M., and Lucy Johnston. "Screening Job Applicants: The Impact of Physical Attractiveness and Application Quality." *International Journal of Selection and Assessment* 8, no. 2 (2000): 76.

Weber, Rene, Ute Ritterfeld, and Klaus Mathiak. "Does Playing Violent Video Games Induce Aggression? Empirical Evidence of a Functional Magnetic Resonance Imaging Study." *Media Psychology* 8, no. 1 (2006): 39–60.

Wheaton, Ken. "Harkin Gives Marketers No Reason to Trust His Words." *Advertising Age* 79, no. 30 (2008): 14.

Wheeler, S. Christian, Melanie C. Green, and Timothy C. Brock. "Fictional Narratives Change Beliefs: Replications of Prentice, Gerrig, & Bailis (1997) with Mixed Corroboration." *Psychonomic Bulletin and Review* 6, no. 1 (1999): 136–41.

Whitlock, Janis L., Jane L. Powers, and John Eckenrode. "The Virtual Cutting Edge: The Internet and Adolescent Self-Injury." *Developmental Psychology* 42, no. 3 (2006): 407–17.

Wilkin, Holley W., Thomas W. Valente, Sheila Murphy, Michael J. Cody, Grace Huang, and Vicki Beck. "Does Entertainment-Education Work with Latinos in the United States? Identification and the Effects of a Telenovela Breast Cancer Storyline." *Journal of Health Communication* 12, no. 5 (2007): 455–69.

Willens, Kathy. "Black College Women Take Aim at Rappers." 2004, available at *USAToday.com*.

Wilson, Clint C., F. Gutierrez, and Lena M. Chao. *Racism, Sexism and the Media: The Rise of Class Communication in Multicultural America.* 3rd ed. Thousand Oaks, CA: Sage, 2003.

Wolf, Naomi. *The Beauty Myth: How Images of Beauty Are Used against Women.* New York: Harper Perennial, 2002.

Wood, Lisa C. and J. Quina Marco. "The Perils of Electronic Filing and Transmission of Documents." *Antitrust* 22, no. 2 (2008): 91.

Yoon, Yeosun, Zeynep Gürhan-Canli, and Norbert Schwarz. "The Effect of Corporate Social Responsibility (CSR) Activities on Companies with Bad Reputations." *Journal of Consumer Psychology* 16, no. 4 (2006): 377–90.

Zachry, Woodie, Marvin Shepherd, Melvin Hinich, James Wilson, Carolyn Brown, and Kenneth Lawson. "Relationship between Direct-to-Consumer Advertising and Physician Diagnosing and Prescribing." *American Journal of Health System Pharmacists* 59 (2002): 42–49.

Zelli, Arnaldo, L. Rowell Huesmann, and Daniel Cervone. "Social Inference and Individual Differences in Aggression: Evidence for Spontaneous Judgments of Hostility." *Aggressive Behavior* 21, no. 6 (1995): 405–17.

Zigler, Edward F., Dorothy G. Singer, and Sandra J. Bishop-Josef. *Children's Play: The Roots of Reading.* Washington, DC: ZERO TO THREE/National Center for Infants, Toddlers and Families, 2004.

Zuwerink, Julia R., and Patricia G. Devine. "Attitude Importance and Resistance to Persuasion: It's Not Just the Thought That Counts." *Journal of Personality and Social Psychology* 70, no. 5 (1996): 931–44.

Index

Active play, 32
Ad Council (AdCouncil.org), 163, 227
Adolescents
    body weight of, 157, 158
    Internet use by, 35
    social fears, 34, 42
    stereotypes and, 108–109
Adult screen time, 6–7
Advertising. *See also* Magazine (print)
        media; Sexuality in advertising
    affects of, 9
    agenda setting theory, 147–148
    athletes in, 159–161, 169, 224
    behaviorism in, 144–145
    body image makeovers, 153–154
    direct-to-consumer, 164–165
    with e-mail, 45–46
    food and fitness, 150, 154–155, 157–161
    on Internet, 149, 158–159, 164
    manipulation, 9, 17, 42, 148–149
    media illusions, 19, 25, 39, 150–151
    obesity and, 155–156, 157
    political, 194–195
    prescription drugs, 163–165
    product placement, 149–150
    Public Service Announcements, 163
    smear ads, 204
    weight-loss products, 161–163
Aesop's fables, 51
African Americans
    media coverage of, 91–94
    movie stereotypes, 14–15, 100
    positive role models, 96, 112
    rap music and, 181–185
    video game portrayals, 97, 185–186
Agenda setting theory, 147–148
Aggression
    childhood studies on, 74–77,
        172–173, 227
    degradation and, 185–186

media violence and, 25, 44, 67–68
mirror neutrons and, 27–28
screen time and, 227
sexuality in children, 172–173
vs. intelligence, 104
video games and, 8, 10
Aggression Research Group, 101
Alda, Alan, 235–236, 238–239
All in the Family (TV show), 7–8
Ambivalent Sexism Theory, 102–103
American Academy for the Advancement
        of Science (AAAS), 237
American Academy of Pediatrics, 227
American Film Institute, 224, 230
American media culture, 134
American Psychological Association
        (APA), 179–180
Anderson, Craig
    aggression studies by, 237
    media violence and, 44–45, 70, 73
    stereotypes and, 96–97, 102, 186
    on video game violence, 79, 81
Anticonformists, 37
Arab stereotypes, 213
Arie, India, 135, 140
Aronson, Elliot, 37
Artistic respect, 65–66
Asian Americans
    media coverage of, 93–94, 115
    stereotypes, 90–91, 99
    underrepresentation of, 115
Assertions
    false, 223
    in fictional narratives, 13–14
    of media research, 49
Athletes
    in advertising, 159–161, 169
    African American portrayal, 94–95,
        185
    in video games, 105

James, William, 27, 85
Jerry Springer Show (talk show), 109
Jost, John, 102
Journalistic freedom, 211
Justice, David, 127
"Just Say No" (drug campaign), 163

Katz, Jonathan, 66–67
Kerry, John, 203, 207, 218
Kilbourne, Jean, 9, 172, 175, 180
King, Martin Luther, Jr, 14–15, 96, 115, 185–186
Korea Education and Research Information Service (KERIS), 235

Lamb, Sharon, 170–171, 173
Lancet (medical journal), 156–157
The Late Show with David Letterman (TV show), 208–209
Latin Americans, media coverage, 91, 93, 99
Lauer, Matt, 175
Learning social lessons, 51–53
Lena, Jennifer, 139
Leno, Jay, 208
Letterman, David, 207–208
Levin, Diane, 172
Lewinski, Monica, 203
Limbaugh, Rush, 197–198, 211
Little Bill (TV show), 113
London Guardian (newspaper), 216
Loveisnotabuse. com, 122

McCain, John
campaign comedy, 207–208, 216–217
image concerns, 207
media coverage, 196, 205
media rankings, 112
on Obama, 213
McCluhan, Marshall, 6, 32, 40, 135, 189, 224–225
Macho man image, 103–104
McKain, Aaron, 210
Maddow, Rachel, 198
Magazine (print) media
degradation in, 110–111
domestic violence and, 125–127, 131–132, 224
exaggerated imagery, 134–135
food and fitness ads, 154–155
gender portrayals, 104, 110
political coverage by, 206–207
sexuality for children, 175–176
weight-loss advertising in, 162–163

Manipulation in advertising, 148–149
Maslow, Abraham, 37
Media apologist, 20–21, 22–23
Media criticism(s)
censorship, 48–50, 110
entertainment value, 46–47
multidimensionality of, 45–46
opinions of, 8–10
Media dieting, 231–232
Media literacy
cultural impact of, 47–48
daily dose of, 233–234
definition of, 41–43
increasing, 234
message controls, 43–45
multidimensionality of, 45
recommendations for, 227–233
Media Literacy (Potter), 42
Media manipulation denial syndrome, 20–25
Media psychology. *See also* Social psychology
body weight and, 15–16, 132–133
evolution of, 17–19, 24
fantasy/reality argument of, 12–15
media criticism and, 8–10
media manipulation denial syndrome, 20–25
research on, 32–36
science of, 72–77
social comparisons of, 36–38
social revolution and, 6
subliminal hints and, 28–30
Media racism. *See* Racial topics, in media; Stereotypes
Mediated culture, 85
Media violence. *See also* Domestic violence; Video game violence
aggression and, 25, 44, 67–68
brain processing of, 81–84
controversy over, 44, 62–64, 76–78
desensitization to, 68, 82
exposure to, 9–11, 77
fear reactions from, 33–35
glamorizing, 105–106, 224
growth of, 77–80
mirror neurons and, 27–28, 85–87
rape, 20, 110–111, 123, 128
research findings, 80–81
research myths, 66–67, 69–72
TV studies of, 32–33, 194–195
vs. artistic respect, 65–66